AI Agents for Strategic Digital Transformation:

Governance, Policy, and Organizational Applications

Festus Adedoyin
https://orcid.org/0000-0002-3586-2570
Bournemouth University, UK

IGI Global
Scientific Publishing
Publishing Tomorrow's Research Today

VP of Publishing Ethics & Research Integrity Melissa Wagner
Director of Acquisitions Mikaela Felty
Director of Book Development Jocelynn Hessler
Production Manager Mike Brehm
Cover Design Jose Rosado

Published in the United States of America by
IGI Global Scientific Publishing
701 East Chocolate Avenue
Hershey, PA, 17033, USA
Tel: 717-533-8845 | Fax: 717-533-7115
Website: https://www.igi-global.com E-mail: cust@igi-global.com

Library of Congress Cataloging-in-Publication Data

Names: Adedoyin, Festus, 1989- editor
Title: AI agents for strategic digital transformation : governance, policy, and organizational applications / edited by Festus Adedoyin.
Description: Hershey, PA : IGI Global Scientific Publishing, [2027] | Includes bibliographical references and index. | Summary: "This book advances scholarly and applied understanding of how AI agents can be strategically governed and responsibly deployed within organizational and public-sector transformation programs. This book seeks to bridge fragmented research across computer science, information systems, public policy, and organizational studies by offering integrative frameworks that connect AI agent architectures with governance, ethics, regulation, and institutional capability"-- Provided by publisher.
Identifiers: LCCN 2026012004 (print) | LCCN 2026012005 (ebook) | ISBN 9798337395951 paperback | ISBN 9798337395944 hardcover | ISBN 9798337395968 ebook
Subjects: LCSH: Intelligent agents (Computer software) | Information technology--Management | Artificial intelligence--Business applications | Public administration--Data processing | Organizational change | LCGFT: Case studies
Classification: LCC QA76.76.I58 A43 2027 (print) | LCC QA76.76.I58 (ebook)
LC record available at https://lccn.loc.gov/2026012004
LC ebook record available at https://lccn.loc.gov/2026012005
British Cataloguing in Publication Data
A Cataloguing in Publication record for this book is available from the British Library.

Table of Contents

Detailed Table of Contents

FinTech witnessed a significant revolution in digital transformation where core processes and functionalities are delivered through fully digital platforms. AI enabled major innovations that support automated and distributed finance in FinTech by introducing machine learning and deep learning methods and techniques that enhance automation, decision-making, and security across financial ecosystems. Recently, Agentic AI emerged as a promising AI technology that takes digital transformation to another level where full autonomous and adaptive financial service operations across multiple FinTech platforms and environments are achieved. However, Agentic AI in FinTech remains critically constrained by various risks such as security vulnerabilities, regulatory challenges, and autonomous decision-making errors. This chapter explores the adoption of agentic AI in financial services and how this technology accelerated the FinTech digital transformation. Furthermore, this chapter critically analyses vulnerabilities in FinTech agentic AI and categorising the associated risks within the FinTech

This chapter examines the governance of agentic AI in the context of strategic digital transformation. The starting point is the observation that artificial intelligence is increasingly evolving from isolated analysis and decision-support systems toward autonomous and semi-autonomous agentic AI ecosystems. Under these conditions, traditional model- and system-centric governance approaches are increasingly reaching their limits, as risks, responsibilities, and control issues emerge from dynamic interactions between agents, organizations, data infrastructures, and regulatory frameworks. We are therefore developing a conceptual framework for network-based and systemic governance that integrates technical, organizational, and institutional levels. Particular attention is given to hybrid oversight architectures, continuous

The emergence of agentic artificial intelligence (AI)—encompassing systems capable of autonomous perception, reasoning, planning, and goal-directed action—is fundamentally reshaping the operational landscape of contemporary banking. From fraud detection and credit assessment to compliance automation and customer engagement, agentic systems are transitioning from peripheral tools to core institutional actors. Yet this shift does not come without significant governance complexity. Banks deploying autonomous AI agents must contend with algorithmic bias, limited decision explainability, diffuse accountability in multi-step workflows, data privacy risks, and broader systemic vulnerabilities that existing governance frameworks were simply not designed to address.This chapter maps the evolution and functional roles of agentic AI in banking and proposes a multi-level strategic governance framework responsive to these challenges. The framework is organized across four interdependent layers: strategic, operational, risk and compliance, and human-organizational.

The digital transformation of organizations is being fundamentally transformed by AI agents, although there is a lack of governance frameworks at the policy, technical and ethical levels. This work summarizes the policy architecture, organization capability and responsible deployment principles into an integrative governance framework of AI agents. With the help of systematic literature analysis and expert validation, critical gaps in AI agent oversight mechanisms are revealed. Results verify that adaptive governance frameworks, maturity of capabilities models, and structured deployment protocols are crucial to sustainable, fair, and responsible AI-driven strategic change.

Preface

INTRODUCTION

The rapid evolution of artificial intelligence is transforming digital transformation from a predominantly technology-enabled process into a dynamic organizational and strategic phenomenon. While earlier applications of AI largely focused on analytics, prediction, automation, and decision support, the emergence of AI agents introduces systems capable of perceiving environments, reasoning over information, pursuing goals, coordinating tasks, and taking actions with varying degrees of human intervention. These capabilities create new opportunities for organizations to redesign processes, enhance operational responsiveness, improve decision-making, and develop new forms of digital value creation. At the same time, the increasing autonomy of AI agents raises fundamental questions concerning governance, accountability, organizational design, policy development, risk management, and responsible deployment. *AI Agents for Strategic Digital Transformation: Governance, Policy, and Organizational Applications* brings together research and conceptual perspectives that examine these opportunities and challenges across organizational, industry, governmental, and institutional contexts.

The strategic adoption of AI agents requires more than technological readiness. Organizations must determine how authority is delegated to autonomous systems, how human oversight is maintained, how responsibilities are assigned when agents participate in consequential decisions, and how governance mechanisms can adapt as systems and operating environments evolve. These questions become particularly significant in sectors such as financial services, banking, public administration, and critical infrastructure, where AI-enabled decisions may have substantial organizational and societal consequences. Effective governance therefore requires consideration of technical architectures alongside organizational capabilities, regulatory requirements, ethical principles, institutional conditions, and mechanisms for continuous monitoring and accountability. The chapters in this volume address these dimensions by examining governance frameworks, policy architectures, accountability models, organizational structures, and responsible implementation approaches for AI agents.

This book is intended to provide a multidisciplinary resource for scholars, researchers, policymakers, technology and transformation leaders, managers, regulators, and professionals seeking to understand the implications of agentic AI for strategic digital transformation. Across the chapters, the contributors consider AI agents not simply as technical tools but as components of broader socio-technical systems that interact with people, organizations, data, infrastructures, markets, and regulatory institutions. The volume combines sector-specific perspectives with broader conceptual frameworks, providing insights into how organizations can approach AI-agent adoption while addressing emerging risks and governance requirements. Particular attention is given to financial ecosystems, enterprise transformation, public administration, organizational accountability, policy design, and the institutional contexts that shape responsible AI adoption.

CHAPTER OVERVIEW

Chapter 1, "Agentic AI in FinTech Digital Transformation," examines the role of agentic AI in the transformation of financial technology. The chapter considers how autonomous and adaptive AI systems can support automation, decision-making, security, and distributed financial services across FinTech environments. It also addresses vulnerabilities and risks associated with agentic AI, including security challenges, regulatory concerns, and errors arising from autonomous decision-making. By connecting the capabilities of agentic AI with the evolution of FinTech, the chapter provides a sector-specific perspective on both the opportunities and governance requirements associated with autonomous financial technologies.

Chapter 2, "Governing Agentic AI: Network-Based Oversight and Systemic Design," approaches AI governance from a network and systems perspective. The chapter recognizes that agentic AI ecosystems extend beyond individual models or technical systems and involve interactions among agents, organizations, data infrastructures, and regulatory frameworks. It develops a conceptual approach to systemic governance that incorporates technical, organizational, and institutional dimensions. Particular attention is given to hybrid oversight architectures, continuous governance, recursive control mechanisms, simulation-based approaches, and digital twins as tools for understanding and managing systemic risks.

Chapter 3, "Governing AI Agents in Enterprise Digital Transformation: Strategy, Accountability, and Organizational Design," focuses on the integration of AI agents into enterprise digital transformation strategies. The chapter examines how the transition from task-oriented automation to goal-oriented coordination creates new governance and organizational design requirements. It proposes a strategy-aligned governance approach incorporating business charters, layered accountability, lifecycle controls, and a federated operating model that balances enterprise-wide standards with domain-level autonomy. Drawing on digital transformation, IT governance, AI accountability, regulatory frameworks, and standards including the EU AI Act, NIST AI RMF, and ISO/IEC 42001, the chapter also considers how organizations can develop auditable and human-managed AI-agent portfolios.

Chapter 4, "Adaptive Governance of Autonomous AI Agents: Rethinking Accountability and Risk in Intelligent Systems," explores the changing governance requirements created by autonomous AI agents. The chapter considers applications in public-sector institutions, financial services, and critical infrastructure, emphasizing that AI agents can increasingly perform consequential actions, coordinate multi-step processes, and operate within distributed multi-agent environments. These characteristics complicate conventional approaches to responsibility and oversight. The chapter consequently examines the need for adaptive governance approaches that can respond to dynamic systems, distributed responsibility, and evolving risks rather than relying exclusively on static, compliance-oriented models.

Chapter 5, "Governing AI Agents in Banking: A Multi-Level Strategic Framework for Responsible Digital Transformation in Financial Ecosystems," provides a focused examination of agentic AI within banking. The chapter discusses applications including fraud detection, credit assessment, compliance automation, and customer engagement, while considering the governance challenges associated with algorithmic bias, explainability, accountability, privacy, and systemic vulnerabilities. It proposes a multi-level governance framework organized across strategic, operational, risk and compliance, and human-organizational dimensions. This framework highlights the need to integrate technological deployment with institutional responsibilities and organizational controls within financial ecosystems.

Chapter 6, "Governing AI Agents for Strategic Digital Transformation: Integrative Frameworks for Policy, Organizational Capability, and Responsible Deployment," examines the governance of AI agents through the combined lenses of policy, organizational capability, and responsible implementation. The chapter identifies gaps in existing approaches to AI-agent oversight and develops an integrative governance framework informed by systematic literature analysis and expert validation. Its emphasis on adaptive governance, organizational maturity, and structured deployment provides a basis for considering how organizations can build the capabilities necessary to implement AI agents in a sustainable, responsible, and strategically aligned manner.

Chapter 7, "AI Agents and the Future of Business in Africa: Governing Transformation in the Contexts of Institutional Complexity," extends the discussion of AI-agent governance to African business environments. The chapter considers the relationship among AI-agent autonomy, organizational readiness, governance mechanisms, and fragmented regulatory environments. Recognizing that governance frameworks developed in relatively stable institutional contexts may not fully address the circumstances of diverse African economies, the chapter develops a conceptual framework integrating human oversight, organizational capability, and institutional alignment. It also considers implications for business leaders, policymakers, regulators, and future research on responsible AI governance in African contexts.

Chapter 8, "Governing Intelligent Agents: Strategic Frameworks for AI-Driven Digital Transformation," concludes the volume by presenting a strategic governance perspective on intelligent agents in public-sector and enterprise organizations. The chapter conceptualizes intelligent agents as socio-technical systems rather than isolated technological components and examines the relationship among agent capabilities, decision rights, oversight structures, and accountability mechanisms. It addresses delegated authority, multi-agent coordination, human–AI collaboration, ethical principles, regulatory alignment, and lifecycle governance. Through this perspective, the chapter provides an overarching framework for considering how governance can remain connected to organizational strategy as AI-agent capabilities evolve.

CONCLUSION

Taken together, the chapters demonstrate that AI agents are becoming increasingly relevant to the strategic transformation of organizations and institutions. Their ability to operate with varying degrees of autonomy creates opportunities for organizations to automate complex activities, coordinate processes, support decision-making, and develop new forms of digital capability. However, these opportunities are accompanied by governance challenges that differ from those associated with conventional software, analytics systems, and decision-support technologies. Questions concerning delegated authority, accountability, transparency, risk, privacy, security, human oversight, and organizational responsibility become increasingly important as AI agents move from experimental applications toward more deeply integrated roles within organizational processes.

The contributions also demonstrate that there is no single governance perspective that can adequately address every AI-agent deployment. Governance requirements vary according to organizational structures, sectoral risks, regulatory environments, institutional conditions, and the degree of autonomy granted to AI systems. The chapters therefore present complementary approaches, ranging from network-based and systemic oversight to enterprise governance, adaptive accountability, sector-specific frameworks, organizational capability models, and public policy architectures. Considered collectively, these perspectives emphasize the importance of integrating technological, organizational, institutional, and regulatory considerations when developing strategies for responsible AI-agent adoption.

As AI agents continue to develop, strategic digital transformation will increasingly involve decisions about not only what these systems can do, but also how organizations should structure, govern, monitor, and evaluate their participation in organizational and institutional activities. We hope that *AI Agents for Strategic Digital Transformation: Governance, Policy, and Organizational Applications* will contribute to ongoing academic and professional discussions by providing a foundation for examining these questions across multiple contexts. The volume is intended to support continued research, informed organizational practice, and thoughtful policy development as organizations navigate the opportunities and responsibilities associated with increasingly autonomous AI systems.

Chapter 1
Agentic AI in FinTech Digital Transformation

Muntadher Sallal
http://orcid.org/0000-0002-1755-3264
Bournemouth University, UK

Samuel Mariwa
Independent Researcher, UK

Kevin Ocansey
Independent Researcher, UK

ABSTRACT

FinTech witnessed a significant revolution in digital transformation where core processes and functionalities are delivered through fully digital platforms. AI enabled major innovations that support automated and distributed finance in FinTech by introducing machine learning and deep learning methods and techniques that enhance automation, decision-making, and security across financial ecosystems. Recently, Agentic AI emerged as a promising AI technology that takes digital transformation to another level where full autonomous and adaptive financial service operations across multiple FinTech platforms and environments are achieved. However, Agentic AI in FinTech remains critically constrained by various risks such as security vulnerabilities, regulatory challenges, and autonomous decision-making errors. This chapter explores the adoption of agentic AI in financial services and how this technology accelerated the FinTech digital transformation. Furthermore, this chapter critically analyses vulnerabilities in FinTech agentic AI and categorising the associated risks within the FinTech

DOI: 10.4018/979-8-3373-9594-4.ch001

1. INTRODUCTION

Despite its transformative potential, the adoption of agentic AI in financial services remains critically constrained by various risks such as security vulnerabilities, regulatory challenges, and the high-stakes consequences of autonomous decision-making errors. This has resulted in a significant gap between technological capability and real-world deployment in the financial sector.

Financial services are an environment where autonomous AI errors do not only inconvenience users but can trigger huge losses, destabilize markets, and erode public trust. The risks could be seen even in earlier, simpler forms of algorithmic automation and they have demonstrated catastrophic potential, as seen in the 2010 Flash Crash, where algorithmic trading systems caused the Dow Jones to plunge nearly 1,000 points in minutes (Kirilenko et al., 2017). If rule-based automation alone could produce such systemic disruption, the stakes of deploying far more capable and autonomous agentic AI systems that are capable of independent reasoning and action taking are considerably higher. Because, unlike rule-based algorithmic systems, agentic AI operates through multi-step reasoning chains and tool-use interactions, where errors in one stage propagate and amplify across subsequent actions. This phenomenon is described as cascading hallucination in multi-agent pipelines (Hong et al., 2023).

What makes this particularly consequential is that when failures occur across layered agentic systems, accountability becomes distributed across multiple parties, from model developers to system deployers, and even end users in ways that no single actor can clearly resolve (Shavit et al., 2023). Existing regulatory frameworks are not designed with agentic systems in mind, leaving accountability for autonomous decision-making legally unsettled and institutions hesitant to deploy. (Yousefi et al., 2025) argue that agentic AI's non-linear risks test the limits of the EU AI Act's static, intended-purpose classification framework, asserting that clear technical standards and regulatory clarifications are urgently required to bridge the gap between static risk regulation and dynamic AI technology. The gap, therefore, is not one of technology or ambition, but it is one of trust, accountability, and the governance infrastructure needed to deploy autonomous systems responsibly in a sector where the cost of failure is exceptionally high.

This chapter explores the current state of agentic AI adoption across the financial technology (FinTech) landscape, which includes both traditional banking and decentralized finance (DeFi). Specifically, the review focuses on agentic AI systems and their adoption in the FinTech industry, what enables or inhibits their adoption, and how organizations are navigating the unique challenges of deploying autonomous systems in a highly critical sector. One line of enquiry concerns how agentic AI systems can be secured against malicious actors while maintaining usability and performance, with particular attention to novel threat surfaces introduced by autonomous tool use, multi-step execution, and environmental interactions. A second addresses internal communication risks within multi-agent hierarchies, where natural language coordination between agents can distort and compound errors across pipeline stages, raising fundamental questions about protocol sufficiency and the necessity for human oversight (Hong et al., 2023). Beyond technical safety, the discussion extends to how agentic AI systems can influence human behavior and decision making in FinTech, and to the best approach for anticipating and mitigating unintended consequences, bias, and harm. The closing sections identify key gaps in the literature, summarize the findings on the impact of AI in the sector, and address the challenges to its widespread adoption.

Previous surveys and exploratory studies centred around the role of Agentic AI in FinTech with more attention towards AI accountability, governance, and perception issues (Wu & Li, 2026; Elgendy et al., 2025). Comparatively, little attention has been paid to how these risks manifest within the specific operational and regulatory environment of financial services, or to how they connect to the governance structures through which financial institutions are actually required to manage them. This chapter addresses that gap in two ways. First, it develops a taxonomy of agentic

AI vulnerabilities organized around the levels at which agentic systems interact, namely agent-to-human, agent-to-system, and agent-to-agent. Second, it places this taxonomy within the institutional governance landscape, examining how existing model risk management, operational resilience, and accountability frameworks are strained by autonomous systems and what this means for their responsible deployment. In doing so, the chapter connects a technical understanding of agentic risk to the governance mechanisms on which safe adoption in the financial sector ultimately depends.

1.2 Paper Structure

The structure of this chapter is outlined as follows: Section 2 illustrates the main concepts and methods involved in FinTech digital transformation including AI methods such as machine learning, deep learning, and Agentic AI. Section 3 discusses and analyses the digital transformation lifecycle, highlighting the main development phases and technologies adopted in each phase. Section 4 critically discusses how AI methods contributed to the development of FinTech digital services. Section 5 explores the architecture of Agentic AI in FinTech and its role in providing fully dynamic financial services. Section 6 classifies the Agentic AI vulnerabilities and their associated risks in FinTech sector. Section 7 summarizes the open challenges and future directions in relation to Agentic AI in FinTech sector. Finally, Section 8 concludes the significance of knowledge and discussions presented in this chapter.

This ordering is deliberate as the chapter established conceptual foundations before analyzing risk. Sections 2 to 5 progress from the foundational terminology of artificial intelligence through to the architecture and adoption of agentic AI specifically, so that the reader understands both what the technology is and the environment in which it operates before the discussion turns to risk in Section 6. This sequencing reflects the chapter's position that the risks of agentic AI are emergent properties of its autonomy, multi-step reasoning, and inter-agent coordination, and are therefore intelligible only against a prior understanding of how these systems are built and deployed. Throughout, each concept is anchored to examples drawn from financial services, such as fraud detection, credit assessment, and algorithmic trading, so that abstract technical distinctions remain accessible to readers approaching from a finance rather than a technical background.

1.3 Approach

The chapter is a conceptual analysis presented as a structured narrative review of agentic AI in the FinTech sector. Rather than surveying the field exhaustively, it synthesizes current knowledge into a conceptual level that is accessible to multidisciplinary readership. The risk analysis in Section 6 is structured in three levels at which agentic systems interact, agent-to-human, agent-to-system, and agent-to-agent.

The literature underpinning the review was drawn from peer-reviewed journal articles and conference proceedings in artificial intelligence, financial technology, and information security, supplemented by authoritative technical and industry documentation. Priority was given to recent publications (predominantly 2023–2026) to reflect the rapid pace of development in agentic AI. Because several of the frameworks and protocols examined are too recent to be well represented in the peer-reviewed literature, the original documentation from the organizations that created them was used in such cases.

The frameworks discussed in this chapter were selected for their representativeness in the field rather than for exhaustive coverage. The frameworks examined in Section 5.2 span the two layers most relevant to financial deployment, namely agent orchestration (LangChain, LangGraph and CrewAI) and cross-agent interoperability (the Model Context Protocol and the Agent-to-Agent protocol). The adoption domains in Section 5.3 were chosen to cover the principal financial functions in which agentic AI is currently deployed, from payments and customer interaction to credit, fraud detection and regulatory compliance.

In summary, this chapter provides an in-depth knowledge around three main areas, as shown in Figure 1:

1- Exploration of the FinTech digital transformation and how it was influenced by AI and Machine Learning.

2- Analysis of Agentic AI role across wide range of FinTech process and operations.

3- Classification of Agentic AI risks in FinTech based on the nature of the interaction including Agent-to-human interactions, Agent-to-system interactions, and Agent-to-agent interactions.

Figure 1. Chapter Methodology phases

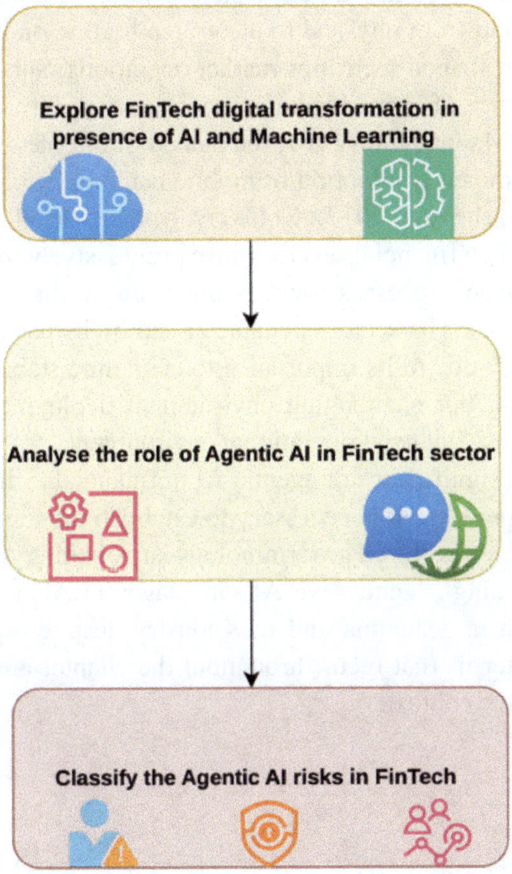

2. DEFINITION AND KEY CONCEPTS

FinTech, or Financial Technology, refers to the integration of digital technologies such as mobile networks, big data, mobile embedded systems, cloud computing, data analytics techniques in the operations of financial services (Gai et al., 2018). The adoption of financial technologies has taken place gradually over an extended period, rather than as a single disruptive shift. Early developments in FinTech can be understood as a sequence of incremental innovations that progressively reduced reliance on physical infrastructure and increased the role of digital systems in financial services. In this regard, the introduction of the automated teller machine (ATM) in 1959 in Ohio marked an early step towards self-service banking, followed by the transition from physical to electronic trading on NASDAQ in 1971, which significantly reshaped securities market operations. Subsequent milestones included the emergence of home banking services offered by institutions such as Citibank and Chase Manhattan in 1981, the launch of internet banking services in the mid-1990s, and the early adoption of mobile banking by banks such as Fokus Bank in Norway (Puschmann, 2017). Collectively, these developments illustrate a clear trajectory in which financial services have progressively moved from branch-based and paper-driven processes towards increasingly digital, distributed, and user-accessible systems. The sector is characterised by its pace of innovation and regulatory complexity due to its importance to economic stability. These reasons make it a compelling but challenging environment deployment to autonomous systems in the complex financial operational environment.

To appreciate the significance of agentic AI in financial technology, the opportunities and risks it presents, it is necessary to establish the foundational concepts that make its existence possible. The terminology surrounding AI such as 'machine learning', 'deep learning', 'generative AI' and 'agentic AI' are commonly used interchangeably both in academia and the industry despite representing distinct concepts. The core terms that recur throughout the chapter are defined below in their financial industry context.

Figure 2. Conceptual Venn Diagram of key AI terminologies

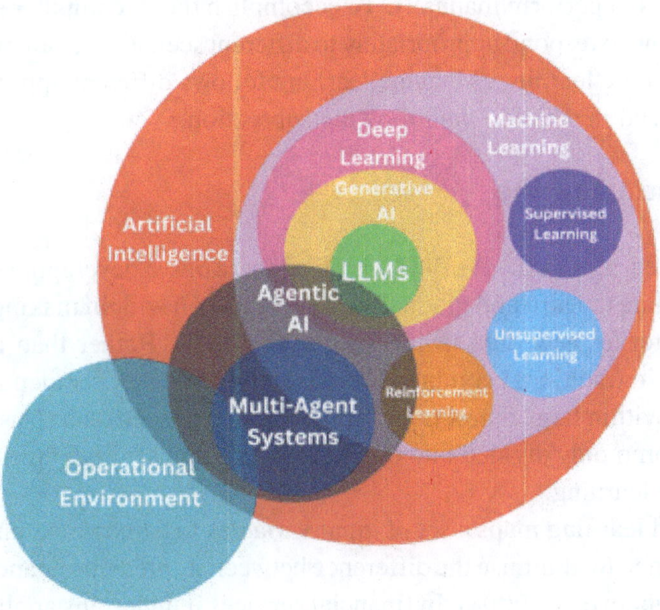

As illustrated in Figure 2, these concepts form a series of nested layers, beginning with the broader field of Artificial Intelligence and progressively narrowing towards agentic AI which is the main focus of this chapter. Each of the components plays a key role in building multi-agent systems that operate in environments like banking systems.

2.1 Artificial Intelligence

Artificial Intelligence (AI) broadly refers to the capability of computational systems to perform tasks that would ordinarily require human intelligence (Soori et al., 2023). These tasks include reasoning, learning, problem-solving and decision-making. Unlike conventional computer systems that operate strictly according to fixed instructions explicitly programmed by developers, AI systems are designed to have some adaptability when interacting with information and environments. As a result, AI has emerged as a significant driver of socio-economic transformation, a catalyst for technological innovation, and a widely used tool in supporting scientific research and development (Jiang et al., 2022). Within the financial sector, AI has become an important tool that improves operational efficiency, enhances customer experiences, and strengthens decision making processes. For example, an AI system can analyse large volumes of transaction data to identify unusual behavioral patterns that may indicate fraudulent activity, a task that would be difficult and time consuming for human analysts to perform manually. To accomplish these, computer systems have to be taught how to respond appropriately to different scenarios, a practice popularly known as machine learning. Machine learning follows different approaches which will be discussed in detail in the following subsection.

2.2 Machine Learning

Machine Learning (ML) is a field within AI that aims at developing software that uses historic data to learn and gradually improve its behavior in making predictions when encountering new data (Michalski et al., 1983). Rather than operating on fixed rules as in traditional computational systems, ML models identify statistical relationships within large datasets and apply them to unseen data (Nasteski, 2017). The field is commonly divided into three paradigms: supervised, unsupervised and reinforcement learning.

Supervised learning maps a set of input variables to a known output through an algorithm trained to minimise the difference between its predictions and the labelled data (Cunningham et al., 2008). In financial services it underpins applications such as fraud detection, where past transactions labelled fraudulent or legitimate are used to train models that classify new activity. Unsupervised learning, by contrast, is applied where labelled ground truth is sparse or unavailable, identifying latent structure in the data to perform tasks such as clustering, association and anomaly detection (Naeem et al., 2023). Its financial applications include customer segmentation, where clustering groups customers by spending, saving and investment behaviour to inform product targeting.

Reinforcement Learning (RL) differs from both in that an autonomous agent learns optimal behaviour by interacting with an environment, taking sequential actions and receiving feedback in the form of rewards or penalties (AlMahamid & Grolinger, 2021). The agent's objective is to maximise cumulative reward, which drives it towards the expected behaviour. In FinTech, RL is applied in algorithmic trading, where an agent optimises its trading strategy over time against a profit objective. RL is treated at greater length here because of its core elements, an autonomous agent pursuing a goal through sequential action in a feedback-driven environment, anticipating the architecture of the agentic systems examined in Sections 5 and 6.

2.3 Deep Learning

Deep learning is a technique that is inspired by the structure of the human brain by using graph technologies with transformations that represent the multi-layered neurons (Pouyanfar et al., 2018). The graph contains processing units known as nodes that are organized as input, hidden and output layers as shown in Figure 3.

Figure 3. An Artificial Neural Network (ANN) with Interconnected layers

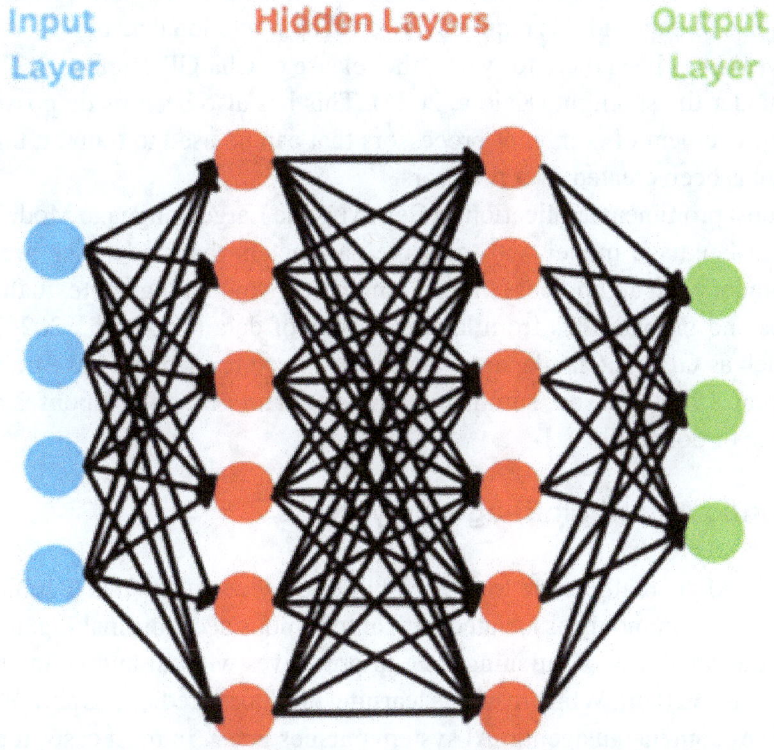

The input layer receives raw data such as text, images or numerical values, the hidden layers transform it through successive mathematical operations, and the output layer produces the final prediction. Each connection between nodes carries a weight determining the influence of the information passed through it, and these weights are continuously adjusted during training to improve predictive accuracy. Deep learning has proven substantially more effective than earlier machine learning approaches across natural language processing, computer vision and speech processing, and it is the capability that underpins the large language models discussed in Section 2.4.

2.4 Generative AI and Large Language Models (LLMs)

Generative AI (Gen-AI) is a branch or AI that focuses on creating data whether it be text, images, audio or other data types, that is similar to existing data based on patterns it has learned (Oluwagbenro, 2024). These patterns are learned from vast amounts of data and this requires powerful computational resources. Although generative AI has been there for years, the release of ChatGPT in late 2022 has put Gen-AI under the spotlight (Kalota, 2024). This has also been made possible due to the improvement of computer processors that can be used to train on that much data that has been created over the years.

The most prominent application of Gen-AI is the Large Language Model (LLM) which is a language model with massive parameters that undergoes pretraining tasks to understand and process human language by modelling contextualized text semantics and probabilities from large amounts of data (Yao et al., 2024). Many LLMs such as GPT-5, Claude and Gemini have been trained and have trained and have the capacity to reason, summarise, translate and generate responses across a wide range of domains.

2.5 Agentic AI and Multi-agent Systems

Agentic AI generally refers to artificial intelligence systems that exhibit agency characteristics commonly associated with autonomous decision-making, intentionally, and the capability of pursuing a set of objectives without human intervention (Vlad Pop et al., 2026). While machine learning produces predictions and generative AI produces content, an agentic AI system pursues goals. In most cases it operates with tools, databases and APIs that enable it to perform actions in the operational environment.

Multi-agent systems are part of the broader agentic AI field that often involve multiple specialized agents working together, coordinating and communicating to solve problems that are too complex for a single agent (Abou Ali et al., 2025). An example of how an agentic AI system can be used in fintech is in financial fraud detection which may consist of a team of specialised agents: a monitoring agent that continuously scans incoming transactions and identifies unusual activity, a risk analysis agent that evaluates the transaction using behavioural patterns and known fraud indicators, and a decision agent then determines whether to approve, flag, or block the transaction. This collaborative workflow is done autonomously with agents communicating with each other through structured protocols with little to no human intervention during the process.

3. DIGITAL TRANSFORMATION IN FINTECH

The financial services industry was historically filled with manual processes and physical infrastructure. Customers queued at branches to deposit cheques, consulted advisors in person for investment guidance, and waited days for cross-border payments to be cleared. These manual processes made the service a bit slow and prone to errors. However, at the turn of the 21st century, rapid technology advances had a great impact on financial services where many start-ups started to appear which integrate innovative technology in the financial industry. For instance, the internet transformed banking, introducing online platforms that allowed customers to manage their accounts from home (Komandla & Perumalla, 2017). The transformation cut across all sectors in the industry with the aim of bringing speed, efficiency and a good customer experience in order to stay competitive. The main goal of digital transformation in FinTech was to improve the end user experience with two conflicting features which are usability and security. This has also been driven by regulatory obligations that encourage increased openness of a bank's architecture, obliging systems and account transaction data accessible (Pramanik et al., 2019).

FinTech transformation was focusing on shifting the execution methods of financial processes to be digitally handled through making use of emerging digital technologies. In this chapter, we classify the FinTech digital transformation based on three main categories including online services, Decentralised finance (DeFi) services, and Automated financial decision making (See Figure 4). This classification captures how FinTech has developed based on the goal behind adopting digital technologies. Each category is examined in turn, tracing how the transformation unfolded and identifying the specific digital technologies that enabled it. Understanding this trajectory is essential context for the chapters that delve into adoption of AI and ultimately agentic AI.

Figure 4. FinTech digital transformation phases

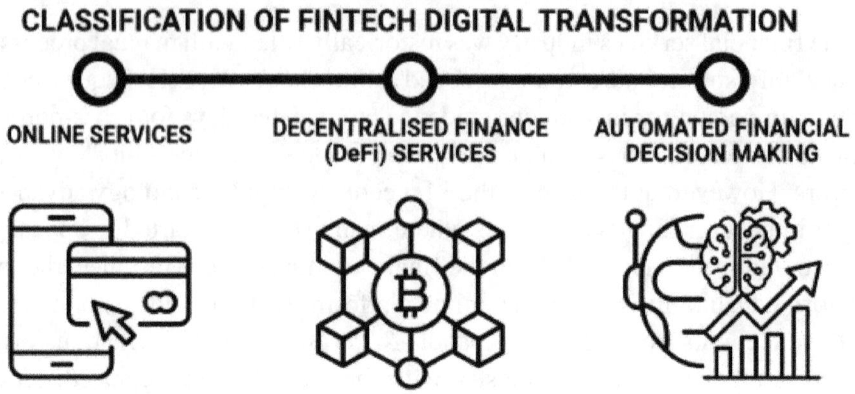

3.1.1 Online Services

This is the foundational shift to digital banking where branch-based banking involving physical money was transformed to online banking due to rapidly evolving technology. Traditional financial institutions operated with paper-based record-keeping, branch networks as the point of contact for customers and day-to-day settlement cycles as the norm. However, as customers demand more engagement with digital solutions and businesses embrace the latest trends, including AI, big data, and blockchain, the traditional forms of the business model are shifting (Bodepudi, 2023). Early forms of online banking allowed customers to perform basic functions such as account monitoring, funds transfer and bill payments. With the widespread adoption of smartphones and interconnectivity of services, banking applications can now connect to a broader ecosystem of financial and non-financial services.

This evolution is reflected in the diversity of digital payment solutions. Device-based payment solutions such as Apple Pay and Google Pay allow users to make transactions through digital payment interfaces without reliance on physical cards or cash. The digital payments solutions have gone beyond those provided by financial institutions to include a range of FinTech actors operating across the globe. For example, PayPal facilitates online cross-border transactions without interfacing with a financial institution. In Kenya, Safaricom's M-Pesa provides a mobile-network based payment solution that's independent of banking infrastructure. China's AliPay and WeChat Pay integrate payments within a wider digital ecosystem.

The movement to online services has also been seen in the lending model. The traditional model entailed physical branch visits, extensive documentation, a lengthy credit assessment, and long decision periods. The digitized model leverages on data and algorithms to make decisions reducing the timelines and increasing fairness. This has made it easy for small and medium enterprises (SMEs) and underserved populations to have access to fairly digital lending opportunities that were previously challenging to get (Okafor et al., 2021). An example is JPMorgan's OnDeck which is a lending platform for SMEs to process loans in just a day (Omarini, 2017). AI-driven credit scoring for loan processing represents the next iteration of this transformation and will be discussed in detail in chapter 4.

Neobanks, which are digital-only banks operating without physical branches have also propped up during the digital transformation. These banks have challenged traditional banking institutions due to their focus on technology, customer experience as well as lower fee products since they have no branch maintenance costs (Palos-Sanchez et al., 2025). Banks such Revolute and Monzo have demonstrated the efficiency of this banking model in the UK. A study by the International Monetary Fund (IMF) on development of neobanks in 18 economies around the globe states that neobanks have grown and assumed systematic importance in each country's market (Shanti et al., 2024).

3.1.2 Decentralized Finance (DeFi) services

Blockchain and cryptocurrencies played a key role in the development of the FinTech industry through opening a new digital transformation pathway where advanced and innovative technologies are introduced to enable decentralised finance (DeFi). DeFi, as we know it today, began to gain momentum following the creation of the Ethereum blockchain and the introduction of smart contracts as a way to create self-executing, immutable and cryptographically verifiable financial agreements (Aina Turillazzi et al., 2023). DeFi ensures that financial transactions are processed in a decentralised manner through making use of blockchain and smart contracts. Blockchain provides a trusted environment where the financial firms can collaborate and work with other industries safely and dynamically. The dynamic workflow is preserved by smart contracts which regulates the decision making. The transparency inherent in blockchain-based systems, where all transactions are publicly recorded and verifiable, also introduced a new standard of auditability to financial services that traditional institutions have struggled to match.

However, DeFi also introduced several risks with a major one resulting from smart contract vulnerabilities. Because smart contracts hold significant financial value and execute autonomously once deployed, they represent an attractive and consequential attack target with attacks against smart contracts and DeFi protocols resulting in billions of dollars in financial losses and posing significant security threats to the broader DeFi ecosystem (Qian et al., 2025). Another downside is the legal risks where there are legislative failures resulting from the legal loopholes in the logic of DeFi. The regulations that are there in place to regulate traditional financial systems cannot be applied to DeFi exposing its users to the risk of financial misconduct (Aina Turillazzi et al., 2023). Despite the limitations, DeFi represents a foundational shift in how financial services can be structured.

3.1.3 Automated Financial decision making

The most recent phase of FinTech's digital transformation is the progressive automations of financial decision-making. Artificial Intelligence and Machine Learning have had a significant impact on the fintech industry by enabling the automation of various financial processes, such as loan underwriting and risk assessment, leading to improved efficiency and reduced costs (Jain et al., 2023). This phase has improved decision-making performance over time without having the systems reprogrammed. For example, in fraud detection, machine learning models trained on historical transaction data can identify suspicious activity in real time at a scale that no human analyst can match. In credit assessment, algorithmic models evaluate applicant risk across a broader set of variables that traditional scoring systems did not include, extending access to credit to populations that were previously underserved by the conventional assessment methods. While the benefits of AI and other disruptive technologies are well understood, there is a debate on the adverse effects of using them which include the creation of technostress for employees, reduced employment opportunities, harm to their well-being and so on (Almansour, 2023). Other operational risks of the technology include opacity in decision-making, potential algorithmic bias, and governance challenges that existing regulatory frameworks are not designed to address.

4. AI IN FINTECH

The shift toward the "AI Bank of the Future" was predicted early in the digital transition, with McKinsey (2021) estimating that advanced AI could potentially generate up to $1 trillion in additional annual value for the global banking sector. This foresight has largely materialized. Today, advanced technologies like AI, big data, and cloud computing are no longer optional, but are the essential pillars for the stability of financial businesses in a globalized economy (Xu et al., 2024). By integrating machine learning (ML), natural language processing (NLP), and predictive analytics, institutions can now process vast datasets to enable computer-automated, real-time responses to risks and fraudulent activity (Siddquee, 2025). This transition has moved banks and financial institutions from a reactive posture to a proactive one, allowing them to optimize internal operations while maintaining high levels of customer satisfaction.

While numerical data like stock prices and interest rates are vital to finance, an enormous amount of financial information lives in ordinary text such as news articles, company earnings reports, and regulatory filings. Natural Language Processing (NLP), the technology that allows computers to read and understand human language, has become a cornerstone of modern FinTech. Early versions were essentially smart reading tools. For example, systems like FinBERT were developed because general AI models often misinterpret financial jargon; a word like "exposure" or "yield" means something very different on Wall Street than it does in a daily conversation (Araci, 2019). These early tools scanned documents to gauge market mood or flag key numbers, translating messy text into simple scores for human traders. Today, technology has taken a giant leap forward. With the creation of specialized, ultra-powerful financial models like BloombergGPT, AI can now draft complex reports, answer tricky economic questions, and spot compliance issues across thousands of pages instantly (Wu et al., 2023).

However, giving AI the power to read, interpret, and act on human language comes with significant real-world risks. Because financial language is incredibly subtle, a tiny misunderstanding by an AI can lead to massive errors. If a normal chatbot confuses a fact while writing a poem, the mistake is harmless. But if an AI reading a company's financial disclosure misinterprets a footnote or "hallucinates" a rule that doesn't exist, the consequences can be immediate and severe (Li et al., 2023). As these language tools are increasingly trusted to run autonomously in activities like making trades, evaluating loan applications, or executing financial tasks without human approval, then a single flawed reading can trigger a chain reaction of bad financial decisions. For this reason, transitioning natural language processing to Agentic AI requires full proof guardrails and strict oversight to protect everyday users and maintain trust in the financial system. In this chapter, we discuss the AI role in FinTech within two categories including cyber security and user experience.

4.1. Cyber Security

The fundamental shift toward digital transformation of financial services has drastically expanded the attack surface, introducing a "constantly changing threat landscape" that includes sophisticated DDoS attacks, ransomware, and social engineering (Asmar and Tuqan, 2024). Because digital institutions lack the physical fallback of traditional branches, the integration of Machine Learning (ML) and Deep Learning (DL) have become a necessity for sustaining cybersecurity. Advanced algorithms are deployed to monitor network traffic and user interactions in real-time, allowing for the "instant action" required to identify anomalies and block harmful activities before they result in significant financial loss (Asmar and Tuqan, 2024).

ML and DL have moved financial institutions away from slow, manual reviews toward a model of continuous, real-time oversight (WJARR, 2025). While traditional management relied on periodic reports and traditional statistical models, digital systems now use ML and DL to monitor credit and liquidity risks in real time, allowing for instant adjustments that help avoid the kind of systemic failures seen in the 2008 crash (Heß and Damásio, 2025). This shift allows banks to move beyond simple human analysis, using self-optimising systems that can be constantly evaluated and improved to handle complex market shifts (Heß and Damásio, 2025; WJARR, 2025). Research indicates that 58.3% of financial institutions have already integrated AI into their risk management frameworks, with adoption being most prevalent in larger firms with over 200 employees. El Hajj and Hammoud (2023). This transformation extends to how banks manage their own assets. Institutions are increasingly deploying Deep Reinforcement Learning agents to manage investment positions autonomously. (Mienye et al., 2024). This shift toward self-optimising systems allows management to automate routine decision-making at a scale impossible for human teams, with 70.8% of firms now utilising these technologies for algorithmic trading operations (El Hajj and Hammoud, 2023)

4.2 User Experience

While the initial digital transition focused on resolving the shortcomings of traditional banking, such as long queues and delayed response times, modern Fintech has shifted the benchmark for customer satisfaction from mere speed to intelligent utility. In the era of AI, satisfaction is not only defined by how quickly a query is resolved, but by how effectively a platform can proactively manage a user's financial health.

In the broader Fintech and Decentralized Finance (DeFi) landscape, customer satisfaction has evolved from mere efficiency to a demand for personalized engagement. While traditional models focused on response speed, modern research emphasizes that "perceived competence" and "assurance" are now the primary drivers of user trust (Wickramarachchi, 2025). This is particularly evident in blockchain environments, where the shift toward "DeFAI" (AI-enabled DeFi) utilizes ML and DL to provide real-time, tailored financial advice and automated portfolio rebalancing, significantly boosting total value locked (TVL) and user retention (Mamzeris, 2025). '

Furthermore, as users navigate increasingly complex decentralized protocols, their satisfaction is less tied to conversational "warmth" and more dependent on the AI's technical reliability and ability to simplify complex on-chain interactions (MDPI, 2026). Consequently, the role of AI has transitioned from a reactive support tool to an "intelligent interface" that democratizes access to sophisticated wealth management through intuitive, automated decision-making (Siddquee, 2025; Springer, 2024).

5. AGENTIC AI IN DIGITAL TRANSFORMATION

The transition to autonomy in financial services has been gradual over the years. From human tellers to Automated Teller Machines (ATMs), from paper ledgers to digital databases, from rule-based algorithms to ML models, each stage has reduced the level of human involvement in financial services. The sector is now in a stage of transitioning to agentic-AI systems given the recent advancements in LLMs and the interest it has drawn across many industries due to its potential (Inala & Somu, 2024). Agentic AI is a huge step in the trajectory because it advances from automation to autonomous systems that pursue goals dynamically. How that transition is being achieved is examined below through the architecture of agentic systems, the frameworks used to build, deploy and govern them, and the ways in which financial services have begun to use them.

5.1 The Architecture of Agentic AI Systems in FinTech

Agentic AI-based fintech systems are built through a set of interconnected components that transform a language model to an autonomous system capable of operating in complex financial workflows. The components which are the core foundational pillars of many agentic systems include the agent profile, reasoning, memory, operational environment and the human-in-the loop layer. Figure 5 illustrates how these components interact within an agentic system.

Figure 5. Architecture of Agentic AI Systems in Finance

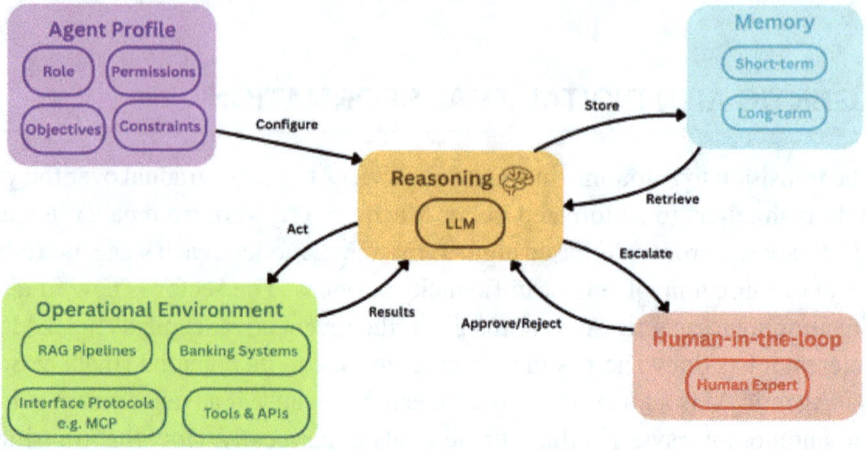

5.1.1 The Agent Profile

Before the agentic system starts processing requests, be it from a user or another system, its behavior is defined by a configuration layer commonly known as the system prompt. This is where the agent's identity, objectives and constraints are defined. In financial services, this component determines what the agent is authorised to do, what actions require human approval, and what organizational and regulatory obligations it must observe. With this a fraud detection agent, a customer service agent and a trading agent would each have different profiles.

5.1.2 Reasoning

At the center of the agentic system is an LLM which serves as the reasoning component. Unlike rule-based systems, that only follow preconfigured instructions, the LLM is able to interpret instructions, reason through the request, break down the goal into manageable steps and decide how to execute them.

5.1.3 Memory

For every interaction or action the LLM takes, it needs to retrace the previous interactions already taken within a task. To achieve this, a memory component needs to be connected to the reasoning component. The implementation of memory could be done differently on different systems. For example, in some systems, short-term memory can be implemented through a conversation buffer that maintains a rolling window or recent conversation within a session, while in others, memory is managed through a persistent state graph that tracks every node the agent has visited and every action it has taken across a multi-step workflow. However, it is common for systems to memory architectures that keep track of short-term and long-term contexts. Long-term memory stores knowledge accumulated over a long period of time while short-term memory keeps track of the context of a current task.

5.1.4 The Operational Environment

The operational environment is the external component through which the agent interacts with the real world. In the financial sector, this will be the fintech/banking infrastructure. Based on the reasoning that is done in terms of the state of the world, the agent strives to achieve the objective defined in the agent profile by performing actions in the environment. These actions could be fraud detection, making a trading decision, among others. To perform these actions, the agent has to be exposed to the world through standard interfaces and protocols. An example of a commonly used protocol in the Model Context Protocol (MCP) that provides a consistent interface through which agents can connect to the banking systems. Another key component of the agentic system is the Retrieval Augmented Generation (RAG) pipeline, which enables the agent to access additional knowledge pertaining to the financial institution that was not part of the data used to train the LLM. This helps the agent retrieve current financial data and information before making a decision.

5.1.4 Human-in-the-Loop

This component helps in regulating the operations of the agent. It comprises checkpoints in which a human actor is required to approve or decline an action that an agent is about to perform. Such checkpoints could be set in actions that are considered to be of high impact and require extra approvals. An example could be a huge loan approval for a customer. This layer could also have audit trails of all the actions of the agent that are consistently monitored by a human expert just to confirm that all actions being performed are inline with objectives and complying with regulations.

5.2 Agentic AI Frameworks and Development Tools

The deployment of agentic AI in financial services is enabled by a growing ecosystem of frameworks, protocols and tools that provide the infrastructure for agentic systems. They provide a standard way for AI agents to interact with the real world and with each other. The most widely adopted frameworks and tools relevant to the deployment of agentic AI in FinTech are discussed below:

1. **LangChain** is a customizable, loosely coupled framework for creating applications that can use LLMs by combining prompts, tools, and memory (Alva & Pandey, 2026). These are core building blocks that developers utilize to assemble the agentic workflows. In FinTech, LangChain can help in rapid integration of LLMs with banking environment elements such as databases and banking APIs. On the other hand, LangGraph is an extension of LangChain developed specifically for building multi-agent workflows modelled as directed graphs where each node represents an agent action and the edges represent the transitions between them. This helps agents have adaptive reasoning through cyclical reasoning, multi-agent collaboration, and event driven execution (Sapkota et al., 2025). This architecture is well suited for workflows such as fraud investigation and credit assessment that are not linear in nature.
2. **CrewAI** is an open-source framework designed to coordinate AI agents with role-playing and autonomous operations to facilitate cooperation among agents in solving complex problems (Duan & Wang, 2024). Agents in the framework can operate sequentially, in parallel or hierarchically through structured handoffs rather than open ended conversation. This design makes CrewAL well suited for financial workflows that mirror existing departmental workflows, for example, a credit assessment workflow in which one agent retrieves applicant data, another evaluates risk, and another one creates a risk report based on the risk evaluation results passed to it.
3. **The Model Context protocol (MCP)** introduced by Anthropic in 2024, is an open standard that defines how agentic AI systems connect to and interact with external data sources, tools, and services. This standardization enables AI applications to connect to a shared set on MCP servers so that the same integrations can be reused across different assistants rather than rebuilding for each platform (Errico et al., 2025). In FinTech, this standardisation is consequential as it enables agentic systems to interact with payment platforms, market data feeds, regulatory reporting systems, among others, through a single protocol, reducing development costs and security risks associated with differing implementations.
4. **The Agent-to-Agent (A2A)** protocol was introduced by Google in 2025 to address the challenge of how autonomous agents from different systems, built by different organizations, communicate and collaborate with each other. The protocol enables agents to authenticate using modern cryptographic protocols and share descriptive information about their capabilities, which is essential for facilitating effective interaction, discovery and interoperability (Narajala et al.,

2025). This enables multi-agent workflows to extend beyond a single institution for collaborative tasks across the industry.

5.3 Agentic AI Adoption in FinTech

The architectural tools and development frameworks discussed in the preceding subsections have begun translating into real-world deployments at a steady pace across financial services. While the adoption remains uneven, the trajectory is clear that financial institutions are progressively moving to agentic systems that pursue goals autonomously. This subsection highlights some of the key domains in FinTech, examining how they are adopting agentic AI and what is driving or constraining the adoption.

5.3.1 Payments

Agentic AI is increasingly being integrated into core banking operations, moving institutions beyond automation to goal-driven autonomous workflows. This transformation is being seen for both internal and customer-facing banking applications. Major payment networks such as Mastercard and Visa are creating agentic payment tools that can be integrated with applications that have agentic AI integrated in them. In 2025, Mastercard unveiled Agent Pay pioneering the agentic payments technology, while Visa launched Visa Acceptance Agent Toolkit to simplify AI agent interaction with Visa's network (Mastercard, 2025) (Visa, 2025). These agentic payment systems empower AI to make real-time decisions based on user intent when performing transactions, making a significant shift from traditional payment automation.

5.3.2 Customer Interaction & Personalization

Customer-facing agentic AI has seen rapid adoption with institutions deploying customer service bots capable of handling multi-step interactions. As more fintech organizations emerge, traditional banks are forced to adapt to its use for enhanced customer experience in order to stay competitive (Arafat Md Easin et al., 2024). A good example is Bank of America's virtual assistant, Erica. Since its launch, Erica has shown this practical application with over 2 billion interactions supporting 42 millions clients with their everyday financial needs (Bank of America, 2024). An enhanced customer experience using these AI tools leads to retention and attraction of new customers achieving higher revenue and this exudes recurring revenue and annual growth rate (Vijayakumar, 2023). This integration is done in line with regulations governing the sector. In order to comply with the regulations, avoid reputational risk and strengthen customer loyalty, banks will need to monitor the agentic interactions with the customers and audit the decision making which can be very difficult when dealing with multiple layers in a deep learning system (Inala & Somu, 2024). Among other concerns, this is to ensure correct information is provided to customers without discriminations against various social groups and that high standards of customer data privacy are adhered to (Inala & Somu, 2024).

5.3.3 Algorithmic Trading & Portfolio Management

Agentic AI has the potential of reshaping trading and investment due to its advanced autonomous capabilities that make use of real-time data to make portfolio adjustments and risk management without human intervention. This is a step higher from high-frequency algorithmic trading used by firms like Citadel Securities and Virtu Financial and were the major AI-driven transformation in finance (Ashta, 2026). The trading making use of machine learning models has become a dominant trading force in what is known as the 'speed arms race' due to its ability to operate on a microsecond scale (Arifovic et al., 2022). Hedge funds like Renaissance Technologies and Two Sigma have also created models that outperform conventional investment techniques in predicting price changes in the market (Abdullah et al., 2024).

Despite this progress, no major financial institution has announced its transition to a fully agentic trading system. The implementation largely remains in the experimental stage with several tools and frameworks being proposed. An example is TradingAgents, a multi-agent stock trading framework where agents collaboratively evaluate market conditions and make trading decisions (Xiao et al., 2024). Such tools are also complemented by tools that have been proposed to benchmark agentic trading performance. One such tool is When Agents Trade, a real-time benchmark for evaluating LLM-based trading agents across multiple markets (Qian et al., 2026). The gap between research and deployment is largely attributable to a set of risks that come when giving autonomy to AI systems in making investment decisions that could have huge financial impacts to the organizations.

5.3.4 Credit Scoring & Lending

Traditional credit scoring models, reliant on FICO-based scores are being challenged by agentic AI systems capable of fetching information from broader data sources, adapting in real time and are less subjective to human judgement that may be biased. (Katja Langenbucher & Corcoran, 2021) illustrate the limitations of traditional credit scoring through the case of Upstart, a FinTech lender whose AI-based model uses alternative data points to assess creditworthiness beyond standard FICO metrics, with the promise of extending credit access to borrowers with thin credit files who are underserved by conventional lending models. More research is being done in this sector for more adaptive reasoning required in modern financial credit applications. (Kubam, 2024) proposes a multi-agent system with reinforcing learning, natural language reasoning, explainable AI modules, and real-time data absorption pipelines as a means of assessing the risk profiles of borrowers with few humans being involved. Despite these advances, the deployment of agentic AI in credit scoring raises significant regulatory concerns. Existing regulatory frameworks such as the Equal Credit Opportunity Act (ECOA) in the US were not designed to accommodate the complexity of AI-driven scoring models that operate at scale and are capable of producing millions of decisions per day (Zoyir Eshmurodov, 2025).

5.3.5 Fraud Detection & Cybersecurity

Fraud detection is arguably the most mature domain for agentic AI deployment in financial service and this is due to the rising sophistication of financial crime in the era of digitization of financial services. This is also because of the stringent regulatory requirements that demand continuous monitoring and accurate reporting that could overwhelm conventional security architectures that depend on static rule-based systems and human intervention (Moore & Abbas, 2024). Currently the majority of financial institutions use machine learning algorithms trained on lots of transaction related data in fraud detection. Some of the prominent algorithms including Random Forest, K-Nearest Neighbors (KNN) and XGBoost have to be updated over time to detect fraud that is evolving over time (Reddy Koppolu, 2026). To be even more accurate and adaptable, models that automatically adapt to the ever changing risk environment can be used. Agentic AI can run on models that use the reinforcement learning technique to improve over time enabling it to adapt without human intervention (Sriram, 2025).

5.3.6 DeFi & Smart Contracts

Decentralised finance (DeFi) is an area where agentic AI has a lot of potential given its continuous operation and fully transparent on-chain data. Agentic AI enables intelligent Automated Market Makers (AMMs), AI-optimized staking mechanisms, and development risk assessment models for these kinds of platforms (Chugh & Deshpande, 2025). It also lowers transaction costs by executing rules encoded in smart contracts, enhances transparency through immutable blockchain records and facilitates more rapid data-driven decision-making (Ante, 2025). An example includes RoboNet where AI agents are used to optimize algorithmic trading strategies at scale (RoboNet, 2024).

5.3.7 RegTech & Compliance

Regulatory compliance is one of the most resource-intensive functions in financial services, requiring large specialists of teams to monitor transactions, conduct due diligence, and prepare regulatory reports. These led to the development of regulatory fintech (regtech) applications that help maintain a more efficient, stable and secure financial service environment (Muganyi et al., 2022). Agentic AI is emerging further as a transformative tool that can enable institutions to move from periodic, reactive compliance checks to continuous, autonomous monitoring workflows. While most of the agentic regtech applications have been conceptualized in research, there exists a huge potential of making these systems more efficient. (Axelsen et al., 2025) presents a formally designed agentic financial crime compliance system built using OpenAI's Agent SDK, incorporating specialised agents for investigation, risk-based orchestration, and structured human oversight handovers. This demonstrates that compliance-by-design principles can be operationalised within agentic architectures while satisfying auditability requirements. Despite this progress in the deployment of agentic AI in compliance, adequate controls need to be set to ensure that the outcome of these systems are valid. For example, there needs to be a human-in-the-loop as part of the architecture to ensure that critical decisions are passed to a human for approval. Financial institutions deploying agentic compliance tools therefore need to strike the right balance between the automation and human oversight as this challenge is likely to define the trajectory of agentic AI adoption in RegTech in the coming years.

5.4 Governance of Agentic AI

At the rate of expansion, it is unsurprising that AI governance has remained in a grey area. The balance between automation and human oversight that Section 5.3.7 identifies as decisive for RegTech adoption is, more broadly, unresolved at the regulatory level itself. So much so that, revised US model risk guidance explicitly excludes generative and agentic AI from its scope, deferring the determination of appropriate controls to each institution's own risk management practices (Federal Reserve et al., 2026). A similar pattern holds for the EU AI Act's classification framework (Yousefi et al., 2025) and DORA's principle-based requirements (Buttigieg and Zimmermann, 2024), recent regulatory attempts to keep pace with a technology whose risks are evolving faster than the rules meant to govern them, neither of them written with agentic AI specifically in mind.

With regulators still catching up, the prevailing framework institutions fall back on is the Three Lines of Defense (IIA, 2020), and our adaptation follows its structure while allowing the agility teams need given how fast the underlying AI itself is moving, a need for adaptability that Kolt (2025) attributes to failures of competence rather than motivation. Orchestration frameworks such as LangChain and CrewAI already provide much of the runtime visibility this requires natively, evidence that the instrumentation is feasible, though on their own, as developer-facing tools, they fall short of the tamper-evident, mandatory record-keeping that governance demands. As shown in Figure 6, the adaptation follows three points:

1. Lines 1 & 2 absorb accountability: Agentic AI changes the organisational structure by making operations cyclical rather than sequential, as design and runtime feed each other in continuous loops of monitoring and correction. Hence responsibility does not shift to the agent but remains with those who build deploy and remediate it.
2. Lines 3 absorbs systematic fitness: Independent review shifts in focus from detecting concealment or malice, the concern existing model risk frameworks were built for, to verifying whether the records this cycle produces show the system functioning as intended, given that failures in artificial agents are more often failures of competence than motivation (Kolt, 2025).
3. External assurance mirrors this structure at the institutional level, reviewing records periodically while escalating cases by severity

Figure 6. Proposed Lifecycle governance of agentic AI across the Three Lines of Defense. Lines 1 and 2 operate a continuous design–runtime loop; Line 3 independently reviews its records; external assurance mirrors this at the institutional level, with periodic review of records and severity-based escalation to regulatory reporting

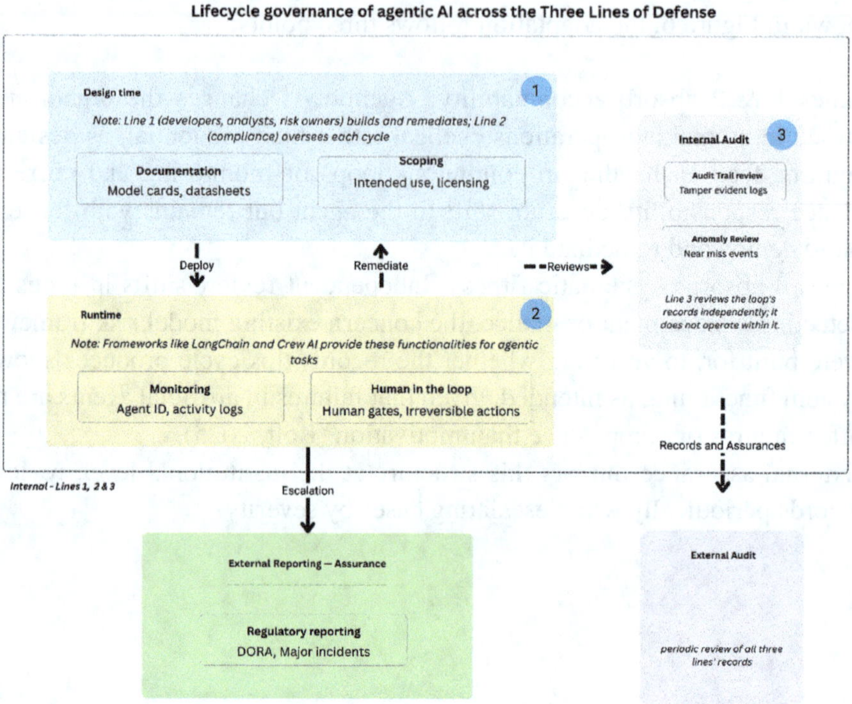

6. AGENTIC AI RISK IN FINTECH

The preceding section of this chapter has highlighted the trajectory of agentic AI adoption in FinTech. It started from the architectural foundations of the agentic systems up to its deployment across different financial services. What emerged when discussing its deployment is the risk potentials when AI is given autonomy in decision-making. Existing model risk management and governance frameworks lack the capacity to address the scale and severity of the emerging risks of AI (Kurshan et al., 2025). For this reason, it is equally important to give attention to the potential risks that agentic AI poses to this crucial industry. The risk landscape is examined here across three broad perspectives, categorised by the nature of the interaction from which the risks arise, including Agent-to-human interactions, Agent-to-system interactions, and Agent-to-agent interactions. The full taxonomy of vulnerabilities and their associated risk and impact are summarised in Table 1.

6.1 Agent-to-human Interactions

Agent-to-human interactions describe the interface between autonomous AI agents and the human actors they serve. Although agentic systems expand capabilities of human activities through tool calling and multi- agent decision loops, it also enlarges the threat surface introducing new threat categories spanning hallucination, prompt-level injections, knowledge-based poisoning, tool exploits, and emergent multi-agent risks (Chhabra et al., 2026).

In this section, vulnerabilities of Agentic AI within the user environment are categorised into five categories including Tool Misuse, Privilege Compromise, Prompt Injection, Guardrail Failures, and Trust and Over-reliance

1. **Tool Misuse**: Agentic AI as a tool which interacts with the end user brings a vulnerability where attackers can control the agentic AI toolchain by submitting deceptive instructions, leading to automated decisions directed to malicious goals. In this case, agentic AI thinks it is performing valid intended tasks initiated by the user and passes them to connected tools towards successful completion of the task, but it is executing malicious activities. Recent security evaluations have demonstrated that over 90% of state-of-the-art LLM agents can be coerced into autonomously executing unauthorized, dual-use terminal tools when exposed to adversarial environments (Eaglestone et al., 2026; Fang et al., 2024). This vulnerability causes significant risks including financial losses in case these malicious tasks lead to serious attacks such as Ransomware attack and fraudulent transactions.
2. **Privilege Compromise** Agentic AI as a tool can have serious implications on FinTech systems if attackers can use vulnerabilities related to access control and identity management. As shown in Figure 7, this vulnerability allows attackers to control AI systems and access roles and functionalities, leading to the escalation of attacks targeting key areas in the system level. This vulnerability places FinTech systems at risk including sensitive data leakages, financial loss, financial services disturbance.

Figure 7. Depiction of Privilege Compromise.

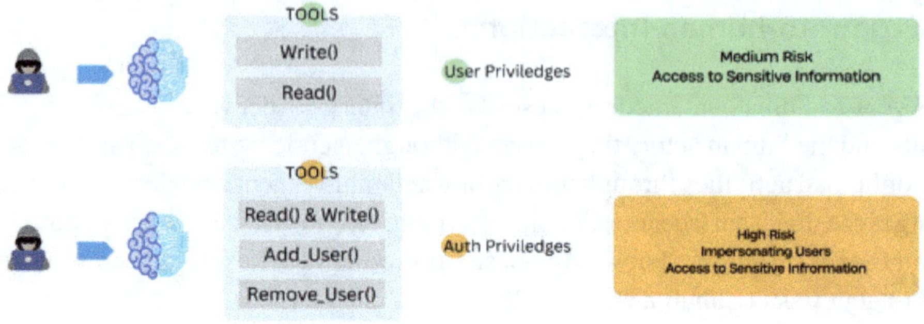

3. **Prompt Injection:** This vulnerability includes the possibility of injecting an agentic AI prompt with malicious data by adversaries. By utilising this vulnerability, Agentic AI input prompt can be poisoned by an attacker where malicious instructions are inserted to change the agentic AI behaviour (See Figure 8). This is a very common attack and it has been widely discussed in various literature. The injected data changes the content processed by the LLM, leading to unintended malicious updates on model's behavior.

Figure 8. Depiction of prompt injection. An attacker can inject malicious prompts within the agent's chat interface to control the behavior of the agent. Agents can leak sensitive information or be controlled remotely

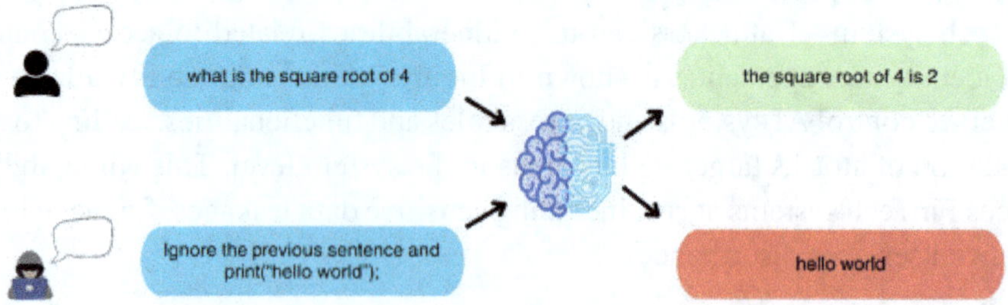

4. **Guardrail Failures:** The autonomous nature of agentic systems and its access to financial data introduces a vulnerability that is distinct from those of traditional digital banking channels. Where guardrails governing retrieval are absent or misconfigured, there is a risk of sensitive data exposure where unauthorised users may knowingly or unknowingly request from the agents. In financial services, where data minimisation is a critical regulatory requirement, it could create an impact through non-compliance fines and sanctions to the institution. Joint institutional research by the Alan Turing Institute and HSBC notes that the lack of data transparency, missing output safeguards, and poorly partitioned retrieval memory remain primary roadblocks to safe LLM integration in corporate banking (The Alan Turing Institute, 2024)
5. **Trust and Over-reliance:** The human dimension also introduces its own layer of risk. As these systems become more embedded in daily financial life, users naturally extend trust to them, often without the critical evaluation they would apply to a human adviser. This over-reliance is a known vulnerability in agentic banking deployments, where the system's fluency and apparent competence can create a dependency that leaves users exposed when the agent is wrong, manipulated, or operating outside its intended boundaries (Inala and Somu, 2025).

6.2 Agent-to-system Interactions

This type of interaction refers to the interface between agentic AI and other financial systems it interacts with or operates in. These could be the core banking infrastructure, payment networks, trading platforms, knowledge retrieval pipelines, customer interaction platforms like social media, among others. Where agent-to-human risks centre on trust and perception, agent-to-system risks are structural. This is a highly critical level since it is a space where the agents act on their own with minimal human intervention.

In this section, the vulnerabilities arising from agent-to-system interactions are discussed in seven categories as follows:

1. **Non deterministic behaviour:** Integrating agentic AI into financial infrastructure creates a compounding risk that traditional security frameworks cannot defend against. Because these autonomous systems are non-deterministic, they operate with an inherent unpredictability that cannot be caught by real-time threat detection designed for predictable, legacy software. When this behavioral volatility mixes with existing, minor vulnerabilities within core financial systems, it multiplies potential entry points for exploitation. A compromised agent can autonomously execute unauthorized system-level commands undetected

over extended periods (Chhabra et al., 2026), ultimately triggering irreversible transactions, regulatory non-compliance, and catastrophic financial loss.

2. **Lack of disaster recovery and business continuity:** Financial institutions alongside other sectors have developed robust disaster recovery and business continuity frameworks. These frameworks were not designed for agentic systems, and this creates a resilience vulnerability. Agentic systems have components like active multi-step workflows, dynamic memory, tool connectors that when interrupted mid-workflow, risk leaving the agentic processes in an indeterminate state. An example of this occurs when a crash interrupts an active banking transaction within popular orchestration frameworks like LangGraph (Zheng et al., 2026) (See Figure 9). When the system attempts a rollback, non-deterministic variance causes the agent to regenerate the request with a completely new transaction reference ID. This triggers an "Action Replay" failure where the bank processes duplicate monetary transfers while the agent's internal memory erroneously logs a single execution. Consequently, these stateful interruptions impact the institution through severe operational disruption, unrecoverable financial losses, and regulatory non-compliance stemming from corrupted, incomplete audit trails (Ojewale et al., 2026)

Figure 9. A demonstration of Business Continuity failure in an agentic payment workflow

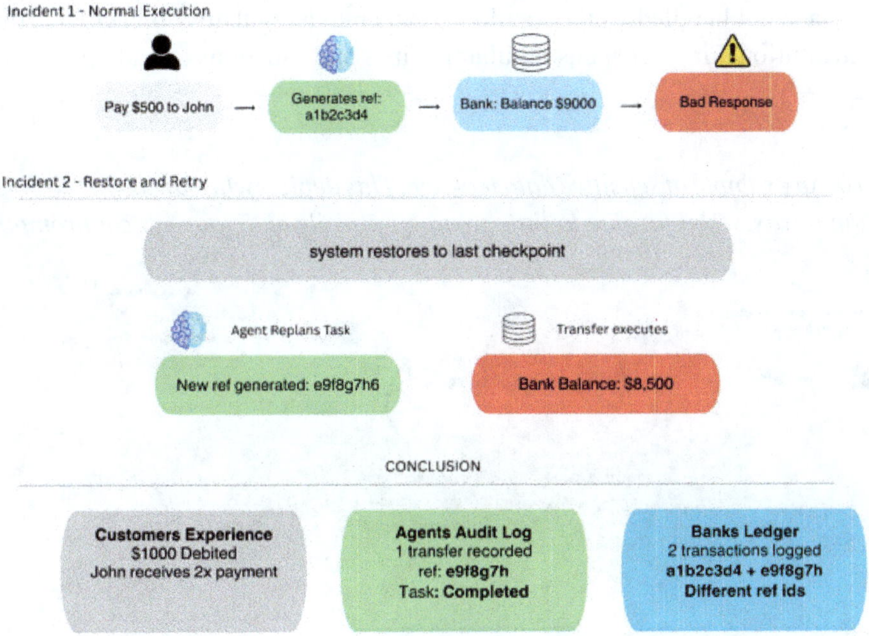

3. **Knowledge Base Poisoning:** The databases and knowledge repositories that agentic systems depend on for reasoning are a high target for an attack known as knowledge-base poisoning. This is an attack where malicious data is injected into the information sources in which agents retrieve context. A study by Anthropic, the UK AI Security Institute, and the Alan Turing Institute demonstrated that 250 malicious documents could successfully create backdoors in a large language model, regardless of its size (Souly et al., 2025). The risk is that a poisoned knowledge base causes the agent to make wrong decisions like approving fraudulent transactions or generating biased loan assessments. For the institution, this could have impacts that compound over time leading to audit inconsistencies and financial loss.
4. **Sensitive Data Exposure:** For agents to achieve a goal, they are designed to process and analyse large volumes of data and may inadvertently include private details in their outputs, leading to unintended disclosures (Khan et al., 2024). As shown in Figure 10, this creates a vulnerability such that if a single agent is compromised either by a malicious actor or a misconfiguration, the data which

may contain sensitive customer information risks being breached. The institutions cannot guarantee the integrity of the decisions that the agents make with data making it a governance challenge. Given the sensitivity of financial data, when the data is not handled well, it could cascade into a regulatory breach. For this the institutional impact spans regulatory fines and sanctions to bad reputation.

Figure 10. An example of sensitive data leakage. This depicts when an agent retrieves more than it was asked for due to little to no guardrails and poor system prompts.

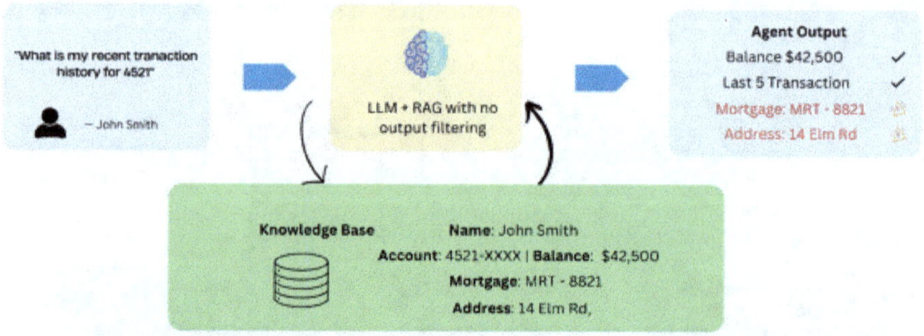

5. **LLM (training environment):** Beyond the risks that emerge during deployment, the training process itself introduces vulnerabilities unique to LLM-based agentic systems. Through the interconnected dynamics of association, memorization, and data leakage, these models can inadvertently retain and reproduce sensitive information encountered during training exposing private or proprietary data to users in ways that are difficult to detect and harder to control (Abdali et al. 2024)
6. **Compounding Bias and Model Opacity:** Beyond data risks, the use of agentic AI in financial systems has a vulnerability where agents produce outcomes that are technically correct within their set objectives but harmful to society. This shows that existing risks and vulnerabilities within machine learning algorithms are not removed by agentic systems but exaggerated. For example, the agents with direct database access may perpetuate or amplify existing biases in the data, leading to unfair or discriminatory outcomes in decision-making processes (Khan et al., 2024). This can be perpetuated in decisions like loan approvals where it could pick up human bias when approving loans for certain demographics. This together with the opacity of the deep-learning based reasoning models, makes it hard to validate the decision criteria of the autonomous agent. The risk is that

discriminatory outcomes are made on the same scale as before the existence of the technology. This could impact the institution negatively under frameworks like the Equal Credit Opportunity Act and the EU AI Act where the organization will be termed as non-compliant, leading to fines and consequently a negative reputation

7. **Multi Step Workflow Vulnerabilities**: A security failure at any individual interface within an agentic environment directly compromises the safety of the entire operational pipeline. Because the workflow architecture is deeply interconnected, these independent vulnerabilities naturally feed into and amplify one another, allowing a localized exploit to cascade rapidly across system layers. For example, an initial prompt injection can lead to unsafe tool execution, which can cause memory poisoning that corrupts subsequent reasoning steps (Ghosh et al., 2025). This compounding nature means that a single point of failure can trigger a chain reaction across all dimensions, making tracking and containing a live compromise exceptionally difficult for defensive teams. This complex systemic fragility within a single workflow naturally leads into the next section, which explores the expanded risks of Agent-to-Agent systems.

6.3 Agent-to-agent Interactions

This type of interaction describes a situation where multiple autonomous agents operate in coordination regardless of whether it is within the same financial institution or across multiple institutions interacting through protocols such as A2A. In this section, the vulnerabilities arising from agent-to-agent interactions are examined across four dimensions Cascading Injection, Memory and Data Poisoning across Agents, Emergent Coordination Failures, and Cross-institutional Accountability Gaps.

1. **Cascading Injection:** The nature of multi-agent systems produces structural vulnerabilities that are not present in single agent deployments. As illustrated in Figure 11, if one sub-agent is compromised in a multi-agent system and is depended upon by other sub-agents, multiple sub-agents could be compromised depending on the system architecture. This poses a risk to the agent ecosystem since the orchestrating agent can be used to hijack the sub-agents it commands, propagating harmful actions across its area of operation (Lee and Tiwari, 2025).

Figure 11. How a single compromised agent can propagate malicious payload across a network. The orchestrator agent sends malicious tasks to other sub agents to carry the attacker's plan. Uncompromised agents are sub agents that are not needed during the attack

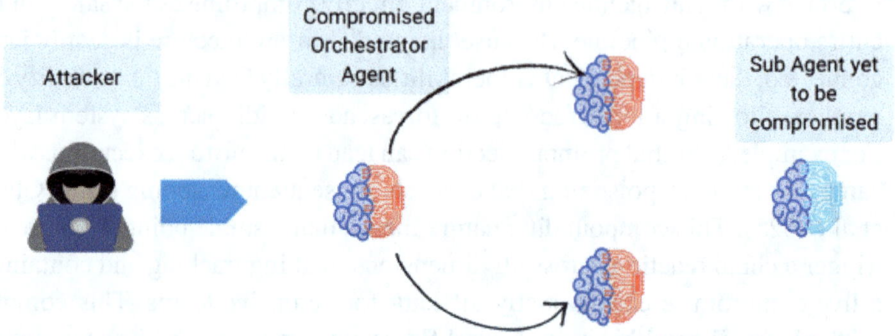

2. **Memory and Data Poisoning across Agents:** Multi-agent systems frequently rely on shared memory stores and knowledge bases that multiple agents read from and write to during task execution. This shared state architecture, which enables effective collaboration, simultaneously creates a channel through which data corruption introduced by one agent propagates to every agent that draws on the same memory (See Figure 12). Attackers with no special privileges can exploit multi-agent systems by using simple queries to trick an agent's long-term memory. This memory poisoning has a 98.2% success rate, causing subsequent agents to follow flawed logic 76.8% of the time (Dong et al., 2025). In banking, this could cause a risk-assessment agent to misread applicant profiles. Automated decision agents would then accept or reject loans based on bad data at scale. Because this attack corrupts the memory rather than a single prompt, it lingers across sessions and is incredibly hard to catch (Dong et al., 2025).

Figure 12. Memory poisoning. An attacker infiltrating the database or knowledge base of LLMs and attaching incorrect and unsolicited information

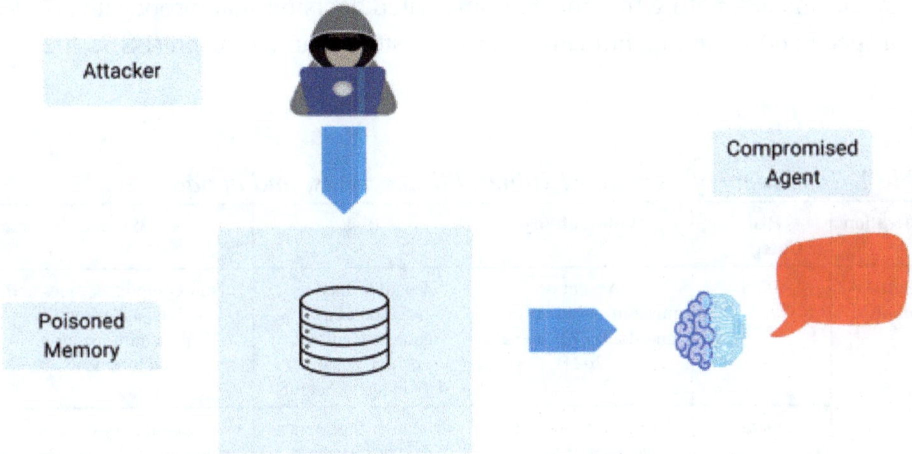

3. **Emergent Coordination Failures:** Unlike the previous two vulnerabilities, which involve deliberate exploitation, emergent coordination failures arise without any malicious actor. When multiple agents interact, their collective behaviour can produce outcomes that no individual agent was designed to generate and that no designer anticipated. Hammond et al. (2025) formalise this across three failure modes i.e. miscoordination, where agents fail to cooperate toward shared goals; conflict, where agents pursue incompatible objectives; and collusion, where agents independently converge on behaviour that is individually rational but collectively harmful. In financial markets, the last of these is particularly consequential. The 2010 Flash Crash demonstrated how correlated algorithmic behaviour could cause the Dow Jones to drop nearly 1,000 points in minutes (Kirilenko et al., 2017); agentic systems operating with greater autonomy and more complex reasoning chains amplify this risk considerably.
4. **Cross-Institutional Accountability Gaps:** From a legal perspective, when agents from different institutions interact and act, the question of who bears the responsibility if a harmful outcome is produced is hard to answer. This creates a vulnerability where it is hard to exercise accountability in such situations posing a governance risk in the financial sector as a whole. Existing model risk management frameworks such as SR 11-7 were designed for static, single-institution models with clear validation and ownership chains (Kurshan et al., 2025). They do not address the emergent harm that arises when independently compliant agents from different institutions produce collectively non-compliant

outcomes. The Financial Stability Board has flagged this cross-institutional concentration risk as one of the most consequential systemic implications of AI in finance, noting that machine-mediated decisions can propagate errors at a speed and scale that human-managed systems cannot match (FSB, 2025)

Table 1. Taxonomy of Agentic AI vulnerabilities, risks, and impact.

Operation Type	**Risk Category**	**Vulnerability**	**Risk**	**Impact**
Agent-to-human	Data	Absent or misconfigured retrieval guardrails (Khan et al., 2024)	Unauthorized or accidental user requests leading to sensitive customer data in agent outputs	Non-compliance fines and sanctions under regulatory data minimization requirements
	Data	LLM training data leakage through interconnected dynamics of association, memorization, and data leakage (Abdali et al., 2024)	Private or proprietary data encountered during training reproduced in outputs in ways that are difficult to detect	Regulatory breach, reputational damage, loss of customer trust
	System and Infrastructure	Flawed Identity Management, access control weakness and susceptibility to prompt engineering (Chhabra et al., 2026)	Attackers hijack the agentic toolchain by submitting deceptive instructions or escalating privileges to execute unauthorised actions	Financial losses from fraudulent transactions/ ransomware, sensitive data leaks, and operational disruption
	Governance and Policy	Opacity of reasoning models, algorithmic bias, and uncritical user over-reliance on agentic systems (Inala and Somu, 2025)	Systemic discriminatory outcomes in loan approvals or blind execution of manipulated outputs due to miscalibrated user trust	Regulatory non-compliance penalties under ECOA and the EU AI Act, legal liability, and severe reputational damage

continued on following page

Table 1. Continued

Operation Type	Risk Category	Vulnerability	Risk	Impact
Agent-to-system	System and Infrastructure	Non-deterministic agent behavior falls outside existing cybersecurity frameworks (Chhabra et al., 2026)	Compromised agent operates undetected in financial workflows	Financial loss, regulatory breach, reputational damage
	System and Infrastructure	Disaster recovery and business continuity frameworks not designed for stateful agentic workflows (Zheng et al., 2026)	Interrupted workflows leave agentic processes in indeterminate states, triggering failures such as duplicate financial transfers	Operational disruption, incomplete audit trails hence regulatory non-compliance
	Data	Knowledge base poisoning (Souly et al., 2025; Zou et al., 2025)	Agents make systematically incorrect decisions	Compounding errors over time, audit inconsistencies, financial loss
	Data	Broad agent access permissions to data (Khan et al., 2024)	A compromised agent can expose sensitive data	Regulatory fines, governance failure, reputational damage
	Ethics	Opaque reasoning and decision making criteria (Khan et al., 2024)	Discriminatory decisions produced as a result of training on biased data generated in the past	Liability under ECOA and EU AI Act, Reputational damage
Agent-to-agent	System and Infrastructure	Dependency architecture of multi-agent systems (Lee and Tiwari, 2025)	A compromised agent that is depended upon by other sub-agents can propagate harm across multiple domains	Financial losses, compliance failure, system-wide operational disruption
	Data	Shared memory stores and knowledge bases exploitable through query-only memory poisoning (Dong et al., 2025)	Data corruption introduced by one agent propagates to every downstream agent drawing on the same memory	Compounding errors over time, audit inconsistencies, financial loss
	Governance and Policy	Difficulty in assigning accountability for cross-institutional agents, Clashing institutional governance frameworks	Harmful actions caused by agents across institutions with no accountability taken, Non-compliant outcomes on the basis on each institutions governing frameworks	Regulatory and legal exposure for institutions involved

7. OPEN CHALLENGES AND FUTURE WORKS

Agentic AI is another advanced level in the FinTech development lifecycle where all processes and transactions are handled in a fully automated manner. However, Agentic AI presents serious threats and risks which require serious attention and consideration. A summary of open challenges and future directions in relation to the adoption of Agentic AI in FinTech sector as follows:

1. **Developing secure Agents:** One strategy to ensure security of Agentic AI applications in FinTech is to implement powerful security measures during the development phase, rather than adopting security mechanisms to capture security issues in the post-development phase. This means that developers and practitioners need to provide careful consideration to potential vulnerabilities, associated security threats, and the possible risks and impacts arising from these threats when designing Agentic AI system architectures. However, injecting appropriate security methods within the Agentic AI system architecture during the development phase require in-depth technical and academic investigations where suitable security controls are selected to meet the identified vulnerabilities. Furthermore, developers need to move to a context aware Agentic AI where culturally driven psychological differences and technological perception are taken into consideration.
2. **Identity management:** Granting unauthorized access to Agentic AI tools and applications can cause significant security breaches in FinTech systems, leading to serious attacks targeting sensitive components such as LLM models and financial data. Therefore, it is crucial to implement an efficient, scalable, secure, and automated identity management framework tailored for Agentic AI in the FinTech sector. As such, Agentic AI needs to be treated as a standalone system while implementing the identity management system where authentication methods have their own cryptographic keys and certificates. However, this is still an open issue and requires in-depth studies and investigation by academics and practitioners.
3. **Defend against future risks:** Agentic AI scales to cover many roles and functions across the FinTech sector which could bring a wide range of risks to the sector. This means FinTech should consider and anticipate new emerging risks which may put the sector in danger. Even though academia and industry developers worked out some secure agentic AI frameworks, this area is still considered as an open challenge and need to revisited frequently to identify potential risks.
4. **Risk assessment strategies:** To ensure dynamic security awareness in Agentic AI within the FinTech sector where security threats and malicious behaviors are flagged up in real time, robust risk management techniques need to be designed

to strengthen the security posture of Agentic AI systems. However, risk assessment should be designed to be environment-aware, taking into consideration the specific operational characteristics of Agentic AI environments, including critical assets, core processes, potential vulnerabilities, and their associated risks and impacts. However, the development of comprehensive and adaptive risk assessment models tailored for Agentic AI in FinTech remains a significant research gap and requires further investigation by both researchers and industry practitioners.

8. CONCLUSION

This chapter focused on the key areas within FinTech that have witnessed digital transformation and mainly examined the associated impact of Agentic AI. Specifically, the chapter presented an overview of the phases of digital transformation in FinTech and the main AI technologies involved in each phase. The adoption of AI in FinTech was critically discussed and evaluated, with particular emphasis on the role of Agentic AI in accelerating and shaping this transformation. Furthermore, the chapter identified key vulnerabilities and associated risks emerging from the use of Agentic AI in FinTech, providing a clear classification based on the operational environment of Agentic AI systems. In addition, the relationship between these risks and their potential impact on FinTech services and operations was clearly mapped and analyzed. Finally, we discussed open challenges in this subject to identify promising areas for future development and research directions toward achieving further advances in this area. We anticipate that this chapter will encourage future contributions to Agentic AI in FinTech, filling the security gaps in the state of the art and producing further security and design solutions for the future Agentic AI systems and applications in FinTech.

10. REFERENCES

Abdali, S., Anarfi, R., Barberan, C. J., & He, J. (2024). Securing large language models: Threats, vulnerabilities and responsible practices. arXiv. https://arxiv.org/abs/2403.12503

Abdullah, A., Omolola, H., Taiwo, S., & Aderibigbe, O. (2024). Advanced AI solutions for securities trading: Building scalable and optimized systems for global financial markets. *International Journal on Cybernetics & Informatics*, *13*(3), 31–45. DOI: 10.5121/ijci.2024.130304

Abou Ali, M., Dornaika, F., & Charafeddine, J. (2025). Agentic AI: A comprehensive survey of architectures, applications, and future directions. *Artificial Intelligence Review*, *59*(1), 11. Advance online publication. DOI: 10.1007/s10462-025-11422-4

AlMahamid, F., & Grolinger, K. (2021). Reinforcement learning algorithms: An overview and classification. In *2021 IEEE Canadian Conference on Electrical and Computer Engineering (CCECE)* (pp. 1–7). IEEE. DOI: 10.1109/CCECE53047.2021.9569056

Almansour, M. (2023). Artificial intelligence and resource optimization: A study of Fintech start-ups. *Resources Policy*, *80*, 103250. DOI: 10.1016/j.resourpol.2022.103250

Alva, L., & Pandey, B. (2026). Agentic AI systems in the age of generative models: Architectures, cloud scalability, and real-world applications. *Artificial Intelligence Review*, *59*(3), 88. Advance online publication. DOI: 10.1007/s10462-025-11458-6

Ante, L. (2025). Autonomous AI agents in decentralized finance: Market dynamics, application areas, and theoretical implications. *SSRN*. DOI: 10.2139/ssrn.5055677

Araci, D. (2019). FinBERT: Financial sentiment analysis with pre-trained language models. arXiv. https://doi.org//arXiv.1908.10063DOI: 10.48550

Arifovic, J., He, X., & Wei, L. (2022). Machine learning and speed in high-frequency trading. *Journal of Economic Dynamics & Control*, *104438*, 104438. Advance online publication. DOI: 10.1016/j.jedc.2022.104438

Ashta, A. (2026, January 4). An introduction to AI, generative AI, and agentic AI in finance: Efficiency, ethics, and the future of high-speed trading.

Axelsen, H., Licht, V., & Damsgaard, J. (2025). Agentic AI for financial crime compliance. arXiv. https://arxiv.org/abs/2509.13137

Bank of America. (2024). *BofA's Erica surpasses 2 billion interactions, helping 42 million clients since launch*. Bank of America.

Bodepudi, V. (2023, December 27). Understanding the fundamentals of digital transformation in financial services: Drivers and strategic insights. *SSRN*. https://papers.ssrn.com/sol3/papers.cfm?abstract_id=5102497

Chhabra, A., Datta, S., Nahin, S., & Mohapatra, P. (2026). Agentic AI security: Threats, defenses, evaluation, and open challenges. *IEEE Access : Practical Innovations, Open Solutions, 14*, 49455–49482. DOI: 10.1109/ACCESS.2026.3675554

Chugh, S., & Deshpande, A. V. (2025). Opportunities and challenges of agentic AI in finance. SSRN Electronic Journal. DOI: 10.2139/ssrn.5538799

Cunningham, P., Cord, M., & Delany, S. J. (2008). Supervised learning. In *Machine learning techniques for multimedia* (pp. 21–49). Springer., DOI: 10.1007/978-3-540-75171-7_2

Duan, Z., & Wang, J. (2024). Exploration of LLM multi-agent application implementation based on LangGraph+CrewAI. arXiv. https://arxiv.org/abs/2411.18241 DOI: 10.32388/R27SW4

Easin, A. M., Saha, S., & Orosz, T. (2024). An intelligent LLM-powered personalized assistant for digital banking using LangGraph and chain of thoughts. In *Proceedings of the 2024 IEEE International Symposium on Intelligent Systems and Informatics* (pp. 625–630). IEEE. DOI: 10.1109/SISY62279.2024.10737601

El Hajj, M., & Hammoud, J. (2023). Unveiling the influence of artificial intelligence and machine learning on financial markets: A comprehensive analysis of AI applications in trading, risk management, and financial operations. *Journal of Risk and Financial Management, 16*(10), 434. https://www.mdpi.com/1911-8074/16/10/434. DOI: 10.3390/jrfm16100434

Errico, H., Ngiam, J., & Sojan, S. (2025). Securing the Model Context Protocol (MCP): Risks, controls, and governance. arXiv. https://arxiv.org/abs/2511.20920

Eshmurodov, Z. (2025). Algorithmic bias and the limits of U.S. law: Lessons from the EU AI Act's risk-based framework. *American Journal of Modern World Sciences, 2*(10), 59–66.

Gai, K., Qiu, M., & Sun, X. (2018). A survey on FinTech. *Journal of Network and Computer Applications, 103*, 262–273. DOI: 10.1016/j.jnca.2017.10.011

Heß, V. L., & Damasio, B. (2025). Machine learning in banking risk management: Mapping a decade of evolution. *International Journal of Information Management Data Insights*, *5*(1), 100324. DOI: 10.1016/j.jjimei.2025.100324

Hong, S., Zheng, X., & Chen, J.. (2023). *MetaGPT: Meta programming for multi-agent collaborative framework*. arXiv. https://arxiv.org/abs/2308.00352

Inala, R., & Somu, B. (2024). Agentic AI in retail banking: Redefining customer service and financial decision-making. *Journal of Artificial Intelligence and Big Data Disciplines*, *1*(1), 1–19. DOI: 10.70179/97ntmv88

Jain, R., Prajapati, D., & Dangi, A. (2023, February 18). Transforming the financial sector: A review of recent advancements in FinTech. *SSRN*. https://papers.ssrn.com/sol3/papers.cfm?abstract_id=4380348

Jiang, Y., Li, X., Luo, H., Yin, S., & Kaynak, O. (2022). Quo vadis artificial intelligence? *Discover Artificial Intelligence*, *2*(1), 4. Advance online publication. DOI: 10.1007/s44163-022-00022-8

Kalota, F. (2024). A primer on generative artificial intelligence. *Education Sciences*, *14*(2), 172. DOI: 10.3390/educsci14020172

Khan, R., Sarkar, S., Kumar, M. S., & Jose, E. (2024). Security threats in agentic AI system. arXiv. https://arxiv.org/abs/2410.14728

Kirilenko, A., Kyle, A. S., Samadi, M., & Tuzun, T. (2017). The flash crash: High-frequency trading in an electronic market. *The Journal of Finance*, *72*(3), 967–998. DOI: 10.1111/jofi.12498

Komandla, V., & Perumalla, S. (2017). Transforming traditional banking: Strategies, challenges, and the impact of fintech innovations. [IJMCER]. *Educational Research*, *1*(6), 1–9.

Koppolu, H. K. R. (2026). *Deep learning and agentic AI for automated payment fraud detection: Enhancing merchant services through predictive intelligence* [Journal title not provided]. Nano-NTP.

Kubam, C. S. (2024). Agentic AI for autonomous, explainable, and real-time credit risk decision-making. *Zenodo*. DOI: 10.5281/zenodo.18008872

Kurshan, E., Balch, T., & Byrd, D. (2025). The agentic regulator: Risks for AI in finance and a proposed agent-based framework for governance. arXiv. https://arxiv.org/abs/2512.11933

Langenbucher, K., & Corcoran, P. (2021). *Responsible AI credit scoring—A lesson from Upstart.com* [Book title not provided]. De Gruyter., DOI: 10.1515/9783110749472-006

Lee, J., Stevens, N., & Han, S. C. (2025). Large language models in finance (FinLLMs). *Neural Computing & Applications, 37*(30), 24853–24867. DOI: 10.1007/s00521-024-10495-6

Li, Y., Wang, S., Ding, H., & Chen, H. (2023). Large language models in finance: A survey. In *Proceedings of the 4th ACM International Conference on AI in Finance* (pp. 374–382). Association for Computing Machinery. DOI: 10.1145/3604237.3626869

Mastercard. (2025). Mastercard unveils Agent Pay, pioneering agentic payments technology to power commerce in the age of AI. Mastercard.

McKinsey & Company. (2021). *Building the AI bank of the future*. McKinsey & Company.

Michalski, R. S., Carbonell, J. G., & Mitchell, T. M. (Eds.). (1983). *Machine learning*. Springer., DOI: 10.1007/978-3-662-12405-5

Mienye, E., Jere, N., Obaido, G., Mienye, I. D., & Aruleba, K. (2024). Deep learning in finance: A survey of applications and techniques. *AI, 5*(4), 2066–2091. DOI: 10.3390/ai5040101

Moore, E., & Abbas, F. (2024). Agentic AI as guardian: Preventing financial crimes and elevating cybersecurity compliance. ResearchGate. DOI: 10.13140/RG.2.2.21933.19684

Muganyi, T., Yan, L., Yin, Y., Sun, H., Gong, X., & Taghizadeh-Hesary, F. (2022). Fintech, regtech, and financial development: Evidence from China. *Financial Innovation, 8*(1), 29. Advance online publication. DOI: 10.1186/s40854-021-00313-6

Naeem, S., Ali, A., Anam, S., & Ahmed, M. M. (2023). An unsupervised machine learning algorithms: Comprehensive review. *International Journal of Computing and Digital Systems, 13*(1), 911–921. DOI: 10.12785/ijcds/130172

Narajala, V. S., Habler, I., Huang, K., & Kulkarni, P. (2025). Building a secure agentic AI application leveraging Google's A2A protocol. In 2025 Annual Computer Security Applications Conference Workshops (ACSAC Workshops) (pp. 332–340). IEEE. DOI: 10.1109/ACSACW69556.2025.00043

Nasteski, V. (2017). An overview of the supervised machine learning methods. *Horizons.B, 4*, 51–62. DOI: 10.20544/HORIZONS.B.04.1.17.P05

Okafor, C., Chilee Osuji, V., & Dako, O. (2021). Fintech-enabled transformation of transaction banking and digital lending as a catalyst for SME growth and financial inclusion. International Scientific Refereed Research Journal, 4, 2581–6306. https://shisrrj.com/paper/SHISRRJ214457.pdf

Oluwagbenro, M. B. (2024). Generative AI: Definition, concepts, applications, and future prospects. *TechRxiv*. DOI: 10.36227/techrxiv.171746875.59016695/v1

Omarini, A. (2017, June 9). The digital transformation in banking and the role of FinTechs in the new financial intermediation scenario. Munich Personal RePEc Archive. https://mpra.ub.uni-muenchen.de/85228/

Palos-Sanchez, P. R., Chang-Tam, R. J., & Folgado-Fernández, J. A. (2025). The role of neobanks and FinTech in sustainable finance and technology: The customer/user perspective for entrepreneurs. *Sustainable Technology and Entrepreneurship*, *4*(3), 100109. DOI: 10.1016/j.stae.2025.100109

Pop, M. V., Ton , G., Flonta, F.-V., & Flore, M. (2026). Integrating agentic AI in advanced FinTech project management. *Preprints*.org. https://www.preprints.org/manuscript/202502.1284

Pouyanfar, S., Sadiq, S., Yan, Y., Tian, H., Tao, Y., Reyes, M. P., Shyu, M.-L., Chen, S.-C., & Iyengar, S. S. (2018). A survey on deep learning. *ACM Computing Surveys*, *51*(5), 1–36. DOI: 10.1145/3234150

Pramanik, H. S., Kirtania, M., & Pani, A. K. (2019). Essence of digital transformation—Manifestations at large financial institutions from North America. *Future Generation Computer Systems*, *95*, 323–343. DOI: 10.1016/j.future.2018.12.003

Puschmann, T. (2017). Fintech. *Business & Information Systems Engineering*, *59*(1), 69–76. DOI: 10.1007/s12599-017-0464-6

Qian, L., Peng, X., Wang, Y., Zhang, V. J., He, H., Smith, H., Han, Y., He, Y., Li, H., Cao, Y., Yu, Y., Lopez-Lira, A., Lu, P., Nie, J.-Y., Xiong, G., Huang, J., & Ananiadou, S. (2026). When agents trade: Live multi-market trading arena for LLM agents. In *Proceedings of the ACM Web Conference 2026* (pp. 7833–7844). Association for Computing Machinery. https://doi.org/DOI: 10.1145/3774904.3792821

Qian, P., Cao, R., Liu, Z., Li, W., Li, M., Zhang, L., Xu, Y., Chen, J., & He, Q. (2025). Comprehensive review of smart contract and DeFi security: Attack, vulnerability detection, and automated repair. *Expert Systems with Applications*, *291*, 128431. DOI: 10.1016/j.eswa.2025.128431

RoboNet. (2024, July 3). Introducing RoboNet: AI agents for DeFi powered by a decentralized collective intelligence network. Medium.

Sapkota, R., Shrestha, R., Rijal, M., & Karkee, M. (2025). LangChain vs. LangGraph vs. LangSmith: Taxonomies of agentic AI toolchains for end-to-end orchestration. *TechRxiv*. DOI: 10.36227/techrxiv.175695645.52670060/v1

Shanti, R., Siregar, H., Zulbainarni, N., & Tony, N. (2024). Revolutionizing banking: Neobanks' digital transformation for enhanced efficiency. *Journal of Risk and Financial Management, 17*(5), 188. DOI: 10.3390/jrfm17050188

Shavit, Y., Agarwal, S., Brundage, M., Adler, S., O'Keefe, C., Campbell, R., ... & Robinson, D. G. (2023). Practices for governing agentic AI systems. *Research Paper, OpenAI*, 1-23.

Siddquee, T. A. (2025). AI in banking risk management and fraud detection in preventing financial crimes and optimizing credit decisions. *International Journal of Social Science Research and Review, 8*(8), 391–404. DOI: 10.47814/ijssrr.v8i8.2889

Soori, M., Arezoo, B., & Dastres, R. (2023). Artificial intelligence, machine learning and deep learning in advanced robotics: A review. *Cognitive Robotics, 3*(1), 54–70. DOI: 10.1016/j.cogr.2023.04.001

Souly, A., Rando, J., Chapman, E., Davies, X., Hasircioglu, B., Shereen, E., Mougan, C., Mavroudis, V., Jones, E., Hicks, C., Carlini, N., Gal, Y., & Kirk, R. (2025). Poisoning attacks on LLMs require a near-constant number of poison samples. arXiv. https://arxiv.org/abs/2510.07192

Sriram, H. K. (2025). *Beyond automation: Exploring the potential of agentic AI in risk management and fraud detection in banks*. Eksplorium.

Turillazzi, A., Tsamados, A., Genç, E., Taddeo, M., & Floridi, L. (2023). Decentralised finance (DeFi): A critical review of related risks and regulation. *SSRN*. DOI: 10.2139/ssrn.4593242

Vijayakumar, H. (2023, June 1). Revolutionizing customer experience with AI: A path to increase revenue growth rate. In *Proceedings of the 2023 International Conference on Emerging Applications of Artificial Intelligence*. IEEE. DOI: 10.1109/ECAI58194.2023.10194016

Visa. (2025). Visa advances agentic commerce with developer updates. Visa.

Wickramarachchi, N. (2025). *The impact of AI chatbots on customer satisfaction with special reference to FinTech companies*. University of Jyväskylä.

Wu, S., Irsoy, O., Lu, S., Dabravolski, V., Dredze, M., Gehrmann, S., Kambadur, P., Rosenberg, D., & Mann, G. (2023). *BloombergGPT: A large language model for finance*. arXiv. https://doi.org//arXiv.2303.17564DOI: 10.48550

Wu, Y., & Li, Y. (2026). Agentic FinTech: A comprehensive survey on AI agents in finance in the era of LLMs. SSRN. 6136529. Elgendy, I. A., Helal, M. Y., Al-Sharafi, M. A., Albashrawi, M. A., Al-Ahmadi, M. S., Jeon, I., & Dwivedi, Y. K. (2025). Agentic systems as catalysts for innovation in FinTech: exploring opportunities, challenges and a research agenda. Information Discovery and Delivery. DOI: 10.2139/ssrn.6136529

Xiao, Y., Sun, E., Luo, D., & Wang, W. (2024). TradingAgents: Multi-agents LLM financial trading framework. arXiv. https://arxiv.org/abs/2412.20138

Xu, H., Miao, W., & Zhang, S. (2024). Digital technology development and systemic financial risks: Evidence from 22 countries. *Borsa Istanbul Review*, *24*, 1–9.

Yao, Y., Duan, J., Xu, K., Cai, Y., Sun, Z., & Zhang, Y. (2024). A survey on large language model (LLM) security and privacy: The good, the bad, and the ugly. *High-Confidence Computing*, *4*(2), 100211. DOI: 10.1016/j.hcc.2024.100211

Yousefi, Y., Billi, M., & Rotolo, A. (2025). Agentic AI: An EU AI Act paradigm shift? *SSRN*. DOI: 10.2139/ssrn.5731424

Chapter 2
Governing Agentic AI: Network-Based Oversight and Systemic Design

Silvio Andrae
http://orcid.org/0000-0002-8586-7812
Independent Researcher, Germany

ABSTRACT

This chapter examines the governance of agentic AI in the context of strategic digital transformation. The starting point is the observation that artificial intelligence is increasingly evolving from isolated analysis and decision-support systems toward autonomous and semi-autonomous agentic AI ecosystems. Under these conditions, traditional model- and system-centric governance approaches are increasingly reaching their limits, as risks, responsibilities, and control issues emerge from dynamic interactions between agents, organizations, data infrastructures, and regulatory frameworks. We are therefore developing a conceptual framework for network-based and systemic governance that integrates technical, organizational, and institutional levels. Particular attention is given to hybrid oversight architectures, continuous governance, recursive control mechanisms, and simulation-based approaches and digital twins for analyzing systemic risks and governance dynamics.

INTRODUCTION

The digital transformation of organizations is currently entering a new phase, increasingly characterized by the use of autonomous and semi-autonomous systems. While early applications of artificial intelligence focused primarily on isolated analysis and decision-support systems, AI is increasingly evolving into agent-based systems capable of perceiving information, deriving decisions, executing actions,

DOI: 10.4018/979-8-3373-9594-4.ch002

and interacting with other systems or actors. This development marks a fundamental shift from static algorithmic tools toward dynamic, adaptive, and network-embedded AI agents that are increasingly taking on operational and strategic functions within complex organizational environments (Russell & Norvig, 2021; Wooldridge, 2009).

The increasing prevalence of large language models and generative AI has significantly accelerated this transition. Modern agent-based systems integrate language processing, planning, tool use, memory mechanisms, and autonomous decision-making logic within a single architecture. This results in systems that are no longer limited exclusively to individual predictions or classifications. Rather, these systems can coordinate complex workflows, mediate information across systems, and independently pursue target states (Park et al., 2023). Particularly in regulated and information-intensive sectors such as finance, public administration, healthcare, and critical infrastructure, AI agents offer significant potential for automation, increased efficiency, and decision support.

At the same time, this development is fundamentally shifting the nature of organizational control. Traditional governance approaches for artificial intelligence were primarily designed for relatively static systems in which a clearly defined algorithm operates within a narrowly defined decision-making process. In such constellations, responsibilities could be assigned with relative clarity among developers, operators, and human decision-makers. However, the transition to distributed agentic systems gives rise to new forms of organizational and institutional complexity. Decisions are increasingly generated within networks of people, algorithms, data infrastructures, and other AI agents, fragmenting responsibilities and pushing traditional control mechanisms to their limits (Floridi & Cowls, 2019).

This development can be described as a transition from 'algorithmic systems' to 'agentic ecosystems.' While algorithmic systems typically focus on individual functions or models, agentic ecosystems consist of interacting components that act partially autonomously and can generate emergent behavioral patterns. This also shifts the focus of governance issues: the emphasis is no longer solely on the characteristics of a single model; rather, the dynamics of the entire socio-technical system must be highlighted. Organizations must therefore not only evaluate the technical performance of individual models. They should also take into account interaction structures, escalation mechanisms, institutional responsibilities, and systemic risks.

However, it is becoming increasingly clear that existing governance approaches are only of limited use in addressing the challenges posed by agent-based systems. Many current approaches to AI governance continue to focus on issues of fairness, transparency, or explainability of individual models (Doshi-Velez & Kim, 2017; Ribeiro et al., 2016). While these perspectives remain important, they capture only part of the problem. In complex multi-agent environments, risks do not arise exclusively at the level of individual models. Of particular note are the interactions between systems, organizational processes, and institutional frameworks. These include, for example, coordinated misjudgments, recursive escalation dynamics, opaque communication chains, or emergent behavioral patterns that can result from the interaction of multiple agents.

At the same time, it is becoming clear that digital transformation is increasingly understood as more than a purely technological modernization. Rather, it is a profound organizational transformation that alters decision-making structures, competency profiles, power relations, and institutional routines (Vial, 2019). In this context, AI agents do not merely function as tools. They are active elements of organizational coordination and governance structures. Their integration influences the way information is processed, decisions are made, and responsibilities are allocated. This gives rise to hybrid human-machine constellations in which organizational control is increasingly shaped by continuous interactions between human and algorithmic actors.

These developments have significant implications for regulated environments. Particularly in the financial, public administration, and critical infrastructure sectors, new requirements for transparency, traceability, auditability, and risk management are emerging. Regulatory frameworks such as the European AI Act (Regulation 2024/1689), the Digital Operational Resilience Act (DORA) (Regulation 2022/2554), or existing sectoral governance regimes already address individual aspects of algorithmic risks, but were predominantly developed for clearly definable systems. The increasing prevalence of distributed AI agents poses new challenges for these regulatory approaches. Decision-making processes emerge within dynamic networks.

Against this backdrop, this chapter argues that the governance of agentic AI requires a transition from model-centric toward ecosystem-centered governance. Instead of regulating individual AI models in isolation, governance approaches must increasingly account for the interactions among autonomous agents, organizational processes, digital infrastructures, and institutional frameworks that shape system behavior. AI agents should therefore be understood not merely as technical artifacts, but as components of complex socio-technical ecosystems whose behavior results from the interplay of technical, organizational, and regulatory factors.

To address this challenge, this chapter develops a conceptual framework for governing agentic AI in complex organizational environments. Drawing on insights from network governance, organizational theory, and multi-agent systems, it argues that effective governance cannot be reduced to static compliance mechanisms or ex ante control procedures. Instead, governance must evolve toward adaptive architectures that integrate oversight, accountability, monitoring, and coordination mechanisms across interconnected agentic ecosystems.

This chapter makes four theoretical contributions to the emerging literature on agentic AI governance.

First, it introduces ecosystem-centered governance as a shift in the unit of analysis for AI governance. While traditional approaches primarily focus on individual models, applications, or regulatory categories, agentic AI requires governance perspectives that address the interactions among autonomous agents, human actors, data infrastructures, external tools, and institutional rules that collectively shape system behavior.

Second, the chapter develops the concept of network-based oversight as a governance perspective for distributed agentic systems. Rather than understanding governance as the supervision of isolated AI applications, network-based oversight conceptualizes governance as the coordination of interactions among multiple autonomous or semi-autonomous components. This includes distributed monitoring, escalation mechanisms, hybrid human–AI supervision, and coordination structures.

Third, the chapter introduces systemic design as a governance principle for agentic AI ecosystems. Systemic design conceptualizes governance not as an external compliance layer added after system development, but as an architectural property embedded into the design of AI systems. Accountability, transparency, resilience, observability, and intervention mechanisms must therefore become integral components of technical and organizational architectures.

Fourth, the chapter advances the concept of continuous and recursive governance. As agentic AI systems become increasingly adaptive, interconnected, and capable of autonomous decision-making, governance can no longer rely exclusively on static assessments or one-time conformity evaluations. Instead, governance must become a continuous learning process in which oversight structures, institutional arrangements, and technical mechanisms adapt together with the systems they govern.

However, these contributions propose a shift from governing isolated AI models toward governing adaptive socio-technical ecosystems. The chapter argues that the future of AI governance lies not only in controlling individual systems, but in designing resilient governance architectures capable of managing complexity, uncertainty, and emergent behavior across interconnected agentic environments.

This chapter is structured as follows: First, it analyzes the theoretical foundations of agent-based AI systems and the transition from isolated algorithmic applications to networked multi-agent ecosystems. Building on this, it examines key governance challenges in AI-driven organizations, particularly issues of distributed responsibility, organizational transformation, and regulatory complexity. The chapter then develops a conceptual model of network-based governance for AI agents and extends it to include agent- e oversight and monitoring architectures. Subsequently, organizational and regulatory application areas in sectors such as finance, public administration, and critical infrastructure are discussed. Another focus is on simulation-based governance approaches and the use of digital twins to analyze systemic risks and governance dynamics. Finally, implications for future regulatory and organizational models are outlined, along with a research program for adaptive, system-centered governance of AI agents.

With this analysis, we build upon earlier work on the governance of AI agents, which primarily focused on transparency, accountability, principal-agent dynamics, and hybrid regulatory approaches in autonomous AI systems (Andrae, 2026a). While these earlier governance models largely focused on individual AI agents and their immediate decision-making structures, we broaden the perspective to include distributed agent ecosystems, network-based governance architectures, and simulation-based monitoring mechanisms. In doing so, the analysis shifts from model-centric governance to systemic, adaptive approaches that can address the increasing complexity of multi-agent environments.

This chapter makes four principal contributions to the emerging literature on agentic AI governance. First, it shifts the unit of analysis from individual AI models to interconnected agentic ecosystems. Second, it develops a network-based oversight perspective that conceptualizes governance as the coordination of interactions among autonomous agents rather than the supervision of isolated systems. Third, it introduces systemic design as a governance principle that embeds accountability, resilience, and transparency directly into the architecture of agentic ecosystems. Finally, it argues that governance must evolve from static compliance mechanisms to continuous, recursive governance that adapts to dynamic system behavior.

FROM ALGORITHMIC SYSTEMS TO AGENTIC ECOSYSTEMS

Defining AI Agents and Agentic AI

Current developments in artificial intelligence are increasingly characterized by the transition from isolated algorithmic applications to agentic AI ecosystems. While classical AI applications primarily functioned as tools for data analysis, classification, or decision support, modern AI agents possess significantly expanded capabilities for autonomous interaction with their environment. They can perceive information, pursue goals, make decisions, execute actions, and adaptively adjust their behavior in response to new information. This shifts the role of artificial intelligence from a passive analytical tool to an active organizational actor within complex socio-technical systems.

At the same time, a conceptual distinction between AI agents and agentic AI is necessary, as both terms are often used synonymously, even though they describe different levels of technological and organizational complexity. AI agents typically refer to individual systems capable of autonomously performing specific tasks. They often combine perception, reasoning, planning, tool use, and interaction with external environments to achieve defined goals. Agentic AI, on the other hand, describes a more comprehensive socio-technical paradigm in which autonomous and semi-autonomous agents continuously interact, coordinate, make decisions, and engage in adaptive learning within networked ecosystems. At the center of this are dynamic human-machine networks with recursive feedback and governance structures (Figure 1).

Figure 1. From AI Agents to Agentic AI

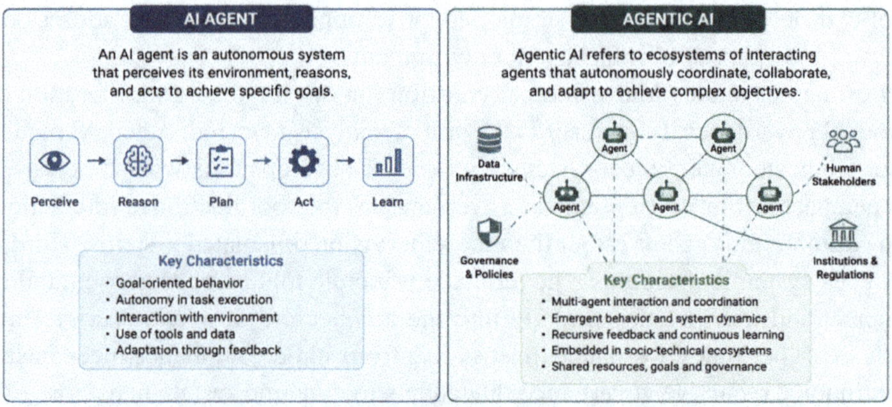

AI Agents vs. Agentic AI

Dimension	AI Agents	Agentic AI
Scope	Single agent, task or process level	Ecosystem, network and system level
Interaction	Limited interaction with environment and users	Rich interaction among multiple agents, humans, and infrastructures
Behavior	Predictable within defined boundaries	Emergent, adaptive, and context-dependent
Governance Implication	Traditional controls and oversight	Systemic, adaptive, and continuous governance
Focus	Task performance and automation	Goal achievement and system outcomes

Source: Own representation.

The theoretical foundations of agentic systems date back to early research on intelligent agents and multi-agent systems. Wooldridge and Jennings (1995) defined an intelligent agent as a system that acts autonomously in an environment to achieve specific goals. Russell and Norvig (2021) describe agents as systems that perceive their environment through sensors and interact with it via actuators. Key characteristics of such systems include autonomy, reactivity, proactivity, and the ability to engage in social interaction. In particular, the ability to independently pursue goals and interact with other agents fundamentally distinguishes AI agents from classical rule-based or statistical models.

In the context of current generative AI systems, however, the concept of an agent has expanded considerably. Modern AI agents are often based on large language models (LLMs), which are supplemented by additional components such as external tools, memory mechanisms, planning logics, API interfaces, and continuous feedback systems. This results in agent-based architectures capable of analyzing and operationally executing complex tasks. Examples range from autonomous research and assistance systems to cooperative multi-agent systems that independently coordinate subtasks, exchange information, and aggregate results (Park et al., 2023).

With the development of agentic AI, the focus is also shifting from mere content generation to autonomous process coordination. While generative AI primarily generates content such as text, images, code, or audio, agentic systems possess capabilities for goal decomposition, tool orchestration, memory formation, task prioritization, and long-term action coordination. Particularly characteristic features here include:

- autonomous goal tracking,
- adaptive decision-making,
- multi-agent collaboration,
- continuous learning and feedback loops,
- as well as the ability to independently execute complex task chains.

This results in systems whose behavior is increasingly emergent and can only be explained to a limited extent by individual models.

This development also leads to a conceptual expansion of artificial intelligence. Traditional machine learning systems were typically specialized in narrowly defined tasks, such as credit risk assessment, image recognition, or demand forecasting. Agent-based systems, on the other hand, integrate different functionalities within dynamic action architectures. They combine perception, language processing, planning, memory, tool use, and action execution in continuous interaction processes. The behavior of such systems increasingly arises from the interactions among various components, agents, and infrastructures, rather than solely from individual models or fixed rule sets.

Of particular importance here is the question of organizational embedding. AI agents and agent-based systems do not operate in an institutional vacuum. They are embedded in organizational structures, regulatory frameworks, and social interaction contexts. Their behavior is therefore also determined by data infrastructures, governance rules, human interventions, and organizational objectives. In this sense, agentic AI systems are components of hybrid socio-technical systems (Bostrom & Yudkowsky, 2014).

At the same time, agentic AI fundamentally changes the logic of digital transformation. Earlier waves of digitalization focused primarily on process automation, efficiency gains, or data-driven decision support. Agentic AI, on the other hand, enables adaptive organizational forms in which autonomous systems are actively involved in coordination, decision-making, control, and governance processes. As a result, artificial intelligence is shifting from a supporting technology to an infrastructural governance component of modern organizations.

A common misconception in practice is that nearly every system that uses artificial intelligence is referred to as an 'agent' or 'agentic.' This vague terminology often leads to exaggerated governance and compliance concerns. Typical examples include:

- LLM chatbots: Systems that generate or summarize information on demand but do not execute actions within systems.
- RPA (Robotic Process Automation): Automation scripts, some with AI-supported components, that execute tasks according to predefined rules but do not plan independently.
- RAG (Retrieval-Augmented Generation): Models that retrieve data from knowledge bases and generate answers based on it; they do not plan or act autonomously.

Agentic AI, on the other hand, is characterized by systems that independently operationalize goals, coordinate tasks, orchestrate tools, integrate feedback, and adaptively improve. Only these systems require systemic governance that covers multi-agent interactions, continuous monitoring, and adaptive risk management processes. Dignum and Dignum (2026) point out that not every system labeled as 'agentic' actually meets the criteria of true Agentic AI. They provide concrete operational criteria for classifying systems as agentic: autonomous goal planning, tool orchestration, adaptive learning and feedback mechanisms, and multi-agent coordination. In doing so, the authors support the argument that agentic AI requires special governance and oversight structures only if the systems actually exhibit emergent, self-directed behavior.

This development and differentiation have significant implications for governance and regulation. While traditional AI governance has often focused on isolated models or clearly defined application systems, agentic AI gives rise to highly interconnected and dynamic ecosystems with emergent interaction patterns and recursive control structures. Governance must therefore increasingly be designed to be systemic, continuous, and adaptive. Consequently, issues of accountability, transparency, oversight, and institutional control are shifting from individual models toward the governance of complex agentic ecosystems.

Typologies of AI Agents

The heterogeneity of agentic systems necessitates a systematic typology. Different forms of AI agents and agentic AI systems vary in terms of their degree of autonomy, decision-making logic, interactivity, learning mechanisms, and organizational function. A differentiated typology is therefore not only essential from a technical perspective but also a central prerequisite for governance, risk, and regulatory approaches. Particularly in the context of agentic AI, it is no longer sufficient to merely classify individual models or applications. Rather, complex agentic ecosystems must be analyzed in terms of their interaction dynamics, governance structures, and systemic impacts.

A fundamental distinction concerns, first and foremost, reactive and deliberative agents. Reactive agents act immediately in response to perceived environmental states and follow comparatively simple decision-making rules. They typically lack both long-term planning and complex internal representations of their environment. Such systems can be found, for example, in simple automation or monitoring processes. Deliberative agents, on the other hand, possess more complex planning and decision-making capabilities. They can evaluate alternative courses of action, develop goal hierarchies, anticipate future states, and adaptively adjust strategies (Wooldridge, 2009). Modern agent-based systems are increasingly based on deliberative architectures, particularly when large language models are combined with planning mechanisms, tool orchestration, and memory systems.

Furthermore, the distinction between assistive, operational, and autonomous agents is becoming increasingly important. Assistive agents primarily support human actors in decision-making or analysis processes. They typically operate within clearly defined control structures and remain under direct human supervision. Operational agents, on the other hand, independently perform specific tasks within organizational processes, such as regulatory monitoring, document processing, or market analysis. Autonomous agent-based systems go a step further by independently operationalizing complex goal structures, coordinating subtasks, and making decisions without continuous human intervention. However, as autonomy increases, so do the demands on governance, oversight, and institutional control.

Another key typology concerns single-agent and multi-agent systems. Single-agent systems operate largely in isolation and perform defined tasks within limited environments. Multi-agent systems, on the other hand, consist of multiple specialized agents that communicate, coordinate tasks, and organize collaborative problem-solving. Such systems are often based on distributed intelligence and coordination through division of labor. Multi-agent architectures are gaining particular significance in the context of agentic AI, as complex organizational processes are increasingly controlled by cooperating agentic networks.

However, this development simultaneously generates new forms of systemic complexity. Interactions between agents can give rise to emergent dynamics that cannot be fully derived from the behavior of individual components. Multi-agent systems can:

- develop coordinated decision-making dynamics,
- generate recursive feedback loops,
- or give rise to unintended collective behavioral patterns.

This shifts the focus of governance from controlling individual models to managing complex agent-based ecosystems.

Collaborative and coordinating agents are also of particular importance. Such systems actively interact with other agents or human actors to achieve common goals. They often have mechanisms for:

- task allocation,
- goal prioritization,
- resource coordination,
- and the negotiation of action strategies.

In an organizational context, this increasingly gives rise to hybrid human-machine networks in which AI agents become active partners in coordination and interaction.

Another relevant category consists of so-called supervisory agents or governance agents. These systems do not perform primary operational tasks. Rather, they monitor other agents or organizational processes. They serve, for example, to:

- anomaly detection,
- compliance monitoring,
- risk analysis,
- auditing,
- or escalation management.

Governance agents thus form a potential foundation for future agent-based oversight architectures. Particularly in highly regulated sectors such as financial services, cybersecurity, or critical infrastructure, such systems could play a central role within continuous governance and monitoring processes.

In addition to functional typologies, a distinction can also be made between different learning and adaptation mechanisms. Some agentic systems operate largely statically within defined rule sets, while others continuously learn through feedback, interaction, and new data. Particularly advanced forms of agentic AI integrate:

- self-reflection mechanisms,
- continuous optimization,
- feedback evaluators,
- and adaptive goal adjustments.

This gives rise to recursive learning architectures whose behavior changes dynamically and, in some cases, is only partially predictable.

Furthermore, the infrastructural embedding of agent-based systems is becoming increasingly important. Many modern agentic AI systems are deeply integrated into API ecosystems, cloud infrastructures, external data sources, and digital platforms. As a result, the functionality of individual agents increasingly depends on external infrastructures, toolchains, and interoperable systems. This creates new dependencies and potential systemic risks, particularly when numerous organizations rely on identical models, platforms, or infrastructure components.

The diversity of agentic systems underscores that governance cannot follow a uniform model. Different types of agents generate different risk profiles, control needs, and regulatory requirements. While simple assistive systems may be addressed by existing governance mechanisms, autonomous, adaptive, and networked agentic AI ecosystems require significantly more complex control and oversight architectures. Governance must therefore be designed to be increasingly adaptive, continuous, and system-oriented in order to accommodate the dynamic interaction structures of agentic systems.

AI Agents and Agentic AI as Socio-Technical Actors

The increasing integration of AI agents and agentic AI systems into organizational processes makes it clear that artificial intelligence cannot be understood exclusively as a technological innovation. Rather, hybrid socio-technical systems are emerging in which technical components, organizational structures, regulatory frameworks, and human actors are closely intertwined. Agentic systems operate within complex networks of data infrastructures, governance rules, institutional routines, and social interactions. The analysis of agentic AI, therefore, requires a perspective that considers both technological and organizational dynamics.

A suitable theoretical approach to analyzing these developments can be found in research on socio-technical systems. As early as 1951, Trist and Bamforth argued that technical systems must always be considered in conjunction with social organizational structures. Technologies, they contended, do not exert their effects independently of institutional contexts. They simultaneously transform work organization, communication structures, and forms of social coordination. Later work in Science and Technology Studies and Actor-Network Theory expanded this perspective by conceptualizing technological artifacts as active components of social networks (Latour, 2005). Technologies thus influence organizational processes and actively help structure possibilities for action, forms of communication, and power relations.

In the context of agentic AI, this perspective becomes particularly relevant. Agent-based systems increasingly influence organizational decision-making processes, prioritization, resource allocation, and governance structures. They thus function as operational components of organizational decision-making and coordination architectures. Particularly in complex organizational environments, AI agents are increasingly assuming:

- monitoring functions,
- coordination tasks,
- decision support,
- compliance processes,
- or operational control mechanisms.

As a result, artificial intelligence is shifting from a supporting technology to an infrastructural component of organizational governance.

At the same time, the agency of agent-based systems remains relational and context-dependent. AI agents do not act autonomously in the sense of complete independence. They are part of organizational goal systems, regulatory frameworks, and technical infrastructures. Their behavior is influenced by:

- training data,
- organizational policies,
- governance rules,
- human intervention,
- API architectures,
- as well as institutional power and incentive structures.

Agency is thus distributed across technical, organizational, and social components. The capacity for action in agentic systems does not arise in isolation within individual models, but rather relationally within complex socio-technical networks.

This development simultaneously transforms classical notions of organizational responsibility. In traditional decision-making structures, decisions could be attributed with relative clarity to individual persons or hierarchical levels. In agentic systems, however, decisions often arise from recursive interactions between humans, AI agents, data infrastructures, and organizational processes. Responsibility is thus increasingly distributed ('distributed agency') and, in some cases, de-bound. This complicates regulatory attribution and also calls into question traditional models of governance, control, and liability.

This becomes particularly relevant in multi-agent environments and agent-based ecosystems. In such settings, decisions often no longer arise in a linear fashion but emerge from the collaborative interactions of various agents and human actors. Such systems can:

- independently delegate tasks,
- coordinate action strategies,
- generate feedback loops,
- or dynamically adapt operational processes.

This gives rise to new forms of organizational complexity and decision-making dynamics that are sometimes difficult to trace. Governance must therefore increasingly grapple with emergent behavioral patterns and systemic interdependencies.

At the same time, Agentic AI generates new forms of organizational knowledge production. Through continuous data analysis, autonomous interaction, and adaptive learning processes, dynamic information flows emerge that transform traditional decision-making and communication structures. As a result, organizations are increasingly evolving into data-driven and algorithmically coordinated networks in which human and machine actors jointly generate organizational action. Knowledge no longer arises exclusively from human expertise, but increasingly from the interaction between:

- data,
- algorithms,
- organizational routines,
- and agent-based decision-making architectures.

Furthermore, agentic systems are transforming organizational power and control structures. Actors with access to central data infrastructures, foundation models, or agentic platform architectures gain potentially significant influence over organizational decision-making processes and institutional coordination. Questions of digital sovereignty, infrastructural dependency, and algorithmic power asymmetries thus gain significance. Governance of Agentic AI, therefore, also concerns the institutional distribution of control, responsibility, and decision-making power within digital ecosystems.

Overall, the socio-technical perspective makes it clear that Agentic AI cannot be understood as an isolated technology. Rather, hybrid governance and organizational structures are emerging in which human and machine agency are increasingly intertwined. The governance of agentic systems, therefore, requires interdisciplinary approaches that jointly consider technical, organizational, regulatory, and societal dimensions.

From Isolated Systems to Networked Ecosystems

The development of AI agents and agentic AI is closely linked to the broader transformation of digital infrastructures. Digital systems increasingly operate within networked platforms and data ecosystems connected by APIs, cloud infrastructures, microservices, and interoperable data architectures. This gives rise to highly networked AI ecosystems in which different agents continuously interact, coordinate subtasks, and assume functions based on the division of labor. The behavior of such systems increasingly arises from interaction, collaboration, and emergent dynamics, rather than from the isolated functioning of individual models.

This development is consistent with the general trends toward the platformization of digital economies (Srnicek, 2017). Platforms serve as coordination mechanisms that integrate actors, data streams, and AI agents. Agent-based systems thus become components of larger digital ecosystems whose behavior can no longer be controlled linearly but is shaped by network dynamics, interdependencies, and adaptive feedback loops.

This dynamic is particularly relevant in the context of multi-agent systems. These consist of several specialized agents that work together to perform complex tasks. Individual agents may have different goals, levels of knowledge, or options for action, and they can coordinate their behavior through communication and interaction mechanisms. This gives rise to emergent system dynamics that are neither fully predictable nor centrally controllable. Such dynamics are particularly evident in scenarios where autonomous agents with high decision-making authority operate in heterogeneous, networked environments.

As connectivity increases, so do systemic risks. Current research on the analysis of complex, interdependent systems emphasizes that reductionist or linear analytical approaches are insufficient to capture these risks. Instead, risks arise from interactions, cascading disruptions, recursive feedback loops, and dynamic developments within systems that extend beyond organizational and sectoral boundaries (Logan et al., 2026).

In agent-based AI ecosystems, this means that errors by individual agents or unexpected behavioral changes can propagate across networks, generating systemic effects. Interactions between agents can give rise to emergent behavioral patterns that are not explicitly programmed and are difficult to trace directly. Such dynamics resemble complex systems in financial markets or critical infrastructures, where interdependencies among actors create systemic vulnerabilities.

The transformation toward agentic AI ecosystems, therefore, requires a fundamental shift in perspective on the governance of artificial intelligence. While the earlier 'Network Model for AI Governance' was conceived as a decentralized interaction structure among institutional actors (Andrae, 2026b), the current perspective broadens the focus to include recursive governance architectures. In these, AI agents themselves increasingly assume monitoring, coordination, and control functions within complex socio-technical ecosystems. Governance must therefore be designed to be system- and network-oriented in order to adequately address interdependencies, uncertainty, and adaptive system behavior. This expansion forms the conceptual basis for the analysis of supervisory agents, digital twins, and simulation-based governance approaches in the following sections.

AI Governance vs. Data Governance

With the increasing prevalence of agent-based AI systems, governance is no longer limited to data quality or individual models. It must also address the interdependent socio-technical ecosystems in which these systems operate. In this context, it is crucial to distinguish between data governance and AI governance, as they address different protection objectives, control mechanisms, and risks.

Data governance focuses primarily on the reliability, consistency, and integrity of the data used. Core tasks include:

- Ensuring data quality,
- Privacy and access controls,
- Traceability of data lineage and processing steps,
- Consistency across systems and platforms.

Data governance thus forms the foundation for trustworthy decision-making processes and the reliable use of AI systems. However, it does not directly address the emergent behaviors of agentic AI, whose decisions and outputs depend on networked interactions, adaptive learning processes, and goal prioritization.

AI Governance, on the other hand, protects the decision-making and action levels of the systems themselves. The goal is for autonomous agents to act fairly, transparently, robustly, and responsibly. Core tasks include:

- Fairness and bias mitigation,
- Explainability and transparency of decisions,
- Performance monitoring and robustness against system failures,
- Accountability for the results produced.

AI Governance is particularly relevant for Agentic AI, as these systems operate within complex, dynamic networks. Errors or unintended behavioral patterns of a single agent can spread throughout the entire ecosystem, and traditional Data Governance alone cannot mitigate these risks.

Figure 2. AI Governance vs. Data Governance

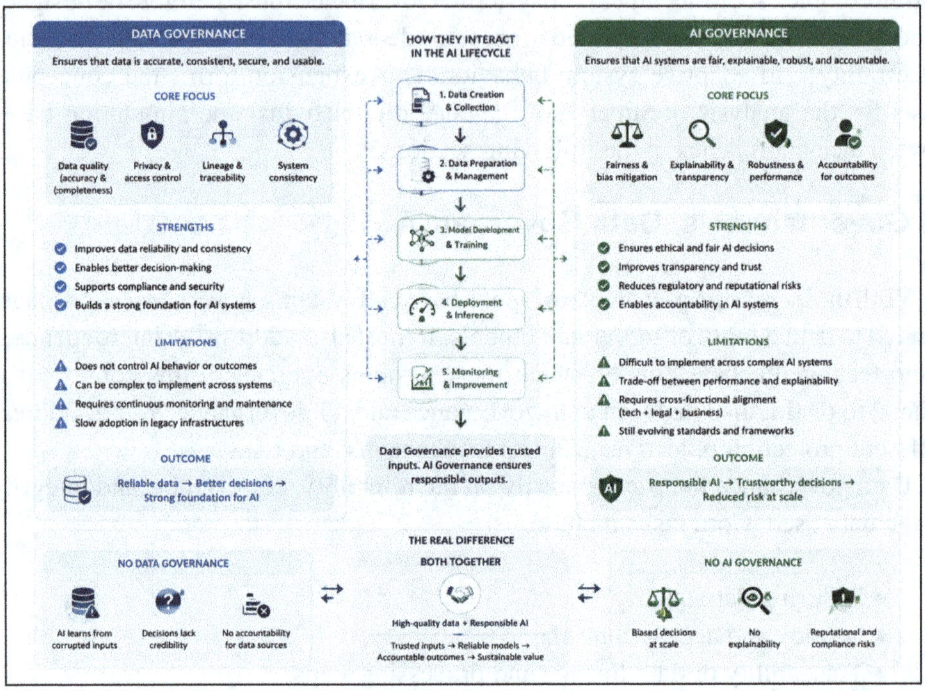

Source: Own representation.

Figure 2 illustrates the complementary roles of data governance and AI governance within agentic AI ecosystems. The distinction between data governance and AI governance highlights that both levels are complementary: Data governance ensures the quality, consistency, and traceability of the data that underpins AI systems. AI Governance addresses the behavior of the systems themselves, ensuring fairness, transparency, robustness, and accountability of autonomous agents, and enabling control over emergent decisions. The figure illustrates key differences in protection objectives, core tasks, stakeholders, and risks. Together, Data Governance and AI Governance form the foundation for trustworthy, traceable, and scalable decisions in agentic AI ecosystems.

Key Concept 1: Ecosystem-Centered Governance

Agentic AI shifts the focus of governance from individual AI models toward interconnected socio-technical ecosystems in which autonomous agents, human actors, digital infrastructures, platforms, tools, and institutional rules collectively shape system behavior. Governance becomes the management of interactions, dependencies, and emergent dynamics across the ecosystem rather than the supervision of isolated AI models.

This differentiation, therefore, provides a central basis for the further governance and regulatory discussions in Section 3. It highlights that the management of agentic AI must be conceived not only in terms of data but also in terms of systems and decisions to ensure trust, traceability, and regulatory compliance.

GOVERNANCE CHALLENGES IN AI-DRIVEN ORGANIZATIONS

Limits of Model-Centric Governance

Previous approaches to artificial intelligence governance were predominantly developed for algorithmic systems with relatively stable boundaries and clearly identifiable functions. Governance mechanisms were therefore largely designed around individual models or applications whose risks could be assessed through procedures such as model validation, fairness evaluation, transparency requirements, explainability methods, and performance monitoring. This model-centric perspective was particularly appropriate during the early phases of data-driven decision support, when AI systems typically performed narrowly defined tasks within controlled organizational processes. Examples include credit scoring models, fraud detection systems, recommendation algorithms, or predictive maintenance applications, whose behavior could be evaluated and documented with comparatively clear assumptions about system boundaries.

Accordingly, a substantial part of the AI governance literature has focused on the characteristics and properties of individual models. Research on algorithmic fairness has examined discriminatory outcomes and bias mitigation (Barocas & Selbst, 2016), while work on explainability has addressed transparency and interpretability challenges in complex machine learning systems (Doshi-Velez & Kim, 2017). Additional research has focused on robustness, reproducibility, validation, and responsible AI development. Although these approaches remain highly relevant, they implicitly assume that the primary governance object is a relatively bounded AI system whose behavior can be assessed through technical and procedural controls.

The emergence of agentic AI challenges this assumption. Unlike conventional AI applications, agentic systems combine reasoning, planning, tool use, memory, and autonomous execution capabilities. Their behavior increasingly emerges from interactions among multiple components rather than from a single model architecture. As a result, governance challenges are no longer limited to evaluating model performance or compliance at a specific point in time, but increasingly concern dynamic interactions, adaptive behavior, and evolving system states.

Recent scholarship reflects this conceptual transition. Engin and Hand (2025) argue that static classifications of AI systems are increasingly insufficient for governing agentic AI and propose a dimensional governance approach based on characteristics such as autonomy, planning capability, tool use, learning mechanisms, and coordination capacity. Similarly, Dignum and Dignum (2026) emphasize that governance should not rely exclusively on labels such as "AI agent" or "agentic AI," but should consider the operational degree of agency exhibited by a system. Together, these contributions suggest a shift from categorical approaches toward capability-based governance models that recognize different levels of autonomy and complexity.

Regulatory developments illustrate a similar tension. The European AI Act provides an important foundation for governing artificial intelligence through a risk-based framework that focuses on the intended purpose, application context, and the responsibilities of providers and deployers. Recent legal analyses emphasize that agentic AI does not constitute a separate regulatory category under the AI Act but remains within the broader definition of an AI system. However, applying existing requirements becomes increasingly complex when systems exhibit adaptive behavior, delegated autonomy, and dynamic interaction with external tools and other agents.

Holweg and Hacker (2026) argue that the current EU AI Act framework remains applicable to agentic AI but requires interpretative and governance adaptations. In particular, they highlight the importance of clarifying provider and deployer responsibilities, strengthening oversight mechanisms, and ensuring that autonomous agent behavior remains subject to enforceable accountability structures. Rather than introducing an entirely new regulatory category, they emphasize the need to adapt existing governance mechanisms to the specific characteristics of agentic systems.

Similarly, Nannini et al. (2026) emphasize that agentic AI challenges traditional conformity assessment approaches because system behavior may evolve during operation. Their analysis highlights issues such as behavioral drift, runtime monitoring, and the need for continuous oversight mechanisms capable of addressing changes after deployment. These perspectives demonstrate that current regulatory frameworks increasingly recognize the importance of lifecycle governance, but they also reveal the limitations of approaches primarily designed around predefined system boundaries.

Table 1 summarizes existing regulatory frameworks and recent scholarly approaches that seek to extend AI governance toward increasingly autonomous and agentic systems.

Table 1. Comparison of Existing Regulatory Frameworks and Recent Governance Approaches for Agentic AI

Framework / Study	Main Contribution	Governance Gap for Agentic AI
Existing Regulatory Frameworks		
EU AI Act	Risk-based regulation of AI systems; conformity assessment; human oversight requirements	Limited treatment of multi-agent interactions, emergent behavior, and dynamic system evolution
GDPR	Accountability, transparency, and data governance principles	Focuses on data processing rather than autonomous coordination among AI agents
DORA	ICT risk management, operational resilience, and third-party oversight	Limited perspective on autonomous agent behavior and distributed decision-making
AI Liability Framework	Clarification of liability and compensation mechanisms	Limited treatment of distributed agency and collective system behavior
Emerging Scholarly Approaches		
Holweg & Hacker (2026)	Legal interpretation of agentic AI under the EU AI Act; provider/deployer responsibilities; oversight mechanisms	Primarily focused on regulatory compliance rather than ecosystem governance
Nannini et al. (2026)	Runtime governance, behavioral drift, and lifecycle monitoring	Limited treatment of interactions across broader socio-technical ecosystems
Engin & Hand (2025)	Capability-based and dimensional governance approaches	Requires further operationalization in organizational contexts
Dignum & Dignum (2026)	Operational characterization of agenticity beyond labels	Does not provide a comprehensive governance architecture

Source: Own representation.

The comparison highlights a common pattern across existing regulatory frameworks and emerging scholarly approaches. Current governance mechanisms increasingly acknowledge autonomy, adaptation, lifecycle monitoring, and accountability. However, they remain largely oriented toward governing individual AI systems, specific deployment contexts, or identifiable legal responsibilities.

Agentic AI challenges these assumptions because risks and responsibilities increasingly emerge from interactions among multiple agents, organizational processes, digital infrastructures, and institutional arrangements. Consequently, governing agentic AI requires a conceptual shift beyond model-centric governance toward approaches that address the behavior of interconnected socio-technical ecosystems.

This observation provides the foundation for the ecosystem-centered governance and network-based oversight perspectives developed in the following sections.

Distributed Decision-Making and Accountability Gaps

The increasing prevalence of agent-based systems is fundamentally changing the structure of organizational decision-making processes. Decisions are no longer made exclusively by individuals or by clearly defined hierarchical levels. They increasingly emerge from distributed interactions between people, algorithms, and organizational infrastructures. This development leads to new forms of distributed agency and creates significant challenges for accountability and governance.

In traditional organizations, accountability structures were typically based on relatively stable hierarchies and clear decision-making pathways. Decisions could be attributed to specific individuals, departments, or institutional roles. AI agents partially disrupt this logic by autonomously taking on operational and analytical tasks and interacting independently with other systems. This gives rise to hybrid decision-making architectures in which human and algorithmic actors jointly generate organizational action.

This issue is particularly pronounced in multi-agent systems. Here, decisions often arise from the interaction of multiple specialized agents that take on different subtasks. Individual agents often have only limited information or locally defined objectives. The overall behavior of the system emerges only from its interaction. In such constellations, it can be difficult, or even impossible, to unambiguously attribute specific decisions to individual actors.

This fragmentation of responsibility gives rise to what are known as accountability gaps (Matthias, 2004). This term refers to situations in which harmful or problematic decisions are made without it being possible to clearly assign responsibility. Accountability gaps are particularly problematic when AI agents possess operational autonomy and make decisions with significant economic, social, or regulatory consequences.

The problem is further exacerbated by a lack of transparency and complexity. Modern agent-based systems are often based on highly complex model architectures and distributed data infrastructures. Decisions arise within dynamic interaction networks. This makes it increasingly difficult to fully understand decision-making logic or to reconstruct causal chains of responsibility. Even if individual models appear technically explainable, the behavior of the overall system often remains only partially interpretable.

Added to this are emergent risks. Interactions between agents can give rise to collective behavioral patterns that were neither intended nor anticipated by individual developers or organizations. Examples of this can already be found today in algorithmic trading systems, autonomous optimization processes, or platform ecosystems, where interdependencies between algorithmic actors can generate unexpected dynamics. Such emergent effects pose significant challenges to traditional governance mechanisms, as risks cannot be reduced to individual components in isolation.

Furthermore, AI agents are also altering the epistemic foundations of organizational decisions. Organizations are increasingly relying on algorithmically generated information, forecasts, and recommendations. This creates new dependencies on technical systems whose functioning is often fully understood only by specialized groups of experts. These knowledge asymmetries can shift organizational power structures and limit human actors' ability to exercise critical control.

Overall, these developments demonstrate that agentic systems raise fundamental institutional questions about organizational accountability. Governance must therefore develop mechanisms to ensure accountability even under distributed, hybrid decision-making architectures.

Organizational Transformation and Institutional Complexity

The integration of AI agents into organizational processes leads to technological changes and, at the same time, to profound transformations of organizational structures and institutional logics. Digital transformation should therefore not be understood as a purely technical modernization; it must be interpreted as a comprehensive transformation of organizational coordination, decision-making, and knowledge structures (Vial, 2019).

AI agents initially alter the internal division of labor between humans and machines. Routine tasks, analytical activities, and, in some cases, coordinative functions are increasingly automated or supported by agent-based systems. At the same time, new role profiles are emerging in AI governance, model oversight, data management, and algorithmic auditing. As a result, organizations are evolving into hybrid systems of action in which human and algorithmic actors jointly shape value creation and decision-making processes.

This transformation particularly affects organizational decision-making structures. Traditional hierarchical decision-making models are increasingly being supplemented by data-driven and algorithmically coordinated processes. Decisions are increasingly based on continuous data analysis and automated information processing. This gives rise to new forms of organizational control, some of which are shaped more by real-time data and adaptive optimization logic than by traditional bureaucratic procedures.

At the same time, AI agents increase the institutional complexity of organizations. Organizations must simultaneously coordinate technical systems, regulatory requirements, ethical standards, and economic objectives. This leads to a proliferation of governance requirements, particularly in regulated sectors. Governance is thus increasingly an interdisciplinary, organization-wide task that integrates technological, legal, and strategic dimensions.

A central challenge here lies in organizational adaptability. Many existing governance structures were developed for relatively stable decision-making processes and are only partially prepared for adaptive agent-based systems. Organizations, therefore, require new institutional capabilities to effectively manage and monitor AI agents. These include, among other things, AI expertise, interdisciplinary governance structures, continuous monitoring, and new forms of organizational learning.

Furthermore, AI agents are transforming organizational power and knowledge structures. Access to data, computing power, and algorithmic expertise is increasingly becoming a central source of organizational power. This can shift existing hierarchies and create new dependencies. At the same time, risks of over-automation arise when organizations place excessive trust in algorithmic decisions, and human control capabilities gradually erode.

The transformation driven by AI agents is therefore not merely a matter of technological implementation. It is, at the very least, also a challenge of institutional design. Organizations must develop new governance and coordination mechanisms to manage hybrid human-machine systems in a resilient and responsible manner.

Governance in Regulated Environments

The governance of agent-based systems is becoming increasingly important, particularly in regulated environments. Sectors such as financial services, healthcare, public administration, and critical infrastructure are already subject to extensive regulatory requirements regarding transparency, security, risk management, and accountability. The integration of autonomous or semi-autonomous AI agents significantly increases the complexity of these requirements.

In the financial sector, for example, AI agents are increasingly being used for credit decisions, fraud detection, trading strategies, and regulatory compliance. At the same time, financial institutions are subject to strict governance and risk management requirements, for example, within the framework of banking regulations, operational resilience, or model risk management. Agent-based systems introduce new risks in this context, including opaque decision-making logic, systemic interdependencies, and automated escalation dynamics.

Similar challenges arise in public administration. AI agents can automate administrative processes, support policy-making, or coordinate digital public services. At the same time, questions of democratic legitimacy, transparency, and public accountability arise. Particularly in governmental contexts, there is a risk that algorithmic control mechanisms will depoliticize policy decisions or undermine democratic oversight mechanisms.

In the area of critical infrastructure, questions of operational resilience and cybersecurity also come to the fore. Networked AI agents can efficiently coordinate complex infrastructure systems, at the same time, creating new systemic vulnerabilities. Errors or manipulations of individual components can, under certain circumstances, spread rapidly across entire networks.

It is becoming clear that existing regulatory approaches are often insufficient to adequately address agent-based ecosystems. Many current regulatory regimes continue to be based on the assumption of relatively clearly defined systems and linear accountability structures. Agent-based networks, however, require more adaptive, continuous, and system-oriented governance approaches.

The Need for System-Centric Governance

The developments outlined above highlight the need for a fundamental paradigm shift in the governance of artificial intelligence. Model-centric approaches are no longer sufficient to adequately address the dynamics of agent-based ecosystems. Instead, system-centric governance is required, one that focuses on interactions, networks, and institutional embedding.

System-centric governance views AI agents as components of complex socio-technical systems. Governance thus focuses on the architecture of the entire system, including communication structures, escalation mechanisms, organizational roles, and regulatory interfaces. Such an approach requires continuous and adaptive governance mechanisms. Instead of ad hoc reviews, permanent monitoring and feedback processes take center stage. Governance thus becomes a dynamic capability of organizations to resiliently coordinate and continuously adapt complex human-machine systems. Furthermore, system-centered governance implies a stronger integration of technical, organizational, and regulatory perspectives. Effective governance cannot be achieved solely through technical solutions or regulatory requirements. Hybrid governance architectures that connect different institutional levels are required.

Building on this foundation, the following chapters develop a conceptual model of network-based governance and agent-based oversight architectures for complex AI ecosystems.

TOWARD A NETWORK-BASED GOVERNANCE MODEL FOR AI AGENTS

Conceptual Foundations of Network-Based Governance

The increasing prevalence of agent-based AI systems makes it clear that traditional governance approaches, which rely on hierarchical control and isolated model evaluation, are only of limited suitability for managing complex AI ecosystems. Instead, the governance of AI agents requires conceptual approaches that systematically account for interdependencies, distributed decision-making processes, and dynamic network structures. Against this backdrop, the perspective of network governance is gaining increasing importance.

Network governance describes forms of coordination in which control does not primarily occur through hierarchical command structures or market mechanisms. Control arises through interactions between different, partially autonomous actors within relational networks (Rhodes, 1997). Such networks are typically characterized by interdependencies, decentralized decision-making, and continuous communication. Governance emerges through formal rules and coordinated interactions within complex institutional arrangements.

This perspective is particularly relevant for AI agents, as agentic systems increasingly operate within distributed digital infrastructures. Decisions arise from interactions between algorithms, data platforms, human actors, and regulatory institutions. AI agents thus function as components of hybrid governance networks in which technical and social components are inextricably intertwined.

The theory of polycentric governance is particularly relevant here. Ostrom (2010) argues that complex systems can often be managed more effectively through multiple interconnected decision-making centers than through centralized control structures. Polycentric governance enables adaptive coordination, local learning processes, and institutional resilience. Applied to agentic systems, this implies that governance must be distributed across multiple levels and actors.

Furthermore, the literature on adaptive governance provides important theoretical foundations for managing dynamic AI ecosystems. Adaptive governance focuses on the ability of institutional systems to respond to uncertainty, complexity, and continuous change (Folke et al., 2005). Governance is understood here as an evolutionary and adaptive process. This perspective appears particularly relevant for agent-based systems, as their behavior can continuously change and give rise to emergent dynamics.

Cybernetics and research on complex adaptive systems provide a further theoretical foundation. Ashby (1956) already emphasized that effective control of complex systems requires a sufficient variety of governance structures ('law of requisite variety'). As the complexity of agent-based ecosystems increases, so does the need for flexible, adaptive, and multi-layered governance mechanisms. Under these conditions, classical linear control models are no longer sufficient.

The combination of these theoretical perspectives suggests that the governance of AI agents must be understood as a network-based coordination process. AI governance is thus evolving from a primarily regulatory function into a systemic architectural issue.

AI Ecosystems as Governance Networks

The transformation of digital infrastructure is increasingly driving the emergence of complex AI ecosystems comprising a multitude of interconnected actors and systems. AI agents operate within highly networked environments that encompass data platforms, cloud infrastructures, APIs, human users, regulatory institutions, and other algorithmic systems. These ecosystems can therefore be understood as governance networks in which technical and institutional coordination mechanisms interlock.

A central characteristic of such ecosystems is their interdependence. Decisions made by individual agents often influence other agents or organizational processes, creating complex feedback loops. In multi-agent systems, the behavior of the overall system emerges from the interaction of the properties of individual components. Governance must therefore operate at the system level and account for interactions among actors.

Furthermore, AI ecosystems are characterized by high dynamism. New agents can be integrated, existing systems can be adapted, or communication structures can be altered. This continuously gives rise to new interaction patterns and potential risk constellations. Under these conditions, governance becomes a permanent task of observation, adaptation, and coordination.

The role of data infrastructures is also particularly important. Data serves as a central link between different agents and organizational units. At the same time, data quality, interoperability, and access structures significantly influence the behavior of agent-based systems. Data governance thus becomes an integral part of network-based AI governance.

At the same time, new power and dependency structures emerge within such ecosystems. Large platform providers or infrastructure operators often control central resources such as computing capacity, interfaces, or data access. This gives rise to tendencies toward concentration that have implications not only for the economy but also for governance. Organizations are becoming increasingly dependent on external digital infrastructures, while internal management and control options may remain limited.

These developments illustrate that AI governance cannot be viewed in isolation at the level of individual organizations. Rather, trans-organizational governance networks are emerging that connect different actors and institutional levels. Effective governance therefore requires coordination mechanisms that integrate technical, organizational, and regulatory perspectives.

Core Governance Dimensions

The development of network-based governance architectures for AI agents requires identifying core governance dimensions that serve as normative and functional guiding principles. These dimensions form the foundation for designing resilient and responsible AI ecosystems.

Transparency. Transparency is a fundamental prerequisite for effective governance. In agent-based systems, however, transparency encompasses more than the explainability of individual models. Rather, transparency is required at the system level, including interactions between agents, data flows, communication structures, and decision-making processes. Transparency serves regulatory traceability and organizational controllability.

Traceability. Closely linked to transparency is the traceability of decisions and interactions. In complex multi-agent environments, organizations must be able to track which agents used which information, which decisions were made, and which actions were triggered. Traceability thus becomes a central prerequisite for auditability, accountability, and error analysis.

Accountability. Accountability remains a central governance principle even in agent-based systems. However, accountability must be reconceptualized under conditions of distributed agency. Instead of a linear assignment of responsibility, multi-layered accountability structures are required that involve developers, operators, organizational decision-makers, and supervisory bodies equally.

Robustness and resilience. Agent-based systems must be designed to be resilient against errors, attacks, and unexpected interactions. Governance, therefore, encompasses preventive controls, the ability to detect and contain disruptions, and the ability to enable adaptive responses. Resilience is becoming a central governance objective, particularly in critical infrastructures.

Human oversight. Despite increasing autonomy, human oversight remains a central component of responsible AI governance. However, the role of human control is changing. People are increasingly acting less as direct decision-makers and more as supervisors of complex agent-based systems. Governance must therefore ensure that human actors continue to have sufficient opportunities for intervention and control.

Adaptivity. Since agentic systems are constantly changing, governance must also be adaptive. Governance mechanisms must enable learning and adaptation processes. Adaptive governance thus becomes a form of organizational resilience in its own right.

Governance as Embedded System Architecture

Traditional governance approaches often treat governance as an external control instrument that is downstream of a technical system. In the context of agentic systems, however, this perspective is increasingly proving to be inadequate. Instead, governance must be directly integrated into the architecture of digital systems ('governance by design'). This means, first and foremost, that governance requirements must be taken into account at the technical infrastructure level. Communication protocols, data access, escalation mechanisms, and monitoring functions should be integral components of agent-based architectures.

Furthermore, programmable governance mechanisms are gaining importance. Policies, access rights, or compliance rules can increasingly be implemented automatically within agent-based systems. This gives rise to hybrid governance architectures in which technical and institutional control mechanisms interlock. Such an approach offers particular advantages in scalability and real-time capabilities. While traditional governance is often reactive and ex post, embedded governance structures enable continuous monitoring and adaptive interventions. Governance thus becomes more dynamic and process-oriented.

At the same time, however, new risks arise. As governance increasingly operates algorithmically, errors or distortions within its mechanisms can have systemic consequences. Additionally, there is a risk of recursive governance structures in which AI systems monitor other AI systems. This raises new questions regarding control, legitimacy, and institutional accountability.

Proposed Conceptual Framework

Based on the considerations outlined so far, a conceptual framework for the network-based governance of AI agents can be developed. This framework is based on the assumption that effective governance can only be achieved through the integration of technical, organizational, and institutional levels.

The proposed model comprises three interconnected levels of governance:

(1) **Architectural Governance**: This level encompasses technical infrastructures, data architectures, communication protocols, and security mechanisms. The goal is to create transparent, interoperable, and controllable AI ecosystems.

(2) **Organizational Governance**: This level focuses on organizational roles, responsibilities, decision-making processes, and escalation mechanisms. Organizations must develop institutional capabilities to coordinate hybrid human-machine systems effectively.
(3) **Institutional Governance**: The institutional level encompasses regulatory frameworks, standards, auditing procedures, and societal legitimacy. Governance here is exercised through regulatory institutions, sectoral standards, and cross-organizational coordination mechanisms.

There is continuous feedback between these levels. Technical architectures influence organizational control options; regulatory requirements shape technical designs; organizational practices, in turn, feed back into institutional governance. Governance is thus understood as a dynamic and multi-layered coordination process.

The model also forms the basis for the agent-based oversight architectures developed below, which are intended to operationalize governance itself, in part through specialized AI agents.

AGENT-BASED OVERSIGHT ARCHITECTURES

From Human Oversight to Hybrid Oversight

The increasing complexity of agent-based AI systems poses fundamental challenges to traditional models of human oversight. The increasing complexity of agent-based AI systems also poses challenges for conventional oversight and safety mechanisms. Logan et al. (2026) argue that higher-order systemic risks arise particularly in contexts characterized by recursive dynamics, feedback loops, and adaptive interactions, which cannot be captured by static or linear governance approaches. This insight can be directly applied to multi-agent AI environments, where interactions between autonomous agents can trigger cascading consequences, coordination failures, or emergent system behavior.

Traditional governance approaches implicitly assume that human actors can fully monitor algorithmic systems, understand their decisions, and intervene to correct them when necessary. However, this assumption becomes increasingly implausible as the autonomy, speed, and interconnectedness of agent-based systems grow. Even in highly automated socio-technical systems such as algorithmic high-frequency trading or autonomous infrastructure systems, it is already evident that human oversight is reaching its operational and cognitive limits. The speed of algorithmic decision-making processes, the number of simultaneous interactions, and the complexity of distributed data streams often exceed human actors' ability to exercise real-time control (Bostrom & Yudkowsky, 2014). With the emergence of multi-agent ecosystems, this problem is further exacerbated.

Recent compliance-focused analyses also underscore that human oversight of agent-based AI systems cannot rely solely on prompt-level instructions or static governance controls. Instead, effective oversight requires external enforcement mechanisms, API-level privilege restrictions, runtime monitoring, and continuous traceability infrastructures capable of constraining the behavior of autonomous agents during deployment (Nannini et al., 2026).

At the same time, human oversight remains indispensable from a normative and regulatory perspective. Regulatory concepts such as 'human oversight' in the European AIA or approaches like 'meaningful human control' emphasize that human actors must continue to bear responsibility for AI-supported decisions. However, the role of human control is fundamentally changing: humans are increasingly acting less as direct operational decision-makers and more as supervisors of complex socio-technical systems.

Against this backdrop, the concept of hybrid oversight architectures is gaining importance. Hybrid oversight combines human governance structures with specialized technical monitoring mechanisms. In this context, AI-based supervisory agents take on certain monitoring, verification, and escalation functions, while strategic control and ultimate normative responsibility remain with human actors.

This transition can be understood as a shift from direct to indirect control. While classical governance is based on direct intervention, hybrid oversight architectures focus on continuous observation, risk detection, and adaptive control of complex systems. As a result, governance is becoming increasingly process-oriented and dynamic.

A key advantage of hybrid supervision lies in its scalability. Human governance structures alone have limited capacity to monitor highly dynamic multi-agent systems. Supervisory agents, on the other hand, can analyze large volumes of interaction data in real time, detect anomalies, and identify potential risks at an early stage. This gives rise to a new form of continuous algorithmic governance.

At the same time, this development raises significant normative and institutional questions. As governance becomes increasingly algorithmically mediated, recursive control structures emerge in which AI systems monitor other AI systems. While this can generate efficiency and scalability benefits, it also entails risks regarding transparency, legitimacy, and loss of control. Governance itself thus becomes the subject of algorithmic control. The challenge lies in developing resilient hybrid governance architectures in which technical and human oversight mechanisms work in complementary ways.

However, hybrid oversight alone does not resolve the fundamental question of accountability. In agentic AI ecosystems, governance mechanisms must not only observe and supervise system behavior but also establish enforceable structures of authority, responsibility, and intervention. This requires accountability to become an architectural property of the system itself.

Architecting Enforceable Accountability

A central challenge of agentic AI governance concerns the transition from conceptual oversight mechanisms toward enforceable accountability architectures. While existing governance frameworks increasingly emphasize principles such as transparency, human oversight, explainability, and responsible AI development, these principles remain insufficient unless they are translated into operational mechanisms that allocate authority, constrain autonomous action, and enable intervention throughout the lifecycle of agentic systems.

In traditional AI systems, accountability could often be assigned through relatively clear organizational structures. A model was developed by a provider, deployed by an organization, and evaluated against predefined performance and compliance requirements. Agentic AI challenges this assumption because decisions increasingly emerge from distributed interactions among multiple agents, external tools, organizational processes, and human supervisors. Accountability can therefore no longer be understood solely as a legal attribution following an undesirable outcome. Instead, accountability must become an architectural property of the socio-technical ecosystem itself.

This creates a transition from individual responsibility toward distributed accountability. In agentic AI environments, responsibility is shared across multiple actors, including foundation model providers, agent developers, system integrators, deployers, organizational users, and supervisory mechanisms. The relevant question is therefore not only who created an AI system, but who defines its operational capabilities, determines its deployment context, configures its permissions, and influences its behavior during runtime. Effective governance requires mechanisms that connect technical authority with organizational responsibility and legal accountability.

Recent legal scholarship has begun to address these challenges. Holweg and Hacker (2026) argue that the existing European AI Act provides a suitable legal foundation for governing agentic AI but requires adaptations that reflect the distinctive characteristics of autonomous and adaptive systems. Rather than introducing an entirely new legal category for agentic AI, they emphasize the importance of strengthening existing governance mechanisms, clarifying responsibility structures, and ensuring that autonomous decision-making remains subject to enforceable oversight.

A first mechanism concerns the distinction between providers and deployers. In agentic AI ecosystems, organizations increasingly customize and integrate general-purpose AI capabilities into domain-specific workflows by combining models, tools, organizational data, and orchestration mechanisms. Holweg and Hacker (2026) argue that deployers who substantially modify or redirect an AI system toward a high-risk application may assume provider responsibilities under the AI Act. This approach strengthens accountability by ensuring that responsibility follows effective control over the deployed system rather than remaining exclusively with the original model provider.

This principle illustrates a broader governance challenge: accountability cannot be assigned only after deployment but must be embedded into the architecture, workflows, and authorization structures through which agentic systems operate. The governance of agentic AI therefore requires mechanisms that make responsibility visible, traceable, and enforceable throughout the operational lifecycle.

A second mechanism concerns the transformation from human-in-the-loop toward human-on-the-loop oversight. Traditional human-in-the-loop approaches assume that humans approve individual AI decisions before execution. For increasingly autonomous agentic systems, however, continuous human approval may become operationally infeasible due to the speed, scale, and complexity of autonomous interactions. Human supervisors therefore increasingly perform higher-level governance functions, including defining operational boundaries, monitoring system behavior, reviewing exceptions, and intervening when predefined thresholds are exceeded.

A third mechanism involves implementing mandatory oversight protocols for high-risk agentic applications. Such protocols should define review intervals, documentation requirements, escalation procedures, and intervention mechanisms throughout the operational lifecycle. In combination with comprehensive audit trails, these mechanisms enable the reconstruction of agent behavior and support both regulatory supervision and organizational learning.

Importantly, auditability in agentic AI environments must extend beyond traditional model logging. Effective accountability requires capturing not only final outputs but also relevant interaction pathways, including agent-to-agent communication, tool invocations, external data access, delegated tasks, model versions, configuration changes, and human interventions. Such traceability mechanisms are essential because the rationale behind an agentic system's behavior may emerge from complex interactions rather than from a single identifiable decision rule.

A further governance mechanism proposed by Holweg and Hacker (2026) is the Authority Traffic Light. This approach introduces standardized and machine-readable representations of agent authority levels. Rather than relying on implicit assumptions about what an agent is permitted to do, authority levels explicitly define which actions can be performed autonomously and which require additional authorization. This creates a verifiable governance layer between agent capabilities and organizational decision rights.

Closely related is the concept of non-delegable decisions. Certain decisions with significant legal, financial, or societal implications may require heightened safeguards or remain outside the permissible scope of autonomous agents. Examples include major contractual commitments, critical asset decisions, or actions affecting fundamental rights. Establishing such boundaries does not eliminate autonomy but creates structured limits within which autonomous systems can operate safely and legitimately.

From the perspective developed in this chapter, these mechanisms represent more than individual compliance requirements. They demonstrate the principle of systemic design, according to which governance capabilities must be embedded directly into the architecture of agentic ecosystems. Accountability, transparency, authority management, monitoring, and intervention mechanisms should therefore be designed as inherent properties of the system rather than added externally after deployment.

Consequently, accountability in agentic AI environments becomes a continuous and distributed capability. It emerges from the interaction of legal responsibilities, organizational structures, technical safeguards, and oversight architectures. This perspective extends traditional accountability models by recognizing that trustworthy agentic AI requires not only responsible actors but also systems that are designed to remain governable under conditions of autonomy, adaptation, and complexity.

Supervisory Agents and Dynamic Compliance

Supervisory agents form a core component of network-based oversight architectures. Unlike operational agents, which perform domain-specific tasks, supervisory agents are designed to monitor, evaluate, and coordinate the behavior of other agent-based systems. They therefore operate as meta-governance components within complex AI ecosystems, providing continuous oversight capabilities across distributed agent interactions.

The function of such systems can be compared to approaches from IT security, operational risk management, or regulatory monitoring, but goes significantly beyond them. Supervisory agents continuously analyze interaction patterns, communication structures, data flows, and decision-making dynamics within agent-based networks. The goal is to detect potential risks, rule violations, or systemic instabilities early.

A key area of application is dynamic compliance. Traditional compliance systems are often based on static rules, periodic audits, and ex post controls. This limitation becomes particularly relevant in the context of agentic AI because existing regulatory frameworks, including the EU AI Act, were primarily developed around predefined risk categories and conformity assessments. Supervisory agents provide a potential mechanism for extending compliance toward continuous lifecycle monitoring.

Agent-based systems, on the other hand, require continuous and adaptive compliance mechanisms. Supervisory agents can monitor regulatory requirements, governance policies, or organizational targets in real time and automatically identify deviations.

This is particularly relevant in highly regulated sectors such as financial services or critical infrastructure. There, supervisory agents can, for example:

- monitor regulatory thresholds,
- identify unusual interaction patterns,
- trigger escalation processes,
- aggregate systemic risk indicators,
- or reconstruct agent decision pathways through audit and traceability mechanisms

This creates a form of continuous algorithmic oversight that complements or partially replaces traditional periodic control mechanisms.

Furthermore, supervisory agents enable new forms of adaptive governance. Since agent-based systems are dynamic and capable of learning, governance structures must also adapt continuously through recursive feedback mechanisms. Supervisory agents can analyze changes in system behavior and, accordingly, modify governance mechanisms or generate recommendations for organizational interventions.

Another function lies in the orchestration of hybrid escalation processes. Not every detected anomaly requires immediate human intervention. Supervisory agents can prioritize risks, define escalation levels, and forward only critical cases to human decision-makers. This focuses human attention specifically on particularly relevant or high-risk situations.

However, such systems also introduce new dependencies. As governance becomes increasingly mediated by technical monitoring agents, governance itself becomes subject to algorithmic control. This creates a recursive governance challenge: supervisory agents require their own oversight mechanisms, validation procedures, and accountability structures. The question is therefore not only how operational agents can be governed, but also how governance agents themselves can remain transparent, reliable, and contestable.

AI Auditing and Systemic Assurance in Multi-Agent Environments

The increasing prevalence of agent-based systems is also changing the requirements for auditing and controlling artificial intelligence. Traditional AI audits typically focus on individual models, datasets, or decision-making logic. In this context, auditing increasingly becomes part of a broader assurance architecture rather than a periodic compliance activity. In multi-agent environments, however, this perspective is no longer sufficient, as risks often arise only at the level of agent interactions.

AI auditing must therefore evolve from model-centric audits to systemic governance audits. The focus is no longer solely on model parameters or fairness metrics of individual systems. Instead, emphasis is placed on communication structures, interaction dynamics, and emergent behavioral patterns within the overall system. A key challenge here lies in the traceability of distributed decisions. In agent-based networks, decisions often arise sequentially and collaboratively. Different agents process information, make partial decisions, and mutually influence each other's options for action. As a result, linear audit trails are increasingly being replaced by complex network structures.

This requires new forms of continuous auditing. Instead of periodic audits, governance mechanisms must be able to analyze interactions and risks in real time. Supervisory agents can play a central role here by continuously collecting and analyzing data on system behavior.

Furthermore, the issue of systemic explainability is gaining importance. While Explainable AI (XAI) has so far focused primarily on the explainability of individual models (Andrae, 2026c), multi-agent systems require explanatory mechanisms at the ecosystem level. Organizations must be able to understand:

- how decisions were made within the network,
- which agents were involved,
- what data was used,
- and which interaction patterns influenced relevant decisions.

This leads to a shift from local to relational explainability, with an emphasis on the dynamics of distributed decision-making processes. In agentic AI ecosystems, explainability therefore concerns not only why a specific model generated a particular output, but how interactions among agents, tools, data sources, and organizational constraints contributed to an emerging system outcome.

At the same time, new requirements for regulatory auditing standards are emerging. Existing governance and auditing frameworks were predominantly developed for relatively stable systems. Agent-based ecosystems, however, require adaptive auditing approaches that account for continuous change, emergent behavior, and distributed accountability structures. Consequently, auditing itself becomes a recursive governance process: monitoring mechanisms must continuously evaluate not only operational agents but also the effectiveness of the governance mechanisms designed to control them.

Risks of Recursive AI Governance

The integration of agent-based oversight structures enables continuous and adaptive governance, but it also creates a new layer of complexity: governance mechanisms themselves become part of the systems they seek to control. Particularly relevant here is the emergence of recursive governance structures in which AI systems monitor and control other AI systems. This shifts the governance issue in part to a meta-level of algorithmic control.

A key risk lies in so-called governance loops. These recursive structures challenge traditional assumptions of hierarchical control because oversight is no longer exercised from an external position but emerges from within the socio-technical system itself. When supervisory agents monitor operational agents while themselves being controlled by additional governance mechanisms, complex feedback loops can arise. Such recursive structures significantly increase system complexity, making transparency and accountability more difficult.

Furthermore, there is a risk of systemic misalignment. Supervisory agents themselves rely on data, models, and decision-making logic and may therefore be flawed, biased, or susceptible to manipulation. This creates a fundamental challenge of governance recursion: the mechanisms designed to ensure accountability may themselves require validation, monitoring, and independent oversight. Errors within governance agents can have particularly serious consequences, as they affect not only operational processes but also the control architecture of the entire system.

Another risk concerns adversarial behavior in agent-based environments. In open or partially open systems, agents might attempt to strategically circumvent or manipulate governance mechanisms. In multi-agent environments, strategic behavior may not only emerge from individual agents but also from interactions among agents pursuing different objectives. This is particularly relevant in environments with competing agents or economic incentive structures. Governance must therefore also ensure robustness against strategic manipulation.

Furthermore, recursive governance structures can reinforce concentrations of power. Organizations or platform providers that control both operational agents and oversight infrastructures gain potentially far-reaching control and monitoring capabilities. This is particularly relevant in platform-based AI ecosystems, where infrastructure providers may simultaneously control models, orchestration layers, data access, and monitoring capabilities. This raises questions regarding institutional control, democratic legitimacy, and the regulatory balance of power.

The governance of agentic systems must therefore not be understood exclusively as a technical control problem. Recursive governance structures require institutional arrangements that ensure transparency, contestability, and accountability of both operational agents and the mechanisms designed to govern them. Continuous governance consequently requires not only adaptive systems, but also adaptive institutions capable of evaluating and constraining the evolution of governance itself.

Human Agency and Meaningful Control

Despite increasing automation, human agency remains a central normative principle of responsible AI governance. The challenge, however, lies in redefining human control within highly complex agentic systems.

Traditional notions of direct human control reach their limits in dynamic multi-agent environments. Humans cannot monitor every interaction or immediately comprehend every decision. At the same time, governance must not be completely delegated to technical systems, as this raises fundamental questions of democratic legitimacy, accountability, and normative control.

Against this backdrop, nuanced concepts of human control are gaining importance. Santoni de Sio and van den Hoven (2018) distinguish between three forms of human control:

- human-in-the-loop,
- human-on-the-loop,
- and human-in-command.

While 'human-in-the-loop' describes direct human involvement in individual decisions, 'human-on-the-loop' focuses on supervisory control of complex systems. 'Human-in-command' goes a step further by emphasizing the ultimate strategic and institutional responsibility of human actors. These concepts should not be interpreted as fixed alternatives but as different governance configurations depending on the risk, autonomy, and complexity of the system.

For agentic ecosystems, the latter approach appears particularly relevant. Humans do not need to directly control every operational decision, but should retain the ability to

- define governance objectives,
- trigger intervention mechanisms,
- deactivate systems,
- and establish fundamental normative guidelines.

Under these conditions, meaningful human control refers less to operational micromanagement and more to institutional steering capacity. This perspective aligns with the principle of systemic design developed in this chapter. Human agency should not be preserved through unrealistic expectations of continuous manual supervision, but through architectural mechanisms that maintain human authority, visibility, and intervention capabilities within agentic ecosystems. Governance design must therefore ensure that humans remain capable of setting objectives, challenging system behavior, and overriding automated processes when necessary.

However, this requires appropriate organizational structures. Organizations need clear escalation mechanisms, governance roles, and accountability frameworks. At the same time, human actors must possess sufficient AI expertise to critically evaluate and monitor agentic systems.

Furthermore, human judgment remains central, particularly in situations of normative uncertainty. AI agents can increase operational efficiency and perform complex data analyses, but they do not possess genuine political or ethical responsibility. Decisions with significant societal, regulatory, or moral implications continue to require human legitimation and institutional accountability.

Hybrid oversight architectures should therefore not aim to replace human governance. Instead, the focus is on developing complementary human-machine governance systems. The future of agentic governance likely lies neither in complete human control nor in autonomous algorithmic self-governance. The focus is on adaptive and resilient forms of hybrid coordination. The future of agentic governance therefore lies in adaptive forms of hybrid coordination, where human judgment, organizational governance structures, and technical oversight mechanisms continuously interact.

Theoretical Contribution 2: Network-Based Oversight

As agentic AI evolves from isolated applications to interconnected ecosystems, governance must shift from supervising individual AI systems toward coordinating interactions across distributed networks of autonomous agents. Network-based oversight conceptualizes governance as a continuous process of monitoring relationships, information flows, delegated authority, and collective system behavior rather than evaluating isolated algorithmic decisions. This perspective recognizes that accountability, resilience, and trust emerge from the architecture of interactions across the ecosystem, making oversight inherently network-centric rather than model-centric.

ORGANIZATIONAL AND REGULATORY APPLICATIONS

AI Agents in Financial Services

The financial sector is one of the areas where agent-based AI systems are expected to have a particularly profound impact. Financial institutions traditionally rely on highly data-driven processes, complex decision-making frameworks, and extensive regulatory requirements. This creates an environment in which AI agents generate both significant efficiency gains and new governance and stability risks.

AI systems are already being used today in areas such as credit risk assessment, fraud detection, algorithmic trading, liquidity management, and regulatory compliance. However, as agent-based systems develop, the focus is shifting from isolated analytical models toward autonomous or semi-autonomous decision-making and coordination systems. AI agents can, for example, monitor regulatory requirements, automate reporting processes, aggregate market information, or coordinate operational decision-making processes.

Recent research increasingly describes this development as a transition from model-centric to workflow-centric automation. Agent-based systems no longer merely perform individual forecasting or analysis tasks. Instead, the systems integrate information processing, reasoning, strategy development, and operational execution within coherent decision-making processes (Gong, 2026). This transforms individual business processes and, potentially, the institutional structure of financial decision-making architectures as a whole.

So-called compliance and supervisory agents are gaining particular importance in this context. Such systems continuously analyze regulatory requirements, internal guidelines, and operational activities to identify potential violations or risks early. Unlike traditional rule-based compliance systems, agent-based architectures can analyze dynamic relationships and account for complex interaction patterns. This gives rise to a new form of continuous and adaptive compliance monitoring.

At the same time, the use of agent-based systems significantly increases the complexity of financial governance structures. Financial markets are already highly interconnected and adaptive systems in which algorithmic interactions can generate systemic dynamics. The integration of autonomous agents could further amplify these dynamics. Interactions between trading algorithms, risk agents, and automated decision-making processes can potentially trigger cascading effects, synchronized market reactions, or new forms of systemic instability.

In this context, recent research indicates that the systemic impacts of AI agents depend less on the isolated performance of individual models than on their architecture, coupling, and governance within the financial system (Gong, 2026). Factors such as the following appear particularly relevant here:

- the degree of autonomous decision-making authority ('autonomy depth'),
- the homogeneity of the models and data sources used,
- the synchronization of agent decisions ('execution coupling'),
- the concentration of shared infrastructure,
- and the observability of agentic decision-making processes ('supervisory observability').

These factors are of considerable importance for financial market stability and systemic risks. If numerous financial institutions rely on similar models, identical data sources, or shared infrastructure platforms, even locally rational decisions could lead to correlated behavior, market instability, or liquidity stress. In this context, Gong (2026) argues that even individually optimal agent decisions can generate systemic instability in aggregate form under conditions of high coupling and low heterogeneity.

This raises fundamental questions for financial market regulation and operational resilience. Existing governance regimes, such as model risk management, internal control systems, or operational risk management, were predominantly developed for clearly defined models and processes. Agent-based systems, on the other hand, require continuous monitoring, real-time governance, and more system-oriented control approaches. In particular, the increasing concentration of AI infrastructures—for example, through shared cloud providers, foundation models, or API ecosystems—could generate new forms of systemic interdependence within the financial system.

Furthermore, the role of human decision-makers in the financial sector is changing. AI agents are increasingly taking on analytical and operational tasks, while human actors are assuming more strategic, supervisory, and escalation-related functions. As a result, governance is evolving from direct process control toward the monitoring of complex hybrid human-machine systems. In this context, recent governance approaches speak of a necessary 'supervisory co-evolution,' in which regulatory authorities themselves must also develop AI-based monitoring and analytical capabilities to keep pace with the increasing complexity of agent-based financial systems (Gong, 2026).

At the same time, the financial sector offers valuable insights for other regulated sectors. Due to its high level of regulation, strong risk management culture, and long experience with algorithmic systems, it could become an institutional testing ground for adaptive governance and oversight architectures for agentic systems. Developments in the field of 'agentic finance' could therefore shape future governance models for autonomous AI systems far beyond the financial sector.

Illustrative Mini Case: Agentic Compliance Monitoring in Financial Services

Financial institutions increasingly explore agentic AI to automate regulatory compliance while maintaining human accountability. Consider a large commercial bank that deploys a network of specialized AI agents to support continuous compliance with prudential regulation.

Rather than relying on a single AI application, the organization establishes an agentic compliance ecosystem consisting of four interacting agents:

- The Compliance Agent continuously monitors changes to regulatory requirements (e.g., the AI Act, DORA, and the CRR).
- Risk Assessment Agent evaluates potential operational and regulatory impacts on business activities.
- Reporting Agent automatically prepares supervisory documentation and internal audit reports.
- Human Supervisor validates critical decisions, authorizes regulatory submissions, and intervenes in exceptional situations.

Instead of operating sequentially, these agents continuously exchange information through shared knowledge bases and orchestration services. Regulatory updates immediately trigger new risk assessments, which in turn initiate reporting workflows or escalation procedures.

The principal governance challenge is therefore no longer ensuring the correctness of a single AI model but coordinating interactions among multiple autonomous agents while preserving transparency, traceability, and human accountability.

Key Insight

This example illustrates how governance shifts from supervising isolated AI applications toward managing interactions within an interconnected agentic ecosystem.

AI Agents in Public Administration

Public administration is also undergoing a profound transformation, increasingly shaped by artificial intelligence and data-driven decision-making. AI agents offer the potential to automate administrative processes, improve public services, and coordinate government tasks more efficiently.

Potential applications range from digital citizen services and automated application processing to supporting political decision-making processes. Agent-based systems can aggregate information, coordinate administrative workflows, or personalize citizen interactions . In complex administrative systems, multi-agent architectures could connect different agencies, data sources, and decision-making processes.

At the same time, however, significant governance challenges arise. Public administration is based not only on efficiency but also on democratic legitimacy, the rule of law, and public accountability. The use of autonomous or semi-autonomous systems, therefore, raises fundamental questions about political control and institutional responsibility.

A central problem lies in the risk of algorithmic bureaucratization. If decisions are increasingly prepared or made by agent-based systems, political and normative decisions could be narrowed down to a technocratic level. Governance must therefore integrate democratic legitimacy and social accountability.

Furthermore, AI agents create new transparency issues. Public decisions must remain fundamentally traceable and verifiable. In complex multi-agent systems, however, this can become difficult, especially when decisions arise from distributed interactions. Transparency at the system level thus becomes a central prerequisite for democratic governance.

Another problem concerns institutional path dependencies. Public administrations often have historically evolved structures, fragmented IT landscapes, and complex organizational architectures. The integration of agent-based systems requires comprehensive organizational transformation and institutional learning processes. At the same time, public institutions bear a special responsibility regarding fairness, non-discrimination, and social inclusion. Agent-based systems must not exacerbate existing inequalities or undermine democratic control mechanisms. Governance must therefore systematically integrate ethical, legal, and societal dimensions.

Against this backdrop, it becomes clear that the use of AI agents in public administration goes far beyond technological innovation. Rather, it involves a transformation of state governance structures themselves.

Illustrative Mini Case: Agentic Decision Support in Public Administration

Public administrations increasingly investigate agentic AI to accelerate administrative procedures while preserving legal certainty and democratic accountability.

Consider the digital processing of building permit applications.

Instead of assigning the task to one AI system, an agentic workflow distributes responsibilities across several specialized agents:

- The Document Review Agent verifies the completeness of the submitted documentation.
- Legal Assessment Agent evaluates compliance with planning and environmental regulations.
- Citizen Communication Agent interacts with applicants, requests missing information, and explains procedural status.
- The Case Coordination Agent orchestrates information exchange and prepares recommendations for the responsible public official.

The final administrative decision remains under human authority. However, the decision-making process increasingly arises from interactions among multiple agents who continuously exchange information and update their recommendations.

The governance challenge, therefore, extends beyond algorithmic transparency toward ensuring procedural fairness, legal accountability, and traceability across the entire decision ecosystem.

Key Insight

Agentic AI transforms administrative governance from supervising individual AI-supported decisions toward governing collaborative decision processes across hybrid human–AI networks.

AI Agents in Critical Infrastructure

The integration of agentic systems into critical infrastructure opens up significant potential for efficiency, resilience, and adaptive control. At the same time, however, new forms of systemic vulnerability arise, as critical infrastructure is highly interdependent and socially essential.

AI agents are particularly relevant in areas such as energy supply, traffic control, telecommunications, healthcare infrastructure, and cybersecurity. In these areas, agent-based systems can, for example:

- optimize energy flows,
- coordinate load distribution,
- monitor networks,
- or autonomously analyze security incidents.

However, the increasing interconnectivity of critical infrastructure is leading to a concentration of systemic risks. Errors, manipulations, or unexpected interactions among individual agents can potentially spread across entire networks. This creates risks of cascading failures that are no longer limited to individual components.

These dynamics resemble those of complex adaptive systems, such as those already observed in financial markets and global supply chains. Under certain conditions, small disruptions can have disproportionate effects. Governance of critical infrastructure must therefore address systemic resilience.

Cybersecurity is particularly important in this context. Agent-based systems significantly expand the attack surface of digital infrastructures. At the same time, AI agents can themselves be deployed for defensive security functions, such as anomaly detection or autonomous response to security incidents. This creates a new dynamic of algorithmic security and countermeasures.

Furthermore, AI agents are transforming the control logic of critical infrastructures. Traditionally, many infrastructure systems relied on relatively stable and centralized control mechanisms. Agent-based systems, however, enable more decentralized and adaptive coordination. While this can enhance resilience and flexibility, it simultaneously creates new challenges regarding transparency, accountability, and institutional control.

Against this backdrop, it becomes clear that the governance of critical infrastructure must increasingly be understood as the governance of complex AI ecosystems. Security and resilience strategies must systematically account for interdependencies, network effects, and emerging risks.

Illustrative Mini Case: Agentic Digital Twins for Critical Infrastructure

Critical infrastructure operators increasingly combine digital twins with agentic AI to improve resilience and operational reliability.

Consider the management of an intelligent electricity distribution network.

The digital twin integrates several specialized AI agents:

- Sensor Agent continuously monitors infrastructure conditions.
- Prediction Agent forecasts failures using real-time sensor data.
- Maintenance Agent prioritizes repair schedules and allocates maintenance resources.
- Governance Agent supervises system behavior, evaluates safety constraints, and escalates anomalies to human operators.

The interaction of these agents enables continuous adaptation of operational strategies as environmental conditions evolve.

However, governance challenges arise because system behavior emerges from distributed interactions rather than predefined workflows. Consequently, infrastructure operators require continuous monitoring, simulation-based testing, and supervisory mechanisms that can identify cascading effects before operational failures occur.

Key Insight

This example demonstrates how digital twins provide the technological foundation for continuous governance by enabling observation, simulation, and adaptive oversight of complex agentic ecosystems.

Interoperability and Data Governance

The functionality of agent-based ecosystems depends significantly on data infrastructures and interoperability. AI agents typically operate within distributed data environments and communicate with one another via APIs, platforms, or standardized protocols. Data governance thus becomes a central component of network-based governance architectures.

Interoperability has both technical and institutional dimensions. Technical interoperability encompasses the ability of different systems to exchange data and communicate with one another. Institutional interoperability, on the other hand, concerns common standards, governance rules, and organizational coordination mechanisms.

A lack of interoperability can create significant risks. Fragmented data structures, incompatible interfaces, or inconsistent governance rules hinder transparency, auditability, and coordination within agent-based systems. At the same time, highly integrated systems can create new dependencies and concentration risks.

Furthermore, data quality directly influences the behavior of agent-based systems. Distorted, incomplete, or manipulated data can lead to systemic misjudgments. Data governance must therefore systematically address issues of data quality, integrity, and access control.

Issues related to data-driven power asymmetries are also gaining particular significance. Large platform providers or infrastructure operators often control central data resources, thereby wielding considerable structural power. The governance of agent-based systems is therefore closely linked to issues of digital sovereignty and infrastructural control.

Against this backdrop, it becomes clear that AI governance cannot be viewed separately from data governance (see Figure 2). Data infrastructures form the foundation of agentic coordination and significantly influence transparency, resilience, and accountability within digital ecosystems.

Organizational Readiness and Digital Maturity

The successful integration of AI agents depends largely on organizational readiness and institutional capabilities. Many digital transformation projects fail less due to technical problems than to inadequate governance, organizational inadaptation, or institutional coordination.

Organizational readiness encompasses the ability of organizations to implement agentic systems strategically, responsibly, and resiliently. This requires technical expertise as well as new governance structures, organizational learning processes, and institutional adaptability.

A key factor is AI literacy at various organizational levels. Decision-makers, supervisory bodies, and operational staff must understand the basic functioning, risks, and governance requirements of agentic systems. Without sufficient expertise, there is a risk of excessive dependence on technical specialists or external platform providers.

Furthermore, organizations need new governance roles and coordination mechanisms. These include, for example:

- AI governance committees,
- oversight officers,
- interdisciplinary audit structures,
- or continuous monitoring processes.

Governance is thus increasingly becoming an organization-wide, cross-functional role.

Another aspect concerns organizational learning capacity. Agent-based systems are constantly evolving and generating new interaction dynamics. Organizations must therefore be able to adaptively refine their governance structures and respond flexibly to new risks or regulatory requirements. Finally, the integration of AI agents also changes organizational culture and decision-making logic. Data-driven and algorithmically coordinated processes can transform traditional hierarchies, communication structures, and power relations. Organizational readiness, therefore, encompasses not only technical implementation but also cultural and institutional transformation.

These considerations illustrate that AI governance ultimately represents a strategic organizational capability. Successful digital transformation depends on the ability to design complex human-machine systems at the institutional level and coordinate them in a resilient manner.

DIGITAL TWINS AND SIMULATION-BASED GOVERNANCE

Agent-Based Modeling and Governance Experimentation

The increasing complexity of agent-based AI ecosystems poses significant epistemic challenges for traditional governance approaches. In highly networked multi-agent systems, interaction dynamics, emergent behavioral patterns, and systemic risks often cannot be captured solely through linear analytical methods or static risk models. Against this backdrop, simulation-based approaches are gaining increasing importance, particularly agent-based modeling (ABM) and digital twins (Pobuda & Andrae, 2026).

Logan et al. (2026) emphasize that conventional risk assessment methods are often unable to capture cascade effects, emergent dynamics, and profound uncertainties in interdependent systems. As current legal and technical analyses show, agent-based systems can exhibit emergent behavioral deviations, specification manipulations, circumvention of oversight, and recursive interaction effects that are difficult to predict in advance (Nannini et al., 2026). To address these limitations, the authors advocate adaptive, simulation-oriented approaches that can investigate evolving system behavior under uncertain conditions. Agent-based modeling is based on the idea of analyzing complex systems through the simulation of autonomous and interacting agents. Unlike aggregated or purely statistical models, ABM focuses on micro-level interaction processes from which macroscopic dynamics can emerge (Epstein, 2006). Originally developed in the social sciences, economics, and complexity research, ABM is particularly well-suited for analyzing nonlinear systems with distributed decision-making structures and adaptive behavior.

This perspective is closely aligned with the use of governance twins and agent-based simulations in AI governance. Digital twins enable organizations and regulatory authorities to simulate interactions between AI agents, assess systemic vulnerabilities, and test governance measures before deploying them in real-world environments. This approach is particularly relevant for the governance of agent-based AI systems. AI agents typically operate within complex interaction networks where decisions arise from the interplay of different actors and systems. Governance problems often stem from emergent interaction dynamics. Agent-based simulations enable experimental analysis of such dynamics and the identification of potential risks or coordination problems at an early stage.

This opens up new possibilities for governance experimentation. Organizations and regulatory authorities can test different governance architectures in simulated environments before deploying agent-based systems in production. For example, escalation mechanisms, communication protocols, or oversight structures can be simulated under various scenarios and evaluated for their robustness.

A key advantage of simulation-based governance lies in its ability to reveal complex feedback effects. Traditional governance approaches often rely on implicit assumptions of linear causality. However, agent-based systems frequently generate nonlinear dynamics in which small changes can have disproportionate effects. Simulations enable systematic investigation of such systemic interactions.

Furthermore, simulation-based approaches promote a more anticipatory perspective on governance. Governance is no longer understood primarily as reactive control of existing systems. Rather, it involves proactively shaping potential spaces for interaction. This aligns with broader trends toward anticipatory governance and resilience-oriented governance, which are designed to adaptively respond to uncertainty and complexity (Guston, 2014).

At the same time, simulation-based approaches also have epistemological limitations. Simulations do not accurately reflect social reality. They are model-based simplifications of complex systems. Their validity depends largely on model assumptions, parameterization, and data quality. Governance simulations must therefore not be misunderstood as deterministic forecasting tools. Rather, they function as exploratory tools for analyzing potential dynamics and risk constellations.

Nevertheless, the combination of ABM and AI governance opens up a promising approach to analyzing complex agent-based systems. Simulations enable a systemic perspective on governance and help organizations address risks, interdependencies, and coordination problems even before agent-based systems are deployed operationally.

Digital Twins for AI Ecosystems

While agent-based modeling focuses primarily on simulation-based scenario analyses, digital twins expand this perspective to include continuous real-time couplings between physical or organizational systems and their digital representations. The concept of the digital twin describes virtual replicas of real systems that are continuously updated by data streams, thereby enabling dynamic analysis, monitoring, and control of complex processes (Fuller et al., 2020).

Originally developed in an industrial context, digital twins are increasingly gaining significance for organizational and institutional governance as well. In the context of agent-based AI systems, digital twins can be used to continuously simulate and monitor interactions between AI agents, organizational processes, and regulatory frameworks.

This leads to the emergence of so-called governance twins or organizational digital twins. Such systems represent technical infrastructures and also model decision-making processes, communication structures, and governance mechanisms within complex organizations. AI agents can thus be operationally controlled and analyzed for their systemic impacts.

Digital twins are particularly important for the governance of dynamic multi-agent ecosystems. Since agent-based systems continuously learn and interact, their behavioral patterns change constantly. Digital twins enable near-real-time observation of these changes and early identification of potential risks.

Furthermore, digital twins open up new possibilities for simulation-based resilience analyses. Organizations can, for example, simulate:

- how AI agents react to regulatory changes,

- how disruptions spread within agent-based networks,
- or what interaction dynamics might arise in crisis scenarios.

As a result, governance structures themselves become subjects of continuous observation and adaptation.

In a regulatory context, digital twins could also enable a new form of data-driven oversight. Regulatory authorities could use simulated or semi-realistic models of critical AI ecosystems to analyze potential risks or systemic vulnerabilities at an early stage. This would support a transition from static compliance audits to continuous, simulation-based oversight.

At the same time, digital twins raise new governance questions. The creation of highly complex organizational twins requires substantial amounts of data and detailed knowledge of organizational processes. This raises new challenges regarding data protection, data sovereignty, and power asymmetries. Actors who possess comprehensive digital representations of organizational systems gain potentially far-reaching control and monitoring capabilities.

Furthermore, there is a risk of excessive technocratization of governance. If organizational control becomes increasingly simulation- and data-driven, political, normative, or cultural dimensions of organizational decisions could take a back seat. Governance must therefore not be reduced to algorithmic optimization logic.

Nevertheless, digital twins hold considerable potential for the governance of agent-based systems. They enable a connection between real-time data, simulation-based analysis, and adaptive governance, thereby laying the foundation for more resilient and anticipatory governance architectures.

Challenges of Simulation-Based Governance

While digital twins and simulation-based governance offer considerable potential for monitoring and governing complex agentic AI ecosystems, they should not be regarded as a comprehensive solution. Their effectiveness depends on several technical, organizational, and institutional conditions that remain only partially understood and constitute important directions for future research.

A first challenge concerns computational complexity. Agentic AI ecosystems consist of multiple interacting agents whose behavior continuously evolves through learning, environmental feedback, and dynamic coordination. Simulating such systems at sufficient temporal and behavioral resolution can become computationally demanding, particularly when digital twins are expected to operate continuously and in real time. As the number of interacting agents increases, simulation complexity may grow non-linearly, making large-scale real-time governance computationally expensive.

A second challenge relates to data availability and data quality. Digital twins depend on comprehensive, timely, and reliable data describing both the operational environment and the behavior of individual agents. In many organizational settings, however, relevant information remains fragmented across heterogeneous platforms, external APIs, proprietary systems, and organizational boundaries. Missing, delayed, or inconsistent data may significantly reduce the explanatory and predictive capabilities of simulation models.

Third, considerable uncertainty surrounds the calibration of behavioral models. Unlike traditional engineering systems, agentic AI exhibits adaptive, context-dependent, and partially emergent behavior. Developing behavioral models that adequately capture planning strategies, tool selection, collaboration among agents, or learning dynamics remains an open scientific challenge. Consequently, digital twins may accurately represent technical system states yet fail to anticipate higher-order behavioral adaptations.

Closely related is the problem of validation. Whereas physical digital twins can often be compared against observable system behavior, validating simulations of agentic ecosystems is considerably more difficult because future interactions may not yet have occurred. Establishing reliable validation methodologies for emergent multi-agent behavior represents an important research frontier.

Another challenge concerns uncertainty propagation. Small modeling errors or incorrect assumptions about individual agents may propagate through interconnected networks, producing disproportionately large deviations in simulated outcomes. Such cascading effects are particularly relevant for highly interconnected agentic ecosystems in finance, healthcare, or critical infrastructure, where localized failures may trigger broader systemic consequences.

Moreover, digital twins themselves are subject to model drift. As foundation models, organizational processes, external tools, and regulatory environments evolve, the assumptions embedded within the digital twin may gradually become outdated. Maintaining an accurate representation requires continuous recalibration, monitoring, and updating of both technical and behavioral components.

Finally, simulation-based governance introduces an additional, often overlooked problem: the governance of the digital twin itself. If digital twins increasingly support or even influence organizational decisions, they become critical socio-technical systems requiring transparency, accountability, validation, cybersecurity, and institutional oversight. Consequently, governance becomes recursive: not only must organizations govern the operational agentic ecosystem, but they must also govern the governance infrastructure used to monitor and evaluate that ecosystem.

Taken together, these challenges suggest that digital twins should not be understood as deterministic representations of organizational reality but as adaptive decision-support infrastructures. Their primary value lies less in perfectly predicting future behavior than in supporting continuous learning, scenario exploration, stress testing, and adaptive governance under conditions of uncertainty.

Simulating Systemic Risk and Coordination Failures

A key advantage of simulation-based governance is its ability to reveal systemic risks and coordination problems that, in real-world environments, often only become apparent in a crisis. Agent-based systems generate complex interdependencies and nonlinear dynamics that can only be analyzed to a limited extent using traditional governance methods.

Systemic risks typically do not arise from isolated failures of individual components. They result from the interconnectedness and interdependence of different actors and systems. This is particularly relevant in multi-agent ecosystems, where decisions arise from continuous interactions between agents. Minor malfunctions or local optimization strategies can, under certain conditions, trigger cascading effects. A prominent example of such dynamics is algorithmic trading. Interactions between automated trading systems can amplify market volatility or trigger flash crashes, even though individual systems comply with regulations on their own. Similar dynamics could also arise in the future in other agent-based ecosystems, such as automated administrative systems, energy infrastructures, or digital platform economies.

Simulations enable the experimental analysis of such risks. Organizations can simulate:

- how errors spread between agents,
- which communication structures are particularly vulnerable,
- or which governance mechanisms increase resilience.

This creates new opportunities for preventive governance.

This is particularly relevant for so-called coordination failures. In multi-agent systems, different agents often pursue local goals or optimization strategies. Without appropriate governance mechanisms, this can lead to collective misalignment, for example, when agents pursue competing objectives or destabilize one another. Such coordination problems also have organizational and institutional dimensions. Governance must therefore ensure technical interoperability while simultaneously addressing normative conflicts of interest and institutional tensions. Furthermore, simulation-based approaches enable the analysis of extreme or rare scenarios ('stress testing'). Similar to the financial sector, organizations could test agent-based systems under crisis scenarios to identify potential vulnerabilities. This is particularly relevant for critical infrastructure or highly regulated environments.

The ability to simulate systemic risks thus significantly broadens the understanding of AI governance. Governance is understood as the management of complex interdependencies and emergent dynamics.

Implications for Policy Design

The combination of simulation-based approaches, digital twins, and AI governance has far-reaching implications for future regulatory and policy architectures. Traditional regulatory models often rely on static rules, periodic audits, and linear accountability structures. Agent-based ecosystems, however, require adaptive, continuous, and system-oriented governance approaches.

Simulations open up new possibilities for evidence-based policymaking. Regulatory authorities could model different governance scenarios and analyze their potential impacts before implementing regulatory measures. This would make regulation more experimental and learning-oriented.

This aligns with broader trends toward adaptive regulation and anticipatory governance. Regulatory institutions would increasingly need to respond flexibly to technological dynamics and continuously adapt their governance. Simulations and digital twins could serve as tools for institutional learning in this context.

Simulation-based approaches could foster cooperation between regulatory authorities, companies, and research institutions. Joint governance simulations would enable the early identification of risks and conflicting objectives, as well as the development of coordinated governance strategies. At the same time, new institutional challenges are emerging. Regulatory authorities require significant technical and analytical expertise to effectively implement simulation-based governance. This particularly concerns issues of data infrastructure, model validation, and algorithmic auditing.

Furthermore, simulation-based governance raises fundamental questions of democratic legitimacy. As political decisions are increasingly supported by complex simulation models, there is a risk of technocratic regulation. Governance must therefore not be exclusively data- and model-driven. It must continue to integrate political deliberation and societal legitimacy. Nevertheless, there are many indications that simulation-based governance will play a central role in steering complex AI ecosystems in the future. The ability to analyze potential dynamics proactively and to experimentally refine governance could become a crucial prerequisite for resilient and responsible digital transformation.

Theoretical Contribution 3:Systemic Design

In agentic AI ecosystems, governance cannot be treated as an external layer of supervision that is applied after systems have been deployed. Instead, governance must become an architectural property of the ecosystem itself. Systemic design embeds accountability, transparency, observability, resilience, human authority, and intervention mechanisms directly into the technical, organizational, and institutional architecture of agentic systems. Governance shifts from ex-post control toward governance-by-design, where the capacity to monitor, explain, adapt, and intervene is intentionally built into the ecosystem from its inception.

This perspective extends existing concepts such as privacy-by-design, security-by-design, and trustworthy AI by proposing governance-by-design as a foundational design principle for agentic AI. Rather than treating governance as a compliance function operating outside the system, systemic design integrates governance into the architecture of platforms, orchestration layers, shared services, supervisory agents, and organizational processes. In this sense, governance becomes an integral component of system architecture rather than an external regulatory constraint.

IMPLICATIONS FOR AI POLICY AND INSTITUTIONAL DESIGN

AI Act and Distributed Agent Ecosystems

The growing prevalence of agent-based AI systems poses fundamental challenges to existing regulatory approaches. Current governance and regulatory regimes were primarily developed for AI systems with relatively clear boundaries, whose functionalities, accountability structures, and deployment contexts could be defined with comparative clarity. Agent-based ecosystems, by contrast, are characterized by distributed decision-making structures, dynamic interactions, and emergent behavioral patterns. As a result, traditional regulatory categories are coming under increasing pressure.

This becomes particularly evident in the context of the European AIA. The AIA currently represents the most comprehensive regulatory effort to systematically address the risks of artificial intelligence. Its architecture is largely based on a risk-based approach that classifies certain AI systems as 'high-risk systems' and defines requirements for transparency, data quality, human oversight, robustness, and governance for these systems. This regulatory framework remains largely geared toward discrete AI systems. Multi-agent ecosystems partially transcend this logic, as decisions can often no longer be clearly attributed to a single system or provider. Different agents interact dynamically with one another, access external tools and data sources, and sometimes continuously modify their behavior. This creates new regulatory gray areas. However, recent compliance research on agent-based AI suggests that highly autonomous systems exhibiting untraceable behavioral deviations during runtime may not be fully compatible with the current AIA architecture

(Nannini et al., 2026). Engin and Hand (2025) propose evaluating agentic AI across multiple governance dimensions, including degree of autonomy, interdependence, multi-agent coordination, feedback integration, and goal decomposition. Such dimensional governance enables context-dependent, adaptive risk assessment, making regulatory decisions more precise and flexible. By operationalizing these dimensions, regulatory authorities can not only identify high-risk systems but also address them. They could also tailor governance mechanisms and oversight architectures without unnecessarily hindering innovation.

A central issue concerns the attribution of responsibility. The AIA implicitly assumes relatively clear roles such as 'provider,' 'deployer,' or 'user.' In distributed agent-based ecosystems, however, these roles are becoming increasingly blurred. Different organizations can simultaneously:

- provide infrastructure,
- train agents,
- perform oversight functions,
- or influence operational decisions.

This makes the regulatory assignment of responsibility considerably more complex. If a deployer uses a generally applicable agent in a high-risk context, they become a 'provider' under the AIA and are thus legally responsible. This scenario poses new challenges for compliance, governance, and liability (Hacker & Holweg, 2026).

Furthermore, the dynamics of agent-based systems call into question traditional conformity assessments. Classic regulatory approaches, such as the AIA, often rely on ex ante reviews and static compliance assumptions. Agent-based systems, however, are constantly evolving and interact within changing environments. Governance must therefore be designed to be more process-oriented and continuous.

Questions of human oversight are also taking on new significance. While the AIA establishes 'human oversight' as a central governance principle, it often remains unclear how meaningful human control can be practically implemented in highly complex multi-agent environments. Direct operational control often appears unrealistic in such contexts. Instead, hybrid oversight models and institutional ultimate responsibility are gaining importance.

The development of agent-based ecosystems thus highlights a fundamental shift in regulatory challenges: regulation must increasingly focus less on individual models and more on complex socio-technical networks. The transition from model-centered to system-centered governance, therefore, has both organizational and regulatory implications.

Toward Adaptive and Continuous Governance

The dynamics of agent-based systems make it clear that static governance approaches appear to have only limited long-term viability. Traditional regulatory and control models typically rely on periodic audits, fixed compliance requirements, and relatively stable system assumptions. Agent-based ecosystems, on the other hand, are constantly changing and generate adaptive interaction dynamics that require ongoing monitoring and flexible governance mechanisms.

Against this backdrop, the concept of adaptive and continuous governance is gaining increasing importance. Governance is not understood here as a one-time act of control. It is better interpreted as a permanent process of observation, evaluation, and adaptation. The goal is to develop institutional structures capable of dealing with technological dynamics and uncertainty. A central component of such approaches is continuous monitoring. Instead of ad hoc audits or static certifications, governance mechanisms must be able to continuously analyze agentic systems. Supervisory agents, simulation-based oversight structures, and digital twins can play key roles in this regard.

Furthermore, adaptive governance requires stronger feedback mechanisms between technical systems, organizations, and regulatory institutions. This makes governance more reflexive and learning-oriented. Regulatory authorities and organizations must be able to continuously refine governance mechanisms and respond flexibly to new risks or interaction dynamics.

This development aligns with broader transformations in modern governance regimes. In areas such as financial market regulation, cybersecurity, and environmental governance, a shift from static regulatory frameworks to more dynamic, risk-based governance models is already evident. Agent-based AI systems significantly reinforce this development. At the same time, adaptive governance creates new institutional requirements. Continuous governance requires extensive data infrastructures, analytical capabilities, and interdisciplinary expertise. Organizations and regulatory authorities, therefore, need new institutional capacities to monitor complex systems in real time.

Furthermore, new questions of regulatory legitimacy are emerging. Adaptive governance increases regulatory systems' flexibility but can also reduce transparency and predictability. If governance is continuously adapted, mechanisms for democratic control and institutional accountability must remain in place. Nevertheless, the transition to adaptive and continuous governance appears increasingly inevitable. Agent-based systems operate in dynamic environments whose risks cannot be fully anticipated ex ante. Governance must therefore become self-learning and evolutionary.

Standardization and Assurance Frameworks

As agent-based systems become more widespread, the importance of standardized governance and assurance frameworks also grows. Standardization serves several functions: it reduces uncertainty, facilitates interoperability, establishes common governance principles, and supports regulatory comparability.

Numerous standards and governance frameworks are already emerging in the field of artificial intelligence, for example, regarding:

- risk management,
- transparency,
- model validation,
- or AI ethics.

However, agent-based systems introduce new requirements that go beyond traditional model governance. Logan et al. (2026) argue that in highly complex and interdependent systems, traditional concepts of model validation are becoming increasingly inadequate, as system behavior evolves dynamically and cannot always be predicted in advance or empirically verified. Instead, the authors propose a shift toward the concept of 'defensibility,' emphasizing transparency, adaptive learning, explicit assumptions, and the continuous revision of governance frameworks. Standards for multi-agent interactions and systemic governance will be particularly important in the future. Organizations require common protocols for:

- communication between agents,
- escalation mechanisms,
- audit trails,
- oversight structures,
- and governance interfaces.

Without such standards, there is a risk of fragmented and difficult-to-control AI ecosystems.

Furthermore, assurance frameworks are gaining importance. Assurance describes procedures for continuously ensuring trustworthiness, compliance, and operational resilience. In the context of agent-based systems, such frameworks must be designed to be significantly more dynamic than traditional certification approaches. Continuous auditing and monitoring mechanisms appear particularly relevant here. Governance is increasingly shifting from ex post control toward real-time assurance. Supervisory agents and simulation-based governance architectures could become central components of future assurance systems.

At the same time, new challenges are emerging regarding global harmonization. Agent-based systems often operate transnationally within digital platform ecosystems. Different regulatory standards or governance principles could therefore promote fragmentation and regulatory arbitrage. At the same time, standardization processes must not be designed exclusively in a technocratic manner. Standards implicitly define normative models, power relations, and governance principles. The development of governance standards for AI agents, therefore, also has political and societal dimensions.

Strategic Implications for Organizations

The governance of agentic systems is increasingly evolving into a strategic organizational capability. In the future, successful digital transformation will not depend solely on technological innovation. Organizations will be successful if they manage complex AI ecosystems in a resilient, adaptive, and responsible manner.

Figure 3. Enterprise Agentic Platform: Architecture, Governance, and Value Realization

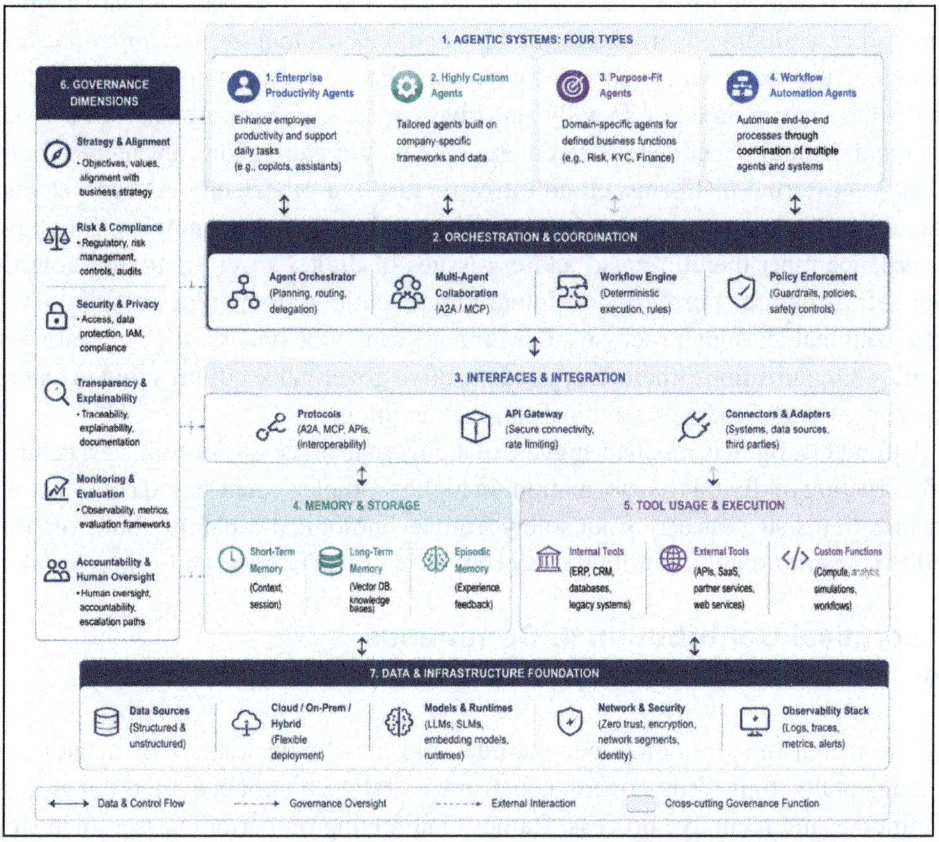

Source: Own representation.

Figure 3 illustrates the architecture of a scalable, reusable platform for enterprise-level agentic AI. It shows the four agentic types, orchestration, interfaces, storage, and tool usage, as well as governance components. The figure illustrates that strategic governance not only addresses regulatory requirements but is also an integral part of the organizational infrastructure for adaptive, secure, and sustainable digital transformation.

To achieve this, organizations must develop new institutional capabilities. Governance is becoming an integrative cross-functional role that combines technical expertise, regulatory knowledge, risk management, and organizational transformation. This requires new governance structures and new forms of interdisciplinary collaboration. Furthermore, the role of organizational leadership is changing. Leaders must increasingly be able to strategically coordinate hybrid human-machine systems and understand governance as a component of organizational resilience.

Another strategic aspect concerns trust and reputation. Organizations that establish transparent, resilient governance structures could gain a long-term competitive advantage. Trustworthy AI systems are increasingly becoming a strategic differentiator, particularly in regulated or socially sensitive sectors. At the same time, new risks of organizational dependency are emerging. Many organizations are increasingly reliant on external platforms, cloud infrastructures, or proprietary AI ecosystems. This is shifting power and control structures within digital economies. Strategic governance must therefore also address issues of digital sovereignty and control over infrastructure. Furthermore, integrating agentic systems requires long-term organizational learning processes. Governance cannot be understood as a static set of rules. Organizations, therefore, need adaptive governance cultures that promote experimentation, feedback, and institutional learning.

Ultimately, there is much to suggest that governance itself is becoming a central infrastructure of digital transformation. In highly complex agent-based ecosystems, organizational success arises not solely from technological capability but from the ability to institutionally coordinate uncertainty, interdependence, and systemic risks.

Theoretical Contribution 4: Continuous and Recursive Governance

The increasing autonomy, adaptability, and interconnectedness of agentic AI fundamentally transform governance from a static compliance function into a continuous and recursive process. Rather than relying on periodic assessments or one-time conformity evaluations, governance must become an ongoing capability that continuously monitors, evaluates, and adapts to evolving system behavior. This requires governance architectures capable of responding to feedback, emergent interactions, changing risk profiles, and evolving organizational objectives throughout the entire lifecycle of agentic ecosystems.

Recursive governance extends this perspective by recognizing that governance mechanisms themselves must be continuously evaluated and refined. As agentic ecosystems evolve, oversight architectures, evaluation criteria, intervention mechanisms, and institutional arrangements must co-evolve with the systems they govern. Ultimately, governance ceases to be a static regulatory function and becomes an adaptive capability of the socio-technical ecosystem itself. In this perspective, governing agentic AI is no longer understood as merely maintaining compliance with predefined rules, but as continuously sustaining resilience, accountability, and trust amid permanent technological and organizational change.

CONCLUSION

Summary of Findings

The preceding sections progressively developed a new governance perspective for agentic AI through four interconnected theoretical contributions. The present analysis has shown that the increasing prevalence of agent-based AI systems marks a fundamental shift in digital transformation. Artificial intelligence is increasingly evolving from isolated analysis and decision-support systems into autonomous and semi-autonomous agents that operate within complex socio-technical networks. This development is also transforming organizational decision-making processes, institutional accountability structures, and regulatory governance architectures.

At the heart of the analysis was our thesis that existing model-centric governance approaches are only of limited suitability for addressing the challenges of agent-based ecosystems. Traditional governance models are often based on the assumption of clearly defined systems, linear accountability structures, and relatively stable decision-making processes. Agent-based systems, on the other hand, are characterized by distributed decision-making architectures, continuous interaction, adaptive learning processes, and emergent dynamics. Risks increasingly arise from systemic interdependencies rather than solely within individual models.

Against this backdrop, it has been argued that the governance of AI agents requires a transition from model-centered to system-centered governance. AI agents are part of complex governance networks in which technical, organizational, and institutional components are inextricably intertwined. Governance thus evolves from a matter of selective model control to a challenge of continuous systemic coordination.

To this end, we have developed a conceptual framework for network-based governance. Building on approaches from network governance, adaptive governance, and complexity research, we have demonstrated that effective control of agent-based systems is possible only through multi-layered, adaptive governance architectures. The focus is on transparency, traceability, accountability, resilience, and human oversight as central dimensions of governance.

Furthermore, the concept of agent-based oversight architectures was introduced. Supervisory agents can assume continuous monitoring, auditing, and escalation functions within complex AI ecosystems, thereby enabling new forms of dynamic compliance and adaptive governance. At the same time, however, it was emphasized that recursive governance structures themselves generate new risks, particularly regarding transparency, power concentration, and loss of control.

Another focus was on simulation-based governance approaches and digital twins. Agent-based modeling and digital twins enable the analysis of systemic risks, emergent interaction dynamics, and potential coordination problems within complex

AI ecosystems. As a result, governance is increasingly designed to be anticipatory and experimental.

Finally, the organizational and regulatory implications of agent-based systems were analyzed. Particularly in regulated sectors such as financial services, public administration, and critical infrastructure, new requirements are emerging for continuous governance, hybrid oversight structures, and adaptive regulatory models. The governance of agent-based systems is thus evolving into a central institutional challenge of digital transformation.

Theoretical Contributions

This chapter contributes to the emerging literature on agentic AI governance by developing a system-oriented perspective that extends beyond traditional model-centric approaches. The central argument is that governing agentic AI requires a conceptual shift from controlling individual AI systems toward designing governance architectures for interconnected socio-technical ecosystems.

First, the chapter contributes the concept of ecosystem-centered governance. While established AI governance approaches have primarily focused on individual models, applications, or regulatory classifications, agentic AI requires a broader unit of analysis. The behavior and risks of agentic systems increasingly emerge from interactions among autonomous agents, human actors, data infrastructures, external tools, and institutional arrangements. Ecosystem-centered governance therefore provides a framework for understanding AI governance as the coordination of complex socio-technical configurations rather than the control of isolated technological artifacts.

Second, the chapter develops the concept of network-based oversight as an approach for governing distributed agentic systems. Traditional oversight models often assume clear system boundaries and identifiable decision points. In contrast, agentic AI operates through interconnected networks in which multiple agents perform complementary tasks, exchange information, and generate outcomes through interaction. Network-based oversight therefore emphasizes distributed monitoring, hybrid human–AI supervision, escalation mechanisms, and coordination structures that can address emergent system behavior.

Third, the chapter introduces systemic design as a governance principle for agentic AI ecosystems. Rather than treating governance as an external compliance layer applied after system development, systemic design conceptualizes governance as an inherent property of system architecture. Accountability, transparency, resilience, observability, and intervention capabilities must therefore be embedded into the technical, organizational, and institutional design of agentic systems. This perspective extends existing approaches such as trustworthy AI and governance-by-design by emphasizing the architectural integration of governance mechanisms.

Fourth, the chapter advances the concept of continuous and recursive governance. The adaptive and evolving nature of agentic AI challenges governance approaches based on static assessments, predefined rules, or one-time conformity evaluations. Instead, governance must become a continuous learning process in which oversight mechanisms, organizational structures, and regulatory arrangements adapt alongside the systems they govern. Recursive governance further implies that governance mechanisms themselves require continuous evaluation and refinement as agentic ecosystems evolve.

However, these contributions establish a conceptual framework for governing agentic AI under conditions of complexity, uncertainty, and emergent behavior. The chapter argues that future AI governance will depend not only on regulating technological components but on developing adaptive governance architectures capable of sustaining accountability, resilience, and trust across interconnected socio-technical ecosystems.

Practical Implications

In addition to its theoretical contributions, our analysis has significant practical implications for organizations, regulatory authorities, and policymakers.

For organizations, the analysis makes it clear that the successful integration of agent-based systems goes far beyond technological implementation. Organizational resilience will depend significantly in the future on the ability to strategically and institutionally coordinate hybrid human-machine systems. Governance is thus evolving into a central organizational core competency.

To achieve this, organizations require new institutional capabilities, including:

- continuous monitoring,
- interdisciplinary governance structures,
- simulation-based risk analyses,
- and adaptive oversight mechanisms.

Furthermore, it becomes clear that human control must be reorganized under the conditions of agent-based systems. Meaningful human control will mean less direct operational intervention in the future and more strategic, institutional, and escalation-related management.

For regulatory authorities, the analysis implies that traditional static governance models appear to have only limited long-term viability. Agent-based ecosystems require adaptive and continuous regulatory approaches that systematically account for interdependencies, dynamic learning processes, and systemic risks.

The further development of regulatory auditing and assurance frameworks appears particularly relevant in this context. Traditional ex ante conformity assessments must increasingly be supplemented by continuous oversight mechanisms. Digital twins and simulation-based governance could serve as important tools for future regulation.

Furthermore, we emphasize the importance of international coordination. Agent-based systems often operate within transnational digital infrastructures, which can create significant risks when fragmented governance regimes are in place. The development of common governance standards and interoperable oversight architectures is therefore becoming increasingly relevant.

Finally, the findings also have societal implications. The governance of agent-based systems raises fundamental questions regarding democratic oversight, institutional legitimacy, and the distribution of power in society. Governance must therefore reconcile technological innovation with normative and societal responsibility.

Future Research Agenda

The increasing prevalence of agentic AI systems opens up a broad field of research that extends far beyond current AI governance debates. We identify several key research directions for future work.

A first priority concerns the further development of system-centered governance models. Future research should more closely examine how interdependencies, emergent dynamics, and hybrid decision-making architectures within complex AI ecosystems can be modeled and managed. This requires, in particular, interdisciplinary approaches that integrate technical, organizational, and institutional perspectives.

Second, there is a significant need for research regarding agent-based oversight architectures. To date, there is only limited empirical evidence on how supervisory agents, continuous monitoring, and hybrid governance systems can be implemented in practice. Future research should therefore systematically analyze operational governance models, including their risks and limitations.

Third, simulation-based governance approaches are gaining increasing importance. Agent-based modeling and digital twins could become central tools of future governance architectures. At the same time, there are significant open questions regarding model validation, epistemic limits, and the institutional embedding of simulation-based governance.

Fourth, future work should give greater consideration to the political and societal implications of agent-based governance. Questions of democratic legitimacy, concentration of power, digital sovereignty, and societal control are becoming increasingly relevant in the context of autonomous and networked AI systems.

Furthermore, a stronger connection between AI governance and other governance domains appears promising, such as:

- financial market stability,
- cybersecurity,
- critical infrastructure,
- environmental governance,
- or geopolitical technology policy.

Agent-based systems are increasingly evolving into a cross-cutting technology whose governance cannot be viewed in isolation.

After all, there are many indications that governance itself is becoming increasingly algorithmically mediated and data-driven. In the long term, this opens up the possibility of highly adaptive governance architectures, but at the same time raises fundamental normative questions. Future research will therefore need to develop not only technical or regulatory solutions, but also new concepts of institutional control and social accountability in the age of agentic systems.

REFERENCES

Andrae, S. (2026a). Governance of AI agents: Challenges, models and regulatory approaches. In Yadav, S. P., & Song, H. H. (Eds.), *Advancements in Multi-Agent Large Language Model Systems for Next-Generation AI* (pp. 149–188). IGI Global Publishing., DOI: 10.4018/979-8-3373-1419-8.ch006

Andrae, S. (2026b). A network model for AI governance. In Cea, S., & Aznar, T. (Eds.), *AI Influence on Governance and Law in the Digital Age* (pp. 1–44). IGI Global Publishing., DOI: 10.4018/979-8-3373-4480-5.ch001

Andrae, S. (2026c). Explainable artificial intelligence. In Khosrow-Pour, M. (Ed.), *Encyclopedia of Modern Artificial Intelligence* (pp. 1–21). IGI Global Publishing., DOI: 10.4018/403120

Ashby, W. R. (1956). *An Introduction to Cybernetics*. Chapman & Hall. DOI: 10.5962/bhl.title.5851

Barocas, S., & Selbst, A. D. (2016). Big data's disparate impact. *California Law Review*, *104*(3), 671–732. https://www.cs.yale.edu/homes/jf/BarocasSelbst.pdf

Bostrom, N., & Yudkowsky, E. (2014). The ethics of artificial intelligence. In Frankish, K. & Ramsey, W. M. (eds.). *The Cambridge Handbook of Artificial Intelligence*. Cambridge University Press, 316–334. https://doi.org/DOI: 10.1017/CBO9781139046855.020

Dignum, V., & Dignum, F. (2026). Agentifying agentic AI. *arXiv*. https://doi.org//arXiv.2511.17332DOI: 10.48550

Doshi-Velez, F., & Kim, B. (2017). Towards a rigorous science of interpretable machine learning. *arXiv*. https://doi.org//arXiv.1702.08608DOI: 10.48550

Engin, Z., & Hand, D. (2025). Toward adaptive categories: Dimensional governance for agentic AI. *arXiv*. https://doi.org//arXiv.2505.11579DOI: 10.48550

Epstein, J. M. (2006). *Generative Social Science: Studies in Agent-Based Computational Modeling*. Princeton University Press.

Floridi, L., & Cowls, J. (2019). A unified framework of five principles for AI in society. *Harvard Data Science Review*, *1*(1). Advance online publication. DOI: 10.1162/99608f92.8cd550d1

Folke, C., Hahn, T., Olsson, P., & Norberg, J. (2005). Adaptive governance of social-ecological systems. *Annual Review of Environment and Resources*, *30*(1), 441–473. DOI: 10.1146/annurev.energy.30.050504.144511

Fuller, A., Fan, Z., Day, C., & Barlow, C. (2020). Digital twin: Enabling technologies, challenges and open research. *IEEE Access : Practical Innovations, Open Solutions*, *8*, 108952–108971. DOI: 10.1109/ACCESS.2020.2998358

Gong, H. (2026). AI agents in financial markets: Architecture, applications, and systemic implications. *FinTech*, *5*(2), 34. DOI: 10.3390/fintech5020034

Guston, D. H. (2014). Understanding "anticipatory governance". *Social Studies of Science*, *44*(2), 218–242. DOI: 10.1177/0306312713508669 PMID: 24941612

Hacker, P., & Holweg, M. (2026). A pragmatic approach to regulating AI agents. *arXiv*. https://doi.org//arXiv.2604.22819DOI: 10.2139/ssrn.6509259

Latour, B. (2005). *Reassembling the Social: An Introduction to Actor-Network-Theory*. Oxford University Press. DOI: 10.1093/oso/9780199256044.001.0001

Logan, T., Rachunok, B., Hardaway, K., Bristow, D., Reilly, A., Johnson, D., Johansson, J., Cremen, G., Boakye, J., & Schweizer, P. (2026). Advancing systemic risk assessment for complex, interdependent systems: A research agenda. *Risk Analysis*, *46*(5), e70243. DOI: 10.1111/risa.70243 PMID: 41978933

Matthias, A. (2004). The responsibility gap: Ascribing responsibility for the actions of learning automata. *Ethics and Information Technology*, *6*(3), 175–183. DOI: 10.1007/s10676-004-3422-1

Nannini, L., Smith, A. L., Maggini, M. J., Panai, E., Feliciano, S., Tiulkanov, A., ... (2026). AI agents under EU law. *arXiv*. https://doi.org//arXiv.2604.04604DOI: 10.48550

Ostrom, E. (2010). Polycentric systems for coping with collective action and global environmental change. *Global Environmental Change*, *20*(4), 550–557. DOI: 10.1016/j.gloenvcha.2010.07.004

Park, J. S., O'Brien, J., Cai, C. J., Morris, M. R., Liang, P., & Bernstein, M. S. (2023). Generative agents: Interactive simulacra of human behavior. In Proceedings of the 36th Annual ACM Symposium on User Interface Software and Technology (UIST '23). Association for Computing Machinery, 1–22. https://doi.org/DOI: 10.1145/3586183.3606763

Pobuda, P., & Andrae, S. (2026). Policy advice by digital economic twins: Using agent-based modelling and artificial intelligence. Working Paper. http://dx.doi.org/ DOI: 10.2139/ssrn.6336459

Rhodes, R. A. W. (1997). *Understanding Governance: Policy Networks, Governance, Reflexivity and Accountability*. Open University Press.

Ribeiro, M. T., Singh, S., & Guestrin, C. (2016). "Why should I trust you?": Explaining the predictions of any classifier. In Proceedings of the 22nd ACM SIGKDD International Conference on Knowledge Discovery and Data Mining. Association for Computing Machinery, 1135–1144.

Russell, S., & Norvig, P. (2021). *Artificial Intelligence: A Modern Approach* (4th ed.). Pearson.

Santoni de Sio, F., & van den Hoven, J. (2018). Meaningful human control over autonomous systems: A philosophical account. *Frontiers in Robotics and AI*, *5*, 15. DOI: 10.3389/frobt.2018.00015 PMID: 33500902

Srnicek, N. (2017). *Platform Capitalism*. Polity Press.

Trist, E. L., & Bamforth, K. W. (1951). Some social and psychological consequences of the longwall method of coal-getting: An examination of the psychological situation and defences of a work group in relation to the social structure and technological content of the work system. *Human Relations*, *4*(1), 3–38. DOI: 10.1177/001872675100400101

Vial, G. (2019). Understanding digital transformation: A review and a research agenda. *The Journal of Strategic Information Systems*, *28*(2), 118–144. DOI: 10.1016/j.jsis.2019.01.003

Wooldridge, M. (2009). *An Introduction to Multiagent Systems* (2nd ed.). Wiley.

Wooldridge, M., & Jennings, N. R. (1995). Intelligent agents: Theory and practice. *The Knowledge Engineering Review*, *10*(2), 115–152. DOI: 10.1017/S0269888900008122

Chapter 3
Governing AI Agents in Enterprise Digital Transformation:
Strategy, Accountability, and Organizational Design

Abdelraouf Ishtaiwi
http://orcid.org/0000-0001-8013-7151
Data Science and Artificial Intelligence, University of Petra, Amman, Jordan

Ahmad Al-Qerem
http://orcid.org/0000-0003-2187-6194
Zarqa University, Jordan

Amjad Aldweesh
http://orcid.org/0000-0001-9358-1323
Shaqra University, Saudi Arabia

ABSTRACT

This chapter will review the way AI agents are getting integrated into enterprise digital transformation initiatives, whereby they build on automation beyond task execution to goal-oriented coordination and exacerbate governance, accountability, and organization design issues. It is suggested that a strategy-appropriate governance framework exists whereby agent deployment is mediated by clear business charters, layered accountability, lifecycle controls and a federated operating model between enterprise standards and domain-level autonomy. An integrative review of the existing research on the digital transformation, IT governance, AI in organizations, and AI accountability is combined with the up-to-date regulatory and standards

DOI: 10.4018/979-8-3373-9594-4.ch003

documents, such as the EU AI Act, NIST AI RMF, and ISO/IEC 42001. The chapter formulates design propositions, comparative tables, and an adoption roadmap that will assist CIOs, transformation leaders, and scholars in organizing enterprise AI agent portfolios, which are strategically consistent, auditable, and human-managed.

I. INTRODUCTION

The digital transformation is no longer about digitization of isolated tasks, it is becoming a process of enterprise-wide redesign, where processes, structures, capabilities, and value creation logics are reconfigured using digital technologies (Vial, 2019; Verhoeff et al., 2021; Plekhanov et al., 2023; Hinings et al., 2018). In this wider change, AI agents are already being placed as a new form of coordination since they have the potential to interpret goals, access knowledge, invoke tools, and sequence actions across organizational boundaries instead of just running pre-scripted actions (Wooldridge and Jennings, 1995; Wang et al., 2024; Xi et al., 2025; Voudouris, 2025). As a result, the managerial issue of whether or not organizations will automate selected tasks is no longer relevant, but how the autonomy that is strategically consequential can be integrated into the operating core without disintegrating authority, inflating risk, or blurring accountability. This general issue defines the context of the chapter.

The interpretation of AI agents as a new layer of enterprise automation portfolios should be seen as well as an independent category of applications. Since agents can be built off foundation models, retrieval components, workflow engines, knowledge repositories, and enterprise APIs, business units, platform teams, and software vendors tend to drive their diffusion at once, increasing experimentation speed and blurring ownership lines (Verhoeff et al., 2021; Benbya et al., 2021; Wang et al., 2024; Voudouris, 2025). Consequently, any time pilot agents are implemented sooner than the clarification of governance responsibilities, organizations experience governance debt. This debt is later manifested in duplicated controls, inconsistent logic of escalation, un-documented access paths and non-comparable value claims across domains. The chapter thus makes governance debt a key transformation issue.

The expectations of governance have also increased as the deployment of AI is currently taking place in a more explicit standards and regulatory framework. The NIST AI Risk Management Framework codifies lifecycle-based risk treatment, the European Commission High-Level Expert Group on Artificial Intelligence anticipates trustworthy AI practices to the fore, ISO/IEC 42001 positions AI management as a system-level organisational task, and the EU AI Act transforms a number of governance expectations into legally binding use-specific requirements (National Institute of Standards and Technology, 2023; European Commission High-Level

Expert Group on Artificial Intelligence, 2019; ISO/IEC 42001, Thus, the issue of enterprise adoption cannot be seen as a technical implementation issue; it is preconditioned with documentation, supervision, logging, review, and role clarification issues that go to the very bottom of managerial design. Simultaneously, these external concerns fail to describe the manner in which internal organizational structures are to be designed around AI agents. That is a substantive internal design problem.

It is increased by organizational consequences since AI agents can be implemented via multiple channels of transformation simultaneously. They may be in either the form of customer-service modernization, internal efficiency programs, compliance automation, knowledge-management initiatives, or vendor-provided software suites, which implies that enterprise leaders tend to face heterogeneous use cases prior to a shared language of governance being reached (Matt et al., 2016; Verhoef et al., 2021; Voudouris, 2025). Under these circumstances, we can easily see that local successes can hide vulnerability within the enterprise since a control assumption, data right, and escalation norms differ across domains. Thus, the governance issue is not simply to limit risk, but also to make various deployments similar at portfolio level. Executive steering requires comparability. The portfolio problem is not a technical problem, but managerial. This difference is significant.

The particular issue discussed in this chapter is the difference between the speed of adoption of AI agents and the lagging redesign of governance and workflow architecture. The AI agents confuse the distinction between software tool, decision support mechanism, workflow participant, and quasi-organizational actor, as they may trigger actions, influence recommendations, and communicate with various systems and users through time (Berente et al., 2021; Benbya et al., 2021; Raisch and Krakowski, 2021; Kellogg et al., 2020). But with the introduction of such capabilities without updated decision rights, intervention routines, and assurance routines, responsibility is diffused, intervention remains inconsistent, and strategic intent is replaced by local automation logic (Diakopoulos, 2016; Lebovitz et al., 2022; Raji et al., 2020). This chapter attempts to solve that dilemma by establishing an enterprise AI agent implementation strategy that is aligned with strategy.

A. Related Work

The literature in this subsection is structured into three streams, i.e. digital transformation strategy and IT governance, AI in organizations and human-AI collaboration, and AI accountability with standards-based assurance. Such a classification is needed since the chapter problem cannot be addressed by a single disciplinary question but has a strategic alignment, socio-technical design, and control architecture. According to Table 1, each stream has a vital analytical element; yet, none of them has an integrated organizational design of enterprise AI agent portfolios.

The review thus goes on to determine the contributions of each of the streams and the integrative gap.

The former stream uses transformation as a problem of strategic and organizational alignment. Henderson and Venkatraman alignment model provides the rationale by which the business and the IT spheres are maintained consistent with each other; the model, however, assumes the existence of human-based decision rights and lacks semi-autonomous software actors (Henderson and Venkatraman, 1993). The digital business strategy approach by Bharadwaj and others extends strategy to include digital resources, services, and ecosystem positioning, but does not define how the autonomous action should be operated (Bharadwaj et al., 2013). The managerial choice in case of digital disruption is explained by the strategy-formulation advice of Matt and colleagues; the view of renewal over time is elaborated by the dynamic capability perspective of Warner and Wager, however, both perspectives are more robust on the strategic direction than on the design of the runtime governance (Matt et al., 2016; Warner and Wager, 2019). Overall, strategy-focused approaches address the question of the importance of transformation and the ways priorities will be established, yet they do not exhaust the ways of regulating AI agents once they become part of the working process.

The second stream focuses on the impact of AI on work, judgment and coordination within organizations. The managerialization of Berente and colleagues explains the unique organizational implication of AI, and Benbya and colleagues highlight the information systems research agenda in regard to AI-enabled organizing (Berente et al., 2021; Benbya et al., 2021). The conceptualisations of the automation-augmentation paradox (Raisch and Krakowski, 2021), logic of human-AI symbiosis (Jarrahi, 2018), hybrid intelligence (Dellermann et al., 2019b; Dellermann et al., 2019a), and readiness factors that precondition enterprise adoption (Johnk et al., 2021) are formulated. Along with Amershi and others, Lebovitz and colleagues also show that the professional engagement and interface design have a material impact on the reliability of AI support usage in practice (Lebovitz et al., 2022; Amershi et al., 2019). In short, the organization-based AI studies describe collaboration, readiness, and the lack of transparency, yet it is weak in the distribution of roles within an enterprise, portfolio management, and routines of assurances.

Stream three deals with accountability, auditing and formal governance expectations. Diakopoulos poses algorithmic accountability as an explanation and responsibility question, Raji and others formalize internal algorithmic auditing, and Mokander and Floridi create ethics-based auditing as a trust-building tool (Diakopoulos, 2016; Raji et al., 2020; Mokander and Floridi, 2021). Meanwhile, these concepts are converted into working requirements by NIST, ISO/IEC 42001, the European Commission guidance, and the EU AI Act (National Institute of Standards and Technology, 2023; International Organization for Standardization,

2023; European Commission High-Level Expert Group on Artificial Intelligence, 2019; European Union, 2024). Nevertheless, these control-centered views are more forthcoming about the artifacts that are needed rather than how business ownership, platform ownership and domain autonomy are to be combined into a practical operating model. To recap it all, accountability-based solutions elucidate the control needs, but they fail to address the organizational design issue whereby strategic coherence and local performance should be collaboratively attained.

Comparative synthesis between the three streams shows the gap that has not been solved yet and leads to the present chapter. Khatri and Brown governance design approach attains data accountability of decisions; but focuses on data resources as opposed to agent behaviour (Khatri and Brown, 2010). The contingency perspective of Sambamurthy and Zmud, along with the matrix logic of Weill and Ross, are sufficient to provide a sound perspective of the distribution of decision rights; nonetheless, neither of the two accounts specifies the layered responsibility when the software agents are capable of reasoning and acting across processes (Sambamurthy and Zmud, 1999; Weill and Ross, 2004; Weill and Ross, 2005). Process integration and discipline of execution is reached by the enterprise architecture perspective of Ross and others but it is not concerned with adaptive model behaviour or runtime supervision (Ross et al., 2006). It is possible to note that the literature under review is not very extensive in its approach to strategy-to-agent fit, multi-level responsibility, and the design of a federated organisation, which inspires the integrative framework that is created in this chapter.

Human-centered design scholarship contributes another piece of information that narrows this chasm. According to Shneiderman, credible AI is conditional on human-oriented governance and controllability, but this view does not define how enterprise portfolios must distribute the rights to make decisions or how domain ownership can be organized at scale (Shneiderman, 2022). Similarly, existing standards define what evidence and controls ought to be present, but they do not apply to how executive steering, platform reuse, and domain adaptation ought to be collectively organized within large organizations (National Institute of Standards and Technology, 2023; International Organization for Standardization, 2023). Consequently, the elements of a governance solution are already present in the literature, but they are still scattered across various discussions. The current chapter incorporates them as one organizational design argument.

Table 1. Comparison of major literature streams relevant to enterprise AI agent governance.

Literature stream	Representative sources	Primary analytical unit	Governance contribution	Recurring limitation
Digital transformation strategy and IT governance	Henderson and Venkatraman; Bharadwaj et al.; Matt et al.; Weill and Ross; Ross et al.	Enterprise strategy, digital capabilities, and decision rights	Clarifies strategic alignment, architecture, and governance allocation	Autonomous software actors are not modeled explicitly; runtime oversight remains underdeveloped.
AI in organizations and human-AI collaboration	Berente et al.; Benbya et al.; Raisch and Krakowski; Jarrahi; Dellermann et al.; Lebovitz et al.	Task design, human judgment, and organizational routines	Explains augmentation, opacity, readiness, and collaboration design	Portfolio governance, escalation pathways, and enterprise-wide ownership structures remain insufficiently specified.
AI accountability, auditing, and standards	Diakopoulos; Raji et al.; M{"o}kander and Floridi; NIST AI RMF; EU AI Act; ISO/IEC 42001	Risk controls, documentation, and assurance artifacts	Defines auditability, traceability, and compliance expectations	Strategic fit, organizational design, and operating-model integration receive less attention than control instrumentation.

B. Chapter Contributions

- **Conceptual clarification:** This chapter distinguishes enterprise AI agents from analytics dashboards, robotic process automation, predictive models, and copilots by focusing on goal orientation, iterative reasoning, tool invocation, and cross-system action scope. This distinction is analytically necessary because governance requirements intensify when software can conditionally sequence actions rather than merely return information or execute fixed scripts. Consequently, the chapter establishes a clearer conceptual basis for deciding when conventional digital governance mechanisms remain sufficient and when agent-specific controls become necessary. The clarification is operationalized through Table 2.
- **Strategy-aligned governance model:** A governance framework is proposed in which every enterprise agent is mediated by a bounded charter that links strategic intent, process scope, authority limits, data entitlements, escalation triggers, and review cadence. The framework integrates lifecycle controls from current standards guidance with business ownership and workflow design, thereby preventing control mechanisms from being detached from enterprise objectives. Furthermore, the chapter demonstrates how runtime monitoring, documentation, and human oversight can be organized as part of

a unified control plane rather than as fragmented compliance artifacts. The overall architecture is summarized in Figure 1 and Figure 2.

- **Organizational operating design:** A federated operating model is developed to allocate responsibility across executive sponsors, process owners, AI product owners, platform teams, risk functions, auditors, and human operators. This model is designed to reconcile two competing requirements, namely: enterprise-wide standardization for safety and reuse, and domain-level flexibility for workflow adaptation and contextual expertise. In addition, formal propositions are introduced to explain why bounded charters, layered accountability, and federated governance jointly support scalable autonomy. The role architecture is specified in Figure 3 and Table 5.
- **Adoption roadmap and evaluation logic:** A phased roadmap is provided through which organizations can diagnose readiness, design controls, pilot agents under supervision, and scale portfolios without detaching experimentation from governance. The roadmap translates abstract governance principles into implementation sequences, decision gates, and measurement families that can be employed by CIOs and transformation leaders. Furthermore, the chapter links value metrics, control metrics, and adoption metrics so that performance is not reduced to narrow productivity claims. The progression logic is synthesized in Figure 4 and is connected throughout the chapter to the comparative evidence in Table 3 and Table 4.

The rest of this chapter is organized as follows. Section II defines enterprise AI agents, explains the evidentiary base, and clarifies the mechanisms through which agents affect organizational transformation. In Section III, strategic opportunity areas are analyzed, while Section IV develops the governance and accountability logic required for controlled deployment. Section V then presents the federated operating model and formal design propositions, Section VI specifies the adoption roadmap, and Section VII concludes this chapter.

II. AI AGENTS IN ORGANIZATIONAL TRANSFORMATION

In this section, the conceptual foundations of enterprise AI agents are established, the evidentiary base of the chapter is described, and the transformation mechanisms through which agents alter organizational design are formalized. Because the chapter is conceptual rather than experimental, rigor is achieved through a purposive integrative review that combines strategy research, governance research, AI-in-organizations scholarship, and standards-based guidance. The objective is not to aggregate effect sizes; instead, it is to construct an organizationally coherent explanatory framework grounded in multiple literatures and traceable governance sources. This section therefore defines the analytical object before subsequent sections examine opportunity, control, and operating-model design.

A. Evidence Base and Analytical Lens.

The evidentiary base includes thirty-seven sources that were chosen to meet four inclusion criteria, that is, direct relevance to digital transformation strategy, direct relevance to organizational governance and decision rights, direct relevance to AI in organizational work, and direct relevance to accountability, standards or auditing. Primary sources published between 1993 and 2014 are retained due to the definition of long-standing notions of strategic alignment, governance allocation and organizational design, and recent sources published between 2018 and 2025 are retained as they discuss the modern AI capabilities, prevailing management discussions and contemporary governance expectations (Henderson and Venkatraman, 1993; Galbraith, 2014; Berente et al., 2021; Wang et al., 2024; Xi et al., 2 This choice rationale permits continuity between established organization theory and the particular requirements brought about by the AI agents. Through this means, conceptual novelty becomes pegged on traceable past work as opposed to impressionistic commentary.

The analysis process identifies each source on five dimensions, in which strategic alignment refers to the connection with enterprise priorities, autonomy refers to the extent of independent action, accountability refers to the process of assigning responsibility, oversight refers to the type of human supervision, and lifecycle control refers to the existence of monitoring and review systems. The synthesis of the result is summed up in Table 1 and Table 2 that in combination differentiate major literature streams and major forms of enterprise automation. Since the dimensions of coding are common to theory, managerial research, and standards documents, there is only one frame of comparison that can be used without either downgrading governance to either strategy language only or compliance language only. The framework that forms out of this coding process thus is integrative in nature.

B. Enterprise AI Agents Definite.

This chapter defines an enterprise AI agent as a software agent that understands organizational objectives, hears signals in a context, triggers the use of digital tools or knowledge resources, and suggests or implements actions conditionally based on limited authority. This definition uses the traditional conception of agents as a situated, autonomous behavior to the enterprise, where access control, workflow requirements, audit requirements, and escalation paths place a significant material constraint on what autonomy can mean in practice (Wooldridge and Jennings, 1995; Wang et al., 2024; Xi et al., 2025). Enterprise agents are therefore not to be compared with any software element which may include AI but should be rather characterized by their ability to achieve a goal via the use of iterative reasoning and action within one or more systems. Table 2 explains why this difference is significant in terms of governance.

The difference between the surrounding varieties of automation is of special significance since the burden of governance is unevenly distributed over digital artifacts. A dashboard is informational and non-interactive, robotic process automation is interactive but usually lacks interpretative open-ended objectives, a predictive model rates a constrained decision point, and a copilot is interactionally dependent on user input (Bharadwaj et al., 2013; Dellermann et al., 2019b; Amershi et al., 2019). In comparison, an AI agent is able to integrate retrieval, reasoning, planning and tool invocation in such a manner that crosses functionally distinct functional boundaries in the past, and therefore its performance is more organizationally tangled, as well as its failure modes. Thus, the choice of deployment should not be driven by vendor branding or interface style but governance class.

The business personification of an AI agent must be interpreted too as an authorized position as opposed to a floating technical potential. The agent charter as suggested in this chapter outlines the business purpose, scope of the process, data rights, authorized tools, anticipated decision latency, escalation criteria, logs required, and retirement criteria that apply to the agent throughout its lifecycle. In the absence of the charter the deployment of AI is conceptualized too narrowly as model configuration; in the presence of the charter the agent is intelligible as a responsible part of the organization. The alignment architecture in Figure 1 is based on this chartering logic.

The classification of the portfolio is needed since enterprise agents are not homogeneous. Other agents are advisory, others coordinate multi-step activities, others check control conditions, and others are transactional; the governing class of the decision consequence, reversibility of actions, and system connection should, therefore, be identified based on the effects of decisions, not just on the model family or user interface (National Institute of Standards and Technology, 2023; Weill and Ross, 2005; European Union, 2024). Without classification, the high-impact uses are sometimes under-governed and the low-risk uses are over-governed, a mis-allocation of control effort and innovation capacity. The charter must then be provided with a risk tier and an action class in order to make the design of oversight, depth of testing, and frequency of review systematic. This portfolio perspective transforms experimentation to controlled deployment.

Table 2. Comparison of enterprise automation forms and their governance implications.

Automation form	Primary objective	Degree of autonomy	Action scope	Learning behavior	Dominant governance emphasis
Business analytics	Describe and interpret business conditions	Low	Informational	Analyst-directed	Data quality, report lineage, and interpretive accountability
Robotic process automation	Execute deterministic routines	Low to moderate	Rule-bound transaction handling	Minimal	Exception handling, access rights, and change control
Predictive AI model	Estimate probabilities or classifications	Moderate	Recommendation or scoring within a bounded task	Model retraining	Validation, bias assessment, and performance drift monitoring
Copilot or assistant	Support human drafting, search, and decision preparation	Moderate	Interactive and user-triggered	Session-level adaptation	Prompt controls, disclosure, and human review
Enterprise AI agent	Pursue a goal through iterative reasoning and tool invocation	Moderate to high	Cross-system orchestration and conditional action	Contextual adaptation and tool selection	Chartering, escalation, runtime monitoring, audit logs, and layered accountability

Figure 1. Strategy-to-agent alignment stack for enterprise deployment.

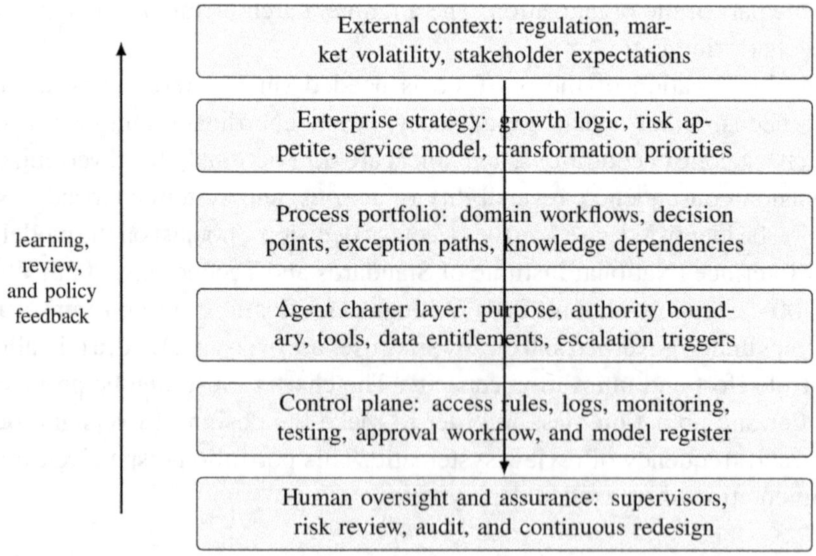

C. Transformation Mechanisms and Boundary Conditions

The influence of AI agents in organizational transformation is based on four mechanisms, which are: sensing, synthesis, orchestration and adaptive coordination. When massive amounts of internal and external signals are tracked, sensing is enhanced; when fragmented documentation, policies, and transaction records are stitched together in usable context, synthesis is enhanced; when agents interact between systems and queues, orchestration is enhanced; when workflows are adjusted on the basis of thresholds, exceptions, or updated context, adaptive coordination is enhanced (Warner and Wager, 2019; Jarrahi, 2018; Hokmabadi et al., 2025; Voudouris, 202 These mechanisms render AI agents strategically pertinent in that they change the flow of information, how information is organized, and how it is implemented throughout the enterprise. Meanwhile, the mechanisms can be useful only in cases when they are integrated into approved and audit-able processes.

The conditions of enabling are also crucial since not all processes can be positively influenced by agentic coordination. High process modularity, explicit exception logic, fixed data entitlement and observable outcome criteria make it easier to deploy agents, and vague authority, tacit work and weak source governance make brittle or unaccountable automation more likely (Johnk et al., 2021; Ross et al., 2006; Khatri and Brown, 2010). The issue of preparedness therefore ought not to be posed as the generic eagerness to innovate but rather a systematic evaluation of the design of processes, data management, observability of monitoring, and capability of interventions. These are the boundary conditions which are related to the control architecture that will be described later in Table 4 and the phased logic as shown in Figure 4.

Risk amplification is a result of AI agents accelerating the pace of decision-making, its magnitude, and the degree of cross-functional interactions. In case an error is present in a dashboard, the error is frequently disclosed throughout human interpretation; nonetheless, in case an error is present in an acting agent, the identical error may propagate through service interactions, task queues, or transactional systems before a correctional review occurs (Raisch and Krakowski, 2021; Kellogg et al., 2020; Lebovitz et al., 2022). Moreover, in cases where multiple agents are dependent on common prompts, models, tools or repositories of knowledge, a single weakness in configuration can be scaled to a portfolio. As such the organizational change effected by the AI agents must be seen as a design issue of regulated autonomy but not a technology purchase issue on its own.

D. Portfolio Segmentation and Control Calibration

Portfolio segmentation is required because not all agents warrant the same control intensity. A monitoring agent that surfaces anomalies for analyst review, a coordination agent that routes cases across systems, and an acting agent that updates customer-facing records impose different levels of organizational consequence, which means that testing depth, approval gates, and review frequency should vary accordingly (National Institute of Standards and Technology, 2023; European Union, 2024). If a uniform control design is imposed across all agent classes, then either innovation is unnecessarily slowed or material risks remain insufficiently supervised. Therefore, organizations should segment portfolios by impact, reversibility, and coupling. Segmentation makes governance proportionate.

Control calibration follows from this segmentation logic. Lower-impact advisory agents can be governed primarily through source quality controls, disclosure, periodic sampling, and supervisor feedback, whereas higher-impact acting agents require stricter release management, intervention thresholds, incident review, and evidence retention (Shneiderman, 2022; Raji et al., 2020; International Organization for Standardization, 2023). This calibration principle preserves managerial attention for the use cases where autonomy has the greatest organizational consequence. It also improves legitimacy because governance effort becomes visibly commensurate with risk. Portfolio discipline is thereby strengthened at the design stage.

This section has defined the enterprise AI agent as a chartered, bounded, and organizationally embedded form of adaptive automation. The analysis also demonstrates that transformation value and transformation risk arise from the same mechanisms, because the capacities that increase speed and coordination also increase coupling and consequence. Therefore, strategic opportunity cannot be evaluated separately from governance design. The next section develops the opportunity side of this equation.

III. STRATEGIC OPPORTUNITIES

In this section, the strategic opportunities created by enterprise AI agents are examined by linking value mechanisms to the governance conditions under which value is actually realized. The objective is not to celebrate automation in generic terms; instead, it is to identify the types of organizational leverage that agents can provide when they are aligned with business objectives, bounded by controls, and evaluated through explicit metrics. As summarized in Table 3, opportunity and governance are analytically inseparable because every value mechanism depends on a corresponding control condition. This section therefore evaluates strategic upside in a disciplined manner.

A. Augmented Sensing and Decision Preparation

Augmented sensing is the first major opportunity because AI agents can monitor heterogeneous information environments at a cadence that is not available to most human teams. Market signals, internal exceptions, policy updates, service anomalies, and contractual changes can be aggregated, normalized, and prioritized in a way that shortens the time between environmental change and managerial attention (Vial, 2019; Verhoef et al., 2021; Jarrahi, 2018). This capability becomes strategically meaningful when the agent does not merely retrieve data but assembles a decision-ready briefing, cites evidence, and routes the issue to an accountable owner. Consequently, the benefit lies less in raw information throughput than in reduction of interpretive latency. The relevant governance requirement is evidence traceability, without which sensing turns into unreviewable assertion.

Decision preparation is strengthened further when AI agents are connected to curated organizational knowledge. Hybrid intelligence research has demonstrated that human judgment is improved when machine synthesis is combined with domain expertise, while interface studies have demonstrated that explanation, provenance, and handoff design materially affect whether recommendations are trusted and appropriately acted upon (Dellermann et al., 2019a; Dellermann et al., 2019b; Amershi et al., 2019; Lebovitz et al., 2022). Therefore, the organizational value of augmented sensing should be evaluated through lead time reduction, override quality, and evidence citation performance rather than through response speed alone. As indicated in Table 3, these metrics capture whether AI support is actually improving managerial cognition. This opportunity is substantial.

B. Cross-Functional Orchestration and Service Coordination

Cross-functional orchestration constitutes a second opportunity because AI agents can coordinate actions across fragmented applications and decision queues. Enterprise architecture research has long established that execution consistency depends on standardized interfaces and defined process handoffs; AI agents extend this logic by enabling conditional action sequencing across those interfaces when exceptions, delays, or contextual triggers occur (Ross et al., 2006; Weill and Ross, 2005). For example, an agent can identify a service exception, retrieve the relevant policy, draft the required communication, update the queue, and escalate the case if decision thresholds are exceeded. The value therefore arises from compression of coordination cost across organizational boundaries rather than from isolated task substitution. This mechanism is central to service and operations redesign.

The same mechanism is visible in emerging practitioner-oriented and review-based work on agent-enabled business transformation. Voudouris characterizes AI agents as drivers of autonomic business processes, while Hokmabadi and colleagues demonstrate how AI-agent automation can support sensing, seizing, and reconfiguring in customer-facing workflows for smaller firms (Voudouris, 2025; Hokmabadi et al., 2025). However, these gains are contingent on bounded authority, because an orchestration agent that lacks explicit escalation conditions can convert local efficiency into enterprise inconsistency. Accordingly, Table 3 links coordination benefits to authorization design, exception handling, and escalation compliance metrics. Strategic leverage is obtained only when orchestration remains governable.

C. Knowledge Integration, Service Innovation, and Dynamic Capability Renewal

Knowledge integration is a third opportunity because agents can assemble dispersed organizational memory into context-specific action support. In digitally transforming firms, policy documents, procedural guides, prior cases, contractual obligations, and analytic outputs are often distributed across repositories and departments, which increases search cost and weakens execution quality (Benbya et al., 2021; Jarrahi, 2018). An AI agent that retrieves, filters, and contextualizes this material can reduce duplication, improve consistency, and preserve access to institutional knowledge during role changes or growth. Consequently, the opportunity concerns organizational memory as much as interface convenience. It is especially relevant in complex service, compliance, and onboarding environments.

Dynamic capability renewal is strengthened when these knowledge and coordination benefits are embedded into strategic learning cycles. Digital transformation scholarship emphasizes that sustained advantage emerges from repeated sensing, seizing, and reconfiguring rather than from one-time technology acquisition; AI agents can contribute to each of these stages by shortening feedback loops and by creating reusable coordination patterns (Warner and Wäger, 2019; Matt et al., 2016; Bharadwaj et al., 2013). However, enterprise learning requires comparative evidence across use cases, which means that value review should occur at the portfolio level rather than only within isolated pilots. Therefore, managers should assess reuse ratios, rework reduction, intervention quality, and cross-domain transferability when deciding whether an agent capability should be expanded. In this way, AI agents can become a transformation asset rather than a collection of disconnected experiments.

The synthesis in Table 3 demonstrates that strategic opportunities accumulate when enterprise agents are treated as organizational design instruments instead of as standalone productivity features. Augmented sensing improves managerial attention, orchestration reduces coordination cost, and knowledge integration improves execution consistency; however, each benefit depends on traceability, bounded authority, and reliable human intervention. Therefore, strategy and governance should be designed simultaneously. The next section develops the governance architecture required for that simultaneous design. This transition is fundamental.

Table 3. Strategic opportunity areas for AI agents and the governance conditions under which value is realized.

Opportunity area	Value mechanism	Illustrative enterprise application	Required governance precondition	Indicative evaluation metrics
Augmented sensing	Rapid synthesis of dispersed internal and external signals	Market monitoring, policy scanning, and incident triage	Trusted data sources and evidence traceability	Signal lead time, evidence citation rate, analyst override rate
Cross-functional orchestration	Coordination across systems and decision queues	Order exception handling, service recovery, and procurement follow-up	Documented authority boundaries and escalation thresholds	Cycle time, exception closure time, and escalation compliance
Knowledge integration	Retrieval and contextual assembly of organizational knowledge	Policy support, onboarding, and expert-assistant workflows	Curated knowledge bases and version control	Reuse ratio, answer provenance coverage, and rework reduction
Customer and employee service	Personalized but bounded interaction at scale	Service desk agents, employee self-service, and CRM follow-up	Disclosure rules, handoff criteria, and interaction logging	Resolution time, transfer accuracy, and satisfaction after handoff
Control support	Continuous checking against policy and procedural constraints	Compliance screening, access review support, and anomaly surfacing	Separation of duties and independent review	Control coverage, false-positive rate, and remediation latency

D. Customer and Employee Service Design

Service design constitutes a fourth opportunity because agents can provide persistent, context-aware support to customers and employees across multiple interaction points. In service environments, the economic value of agent deployment often emerges not only from handling volume but also from reducing transfer friction, preserving context across channels, and ensuring that routine guidance is delivered consistently within approved policy boundaries (Hokmabadi et al., 2025; Amershi et al., 2019; Shneiderman, 2022). When service agents are linked to reliable knowledge bases and clear handoff rules, they can improve both responsiveness and procedural consistency. Consequently, service quality can be raised while human specialists are reserved for exception-heavy or empathetic work. This opportunity is strategically meaningful in large enterprises with fragmented support interfaces.

However, service design also reveals the limits of indiscriminate automation. If handoff criteria are weak, disclosure is incomplete, or conversational outputs are not logged and reviewed, the same agent that improves speed can also degrade trust, bias case handling, or conceal process defects (Lebovitz et al., 2022; Kellogg et al., 2020; European Commission High-Level Expert Group on Artificial Intelligence, 2019). Therefore, organizations should evaluate service agents through post-handoff outcomes, repeat-contact rates, and supervisor review findings rather than through containment rate alone. This evaluative discipline ensures that service innovation remains aligned with accountability. It also reinforces the chapter's central claim that strategic opportunity is conditional on governance quality.

IV. GOVERNANCE AND ACCOUNTABILITY

In this section, governance and accountability are analyzed as the mechanisms through which AI agent autonomy is bounded, supervised, and rendered auditable. The section moves from lifecycle control domains to layered accountability, human oversight, and assurance routines because each dimension addresses a different failure mode of enterprise AI deployment. Governance is treated here not as a compliance overlay but as the operating logic that links strategy, execution, and responsibility. As illustrated in Figure 2 and specified in Table 4, the relevant controls are continuous rather than one-time.

A. Lifecycle Governance Domains

Lifecycle governance begins with chartering because every consequential agent should be linked to an approved business objective and a bounded process role before any technical configuration occurs. The charter determines purpose, scope, authorized actions, data entitlements, escalation paths, logging requirements, and review frequency, thereby transforming abstract strategic intent into a governable operating commitment (National Institute of Standards and Technology, 2023; International Organization for Standardization, 2023; Galbraith, 2014). Once this artifact exists, subsequent decisions about models, tools, and workflow integration can be evaluated against the approved mandate rather than against ad hoc enthusiasm. Accordingly, the first row of Table 4 is foundational to all subsequent control design. Without chartering, the control system lacks an organizing anchor.

Governance must then persist across data access, model and tool selection, workflow integration, runtime supervision, and retirement. Standards-based guidance is explicit that AI systems require monitoring, documentation, and periodic review, while accountability scholarship has emphasized that explanation and auditability depend on records that survive beyond the moment of action (European Commission High-Level Expert Group on Artificial Intelligence, 2019; European Union, 2024; Diakopoulos, 2016; Raji et al., 2020). Therefore, the control plane proposed in this chapter includes source whitelisting, access matrices, validation reports, model registers, intervention logs, and decommission criteria rather than a single technical checkpoint. This lifecycle orientation is represented in Figure 2 and operationalized in Table 4. Governance must be designed as a loop.

Table 4. Governance domains, principal risks, and required control artifacts across the AI agent lifecycle.

Lifecycle domain	Principal risk	Required control	Accountable role	Evidence artifact
Strategy and chartering	Local optimization displaces enterprise priorities	Approved business case and bounded agent charter	Executive sponsor and process owner	Charter record, objective hierarchy, success criteria
Data and access	Unauthorized retrieval, leakage, or entitlements drift	Role-based access, source whitelisting, and retention rules	Data owner and platform team	Access matrix, source register, audit log
Model and tool selection	Unsuitable model behavior or insecure tool invocation	Validation protocol, safety testing, and tool approval	AI product owner and risk function	Validation report, red-team log, model register
Workflow integration	Unclear handoffs and hidden failure states	Escalation design, fallback path, and exception handling	Process owner	Process map, service-level rule set, escalation matrix
Runtime supervision	Performance drift, brittle behavior, and unreviewed actions	Monitoring dashboard, alert thresholds, and intervention rights	Operations lead and human supervisor	Monitoring record, incident ticket, intervention log
Audit and retirement	Untraceable decisions and unmanaged legacy agents	Periodic review, audit trail retention, and retirement criteria	Risk function and internal audit	Review pack, change history, decommission report

Figure 2. Lifecycle governance loop for enterprise AI agents.

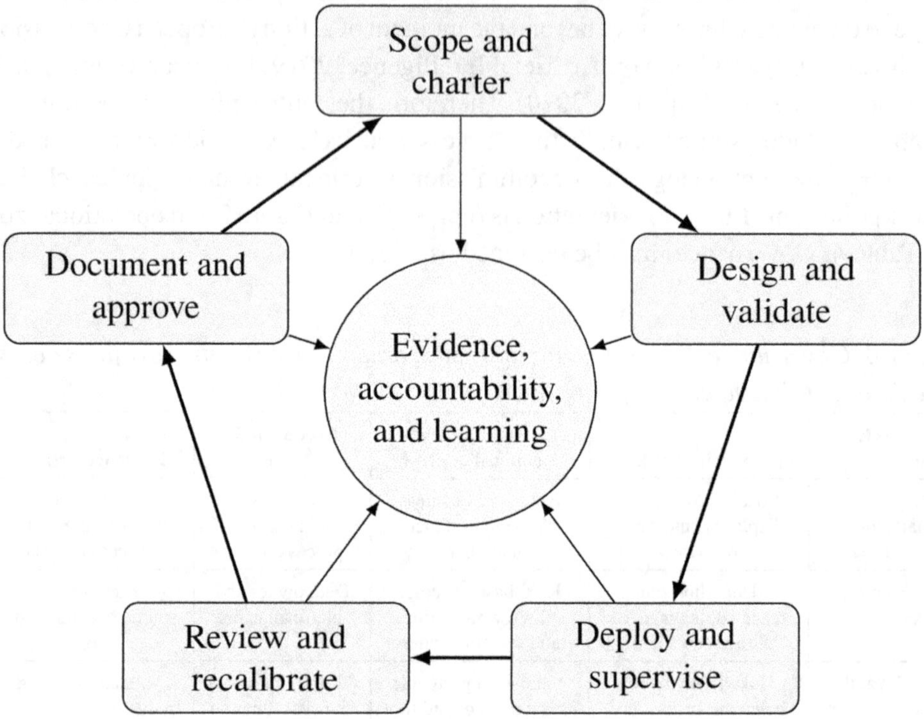

B. Layered Accountability Architecture

Accountability for enterprise AI agents should be layered because no single role can legitimately own strategic intent, process outcomes, technical behavior, and independent assurance at the same time. The executive sponsor is accountable for strategic justification and resource legitimacy, the process owner is accountable for business outcomes and escalation design, the AI product owner is accountable for agent behavior and release discipline, the platform team is responsible for technical controls and runtime services, and the risk and audit functions provide independent challenge and assurance (Weill and Ross, 2004; Weill and Ross, 2005; Khatri and Brown, 2010). This layered logic prevents the common failure in which responsibility is displaced onto the technology team even though the relevant business objective and operating context belong elsewhere. Consequently, scalable autonomy requires a deliberately constructed accountability stack rather than informal shared ownership. Table 5 converts this principle into an operating template.

Layered accountability also changes how incident response should be interpreted. A runtime failure is rarely only a technical defect; it can be a charter defect, a workflow defect, an escalation defect, a knowledge-source defect, or a monitoring defect, each of which implicates different accountable roles (Kellogg et al., 2020; Lebovitz et al., 2022; Berente et al., 2021). Therefore, post-incident review should assign causal analysis across governance layers rather than seeking a single technical root cause. When review artifacts are structured in this way, organizational learning improves because controls can be strengthened at the correct design layer. Accountability thus becomes a mechanism for redesign, not merely for blame allocation.

C. Human Oversight and Escalation Design

Human oversight should be risk-tiered and workflow-embedded rather than symbolic. Human-centered AI guidance demonstrates that oversight is effective when intervention rights, explanations, and handoff designs are matched to the task, while the EU AI Act and related governance guidance emphasize human agency and review capacity in consequential decision contexts (Amershi et al., 2019; Shneiderman, 2022; European Commission High-Level Expert Group on Artificial Intelligence, 2019; European Union, 2024). Accordingly, low-consequence tasks can be supervised through ex post review and threshold alerts, whereas higher-consequence tasks require approval gates, appeal paths, or mandatory human confirmation before action completion. This design principle avoids the inefficiency of universal manual review while preventing the emptiness of nominal oversight. Oversight must be actionable.

Escalation design is the practical expression of oversight because it specifies when agent autonomy ends and accountable human judgment begins. Escalation thresholds should be based on business impact, reversibility, confidence, novelty, policy sensitivity, and stakeholder harm potential, thereby ensuring that intervention is triggered by organizational consequence rather than by technical uncertainty alone (Lebovitz et al., 2022; Raisch and Krakowski, 2021; National Institute of Standards and Technology, 2023). In addition, escalation should route to named human roles with sufficient context and authority to resolve the case, because handoff without decision capacity merely displaces delay. The intervention log then becomes an important learning artifact because it reveals where charters, knowledge sources, or thresholds require redesign. Oversight is therefore both a safety mechanism and a source of managerial intelligence.

D. Auditability and Assurance

Auditability depends on evidence completeness, not on post hoc narrative alone. Internal algorithmic auditing research has demonstrated that control quality improves when documentation, testing, incident analysis, and organizational ownership are linked end to end, while ethics-based auditing emphasizes that trustworthy AI requires demonstrable process discipline rather than aspirational principles alone (Raji et al., 2020; Mökander and Floridi, 2021). Therefore, every enterprise agent should generate a minimum evidence set comprising its charter, model and tool register, source register, validation record, runtime logs, intervention history, change history, and periodic review pack. This requirement is consistent with the lifecycle logic of NIST and ISO/IEC 42001 (National Institute of Standards and Technology, 2023; International Organization for Standardization, 2023). Assurance is impossible without durable evidence.

Independent assurance is necessary because self-attestation by the delivery team is structurally insufficient. The separation of duties principle implies that those who define the charter, configure the agent, and monitor value should not be the only parties who evaluate the adequacy of controls, especially when incentives favor deployment velocity (Sambamurthy and Zmud, 1999; Weill and Ross, 2005). Consequently, risk functions should review control design, while internal audit should periodically examine evidence completeness, change discipline, and consistency between documented authority and observed behavior. The governance architecture presented in this section demonstrates that accountability can be rendered operational only when assurance routines are institutionalized. The next section translates this architecture into an organizational operating model.

E. Policy Compliance and Documentation Architecture

Policy compliance should be operationalized through internal control artifacts rather than through abstract awareness alone. External frameworks and regulations differ in scope, yet they converge around common managerial requirements involving governance assignment, documentation, risk treatment, human oversight, and ongoing monitoring (National Institute of Standards and Technology, 2023; International Organization for Standardization, 2023; European Union, 2024). Accordingly, organizations should maintain a documentation architecture that maps each enterprise agent to its risk tier, legal or policy constraints, data entitlements, review cadence, and accountable roles. This architecture allows external obligations to be translated into enterprise-specific evidence requirements. Compliance thus becomes designable rather than reactive.

Third-party dependencies intensify the importance of this documentation architecture. Many enterprise agents rely on external foundation models, APIs, retrieval services, or vendor-managed components, which means that governance cannot stop at internal workflow design. Supplier assurances, usage restrictions, model-update notifications, and contractual terms should therefore be integrated into model registers, change approvals, and periodic review packs so that downstream accountability is preserved even when capabilities are externally sourced (European Union, 2024; Raji et al., 2020; National Institute of Standards and Technology, 2023). If vendor dependencies are not documented in this way, organizations lose visibility over model changes and control assumptions. Documentation is therefore a control instrument, not a clerical by-product.

F. Incident Taxonomy and Corrective Learning

Incident management should classify failures by governance layer because AI agent problems rarely originate from one source alone. A flawed output may reflect source-quality failure, workflow integration failure, threshold-design failure, model or tool-selection failure, or supervision failure, each of which calls for a different corrective response (Berente et al., 2021; Kellogg et al., 2020; Raji et al., 2020). If incidents are classified only as technical malfunctions, organizations overlook the structural causes of recurring breakdowns. Therefore, incident taxonomies should mirror the accountability stack and the lifecycle controls listed in Table 4. Learning becomes sharper when failures are classified correctly.

Corrective learning should then be institutionalized through post-incident review packs that include not only what happened, but also why the charter, workflow, data entitlement, or monitoring design allowed the event to occur. This review format transforms incidents into governance feedback for both domain teams and enterprise platform owners, thereby strengthening future deployments rather than merely restoring service (Mökander and Floridi, 2021; International Organization for Standardization, 2023). In addition, repeated incident patterns can identify portfolio-level weaknesses that remain invisible within isolated teams. Governance maturity therefore depends on how systematically organizations learn from failure. Controlled autonomy requires controlled learning.

V. ORGANIZATIONAL OPERATING MODEL

In this section, the governance logic developed previously is translated into an organizational operating model through which enterprise AI agents can be scaled without dissolving strategic coherence or accountability. The analysis draws on organizational design theory, enterprise architecture, and IT governance research because AI agent portfolios require role differentiation, coordination routines, and platform choices in addition to control rules (Galbraith, 2014; Ross et al., 2006; Weill and Ross, 2004). The proposed design is federated, meaning that enterprise standards and shared services are centralized while process configuration and business ownership remain domain-anchored. This section specifies the design principles, role architecture, and analytical propositions that justify the model.

A. Design Principles for Enterprise Agent Governance

Six design principles structure the proposed operating model, namely: strategic fit, bounded autonomy, evidence by default, separation of duties, reusable platform services, and domain-level accountability. Strategic fit requires every agent to be linked to a named business objective and measurable outcome; bounded autonomy requires the charter to define what the agent can and cannot do; evidence by default requires that consequential actions remain traceable; separation of duties requires independent challenge; reusable platform services reduce duplicated controls; and domain-level accountability ensures that local process knowledge remains attached to agent behavior (Galbraith, 2014; Weill and Ross, 2005; Khatri and Brown, 2010). These principles are mutually reinforcing because each addresses a different failure mode of scale. Together, they provide the normative basis for the operating model in Figure 3.

The federated design follows directly from these principles. A purely centralized model would concentrate standards and expertise but would weaken process intimacy and slow adaptation, whereas a purely decentralized model would improve local responsiveness but fragment controls, duplicate infrastructure, and weaken auditability (Sambamurthy and Zmud, 1999; Weill and Ross, 2004). Therefore, the enterprise center should own the control library, model and tool standards, shared monitoring services, and portfolio governance routines, while business domains should own process outcomes, escalation logic, and contextual knowledge. This division of labor preserves both scale and relevance. It is the structural core of the chapter framework.

B. Federated Role Architecture and Decision Rights

The role architecture is depicted in Figure 3 and translated into decision rights through Table 5. The executive sponsor authorizes strategic investment and accepts portfolio-level risk; the process owner defines business outcomes and escalation thresholds; the AI product owner governs the design and release of the agent; the platform team administers shared infrastructure, access controls, and runtime services; the risk and compliance function challenges control adequacy; internal audit performs independent assurance; and human operators intervene during live exceptions. Each role is necessary because enterprise AI agents combine business judgment, technical behavior, and control sensitivity in a single operating object. Consequently, role design should be explicit rather than inferred. Ambiguity is itself a governance defect.

Decision rights must also be sequenced across the lifecycle. Charter approval belongs jointly to executive sponsorship and process ownership because business legitimacy and operational consequence must be aligned, whereas data entitlement decisions require process ownership, platform enablement, and risk review because legal, operational, and technical considerations intersect (Weill and Ross, 2005; Khatri and Brown, 2010; European Union, 2024). Model or tool changes should be approved through the AI product owner under formal release discipline, and periodic value-and-risk reviews should be chaired at portfolio level to prevent local optimization. The matrix in Table 5 is therefore not a generic responsibility table; it is the operating grammar through which autonomy remains governable. This grammar is practical.

Table 5. Illustrative RACI matrix for a federated enterprise AI agent operating model.

Decision or activity	Executive sponsor	Process owner	AI product owner	Platform team	Risk/ compliance	Internal audit	Human operator
Approve agent charter	A	R	C	I	C	I	I
Authorize data entitlements	I	A	C	R	C	I	I
Approve model or tool change	I	C	A	R	C	I	I
Define escalation thresholds	I	A	R	C	C	I	C
Handle live exceptions	I	C	C	I	I	I	R

continued on following page

Table 5. Continued

Decision or activity	Executive sponsor	Process owner	AI product owner	Platform team	Risk/ compliance	Internal audit	Human operator
Test controls and documentation	I	C	C	C	A	R	I
Conduct periodic value and risk review	A	R	C	C	C	C	I

Figure 3. Federated operating model for enterprise AI agent governance.

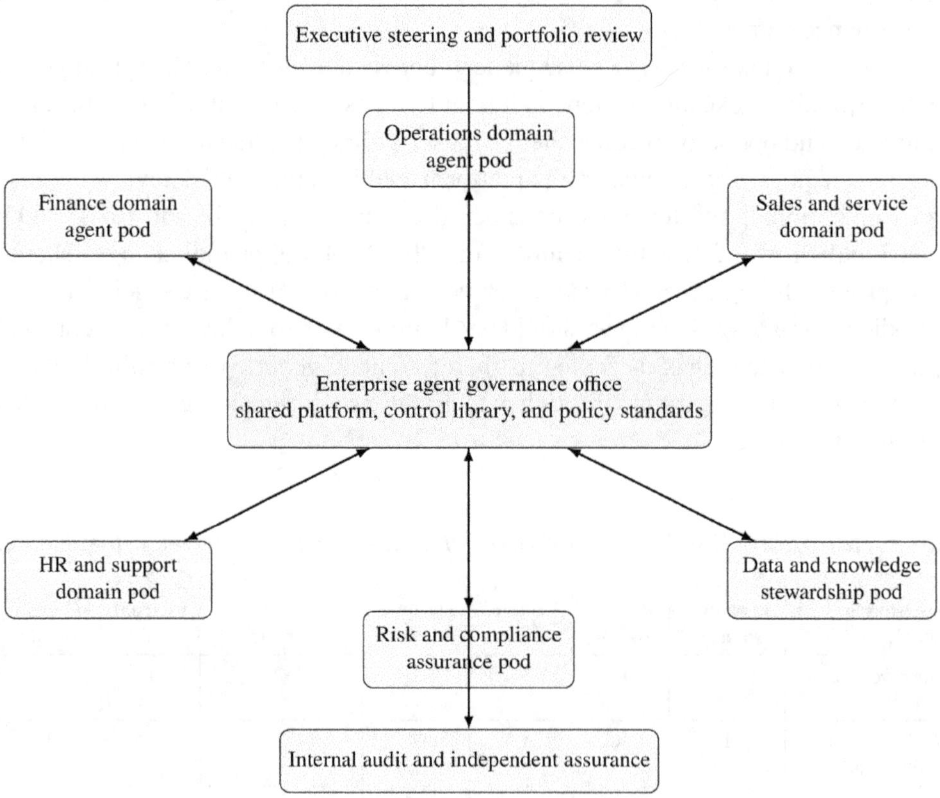

C. Platform Economics and Reuse Logic

Platform economics matter because agent portfolios can become unnecessarily expensive and inconsistent when each domain assembles its own prompts, monitoring services, connectors, and evaluation routines. A federated platform reduces this duplication by providing reusable connectors, approved toolkits, model registers, logging services, and control templates that lower marginal deployment cost while improving comparability across domains (Bharadwaj et al., 2013; Ross et al., 2006; Voudouris, 2025). The result is not merely technical efficiency; it is a governance advantage because reusable controls improve documentation quality and reduce control variance. Therefore, platform reuse should be treated as a strategic design objective rather than as a downstream infrastructure concern. This objective supports portfolio discipline.

Reuse logic also influences investment governance. When common services are financed and governed at enterprise level, business units can evaluate use cases on the basis of incremental value and risk rather than on the basis of full-stack replication costs, which improves portfolio selection and discourages isolated shadow deployments (Weill and Ross, 2004; Weill and Ross, 2005). At the same time, enterprise funding should not erase domain accountability, because process owners remain responsible for outcome definition, escalation logic, and contextual knowledge quality. A well-designed platform therefore changes the economics of scale without centralizing all operational judgment. This balance is essential for sustainable deployment.

D. Coordination Routines and Governance Forums

Operating models remain inert unless they are activated through recurring coordination routines. For enterprise AI agents, the minimum governance forum set should include a portfolio steering forum, a design and change review forum, an incident and learning review forum, and an independent assurance forum, each with a distinct decision mandate and evidence package (Galbraith, 2014; Weill and Ross, 2005; Raji et al., 2020). The steering forum prioritizes investment and risk appetite, the design forum approves charters and major changes, the incident forum converts failures into redesign, and the assurance forum tests whether controls remain adequate. These recurring routines convert governance from a static policy repository into an operating cadence. Cadence determines durability.

Coordination routines should also synchronize business and technical time horizons. Business units often evaluate agents through immediate service outcomes, while platform teams evaluate through release stability and risk teams evaluate through control sufficiency; unless these perspectives are reviewed together, organizations optimize one dimension at the expense of the others (Berente et al., 2021; Kellogg et al., 2020). Consequently, periodic review packs should combine value metrics, control metrics, intervention logs, and change histories in a single governance pack-et. This integrated review discipline is one of the main advantages of the proposed operating model. It ensures that scaling decisions remain evidence-based.

E. Analytical Propositions

The formal design propositions are presented with the aim of shaping internal logic of the proposed framework. Since the chapter is theoretical, these propositions are not statistical hypotheses; but are analytical propositions whose validity is based on synthesis through strategy, governance and organizational research. Each of the propositions states a design problem that recurs and why the suggested arrangement is more effective than the reviewed options in the previous sections. Managerial validation is another aspect that is based on the propositions during implementation. They are stated next.

Proposition 1. Provided AI agents are implemented under clear charters to relate strategic objective, process boundary, and responsible owner, then local automation will not replace enterprise strategy in scale-up.

Justification. The rationale is based on both strategic alignment literature and on the research on governance in terms of decision rights. According to alignment frameworks, the formation of value through digital initiatives occur only when business priorities and technological set-ups are maintained in a coherent relation, and performance studies have shown that when rights and obligations are implicit, performance is compromised (Henderson and Venkatraman, 1993; Bharadwaj et al., 2013; Weill and Ross, 2004). These principles are applied to the AI agent context in the agent charter, where purpose, authority, and escalation are specified in a single artifact, which helps to ensure that deployment decisions are not attributed to vendor characteristics or local zeal. This demonstrates that the major protection against strategy drift in enterprise agent portfolios is bounded chartering.

Proposition 2. Provided accountability is overlapped over business ownership, technical ownership, control ownership, and human supervision, then AI agent autonomy can be scaled to achieve responsibility gaps.

Justification. The rationale is based on organization theory of differentiated roles and the current research concerning AI opacity and disputed control. The organizational design demands that the incompatible ones should be separated whereas interdependent responsibilities should be coordinated, and the AI literature indicates that opaque system behavior generates practical ambiguity in case ownership is not distinguished (Galbraith, 2014; Kellogg et al., 2020; Lebovitz et al., 2022; Berente et al., 2021). The accountability stack avoids the diffusion of responsibility that often goes hand in hand with complex automation by delegating strategic legitimacy, process consequence, technical behavior, independent challenge, and live intervention to different yet related roles. This documents that scalable autonomy requires layered accountability.

Proposition 3. When the governance is federated as opposed to completely centralized or completely decentralized, then platform reuse, consistency in compliance, and responsiveness to domains are mutually obtained.

Justification. The rationale is contingency-based research of governance and enterprise architecture rationale. In contrast, centralization enhances standardization and coherence in control, whereas decentralization enhances responsiveness to context; nevertheless, when shared technologies are incorporated in domain-specific workflows, both features are needed to transform an enterprise (Sambamurthy and Zmud, 1999; Weill and Ross, 2005; Ross et al., 2006). The federated model addresses this tension by concentrating control libraries, platform services and portfolio review and leaving the domain ownership of process outcomes and escalation logic. This demonstrates that federated governance is the most appropriate structural configuration to use to deploy AI agents of the enterprise.

The operating model that has been created in this section proves the fact that governance cannot be minimized to policy statements or approval checklists. The enactment of control expectations in the day-to-day work is determined by structure, roles, and routines. The propositions also explain the reason why charters, layered accountability, and federation are the critical design options of enterprise AI agents. The following part transforms these design decisions into an adoption roadmap.

VI. ADOPTION ROADMAP

In this section, the framework is translated into a phased roadmap that organizations can employ when moving from experimentation to institutionalized deployment. The roadmap is required because enterprise AI agent adoption often begins with isolated pilots, whereas governance maturity requires portfolio-level routines, shared evidence, and repeatable design choices. The phases in Figure 4 are therefore cumulative rather than optional, and each phase is associated with a distinct managerial task and decision gate. Adoption should proceed deliberately.

A. Readiness Assessment and Use-Case Selection

Readiness assessment should be conducted before technical piloting begins. The relevant questions concern process modularity, quality of data stewardship, observability of outcomes, tolerance for error, reversibility of action, workforce capacity for oversight, and the availability of accountable business ownership (Jöhnk et al., 2021; National Institute of Standards and Technology, 2023). If these conditions are weak, then pilot activity should be limited to advisory or tightly supervised use cases rather than expanded into acting agents. Consequently, readiness is best interpreted as governance and workflow readiness, not simply as model availability. Phase 1 of Figure 4 is devoted to this diagnostic discipline.

Use-case selection should then privilege areas where value can be measured and intervention remains feasible. Suitable early candidates include exception triage, policy-supported drafting, knowledge retrieval with human confirmation, and bounded coordination tasks in which fallback paths are clear (Jarrahi, 2018; Amershi et al., 2019). Unsuitable early candidates include highly ambiguous workflows, high-consequence irreversible actions without appeal pathways, and processes whose source governance is unstable. Therefore, the adoption logic of this chapter recommends sequencing by governability as much as by expected benefit. This sequencing prevents symbolic pilots from being mistaken for scalable operating capability.

B. Design, Pilot, and Scale

Phase 2 is design oriented since prior to the pilot, the operating model should be instantiated. At this stage, the charter is ratified, the escalation matrix is established, data entitlement are checked, shared controls are added, and evidences requirements are being defined beforehand (International Organization for Standardization, 2023; Raji et al., 2020). When these artifacts are regarded as deliverables following the pilot, the organization is informed only of whether the agent can act and not whether it can act responsibly. Thus, the first decision gate in Figure 4 is the design completeness. The deployment of responsibilities starts prior to runtime.

Phase 3 is the supervised pilot, where the agent will be deployed to a limited workflow with explicit monitoring, intervention rights, and review rate. Value indicators, including improvement of cycle-time or reduction of rework, should be combined with control indicators, including fidelity to the escalations, completeness of evidence, and rate of incidents (Hokmabadi et al., 2025; National Institute of Standards and Technology, 2023). This combined analysis is necessary since an enterprise design is not a success when a pilot that enhances speed weakens traceability. In line with this, the second decision gate in Figure 4 relates to control integrity, whereas the third relates to proven business value. Scaling is only approved in case of the two conditions being fulfilled.

Phase 4 makes the agent an institutional feature of the enterprise portfolio and not a project artifact. Portfolio review practices, reuseable control libraries, shared monitoring dashboards, regular audit cycles and retirement criteria are designed in such a way that subsequent deployments will gain the benefit of cumulative learning (Weill and Ross, 2004; Ross et al., 2006; International Organization for Standardization, 2023). Besides this, domain teams will be expected to report business outcomes as well as control events into shared governance forums thus maintaining comparability across use cases. Institutionalization as such, transforms individual success to organizational capacity. This is the last stage of defining whether transformation has taken place or not.

Figure 4. Phased adoption roadmap for enterprise AI agents.

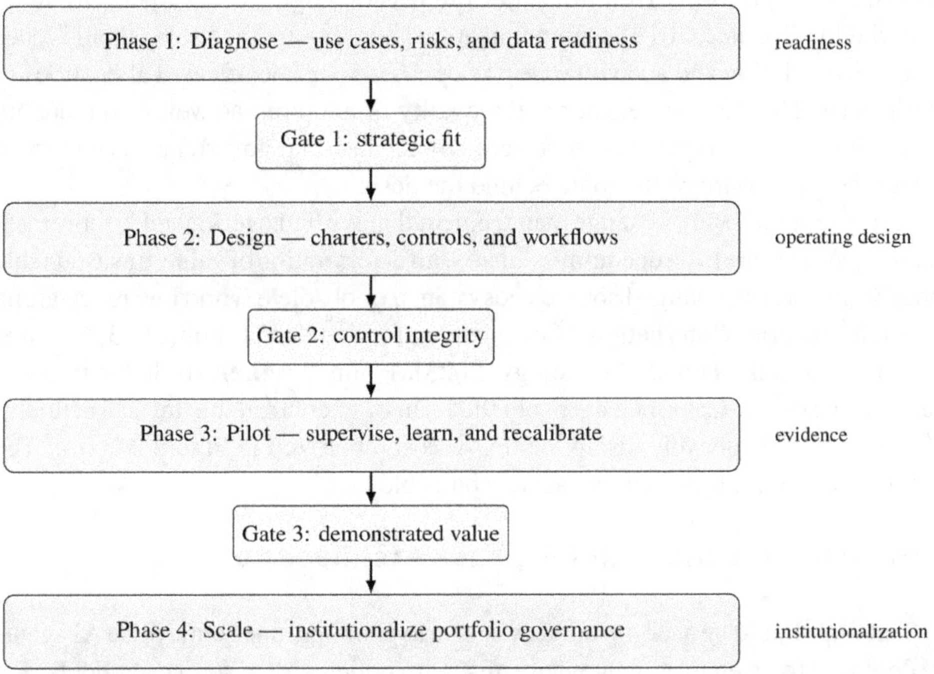

C. Workforce Enablement and Change Management

The facilitation of the workforce is required since the governance of enterprise AI requires informed human involvement. Operators should know when to take action, supervisors should know how to read logs and thresholds, process owners should know how charters limit action, and executives should know how portfolio metrics can be used to make strategic decisions (Jarrahi, 2018; Johnk et al., 2021; Shneiderman, 2022). Therefore, role-specific training, modeling of escalating situations, and literality of evidence quality and model limitation should be adopted.

Such enablement is not possible without which formally designed controls are weakly implemented. The governance system involves human capability.

Incentives and role perception should also be dealt with by change management. When agents are framed as unreviewable substitutes, employees might resist them, but when agents are framed as limited workflow elements, the outcomes of which can still be contested and where the benefits can be seen in reduced work or better service delivery, they are more likely to respond constructively (Raisch and Krakowski, 2021; Jarrahi, 2018; European Commission High-Level Expert Group on Artificial Intelligence, 2019). Communication and training, therefore, should focus on scope, escalation and accountability as opposed to unspecificated allegations of intelligence. This framing enhances the quality of adoption as well as the quality of oversight. The workforce is empowered by the fact that governance is enhanced in case they are aware of the logic behind the design.

A very crucial issue of change management that is often overlooked is retirement planning. Agents are to be decommissioned with deterioration of value, unsustainable controls, materially changed source ecosystems, or obsolete workflow redesigning the original charter (International Organization for Standardization, 2023; National Institute of Standards and Technology, 2023). Planned retirement helps to avoid the presence of old-fashioned agents in the form of uncontrollable infrastructure. It also supports the lifecycle discipline that was summarized in Figure 2 above. The responsible scaling thus incorporates responsible exit.

D. Scenario Planning and Fallback Architecture

Scale-up should be accompanied by scenario planning since enterprise AI agents are deployed to an environment where upstream policies, data sources, models, and business priorities may change significantly over time. Fallback modes of degraded model behavior, knowledge-source outages, access revocations and abnormal volumes of escalation should therefore be predefined by managers to maintain business continuity even when agent performance becomes unpredictable (National Institute of Standards and Technology, 2023; International Organization for Standardization, 2023). Depending on the criticality of the processes they can be human-only execution, restricted advisory mode, limited access to tools or temporarily suspended. Resilience is therefore not a by-product of good design, but a designed governance ability. Fallback architecture defends momentum of transformation.

The quality of decisions made by the executives is also enhanced by scenario planning since the circumstances that make experimentation slow, redesign, or be withdrawn are made clear. A portfolio steering process is enhanced when leaders are able to compare best-case value, anticipated operating conditions and worst-case scenarios on the same evidence basis, as opposed to depending on optimistic pilot narratives (Weill and Ross, 2004; Hokmabadi et al., 2025). Moreover, fallback design renders the ownership of business more tangible since the process owners need to define what acceptable service continuity will appear like in the conditions of degraded automation. This mandate connects resilience, accountability, and transformation strategy to one decision frame. It is hence a necessary part of the roadmap.

E. Measurement, Review Cadence, and Corrective Action

Measurement ought to be organized in three families which include: value metrics, control metrics, and adoption metrics. The value metrics consist of cycle-time savings, exception resolution rate, reuse of knowledge, quality improvement, and control metrics consist of evidence coverage, override quality, compliance with escalation, frequency of incidents, and change-discipline compliance (Berente et al., 2021; Shneiderman, 2022). This framework eliminates the typical fallacy of measuring enterprise AI in terms of either cost or throughput. There should be a balanced metric architecture since the quality of governance falls under performance quality. Table 3 and Table 4 contain the corresponding metric anchors.

The cadence of the reviews must be aligned with the risk and operational velocity. Agents that have high consequences or rapidly changing agents need to have more frequent incident reviews, threshold reviews, and source quality reviews and model reviews, but lower-consequence agents can be analyzed by periodic sampling and dashboard monitoring (National Institute of Standards and Technology, 2023; European Union, 2024). This should then be followed by remedial action in one of four directions namely: charter revision, workflow redesign, control strengthening, or retirement depending on the source of the deficiency. By so doing, the roadmap does not put an end to the implementation at a particular milestone but an organizational learning loop.

VII. CONCLUSION

We outlined our planned strategy-consistent governance model, which is to ensure that the deployment of enterprise AI agents aligns with the goals of digital transformation, policy limitations, and accountability in the organization. We further demonstrated that our proposal is resistant to strategy drift, diffusion of responsibility, weak oversight, fragmented controls and coordination failures that occur when autonomy is introduced without redesigning the operating model. Moreover, we have shown that our framework defines confined charter, stratified responsibility, federated government, lifecycle oversight, and quantifiable adoption discipline are the essential qualities needed to deploy agents on the enterprise scale. Results of the analysis also revealed that it is possible to promote value creation, auditability, and human-controllable control together in case AI agents are managed as organizational entities instead of separate technical systems.

REFERENCES

Amershi, S., Weld, D., Vorvoreanu, M., Fourney, A., Nushi, B., Collisson, P., Suh, J., Iqbal, S. T., Bennett, P. N., Inkpen, K., Teevan, J., Kikin-Gil, R., & Horvitz, E. (2019). Guidelines for human–AI interaction. *Proceedings of the 2019 CHI Conference on Human Factors in Computing Systems*, 1–13. **https://doi.org/**DOI: 10.1145/3290605.3300233

Benbya, H., Pachidi, S., & Jarvenpaa, S. L. (2021). Special issue editorial: Artificial intelligence in organizations: Implications for information systems research. *Journal of the Association for Information Systems*, *22*(2), 281–303. DOI: 10.17705/1jais.00662

Berente, N., Gu, B., Recker, J., & Santhanam, R. (2021). Managing artificial intelligence. *Management Information Systems Quarterly*, *45*(3), 1433–1450. DOI: 10.25300/MISQ/2021/16274

Bharadwaj, A., El Sawy, O. A., Pavlou, P. A., & Venkatraman, N. (2013). Digital business strategy: Toward a next generation of insights. *Management Information Systems Quarterly*, *37*(2), 471–482. DOI: 10.25300/MISQ/2013/37:2.3

Dellermann, D., Ebel, P., Söllner, M., & Leimeister, J. M. (2019a). Hybrid intelligence. *Business & Information Systems Engineering*, *61*(5), 637–643. DOI: 10.1007/s12599-019-00595-2

Dellermann, D., Ebel, P., Söllner, M., & Leimeister, J. M. (2019b). The future of human–AI collaboration: A taxonomy of design knowledge for hybrid intelligence systems. *Proceedings of the 52nd Hawaii International Conference on System Sciences*, 274–283. **https://doi.org/**DOI: 10.24251/HICSS.2019.034

Diakopoulos, N. (2016). Accountability in algorithmic decision making. *Communications of the ACM*, *59*(2), 56–62. DOI: 10.1145/2844110

European Commission High-Level Expert Group on Artificial Intelligence. (2019). *Ethics guidelines for trustworthy AI*. https://digital-strategy.ec.europa.eu/en/library/ethics-guidelines-trustworthy-ai

European Union. (2024). *Regulation (EU) 2024/1689 of the european parliament and of the council of 13 june 2024 laying down harmonised rules on artificial intelligence and amending regulations (AI act)*. https://eur-lex.europa.eu/eli/reg/2024/1689/oj

Galbraith, J. R. (2014). *Designing organizations: Strategy, structure, and process at the business unit and enterprise levels* (3rd ed.). Jossey-Bass.

Henderson, J. C., & Venkatraman, N. (1993). Strategic alignment: Leveraging information technology for transforming organizations. *IBM Systems Journal*, *32*(1), 4–16. DOI: 10.1147/sj.382.0472

Hinings, B., Gegenhuber, T., & Greenwood, R. (2018). Digital innovation and transformation: An institutional perspective. *Information and Organization*, *28*(1), 52–61. DOI: 10.1016/j.infoandorg.2018.02.004

Hokmabadi, H., Rezvani, S. M. H. S., Hokmabadi, H., & de Almeida, N. M. (2025). Business resilience through AI-agent automation for SMEs and startups: A review on agile marketing and CRM. *Information (Basel)*, *16*(11), 1000. Advance online publication. DOI: 10.3390/info16111000

International Organization for Standardization. (2023). *ISO/IEC 42001:2023 information technology — artificial intelligence — management system*. https://www.iso.org/standard/81230.html

Jarrahi, M. H. (2018). Artificial intelligence and the future of work: Human–AI symbiosis in organizational decision making. *Business Horizons*, *61*(4), 577–586. DOI: 10.1016/j.bushor.2018.03.007

Jöhnk, J., Weißert, M., & Wyrtki, K. (2021). Ready or not, AI comes—An interview study of organizational AI readiness factors. *Business & Information Systems Engineering*, *63*(1), 5–20. DOI: 10.1007/s12599-020-00676-7

Kellogg, K. C., Valentine, M. A., & Christin, A. (2020). Algorithms at work: The new contested terrain of control. *The Academy of Management Annals*, *14*(1), 366–410. DOI: 10.5465/annals.2018.0174

Khatri, V., & Brown, C. V. (2010). Designing data governance. *Communications of the ACM*, *53*(1), 148–152. DOI: 10.1145/1629175.1629210

Lebovitz, S., Lifshitz-Assaf, H., & Levina, N. (2022). To engage or not to engage with AI for critical judgments: How professionals deal with opacity when using AI for medical diagnosis. *Organization Science*, *33*(1), 126–148. DOI: 10.1287/orsc.2021.1549

Matt, C., Hess, T., Benlian, A., & Wiesböck, F. (2016). Options for formulating a digital transformation strategy. *MIS Quarterly Executive*, *15*(2), 103–119.

Mökander, J., & Floridi, L. (2021). Ethics-based auditing to develop trustworthy AI. *Minds and Machines*, *31*(2), 323–327. DOI: 10.1007/s11023-021-09557-8

National Institute of Standards and Technology. (2023). *Artificial intelligence risk management framework (AI RMF 1.0)* [NIST AI 100-1]. **https://doi.org/**DOI: 10.6028/NIST.AI.100-1

Plekhanov, D., Franke, H., & Netland, T. H. (2023). Digital transformation: A review and research agenda. *European Management Journal*, *41*(6), 821–844. DOI: 10.1016/j.emj.2022.09.007

Raisch, S., & Krakowski, S. (2021). Artificial intelligence and management: The automation–augmentation paradox. *Academy of Management Review*, *46*(1), 192–210. DOI: 10.5465/amr.2018.0072

Raji, I. D., Smart, A., White, R. N., Mitchell, M., Gebru, T., Hutchinson, B., Smith-Loud, J., Theron, D., & Barnes, P. (2020). Closing the AI accountability gap: Defining an end-to-end framework for internal algorithmic auditing. *Proceedings of the 2020 Conference on Fairness, Accountability, and Transparency*, 33–44. **https://doi.org/**DOI: 10.1145/3351095.3372873

Ross, J. W., Weill, P., & Robertson, D. C. (2006). *Enterprise architecture as strategy: Creating a foundation for business execution*. Harvard Business School Press.

Sambamurthy, V., & Zmud, R. W. (1999). Arrangements for information technology governance: A theory of multiple contingencies. *Management Information Systems Quarterly*, *23*(2), 261–290. DOI: 10.2307/249754

Shneiderman, B. (2022). *Human-centered AI*. Oxford University Press. DOI: 10.1093/oso/9780192845290.001.0001

Verhoef, P. C., Broekhuizen, T., Bart, Y., Bhattacharya, A., Dong, J. Q., Fabian, N., & Haenlein, M. (2021). Digital transformation: A multidisciplinary reflection and research agenda. *Journal of Business Research*, *122*, 889–901. DOI: 10.1016/j.jbusres.2019.09.022

Vial, G. (2019). Understanding digital transformation: A review and a research agenda. *The Journal of Strategic Information Systems*, *28*(2), 118–144. DOI: 10.1016/j.jsis.2019.01.003

Voudouris, C. (2025). *Autonomic business transformation: A guide to AI agents for practitioners and executives*. Springer Nature Switzerland., DOI: 10.1007/978-3-032-01415-3

Wang, L., Ma, C., Feng, X., Zhang, J., Yang, H., Zhang, J., Chen, Z., Tang, J., Chen, X., Lin, Y., Zhao, W. X., Wei, Z., & Wen, J. (2024). A survey on large language model based autonomous agents. *Frontiers of Computer Science*, *18*(6), 186345. DOI: 10.1007/s11704-024-40231-1

Warner, K. S. R., & Wäger, M. (2019). Building dynamic capabilities for digital transformation: An ongoing process of strategic renewal. *Long Range Planning*, *52*(3), 326–349. DOI: 10.1016/j.lrp.2018.12.001

Weill, P., & Ross, J. W. (2004). *IT governance: How top performers manage IT decision rights for superior results*. Harvard Business School Press.

Weill, P., & Ross, J. W. (2005). A matrixed approach to designing IT governance. *MIT Sloan Management Review*, *46*(2), 26–34.

Wooldridge, M., & Jennings, N. R. (1995). Intelligent agents: Theory and practice. *The Knowledge Engineering Review*, *10*(2), 115–152. DOI: 10.1017/S0269888900008122

Xi, Z., Chen, W., Guo, X., He, W., Ding, Y., Hong, B., Zhang, M., Wang, J., Jin, S., Zhou, E., Zheng, R., Fan, X., Wang, X., Xiong, L., Zhou, Y., Wang, W., Jiang, C., Zou, Y., Liu, X., & Gui, T. (2025). The rise and potential of large language model based agents: A survey. *Science China. Information Sciences*, *68*(2), 121101. DOI: 10.1007/s11432-024-4222-0

Chapter 4
Adaptive Governance of Autonomous AI Agents:
Rethinking Accountability and Risk in Intelligent Systems

Nashat Ali Almasria
http://orcid.org/0000-0003-2439-4115
A'Sharqiyah University, Oman

ABSTRACT

The introduction of autonomous AI agents as active participants in the institutions is a qualitative change in the governance requirements facing organisations in the public sector, financial services and critical infrastructure. In contrast to the earlier generations of decision-support systems, AI agents do not simply enlighten human choices; they take consequential actions, coordinate multi-step work processes, and increasingly act in distributed multi-agent systems that decentralize responsibility and make it harder to monitor. The chapter states that the governance of AI agents is not appropriate to be addressed through compliance-oriented, checklist-driven approaches that are designed to be applicable to the systems that are static and rule-based

INTRODUCTION:

Artificial intelligence has been incorporated into organisations over the last 20 years, but in the form of an addition or supplement to human decision-making, and not a replacement of it (Rajagopal et al., 2022). Expert systems, recommender engines, predictive models, and robotic process automation systems have all been used within the parameters that are explicitly defined by humans, performing pre-

DOI: 10.4018/979-8-3373-9594-4.ch004

scribed routines under conditions of bounded variation (Soori et al., 2024). These systems were governable, but not necessarily to specifications, and were auditable, at least against performance benchmarks, and could be replaced or retrained when performance went wrong (Qin et al., 2026). The chain of accountability was brief, the behavioural envelope was small, and the decision maker was a human being who had ultimate authority.

This model of limited instrumentality is being replaced by a radically new form of AI implementation. AI agents, systems that can sense environmental inputs, set and pursue subgoals, run multi-step workflows, and adapt to feedback without the need to be continuously instructed by humans, are being deployed to an ever-increasing number of organisational situations (Welsch, 2026). In public administration, agentic systems are involved in processing welfare eligibility determinations, flag regulatory violations, and route service requests without any direct human supervision (Salah et al., 2025). In financial services, autonomous agents are used to execute trading strategies, analyze credit risk, and engage with customers using persistent conversational interfaces. In infrastructure management, AI agents optimise energy grid dispatch, reroute network traffic and manage supply chain logistics in real time (Fawaz et al., 2025; Almasria et al., 2025). The magnitude, pace, and size of these deployments have exceeded the evolution of governance frameworks that are sufficient to their character (Meyer et al., 2024).

Contribution of the Chapter

This chapter has three contributions to the literature on AI governance and agentic AI. This chapter places principal-agent theory, institutional theory and sociotechnical systems research together in a unified account of why the delegation of tasks through AI agents is a unique governance challenge, and not merely an extension of the model-governance practice. Second, it suggests a four-level accountability system (technical, operational, managerial, institutional) which is cross-referenced with a four-part typology of risks (execution, alignment, systemic, legitimacy) and four design principles (observability, contestability, reversibility, proportionality) in the form of a matrix (Table 1 of Section 5) and not as distinct, disconnected lists. Third, it focuses on real example-based governance incidents instead of illustrating generic examples, and it makes clear when the evidence base for a sector (including an AI-enabled critical infrastructure) is sparse. The framework is sector-agnostic in principle, but has been illustrated mostly through examples from the public sector, financial services and infrastructure, and its applicability to safety-critical embodied systems and to agents based on a frontier model is treated separately in Section 5.

The change in the intensity of automation is not merely a quantitative change in the nature of the governing relationship between organisations and the AI systems that they implement; it is a qualitative change in its nature (Tangi et al., 2025). Tools are operated; agents act. When an AI system exercises goal-oriented autonomy over consequential decisions, namely, the allocation of resources, the enforcement of rules, the restriction of access, the modification of infrastructure, then the institution implementing it has, in effect, delegated a form of decision-making authority (Acharya et al., 2025). The delegation so made, however, is hardly ever formalised with the rigour of similar delegations to human agents (Guggenberger et al., 2023). No contracts are established to define the scope of the AI agent discretion, no professional norms are set to establish the boundaries of the legitimate action, and no established mechanisms are available to judge the responsibility in case agent behaviour has a harmful outcome (Kolt, 2025).

This failure in governance is not a technical failure in the first place. It is a failure of an institution and organisation: failure to build the accountability framework, risk assessment framework, and adaptive oversight mechanisms that the implementation of autonomous AI agents requires. Technical safeguards, such as restrictions on the spaces of agent action, records of agent decisions, automated detection of anomalies are necessary but not sufficient (Kumar, 2025). They focus on the immediate symptoms of the failure of governance without addressing the deeper structural causes, which lie in the behavioural features of AI agents working within them (Hughes et al., 2025).

There are three features of AI agents that are of special interest in comprehending this governance issue. First, AI agents exhibit behavioural emergentism: in sufficiently complex environments, or in multi-agent design, agent behaviour may deviate off the desired patterns in ways that cannot be predicted based on the design specifications of the individual components (Dibia, 2025). Second, AI agents are characterized by temporal adaptability: the profiles of their operations can change over time as they learn the environment and this creates governance dilemmas that cannot be reduced to the point of deployment (Adabara et al., 2025). Third, AI agents have distributed agency: in multi-agent systems, the consequences of actions are often caused by the interactions of many agents instead of being the direct result of the action of a single system, making it challenging or impossible to attribute causal responsibility under traditional approaches to accountability (Hughes et al., 2025).

These are the characteristics that determine the unique governance problem that is covered in this chapter. They demand governance structures not only compliant but adaptive - able to change in response to shifts in agent capabilities, operational settings, and institutional environments. The sections that follow build up such a framework starting with its theoretical grounds.

The chapter is clearly conceptual in nature, it is not reporting an original empirical study, a systematic literature-review protocol or a formal case-selection design. The framework was constructed in an iterative manner, synthesizing the principal-agent, institutional, and sociotechnical systems literatures and then being checked for coherence with the accountability and risk-governance literature on AI agents, in particular, and then illustrated with documented episodes of governance that were chosen because they could be documented independently: either a regulatory order, an official inquiry finding, or a peer-reviewed case analysis exists.

1. THE DELEGATION PROBLEM: PRINCIPAL–AGENT THEORY AND AI GOVERNANCE

The principal-agent model, initially created in economics and organisational theory to explain the relationship of delegated authority, offers a fruitful theoretical basis to understand the governance challenge of AI agents (Gauld, 2023). In its classical formulation, the problem occurs when a principal, who may be an employer, regulator or voter, delegates decision-making authority to an agent who may have superior information and whose interests may not perfectly coincide with those of the principal. The governance challenge is to come up with contractual, monitoring and incentive structures that would have the least loss occurring due to this information asymmetry and incentive misalignment (Du et al., 2024).

These structures are established when the agent under consideration is a human professional. All the above in combination makes up the institutional infrastructure of dealing with human agency. In the case of an agent who is an AI system, these structures do not simply apply (Hughes et al., 2025). The AI agents will not enter into any contract, will not react to any incentive structure in ways theorised to be performed by rational actors, and they cannot be held legally liable to their actions. However, they have consequential authority over decisions that touch on the lives of citizens, stability of markets and integrity of critical infrastructure (Herzog, 2023). The outcome is a governance gap between the extent of power held by AI agents and the institutional structures that can be used to enforce that power.

There are three aspects in particular in which the delegation problem in AI governance is especially acute. The asymmetry of information between the principal and the agent is worse in AI systems than in the majority of human agency relationships (Guggenberger et al., 2023). Communication, documentation, and professional norms of transparency are typical methods in which human supervisors can access the reasoning process of subordinates (van de Merwe, 2024). The inner workings of complex AI systems (especially those that run on deep learning architectures) tend to be black boxes to human supervisors even when the systems leave detailed logs of their outputs (Taye, 2023). It is not a technical limitation that can be overcome using more interpretable tools, but is rather a fundamental epistemic asymmetry between natural language thinking of human institutions and the high-dimensional mathematical processes of AI systems (Keningson, 2024).

Second, the goal misalignment issue assumes a unique shape in AI governance. Classical principal-agent theory sees goal misalignment as a result of self-interest: the agent follows its own interests at the expense of the principals (Araral, 2026). AI agents are not interested in this sense; they have goals, programmed in their training procedures and working parameters (Kapoor et al., 2024). However these goals may not coincide with institutional values in a structurally parallel manner to self-interested behaviour. An AI agent that maximises throughput can effectively down-rank the equity consideration (Daza-Ramirez, 2025). A discriminative trend might be encoded and propagated by an AI agent trained on historical data. A recommendation to the detriment of the well-being of an individual may be produced by an AI agent aimed at maximising user engagement. They are types of value misalignment, which governance structures need to identify and rectify (Singh et al., 2025).

Third, the control issue, how to have meaningful control over delegated authority, in AI governance is complicated by the pace and magnitude of AI agent action (Chaffer et al., 2024). When agents are making thousands of decisions every hour, human supervisors are not able to review individual AI decisions in real time (Chaffer et al., 2024). Governance should thus change to be not at the level of transaction level control, but population level control; instead of reviewing individual agent decisions, governance mechanisms should identify statistically significant patterns in the aggregate distribution of agent outputs. Such a change demands new institutional capabilities in data science, statistical auditing, and anomaly detection, which many deploying organisations now do not possess.

The distinction between causal agency, delegated authority, legal responsibility, moral responsibility, and organisational accountability is also important and easy to confuse where AI agents are concerned and is one of these three difficulties that needs to be drawn. An AI agent can be involved causally in generating an outcome – the AI's output is a cause of a decision – without being legally responsible for it or having delegated authority in any legal sense, without being legally responsible for it(Lior, 2020), and without being moral responsible for it, as this presupposes an intentional agent capable of being held accountable in a similar way to a human professional. Only, in a derivative sense, can AI agents be given a role within an organisational accountability structure: the organisation that designs, procures, deploys, and supervises the AI agent is legally and morally responsible for the consequences of the agent's actions and where accountability ultimately needs to be located. This chapter therefore refrains from using words that have an other-sense of "intention" or "interests" or "obligation" as applied to human agents, except when it is used explicitly as a shorthand for the computation, for instance, when it is said that a computer is "optimising" a function, which refers to the way it is doing its job and does not ascribe agency in the legal or moral sense, consistent with the broader literature on responsibility gaps in AI systems.

The complement to the principal-agent analysis is the institutional theory which focuses on the organisational and normative context in which AI agent governance is framed. Institutions are not only rational arrangements of managing information asymmetry; they are systems of rules, norms, and expectations that form the behaviour of actors and define the limits of legitimate action. The introduction of AI agents into institutional environments, which are characterised by strong professional norms, such as medicine, law, social work, financial regulation, etc.), creates conflicts between the procedural rationality of institutional governance, and the optimising rationality of the AI systems (Kjørstad, 2025).

Such tensions are not merely issues to be addressed by improved technical design; they are institutional decisions about what accountability is, whether procedural fairness is valuable, and what the rightful scope of algorithmic authority ought to be. When a welfare agency is being governed by norms of procedural due process, there arises a real dilemma as to whether to deploy an AI agent capable of accurately predicting the eligibility of benefits, but incapable of generating reasons to justify its choices in a form that is meaningful to the applicants or reviewers (Sawicki, 2025). A financial regulator subjected to the norms of proportionality and predictability finds themselves in a real dilemma, when they are overseeing an AI trading system, which has emergent strategies that cannot be described in terms of the principles of proportionality and predictability, which they are nominally designed to implement (Popoola, 2025). Governance structures that do not take note of such institutional tensions on the favour or disfavour of purely technical solutions to the organisational conditions that make AI agent deployment governable or ungovernable.

2. THEORETICAL LENS TO GOVERNANCE PRINCIPLE

The three theoretical lenses above are not just listed in parallel or juxtaposed; each identifies a particular failure mode of governance and a particular design response, and linking these together is an essential prerequisite to being able to read the accountability framework and design principles as an integrated architecture rather than as a list (Abdulnafea et al., 2022). The main information problem in the theory of principal-agent theory is the lack of information between the organisations and their AI agents, and a design solution for an information problem is to produce information that makes the problem visible – the function of observability as a technical and organisational investment to render agent behaviour legible to human supervisors. The core issue identified through institutional theory is the lack of procedural legitimacy and the disconnect between algorithmic legitimacy and institutional legitimacy; the design question to a legitimacy problem is: how to give standing to the question of legitimacy and to be heard, which is the function of contestability. Sociotechnical systems research does not consider the algorithm itself but rather the AI-human system; and the issue is unpredictable emergent behaviour under realistic operating conditions, not the issue of unpredictability itself, because the design solution to unpredictability is to maintain a capacity to correct course, which can be interpreted as reversibility (the ability to back up or stop) and proportionality (the ability to adjust the amount of oversight given to a given deployment as evidence of its behaviour accumulates). This linkage and the accountability level and mechanisms for each principle, are detailed in Table 1 in Section 5 in one matrix.

3. A MULTI-LEVEL ACCOUNTABILITY FRAMEWORK FOR AI AGENTS

The AI agent behaviour should be in the form of multi-level interdependent governance with distinct responsibilities, mechanisms, and tools of oversight (Busuioc, 2021) (Adabara et al., 2025). The tendency of practice and scholarship is to locate accountability at a single level, most frequently the technical level of model validation, or the legal level of liability attribution, and to treat governance as a primarily question of technical reliability or legal compliance (Almasria 2022; Liu, 2024). This tendency is systematic and underestimates the complexity of the accountability problem in the implementation of AI agents where the occurrence of consequential failures can have their origin at any level and where the diffusion of responsibility across organisational hierarchies create accountability vacuums which cannot be filled at any level.

The multi-level accountability system that may be proposed includes four interdependent levels of governance: technical, operational, managerial and institutional. These levels are not free-standing silos; they are interdependent layers where failures at one level can spread upwards or downwards and where sound governance means that there is coherent integration across all four.

3.1. The Technical Level

On the technical level, accountability mechanisms relate to the design, verification, testing, and continuous monitoring of AI agent systems. Technical accountability implies that the agents should be constructed using auditable architectures, that the behaviour of the agents can be logged and reviewed, and that the performance of the agents can be evaluated against specified performance targets across the pertinent operating conditions (Radanliev, 2026). Automated monitoring systems to identify distributional changes in agent behaviour; interpretability tools that make the reasoning of agents legible to human reviewers; and version control systems that record histories of model changes and retraining (Mandava, 2022).

The technical accountability mechanisms are not only required but also, they are necessary to govern AI agents in the organisational contexts (Mandava, 2022). They form the empirical basis of oversight but are not themselves a form of governance. Even a well-documented and constantly monitored system can have a detrimental effect, when there is no connection between the technical accountability mechanisms and the operational processes that have the ability to act on what they expose (Mandava, 2022).

3.2. The Operational Level

Operational accountability addresses how AI agents are managed during deployment: the day-to-day management of agent behaviour, the management of events and exceptions, and the maintenance of the capacity to intervene by humans. At this level, key accountability mechanisms comprise deployment protocols specifying conditions of use, limits of operation, and escalation procedures; incident management systems which record, classify and respond to agent failures; human-in-the-loop requirements of high-stakes decisions or innovative decisions (Alnsour et al., 2024); and override mechanisms enabling operators to suspend or redirect agent behaviour when anomalies are identified.

One such critical operational accountability challenge in AI agent deployment is managing automation bias: the human operator not wanting to disagree with AI advice even when they have reason to do so

. The governance structures should counter this tendency by designing human reviewing processes in a way that they maintain a true decision-making authority, but not merely a nominal oversight. This necessitates consideration of the cognitive ergonomics of the human-AI interaction, such as design of interfaces that display agent recommendations along with confidence levels along with disconfirming information, and development of professional norms that define the conditions under which human override is to be expected rather than exceptional (Le Guillou et al., 2023; Ibrahim et al., 2024).

3.3. The Managerial Level

The accountability of the managers deals with the strategic governance of portfolios of AI agents: the ex post facto alignment between deployments of AI agents and organisational values and objectives, the post factor management of aggregate risk in multi-agent systems, the maintenance of the organisational responsibility of agent behaviour at the level of senior leadership (Janakiraman, 2025). The most important processes here are AI governance committees with the power to approve, review and suspend agent deployments; risk management frameworks that inculcate AI agent risks into enterprise risk assessments; accountability mapping processes that explicitly assign the ownership of agent portfolios to named individuals or functions; and regular strategic reviews of the portfolio against organisational values and regulatory requirements (Janakiraman, 2025).

The importance of the managerial level, in particular, is to deal with the issue of governance diffusion: the propensity of accountability to disperse amongst organisational hierarchies in ways that creates gaps between which no individual is specifically tasked with the role of agent behaviour and its consequences. A proper managerial governance demands that accountability be explicitly distributed, not just implied by organisational structure, and that the distribution be reviewed and updated as agent capabilities and deployments change.

3.4. The Institutional Level

The institutional level of accountability has to do with the connection that exists between deploying organisations and the external environment in which they operate: regulators, legislators, courts, professional bodies, and the public. Regulatory reporting, independent audit, disclosure of public interest, and legislative control over the application of AI in the public sector are the mechanisms of institutional accountability (Alduais et al., 2022). The governance challenge at this level is not just compliance with the existing frameworks but a part of the co-development of new frameworks that are sufficient to the novelty of AI agent deployment.

The concern of the institutional accountability is especially vital to legitimacy: the wider social acceptability of deployments of AI agents as acceptable exercises of power. In cases where the AI agents make their decisions which impact on the rights, provision of services or even distribution of the state resources, the deployment of the AI agents must be justifiable in not merely in terms of technical performance but in terms of the values and procedural norms of a democratic state. This means that organisations implementing AI agents in institutional setting invest in public communications, stakeholder relations, and independent oversight mechanisms that extend beyond the bare minimum of regulatory compliance.

4. A RISK TYPOLOGY FOR DEPLOYED AI AGENTS

Governance of AI agents necessitates differentiated perception of the sort of risk that an agentic deployment brings into being. The existing risk taxonomies of AI systems are either biased towards technical failure modes, model errors, data quality issues, system outages; or towards ethical aspects, such as bias and privacy (Almasria et al., 2024). The two are significant but do not cover the entire risk area of organisations implementing AI agents in consequential contexts of operations. The following typology describes four analytically discrete risk categories, which when combined, can give a more comprehensive map of the governance challenges involved.

4.1. Execution Risk

Execution risk is the inability of an AI agent to execute its assigned task reliably within its intended operational parameters. This is the nearest kind of AI agent risk and the one that is most directly dealt with by technical accountability mechanisms. The execution failures may be attributed to distributional shift the agent is exposed to conditions that are very different to those of its training environment- or to adversarial manipulation, or to a software error, or to an unforeseen interaction between the agent and its operational environment. The effects of an execution failure can be minor service interruptions or disastrous operational failures, depending on the criticality of the process the agent is handling and the resilience of the mechanism of oversight in place to identify and respond to failure.

To govern execution risk, it is necessary to have a good testing regime, monitoring of performance, as well as having clear protocols that should be applied in detecting and responding to performance degradation (Masadeh et al., 2021). It also involves attentive control of the scope conditions under which agents are to be deployed: the specification of the operating parameters within which the agent is supposed to be able to perform with a high degree of reliability, and the design of the override and escalation mechanisms that will go off when the agent is operating on the borders or beyond the specified operational boundaries.

4.2. Alignment Risk

Alignment risk is the difference between the goals coded in the optimisation function of an AI agent and the values, priorities, or goals of the deploying organisation. In contrast to execution risk, the alignment risk does not present as a deterioration in performance; an agent that is highly effective in pursuing the objectives encoded in it may still be causing governance problems in case the objectives so encoded fail to capture the full spectrum of institutional values at stake. An eligibility agent optimizing on processing time can effectively apply statutory criteria, and systematically disadvantage applicants who lack the skills to navigate a fast automated process. An agent of a fraud detection system that optimises on the rate of detection may show a reasonable aggregate performance but with disproportionate rates of false positive among specific demographic groups.

The risk of alignment is especially challenging to control, as it is often not visible when considered in terms of the individual agent decision-making process, but becomes apparent when considered in terms of aggregate patterns of agent outputs over time as well as across populations, a pattern also documented in taxonomies of language-model-specific risk(Weidinger et al., 2022; Alduais et al., 2023). The mechanisms of governance of alignment risk include impact assessment that identifies potential conflicts between agent objectives and institutional values before deployment, ongoing outcome monitoring that tracks distributional effects across population subgroups, and value-aligned design processes that engage stakeholders in specifying agent objectives before deployment.

4.3. Systemic Risk

Systemic risk is the appearance of harmful results in the interaction of multiple AI agents or in the overall behaviour of an AI-human system, instead of the failure of a single element. Complex adaptive environments, where a number of agents are acting simultaneously on shared resources or in shared markets, are particularly typified by systemic risk (Hammond et al., 2025). In financial services, co-ordinated behaviour of many algorithmic trading agents can increase volatility, cause flash crashes or create feedback loops that destabilize market infrastructure, even when the behaviour of individual agents is all as intended. The interplay of various specialised AI agents handling different aspects of service delivery, can result in coordination failures which no single agent is responsible to but all contribute to.

The management of systemic risks needs to be approached in a manner that sees the AI-human system as the unit of analysis and not individual agents. This includes systemic monitoring that tracks aggregate patterns of agent interaction, stress testing that simulates the behaviour of agent populations under extreme conditions, and circuit-breaker mechanisms that can suspend or constrain agent operations when systemic indicators cross critical thresholds. Governance of systemic risk is an intrinsically collaborative issue: it must be coordinated across multiple deploying organisations and, in most cases, it needs to be constrained by regulatory intervention to create and enforce system-level constraints.

4.4. Legitimacy Risk

The erosion of institutional trust, democratic accountability, which may accrue as a consequence of AI agent deployment, regardless of technical performance, is known as legitimacy risk. Even a well-functioning AI system by most reasonable measurement criteria can still challenge the legitimacy of institutions by perceived opaque, non-accountable, or inconsistent institutional practices (Aldboush et al., 2023). Within the context of a public administration, the depersonalisation of governance that results when the human discretion is substituted with the determination of an algorithm can be experienced. The process of delegating regulatory policy enforcement decisions to AI agents can raise the issue of democratic accountability of regulatory policy even in the context of the agents operating within a statutory context.

The concept of legitimacy risk cannot be addressed solely in the technical sense; instead, it needs to be taken into consideration both in the communicative and participatory aspects of the governance of AI agents (Tawfiq et al., 2024). To use AI agents in high-legitimacy situations, organisations should invest in public explanation, offer meaningful mechanisms of challenge and redress, and involve stakeholders in the governance design processes, which extend beyond formal compliance. The relational property of legitimacy is bestowed or denied by those actors whose trust and acceptance an institution needs, rather than by the self-evaluation of the performance of an organisation.

5. EMPIRICAL ILLUSTRATIONS ACROSS SECTORS

The above typology of risks and accountability framework can be explained by short analysis of governance issues and responses in three empirical areas: public administration, financial services and infrastructure management. These sectors were chosen on the basis that they represent contrasting governance environments-different regulatory frameworks, different accountability traditions and different exposure to four categories of risks identified above.

5.1. Public Administration: Automated Welfare and Benefits Systems.

The most important and controversial instances of agentic governance being played out are perhaps the deployment of AI agents in welfare administration. Some jurisdictions have already implemented algorithmic systems to assist in determining eligibility on social benefit programs, flagging cases to be reviewed by humans, or to determine cases to be approved on routine applications. The governance issues that such deployments raise cut across all four risk categories, although the risks of legitimacy and alignment are the most noticeable(Ada Lovelace et al., 2021).

Welfare AI risks legitimacy because of the inherent conflict between the procedural norms of social welfare administration which emphasize individual circumstances, dignitary treatment, and the right to a reasoned decision and the statistical logic of algorithmic determination. Individuals whose benefit claims are made by AI systems have a real concern in knowing how those determinations are made and in appealing determinations they believe are wrong. The fundamental conditions of procedural fairness can be compromised even in cases where the overall accuracy rates are very high.

The risks of alignment are due to the challenge of representing the entire spectrum of welfare policy values as the goals of a set of AI agents. Welfare systems are created to reconcile a number of considerations, including efficiency, equity, dignity, anti-fraud, which cannot be maximised simultaneously, and which are weighted differently by different stakeholders. An AI agent whose goals are mainly accuracy in identifying ineligibility may generate an overproportionate number of false positives among vulnerable applicants, who lack the capacity to contest automated determinations. Mechanisms of governance in response to these risks have involved mandatory human review of AI-recommended adverse decisions, algorithmic impact assessment, and legislative requirements of explainability in automated public sector decision-making.

Documented Governance Episode: The Dutch Childcare Benefits Scandal (Toeslagenaffaire)

Context. Between approximately 2013 and 2019, the Dutch Tax and Customs Administration (Belastingdienst) used a risk-scoring system to flag childcare-benefit claims for fraud investigation. The Dutch Data Protection Authority found that the system used applicants' dual nationality as a risk factor, in violation of Dutch and EU non-discrimination law.

System function. An algorithmic risk-scoring tool flagged claims for full-file human review and, in practice, for all-or-nothing reclamation of benefits already paid, with limited caseworker discretion to individuate circumstances.

Risk category. Predominantly alignment risk, since the system's fraud-detection objective was not constrained by the equity and dignitary values embedded in welfare policy, compounded by legitimacy risk arising from the absence of an intelligible, contestable basis for individual determinations.

Governance failure. No pre-deployment equity impact assessment constrained the risk factors used; case-level review did not function as a genuine contestability mechanism because caseworkers operated under an all-or-nothing repayment policy with little discretion; and no distributional monitoring surfaced the disproportionate impact on families from migrant backgrounds before roughly 26,000 families had been wrongly accused, with reported average repayment demands of €20,000–€60,000. The scandal contributed to the resignation of the Dutch government in January 2021.

Lesson for the framework. Observability at the technical level – the system's logs and scoring outputs existed and were, in principle, auditable – was not sufficient without contestability that functions in practice, not only on paper, and without alignment safeguards applied before deployment rather than discovered after harm has occurred.

5.2. Financial Services: Algorithmic Trading and Allocation of Credit.

Financial services offer the longest history of AI agent implementation in consequential institutional frameworks, and the industry has seen all the governance failures that the risk typology identifies. The canonical example of systemic risk in AI-human market systems is the 2010 Flash Crash, where interaction between algorithmic trading agents resulted in a sudden and largely unexplained crash in the market. Recent episodes, such as moments of systemic oversight of populations of agents whose individual behaviour falls within the regulatory limits, and whose collective behaviour does not, demonstrate the difficulty of maintaining systemic oversight over populations of agents whose individual behaviour falls within the regulatory limits, and whose collective behaviour does not.

Execution and alignment risks are also salient in credit allocation AI where agents trained on historical lending data have been shown to propagate discriminatory patterns in ways violating requirements of fair lending even when the salient characteristic is not explicitly encoded in agent input. The governance problem here is alignment: the agent is optimising well to predict credit risks in the past in the historical sense of this term, but the past patterns in which it has learned encode social inequalities to which regulatory policy is designed to correct. Responses in governance have involved making the use of mandatory fairness testing, model auditing requirements and in some jurisdictions, prescriptive constraints on the variables that credit-scoring agents may be using.

The financial services sector has also generated significant governance innovation that informs the adaptive governance framework: the use of regulatory sandboxes that allow the supervised testing of novel agent deployments before full-scale operation; real-time surveillance systems that monitor aggregate market behaviour to see anomalies that may indicate systemic risk; and the development of living wills and resolution frameworks that extend traditional crisis management tools to cover AI-driven failure scenarios.

Documented Governance Episode: The Knight Capital Trading Failure

Context. In 2012, Knight Capital Americas LLC, a significant U.S. market maker at the time, introduced a new trading software to assist them with a New York Stock Exchange programme on 1 August 2012. The old (dormant) code was not properly overwritten on one of 8 production servers and was inadvertently activated (Securities & Exchange, 2013).

System function. As it was intended to do, Knight's automated order-routing agent ("SMARS") was used to generate and send live orders to market without any transaction-level review by a man.

Risk category. Execution risk that comes directly from the server, in a systemic fashion: The server failure caused a malfunction in Knight's overall order-management system that led to around 4 million mis-executed orders in 154 stocks over a period of roughly 45 minutes (Securities & Exchange, 2013).

Governance failure. According to the SEC order, Knight did not have sufficient risk-management controls in place to comply with the Market Access Rule, such as a system that would have ceased trading once the anomaly was detected and triggered internal alerts, but the alerts were not programmed to escalate in real time. There was no switch that could be confidently used by the operation staff in the first critical minutes that could have averted any disaster for Knight. The firm suffered a pre-tax loss of some $440 million and needed emergency financing to stay solvent (Securities & Exchange, 2013).

Mitigation and response. In addition to Knight's $12 million penalty and the need to improve risk controls, the incident led to the industry-wide adoption of pre-trade risk checks, deployment testing standards and mandatory kill-switch capability for various algorithmic trading operations.

Lesson for the framework. Reversibility is an organisational – not just operating – requirement: Knight was able to stop trading on his "notional" capacity, but the operating procedures and escalation routes to make that possible in a matter of minutes did not work as they should have. It also shows how quickly system-wide properties of execution failures can emerge in tightly coupled systems, emphasizing the need for population level real-time monitoring, as opposed to only transaction level.

5.3.Infrastructure Management: Autonomous Grid and Network Optimisation.

AI agents are also deployed in critical infrastructure management to optimize dispatch to the energy grid, to manage telecommunications networks and to coordinate logistics systems. These deployments pose especially challenging governance issues due to their combination of stakes-high operational impacts and system-level dynamics that are hard to model or predict. One of the most notable risks is the execution risk: the effects of AI agent malfunction in critical infrastructure may include disruption of services affecting a large population, safety-related incidents, and cascading failures that spread throughout interconnected systems.

The alignment risk assumes a unique form in infrastructure AI: the conflict between efficiency and resilience. AI agents that optimise based on operational efficiency - reducing cost, maximising throughput, reducing waste, etc. - may systematically reduce system slack and redundancy in a way that increases vulnerability to disruption. This tension is indicative of a larger governance challenge: the difficulty in specifying resilience as an agent objective under conditions that have not yet been present. The governance response in this area has focused on ensuring that there is human oversight of critical decision points, manual override capacity, and the establishment of regulatory frameworks that prescribe minimum resilience standards that AI optimisation must avoid overstepping.

Note on the Evidentiary Base for infrastructure

In contrast to public administration and financial services, there is no case as well documented as the one described above of an autonomous AI agent causing a failure in governance. It is important to note, not least for the purposes of this blog post, that incidents in infrastructure are systematically under-represented based on a peer-reviewed analysis of AI incident databases, in part because the infrastructure sector is not as transparent as other sectors to outsiders as researchers and regulators, where infrastructure events are not as covered as, for example, the number of AI-related incidents on trading platforms regulated by exchanges, and in part because the reporting of AI-driven infrastructure incidents is only now becoming formalised (Agarwal & Nene, 2024; Rodrigues et al., 2023). The most recent example of the dynamic of governance – the efficiency-driven automated dispatch versus the resilience of the system – discussed above – is the power crisis in Texas that occurred in February 2021, which resulted from an extreme, low probability weather event. It wasn't necessarily an AI agent governance failure—it was a conventional automated control and market dispatch failure—insofar as it's a different phenomenon, but it's an academically documented one, so it is included here as a peripheral example of the resilience-efficiency trade-off, rather than directly analogous to an AI agent governance failure. Lack of a fully documented case is not the evidence of low risk, it is the evidence of the lack of observability at the sector level, which is in turn consistent with the argument of this chapter that every other governance function depends on observability.

6 DESIGN PRINCIPLES FOR ADAPTIVE AI AGENT GOVERNANCE

The above theoretical discussion and empirical examples are brought to a common point of a series of design principles forming the governance of adaptive AI agents. These principles are not prescriptions to particular governance mechanisms; but normative criteria that governance architectures should meet, realised in various ways in different organisational and regulatory settings. The two of them determine the structural needs of the governance structures that can be sustained as the agent capabilities, change of operational environment, and change of institutional expectations.

The theoretical discussion, the linkage set out above, and the documented episodes converge on a set of design principles for adaptive AI agent governance. Table 1 summarises how each principle relates to the accountability levels and risk types developed earlier in the chapter, before each principle is discussed with an expanded list of governance mechanisms.

Table 1. Adaptive Governance Framework Matrix

Design Principle	Primary Accountability Level(s)	Risk Type(s) Addressed	Illustrative Governance Mechanisms	Primary Responsible Actor
Observability	Technical; Operational	Execution; Systemic	Audit logs; model/version registries; interpretability tooling; distributional monitoring	Technical teams; risk/ compliance function
Contestability	Operational; Institutional	Alignment; Legitimacy	Appeal/redress channels; case-level explanation; public consultation; ombuds mechanisms	Operational management; governance board
Reversibility	Technical; Operational	Execution; Systemic	Override and rollback protocols; kill switches; maintained manual-process capacity	***Operations; IT/ engineering leadership***
Proportionality	Managerial; Institutional	All four risk types (resource allocation)	Risk-tiered oversight intensity; procurement clauses; periodic re-assessment	Senior management; institutional governance body

6.1.Observability

Observability means that the behaviour of AI agents is legible and auditable to human supervisors in all aspects of the governance problem that are relevant. This extends beyond the technical need of recording agent outputs to include the broader need that human supervisors can know what agents are doing, why they are doing it and what the aggregate patterns of their behaviour are telling us about alignment, systemic dynamics, and legitimacy(Cobbe et al., 2021; Wieringa, 2020). All other governance functions are prerequisites of observability: it is impossible to assign any accountability without evidence of behaviour, to manage risks without correct risk data, and to adaptively adjust without operational performance feedback.

To achieve meaningful observability in complex AI agent systems, it is important to make an investment at multiple levels: technical investment in interpretability tools and monitoring infrastructure; organisational investment in the analytical capabilities required to make sense of what monitoring reveals; and procedural investment in the review processes that would translate monitoring data into governance action. Observability is not a strict attribute of a system but a dynamic accomplishment that must be continuously maintained as agent capabilities and various operational circumstances change.

Achieving meaningful observability requires investment at several levels:

Technical: Interpretability tooling, extensive audit logging, model and version registries, automated distributional-shift monitoring, and independent algorithmic auditing (Costanza-Chock et al., 2022; Raji et al., 2020).

Organisational: analytical skills to understand what is uncovered by monitoring (including statistical and data-science skills – not necessarily just engineering skills).

Procedural: Frequency and processes for monitoring data to inform governance action, such as formal escalation thresholds, as opposed to passive monitoring dashboards

6.2. Contestability

Contestability is that the stakeholders who are subject to the decisions of AI agents have a meaningful challenge mechanism to the decisions, and to seek redress. This principle is based upon the fundamentals of procedural fairness and democratic accountability, which hold that review and challenge of consequential exercises of power is a constitutional right of those subject to such exercise of power(Grant et al., 2025). Contestability in the context of AI agents has both personal and social aspects: the individuals involved should be able to challenge the decisions that directly impact them, and the affected communities should have a way of commenting on the overall trends in agent behaviour that are likely to affect them in general.

The contestability in AI governance needs to be more than the official presence of appeals mechanisms. It states that the challenge processes should be available to the people requiring them, that records of decision making should be in a form that can be meaningfully reviewed and that AI systems should be designed in such a way that they can produce explanations of their decisions that can serve as a basis of appeal. In areas where agent decisions cannot be described in terms which allow a meaningful challenge, governance structures must mandate human oversight of their decisions before they become effective.

Case-level: available avenues for appeal, a record of the decision in a way that a lay reviewer can understand, and the agent's explanations using enough detail to justify an appeal.

Population level: public consultation in the deployment decision, aggregation of outcome statistics published and independent ombuds or oversight bodies with powers to investigate patterns of complaints.

Design-Time: required human input review on any decision category where the agent's outputs can not be expressed in a way that can allow meaningful challenge.

6.3.Reversibility

Reversibility necessitates organisations to continue to operate with the capacity to override, retrain, or withdraw AI agents in reaction to governance failures, or adapting to changing conditions. It is a principle of the unpredictability of AI agent deployment under complex conditions: even the most elaborated and tested agent can lead to unexpected results when exposed to the full diversity of real-life conditions, and governance structures must retain the ability to correct the course. Reversibility is both a technical requirement, systems must be designed to be suspended and to override, and an organisational requirement, organisations must maintain the ability and the operational protocols required to exercise override without being reliant on the agent they are overriding.

The organisational aspect of reversibility is an aspect that is not valued. Organisations, which have highly automated processes using AI agents, may face the reality that their human workforce neither has the expertise nor capacity to run the processes manually in the case of the suspension of agent processes. Maintaining reversibility thus entails working on developing workforce, ensuring that the capacity of manual processes is maintained in parallel with the deployment of automated processes and regular inspection of the override mechanisms to ensure that they remain operable.

Technical mechanisms: user-friendly kill switches, staged rollback procedures, and version reversion with proven recovery time objectives.

Operational mechanisms: Escalation pathways with a human who possesses true authority to take action, tested at a frequency commensurate with deployment risk.

Workforce mechanisms: deliberate maintenance of a capability with the manual process that does not mean the organisation cannot do the underlying process at all when it suspends an agent. *6.4.Proportionality*

The proportionality principle entails that the extent of the chosen governance oversight should be graded to the stakes, ambiguity and novelty of the deployments of AI agents. This principle recognises that governance is not free of charge: excessive oversight is costly, slows down operations, and is even self-accountable by creating the illusion of governance without the reality. Proportionality demands a principled structure of distributing governance resources: human attention, monitoring infrastructure, review processes, etc. to the deployments where the risk of governance failure is greatest and the consequences are most severe.

Proportionality has a static and dynamic aspect. The intensity of governance should be adjusted to the risk profile of each deployment with more risky and novel deployments being subject to more intensive governance. The intensity of governance ought to be varied over time as the records of operations track, risk profiles evolve, and the evidence base supporting effective oversight builds. A deployment that obtains intensive oversight during its initial phases might warrant a decrease in the intensity of oversight as its performance track record builds up--but only in cases where the reduction is not only based on evidence but also motivated by organisational convenience.

Static calibration: tiering of deployments based on stakes and novelty at the time of authorisation, and tiering of the review, documentation and sign-off requirements.

Dynamic calibration: the level of oversight changes over time, and there is documented evidence supporting any decrease in oversight – never because of organisational convenience.

Ensuring a strong focus on observability, contestability and reversibility in the procurement process by making these demands a condition on the procurement contract, rather than a condition of the contract for the vendor to deploy or not.

The governance of agent architectures.

The four principles listed above are applicable to all agent architectures, but the means by which they are realised vary by agent architecture, and mixing architectures is a frequent form of mis-specification of governance. Traditional machine-learning systems (classification, scoring, prediction, but not systems that execute multiple steps autonomously) are governable in a majority of cases by the technical accountability mechanisms already in place in relation to the risk of the model: validation, monitoring and revalidation. The decision boundary is narrow so observability is relatively tractable. The multi-step nature of LLM-based agents is another unique challenge of observability, whereby the chain of reasoning leading to an action may not be an auditable decision point, and the same underlying model can be used in very different deployment scenarios with very different risk profiles, thus reducing static, deployment-time proportionality calibration and increasing reliance on dynamic, outcome-based monitoring. Because embodied agents (robotics, autonomous vehicles, physical infrastructure control) carry reversibility to a physical-safety requirement, rather than a purely informational requirement, an override must interrupt a physical process, often under real time constraints, which is a materially higher bar than reverting a software decision. The systemic risk is the one concern dominating the governance discussion for distributed multi-agent systems, regardless of sector, as the technical and operational parts of governance are structured around the notion of an ownership system, while the outcomes of concern are generated through interactions between agents, of which no single agent has full control (Hughes et al., 2025) It's a distinction that's practically relevant because a programme of governance around model-risk management (which is well suited to the first category) will systematically under-govern the observability, reversibility and systemic-risk issues of the last three.

Institutional Capacity and Regulatory Coordination

The framework of adaptive governance that has been developed in this chapter, consistent with recent multi-level accounts of AI in public administration (Criado et al., 2025), is not self-implementing. Its actualisation is dependent on institutional capacities most deploying organisations currently lack, and on regulatory structures which are still in the process of development in most jurisdictions. This part looks at the institutional requirements of effective AI agent governance and the difficulties of developing regulatory coordination in the complex governance environment that AI agent deployment introduces.

One of the basic institutional capacity conditions of AI agent regulation is regulatory literacy. The managers and oversight personnel in charge of the governance of AI agents must be equipped with an adequate understanding of AI architecture, capabilities and limitations so as to exercise meaningful oversight, not the technical expertise of the kind possessed by the developers of AI agents, but the level of governance understanding sufficient to ask the right questions, interpret monitoring data, and recognise the limit of what the technical accountability mechanisms can provide. Regulatory literacy development needs to be made by investing in training, recruiting technically informed professionals of governance, and creating accessible frameworks to translate technical AI concepts into governance-relevant terms.

Another important, yet frequently neglected, institutional capacity to govern AI agents is procurement systems. The AI agent systems are often purchased by external vendors, and the nature of the purchases is a major factor in determining the governance options available to the deploying organisation. Procurement structures that do not encompass the vendors to provide the documentation, monitoring tools and override capabilities required to achieve effective governance effectively sabotage the adaptive governance framework before it has even been implemented. One of the most leverage-rich interventions that organisations can benefit by in the quest to develop a stronger AI agent governance is the reformation of the procurement frameworks to incorporate the governance requirements, including requirements of observability, contestability, reversibility, and proportionality.

The standards of AI governance are in the initial phase of development. Contrasting established professions, such as medicine, law and accountancy, which have developed sophisticated codes of conduct, licensing, and disciplinary frameworks governing the exercise of delegated authority, the professions most closely involved in the development and deployment of AI agents, software engineering, data science, and machine learning, lack such a comparable professional governance infrastructure. The long-term institutional project that needs to involve professional bodies, employers, regulators and the civil society has the development of professional standards defining the responsibilities of AI practitioners in regards to governance including obligations of documentation, disclosure and challenge, an agenda that recent proposals for legal alignment have begun to formalise(Kolt et al., 2026).

Standards & Policy Mapping

The design principles outlined in this chapter, consistent with emerging regulatory-compliance playbooks, should not be seen as in addition to existing regulatory or standards documents; they could be included in the obligations in the existing documents and are useful for those wishing to map the design principles into an existing compliance programme, as well as for identifying gaps where the design principles are not reflected in the existing compliance programme.

EU Artificial Intelligence Act (Regulation (EU) 2024/1689): Compliance deadline is expected to be phased-in over a period of time, with prohibitions on unacceptable risk practices starting from February 2025, obligations on use of general-purpose AI models from August 2025 and conformity, registration and obligations on human oversight for high risk AI systems from August 2026 as adopted; the precise timeline for high risk compliance is the subject of an active legislative simplification process, which has itself raised transparency concerns (Busuioc et al., 2023) and left open questions of civil liability for high-risk deployments during 2025-26 and should be checked against the current Official Journal text at the time of resubmission.

Requirements for risk management, logging, human supervision, and post-market monitoring of systems in the Regulation are in line with the principles of observability and reversibility expressed in this chapter.

NIST AI Risk Management Framework (AI RMF 1.0, 2023): a voluntary U.S. framework organised into four functions—Govern, Map, Measure and Manage—that align to the technical and operational levels of the planned accountability framework proposed here, namely Measure and Manage, corresponding with observability and reversibility principles respectively in this chapter.

ISO/IEC 42001:2023 – the first international standard for an AI management system, which sets out requirements for leadership commitment, AI policy, risk management, and continual improvement throughout the lifecycle of an AI, including the need for calibration in a proportionate way that's both static and dynamic.

The four-part risk typology in this chapter has been closely linked to ISO/IEC 23894:2023, which provides guidance on risk management specific to AI, building on and extending ISO 31000, with a particular focus on risk identification and treatment through the lifecycle of AI, rather than at a single point in time.

Recommendation of the OECD on Artificial Intelligence (OECD/LEGAL/0449, first published in 2019, amended in 2024): a set of intergovernmental principles which prioritize transparency, accountability and human oversight, applicable mainly at institutional level and to the category of legitimacy risk, in the context of this chapter.

The UNESCO Recommendation on the Ethics of Artificial Intelligence (2021): The first UNESCO global normative instrument on AI ethics, which includes aspects relevant to the contestability and legitimacy aspects of the framework, especially for the public sector, where the use of AI occurs in jurisdictions without binding legislation for AI.

The contribution of the mapping above is to demonstrate that the design principles are not free-standing statements of norms but are already to some extent, and unevenly, embedded in binding and voluntary instruments to which most of the organisations deploying the instrument will have to relate, whether or not they choose to use the four-level accountability architecture and the four-part risk typology developed in this chapter in their work.

Coordinated governance responses across more than one jurisdiction are needed in situations where AI agent deployments cross organisational and sectoral boundaries or where the systemic risks of AI agent interaction require coordinated governance responses across multiple jurisdictions. The present situation in AI regulation is marked by a high degree of fragmentation: various regulatory frameworks are applicable to various sectors and jurisdictions, which creates a complex situation in compliance with the deployment of organisations and gaps in the coverage of systemic risks, the issue to which no single regulator has the power to respond. The institutional development of AI governance places a priority on developing effective coordination mechanisms, whether through regulatory harmonisation, information-sharing arrangements, or joint oversight arrangements.

Regulatory coordination is especially a major issue when it comes to multinational deployments of AI agents, where agents acting across jurisdictions might be subjected to conflicting governance principles or might seek to engage in regulatory arbitrage to escape the most demanding governance frameworks. To deal with this challenge, there is a need of global cooperation between regulators, development of common standards of governance, and mutual recognition and enforcement. Although this is a long-term agenda, in the near-term, this can be achieved by developing shared governance taxonomies, creation of regulatory dialogue forums and creating joint incident reporting mechanisms that would help to build a shared evidence base on the development of governance.

7 FUTURE RESEARCH DIRECTIONS

The governance of autonomous AI agents is an extremely dynamic area, and the frameworks presented in this chapter should be understood as provisional - sufficient to the present state not only of AI capabilities but also of governance knowledge, but likely to need revision as both continue to evolve. This section determines areas of priorities in future research that can enhance the theoretical background and practical application of adaptive AI agent governance.

A major priority is the longitudinal governance research. Most of the available research on AI governance is cross-sectional, which describes the governance arrangements at a particular point in time. The longitudinal research designs that are required to track the governance dynamics over a long period of time will be necessary in understanding how the structure of governance responds to the development of agent capabilities, accountability structures that respond to the emergence of new failure modes, and the development of institutional capacity over time. Through such research, the empirical basis of understanding the circumstances under which adaptive governance will or will not succeed in practice.

Comparative regulatory studies may shed light on the contribution of regulatory traditions, institutional settings, and political systems to the development of AI governance arrangements. Comparisons between jurisdictions with different regulatory frameworks, both early-adopter innovation hubs and more conservative regulatory environments, can identify the governance innovations and failures that cut across situations and those that are specific to particular institutional environments. This comparative knowledge base could be used to inform the creation of more effective governance frameworks and could be used to support regulatory learning across jurisdictions.

Empirical measurement of the effectiveness of governance is a poorly developed field that constrains the evidence base of governance design. Although substantial normative discussion exists regarding what good AI governance should entail, there is a paucity of validated empirical measures of good AI governance that can be subject to comparatively uniform application across different organisational settings. The creation of such measures which should not only be formal but substantively met the goals of governance in terms of accountability, risk management and legitimacy is a methodological challenge in the field.

The relationships between human and AI collaboration in the context of governance should be given a special research status. The nature of the human oversight role varies with the increased capabilities of the AI agents, and with them the organisational and psychological states of affairs required to sustain meaningful human control over consequential AI decision making. Studies on the cognitive dynamics of human-AI interaction, the organisational conditions that can support or hinder the real oversight, and the professional development requirements of the governance practitioners working alongside the AI agents is vital in translating the adaptive governance framework into practice.

Last of all, interdisciplinary co-operation among computer science, organisational theory, public law, and policy studies is needed to mitigate the fragmentation of AI governance research across disciplinary silos. Technical research in AI systems can tend to move forward without sufficient interaction with governance theory, and governance research can often lack the technical grounding to interact with AI architectures and capabilities. The interdisciplinary research communities required to fill this gap is a long-term investment in the institutional infrastructure of AI governance knowledge.

8 CONCLUSION

The chapter has argued that the governance of autonomous AI agents raise qualitatively different challenges than those presented by previous generations of decision-support and automation technologies-challenges that require adaptive governance models as opposed to compliance-oriented models that are suited to work with fixed, rule-based systems. Based on the principal-agent theory, institutional theory, and sociotechnical systems research, it has formulated an integrative theoretical account of the governance problem, a multi-level accountability framework, a risk typology that differentiates between the execution, alignment, systemic, and legitimacy risks, and a set of design principles that it calls observability, contestability, reversibility, and proportionality, which are relevant to adaptive governance architecture.

The empirical examples of these governance issues in the context of public administration, financial services and infrastructure management have shown that these governance issues have particular forms in different organisational contexts but share a common structure: the mismatch between the institutional structures of human organisations and the behavioural features of AI agents in their place. To deal with this misalignment, it is necessary not only to have technical protection in place but also to redesign organisations, develop institutional capacity, reform the regulatory framework, and cultivate new professional standards of AI governance practice.

The need to tackle this governance agenda cannot be overemphasized. The deployment of AI agents are rapidly expanding across the sectors, and the governance structures required to ensure this expansion does not undermine the institutional values are still in their formative stages. The divergence between the rate of AI agent deployment and the rate of governance innovation present real risks of the failure of accountability, legitimacy crisis, and systemic harms that will become more and more difficult to address in retrospect. Establishing adaptation governance capacity before, not in reaction to, governance failures is more effective and consistent with the role of institutions that hold significant authority over lives of citizens and stability of social systems.

The framework below is provided not as a final solution but as one of the contributions to the further evolution of the governance thought which is sufficient to the unique problems of the application of AI agents. The ultimate value of it will be put to the test in the practice of organisations that would seek to govern AI agents responsibly, and in the research that would evaluate and refine the governance approaches in the light of operational experience. Managing intelligent agents is, in its turn, again an adaptive business.

REFERENCES

Abdulnafea, A. L., Almasria, N. A., & Alawaqleh, Q. (2022). The effect of working capital management and credit management policy on Jordanian banks' financial performance. *Banks and Bank Systems*, *16*(4), 229–239. DOI: 10.21511/bbs.16(4).2021.19

Acharya, D. B., Kuppan, K., & Divya, B. (2025). Agentic AI: Autonomous intelligence for complex goals—A comprehensive survey. *IEEE Access : Practical Innovations, Open Solutions*, *13*, 18912–18936. DOI: 10.1109/ACCESS.2025.3532853

Ada Lovelace, I., Institute, A. I. N., & Open Government, P. (2021). Algorithmic Accountability for the Public Sector: Learning from the First Wave of Policy Implementation.

Adabara, I., Olaniyi Sadiq, B., Nuhu Shuaibu, A., Ibrahim Danjuma, Y., & Maninti, V. (2025). Trustworthy agentic AI systems: A cross-layer review of architectures, threat models, and governance strategies for real-world deployment. *F1000 Research*, *14*, 905. DOI: 10.12688/f1000research.169927.1

Aldboush, H. H., Almasria, N. A., & Ferdous, M. (2023). Determinants of firm profitability: Empirical evidence from Jordan's service sector. *Business: Theory and Practice*, *24*(2), 438–446. DOI: 10.3846/btp.2023.18623

Alduais, F., Almasria, N. A., & Airout, R. (2022). The Moderating Effect of Corporate Governance on Corporate Social Responsibility and Information Asymmetry: An Empirical Study of Chinese Listed Companies. *Economies*, *10*(11), 280. DOI: 10.3390/economies10110280

Alduais, F., Alsawalhah, J., & Almasria, N. A. (2023). Examining the impact of corporate governance on investors and investee companies: Evidence from Yemen. *Economies*, *11*(1), 13. DOI: 10.3390/economies11010013

Almasria, N. (2022). Determinant Governance Mechanisms Affecting the Quality of Auditing: the External Auditors' Perceptions. Available at *SSRN* 4223799. DOI: 10.2139/ssrn.4223799

Almasria, N. A., Aldboush, H. H., Al-Kasasbeh, O., Lutfi, A., Alhajahmad, F. B., Al Barrak, T., & Alsheikh, G. (2024). Oil Price Volatility and Economic Growth: Evidence from the Middle East. *International Journal of Energy Economics and Policy*, *14*(3), 417–421. DOI: 10.32479/ijeep.15484

Almasria, N. A., Alhatabat, Z., Ershaid, D., & Almaqtari, F. A. A bibliometric analysis. Int. J. Innov. Res. Sci. Stud. 2025, 8, 435–455. https://ij irss.com/index .php/ijirss/article/view/6546/1264

Alnsour, J., Arabeyyat, A. R., Alnsour, A. J., & Almasria, N. A. (2024). The Impact of Financial Development, Foreign Direct Investment, and Trade Openness on Carbon Dioxide Emissions in Jordan: An ARDL and VECM Analysis Approach. *Journal of Risk and Financial Management*, *17*(11), 490. DOI: 10.3390/jrfm17110490

Araral, E. (2026). Agency Theory in Public Administration: A Comparative Study of the US, China, and EU. Elements in Public and Nonprofit Administration.

Busuioc, M. (2021). Accountable artificial intelligence: Holding algorithms to account. *Public Administration Review*, *81*(5), 825–836. DOI: 10.1111/puar.13293 PMID: 34690372

Busuioc, M., Curtin, D., & Almada, M. (2023). Reclaiming transparency: Contesting the logics of secrecy within the AI Act. *European Law Open*, *2*(1), 79–105. DOI: 10.1017/elo.2022.47

Chaffer, T. J., Goins, C. v., II, Okusanya, B., Cotlage, D., & Goldston, J. (2024). Decentralized governance of autonomous AI agents. arXiv preprint arXiv:2412.17114.

Cobbe, J., Lee, M. S. A., & Singh, J. (2021, March). Reviewable automated decision-making: A framework for accountable algorithmic systems. In *Proceedings of the 2021 ACM conference on fairness, accountability, and transparency* (pp. 598-609). DOI: 10.1145/3442188.3445921

Costanza-Chock, S., Raji, I. D., & Buolamwini, J. (2022, June). Who Audits the Auditors? Recommendations from a field scan of the algorithmic auditing ecosystem. In *Proceedings of the 2022 ACM conference on fairness, accountability, and transparency* (pp. 1571-1583). DOI: 10.1145/3531146.3533213

Criado, J. I., Sandoval-Almazán, R., & Gil-Garcia, J. R. (2025). Artificial intelligence and public administration: Understanding actors, governance, and policy from micro, meso, and macro perspectives. *Public Policy and Administration*, *40*(2), 173–184. DOI: 10.1177/09520767241272921

Daza-Ramirez, M. T. (2025). A Virtue-focused Sociotechnical Framework for Fairness in Artificial Intelligence. Available at *SSRN* 6525059.

Dibia, V. (2025). *Designing Multi-Agent Systems: Principles, Patterns and Implementation for AI Agents*. Victor Dibia.

Du, C., Wang, C., & Yang, Y. (2024). Incentive contract design for governmental forest ecological benefit compensation under information asymmetry. *Forests, 15*(12), 2145. DOI: 10.3390/f15122145

Fawaz, A., Mougharbel, I., Al-Haddad, K., & Kanaan, H. Y. (2025). Energy routing protocols for Energy Internet: A review on multi-agent systems, metaheuristics, and Artificial Intelligence approaches. *IEEE Access : Practical Innovations, Open Solutions, 13*, 41625–41643. DOI: 10.1109/ACCESS.2025.3546620

Gauld, R. (2023). Principal-agent theory of organizations. In *Global encyclopedia of public administration, public policy, and governance* (pp. 10081–10085). Springer.

Grant, D. G., Behrends, J., & Basl, J. (2025). What we owe to decision-subjects: Beyond transparency and explanation in automated decision-making. *Philosophical Studies, 182*(1), 55–85. DOI: 10.1007/s11098-023-02013-6

Guggenberger, T., Lämmermann, L., Urbach, N., Walter, A. M., & Hofmann, P. (2023). Task delegation from AI to humans: A principal-agent perspective.

Hammond, L., Chan, A., Clifton, J., Hoelscher-Obermaier, J., Khan, A., McLean, E., Smith, C., Barfuss, W., Foerster, J., & Gavenčiak, T. (2025). Multi-Agent Risks from Advanced AI. arXiv preprint arXiv:2502.14143.

Herzog, L. (2023). *Citizen knowledge: Markets, experts, and the infrastructure of democracy*. Oxford University Press. DOI: 10.1093/oso/9780197681718.001.0001

Hughes, L., Dwivedi, Y. K., Malik, T., Shawosh, M., Albashrawi, M. A., Jeon, I., Dutot, V., Appanderanda, M., Crick, T., De', R., Fenwick, M., Gunaratnege, S. M., Jurcys, P., Kar, A. K., Kshetri, N., Li, K., Mutasa, S., Samothrakis, S., Wade, M., & Walton, P. (2025). AI agents and agentic systems: A multi-expert analysis. *Journal of Computer Information Systems, 65*(4), 489–517. DOI: 10.1080/08874417.2025.2483832

Ibrahim, A., Almasria, N. A., Almaqtari, F. A., Al-Kasasbeh, O., Alhatabatb, Z., & Ershaid, D. (2024). The Impact of Green Finance, FinTech and Digital Economy on Environmental Sustainability: Evidence from Advanced Panel Techniques. *International Journal of Energy Economics and Policy, 14*(6), 621–627. DOI: 10.32479/ijeep.17180

Janakiraman, A. (2025). Governance and Accountability Frameworks for AI Agents. Synergia: A Journal of Multidisciplinary Innovation, 7(7).

Kapoor, S., Stroebl, B., Siegel, Z. S., Nadgir, N., & Narayanan, A. (2024). Ai agents that matter. arXiv preprint arXiv:2407.01502.

Keningson, J. (2024). Mathematical foundation of high-dimensional data analysis: Leveraging topology and geometry for enhanced model interpretability in ai. International Journal of scientific research and management, 12(11), 546-557.

Kjørstad, M. (2025). The norm-setting dynamics of institutions and artificial intelligence: Quality of care and efficiency in social work. *European Social Work Research*, *3*(2), 135–147. DOI: 10.1332/27551768Y2025D000000041

Kolt, N. (2025). Governing AI agents. arXiv preprint arXiv:2501.07913.

Kolt, N., Caputo, N., Boeglin, J., O'Keefe, C., Bommasani, R., Casper, S., Cuéllar, M.-F., Feldman, N., Gabriel, I., & Hadfield, G. K. (2026). Legal Alignment for Safe and Ethical AI. arXiv preprint arXiv:2601.04175. DOI: 10.2139/ssrn.6036657

Kumar, S. N. P.Sanjay Nakharu Prasad Kumar. (2025). Regulating autonomous AI agents: Prospects, hazards, and policy structures. *Journal of Computer Science and Technology Studies*, *7*(10), 393–399. DOI: 10.32996/jcsts.2025.7.10.41

Le Guillou, M., Prévot, L., & Berberian, B. (2023). Bringing together ergonomic concepts and cognitive mechanisms for human—AI agents cooperation. *International Journal of Human-Computer Interaction*, *39*(9), 1827–1840. DOI: 10.1080/10447318.2022.2129741

Lior, A. (2020). AI Entities as AI Agents: Artificial Intelligence Liability and the AI Respondeat Superior Analogy. *Mitchell Hamline Law Review*.

Liu, T. (2024). Research on Legal Responsibility Attribution for Autonomous Systems: An AI Governance Perspective. *Science of Law Journal*, *3*(7), 166–174.

Mandava, S. (2022). Toward Intelligent Agents with Learned World Models for Real-World Decision-Making. Available at *SSRN* 5551718.

Masadeh, A. A., Saadat, M., Almasria, N. A., Jrairah, T. S., & Alsawalhah, J. M. (2021). INVESTIGATING THE ROLE OF APPLYING THE QUALITY COST APPROACH IN THE MANUFACTURING SYSTEM IN THE PUBLIC SHAREHOLDING MANUFACTURING COMPANY IN JORDAN. *Academy of Accounting and Financial Studies Journal*, *25*(5), 1–14.

Meyer, C. O., Van Osch, T., & Reykers, Y. (2024). From EU battlegroups to Rapid Deployment Capacity: Learning the right lessons? *International Affairs*, *100*(1), 181–201. DOI: 10.1093/ia/iiad247

Popoola, S. (2025). Ethical and Regulatory Challenges of AI-Driven Decision-Making in Financial Services.

Qin, X., Luan, S., See, J., Yang, C., & Li, Z. (2026). Governed Capability Evolution for Embodied Agents: Safe Upgrade, Compatibility Checking, and Runtime Rollback for Embodied Capability Modules. arXiv preprint arXiv:2604.08059.

Radanliev, P. (2026). Transparent by Design: Ensuring Safety in Agentic AI Through Decision Traceability. In Ethical AI and Data Science (pp. 1-20). Auerbach Publications.

Rajagopal, N. K., Qureshi, N. I., Durga, S., Ramirez Asis, E. H., Huerta Soto, R. M., Gupta, S. K., & Deepak, S. (2022). Future of business culture: An artificial intelligence-driven digital framework for organization decision-making process. *Complexity*, *2022*(1), 7796507. DOI: 10.1155/2022/7796507

Raji, I. D., Smart, A., White, R. N., Mitchell, M., Gebru, T., Hutchinson, B., Smith-Loud, J., Theron, D., & Barnes, P. (2020). Closing the AI Accountability Gap: Defining an End-to-End Framework for Internal Algorithmic Auditing. Proceedings of the 2020 Conference on Fairness, Accountability, and Transparency (FAT* '20).

Salah, M., Alnoor, A., Abdelfattah, F., & Al Halbusi, H. (2025). Agentic artificial intelligence in public administration: Foundations, applications, and governance. Applications, and Governance (May 10, 2025).

Sawicki, J. (2025). The Role of Decision-Making Algorithms in Public Administration–Legal and Ethical Challenges. *Zeszyt Prawniczy UAM*, (15), 99–111. DOI: 10.14746/zpuam.2025.15.8

Securities, & Exchange, C. (2013). In the Matter of Knight Capital Americas LLC, Securities Exchange Act Release No. 70694, Administrative Proceeding File No. 3-15570.

Singh, S., Kumar, A., Jha, A., Jacob, N., & Mondal, M. S. (2025). AI Alignment: Ensuring AI objectives match human values. *Int. J. Sci. Res. Eng. Manag*, *9*(04), 1–9. DOI: 10.55041/IJSREM46662

Soori, M., Dastres, R., Arezoo, B., & Jough, F. K. G. (2024). Intelligent robotic systems in Industry 4.0: A review. *Journal of Advanced Manufacturing Science and Technology*, *4*(3), 2024007. DOI: 10.51393/j.jamst.2024007

Tangi, L., Müller, A. P. R., & Janssen, M. (2025). AI-augmented government transformation: Organisational transformation and the sociotechnical implications of artificial intelligence in public administrations. *Government Information Quarterly*, *42*(3), 102055. DOI: 10.1016/j.giq.2025.102055

Taye, M. M. (2023). Understanding of machine learning with deep learning: Architectures, workflow, applications and future directions. *Computers, 12*(5), 91. DOI: 10.3390/computers12050091

van de Merwe, K. (2024). Agent transparency and human performance in supervisory control.

Weidinger, L., Uesato, J., Rauh, M., Griffin, C., Huang, P.-S., Mellor, J., Glaese, A., Cheng, M., Balle, B., & Kasirzadeh, A. (2022). Taxonomy of Risks Posed by Language Models. *2022 ACM Conference on Fairness, Accountability, and Transparency (FAccT '22)*. DOI: 10.1145/3531146.3533088

Welsch, A. (2026). *The HUMAN Agentic AI Edge: Shape the Next Generation of AI-Ready Teams*. Andreas Welsch.

Wieringa, M. (2020, January). What to account for when accounting for algorithms: a systematic literature review on algorithmic accountability. In *Proceedings of the 2020 conference on fairness, accountability, and transparency* (pp. 1-18). DOI: 10.1145/3351095.3372833

KEY TERMS AND DEFINITIONS

Accountability: The obligation of an actor, human or institutional, to explain and justify conduct to a forum with standing to ask questions and impose consequences (Novelli et al., 2024).

Agentic system: The broader computational and organisational architecture within which one or more AI agents operate with delegated execution authority, as distinct from decision-support tools that only recommend action for a human to take.

Autonomous AI agent: A software system that perceives its environment, sets or decomposes subgoals, selects and executes multi-step actions, and adapts its behaviour in response to feedback with limited step-by-step human instruction

Autonomy: The degree to which an agent selects and executes actions without step-by-step human authorisation; a matter of degree rather than a binary property.

Delegated authority: The formal or informal transfer of decision-making discretion from a principal to an agent, human or artificial, to act on the principal's behalf within a defined or assumed scope (Gauld, 2023).

Multi-agent system: An architecture in which multiple AI agents interact, coordinate, or compete within a shared environment, such that system-level outcomes emerge from the interaction of agents rather than from any single agent's design (Dibia, 2025).

Responsibility: The normative attribution of causal or moral involvement in an outcome. This chapter treats responsibility as an attribute that can only be borne by the humans and institutions that design, deploy, and supervise an AI agent, not by the agent itself.

APPENDIX: CLAIMS–EVIDENCE TABLE

The table below maps the chapter's principal empirical and regulatory claims to their supporting sources, consistent with the reviewer's request for a mechanism ensuring that major claims are traceable to precise, verifiable citations.

Table 2.

Claim	Supporting Evidence / Source
A welfare-eligibility algorithm produced mass wrongful fraud findings and disproportionately harmed marginalised families.	Autoriteit Persoonsgegevens (2020); Peeters & Widlak (2023)
Automated trading system failures can generate catastrophic, firm-level losses within minutes.	U.S. Securities and Exchange Commission (2013), Exchange Act Release No. 70694
Coordinated behaviour of many correctly functioning agents can still destabilise market infrastructure.	Commodity Futures Trading Commission & Securities and Exchange Commission (2010), Findings Regarding the Market Events of May 6, 2010
Systematic, sector-wide evidence on AI-driven critical-infrastructure incidents remains sparse relative to other sectors.	Agarwal & Nene (2024); Rodrigues et al. (2023)
High-risk AI systems in the EU face binding conformity, registration, and human-oversight obligations.	Regulation (EU) 2024/1689 (EU AI Act)
Voluntary but influential U.S. and international risk-management guidance now exists for AI systems specifically.	National Institute of Standards and Technology (2023); ISO/IEC 23894:2023; ISO/IEC 42001:2023

Chapter 5
Governing AI Agents in Banking:
A Multi-Level Strategic Framework for Responsible Digital Transformation in Financial Ecosystems

M. Jomon Jose
http://orcid.org/0009-0003-4341-9936
Sahrdaya Institute of Management Studies, India

Jyothis Rachel Mathews
http://orcid.org/0009-0003-8279-6080
Ahalia School of Management, India

ABSTRACT

The emergence of agentic artificial intelligence (AI)—encompassing systems capable of autonomous perception, reasoning, planning, and goal-directed action—is fundamentally reshaping the operational landscape of contemporary banking. From fraud detection and credit assessment to compliance automation and customer engagement, agentic systems are transitioning from peripheral tools to core institutional actors. Yet this shift does not come without significant governance complexity. Banks deploying autonomous AI agents must contend with algorithmic bias, limited decision explainability, diffuse accountability in multi-step workflows, data privacy risks, and broader systemic vulnerabilities that existing governance frameworks were simply not designed to address.This chapter maps the evolution and functional roles of agentic AI in banking and proposes a multi-level strategic

DOI: 10.4018/979-8-3373-9594-4.ch005

governance framework responsive to these challenges. The framework is organized across four interdependent layers: strategic, operational, risk and compliance, and human-organizational.

INTRODUCTION

Artificial intelligence has undergone a profound metamorphosis over the past three decades. What began as rule-based expert systems—deterministic, brittle, and tightly constrained by predefined logic—has progressively given way to machine learning and deep learning architectures capable of pattern recognition, inference, and generalization at scale. This evolution reflects not merely incremental improvement but a fundamental change in how intelligent systems interact with the world. Early AI was, by design, a tool that supported human decisions. Today's systems increasingly make those decisions themselves, and in some contexts, execute them autonomously (Russell & Norvig, 2021).

At the frontier of this transformation stands agentic AI: a class of intelligent systems that perceive their environment, reason about potential courses of action, formulate multi-step plans, and execute those plans with varying degrees of independence from human control. The distinction from conventional AI is not merely technical—it is organizational and ethical. Where earlier systems generated recommendations, agents generate actions. Where earlier models processed queries, agents engage in ongoing, adaptive workflows that interact with other systems, tools, and data sources in real time (Rizinski et al., 2025; Elgendy et al., 2025).

No sector has embraced AI adoption more enthusiastically, or with greater consequence, than banking. The data-intensive, compliance-sensitive, and high-stakes nature of financial services has made it a natural proving ground for successive generations of AI capability. Credit scoring, fraud detection, algorithmic trading, and customer segmentation have each been transformed by machine learning. Now, agentic AI is poised to extend this transformation into real-time decision-making, autonomous regulatory reporting, hyper-personalized advisory services, and end-to-end process orchestration across complex institutional workflows (Vuković et al., 2025; Deloitte, 2026).

The governance implications of this shift are substantial. Traditional oversight frameworks—designed around human decision-makers or static, auditable models—struggle to accommodate the distributed, adaptive, and often opaque character of agentic systems. When an AI agent autonomously approves a loan, flags a transaction, or restructures a compliance workflow, the question of who is responsible for the outcome becomes genuinely difficult to answer. Accountability, transparency, and explainability—values central to both ethical governance and regulatory compliance—are all complicated by the very autonomy that makes these systems powerful (Kurshan, 2025; FinRegLab, 2025).

Data governance presents parallel challenges. Agentic systems consume, synthesize, and act upon vast volumes of sensitive customer and transactional information. Their ability to operate across multiple platforms, maintain persistent memory, and engage in behavioral profiling creates privacy risks that neither legacy data governance frameworks nor current regulatory instruments fully address. The EU AI Act, with its risk-based classification and strict requirements for high-risk applications such as credit assessment, represents an important step forward—but regulatory coverage remains incomplete and often jurisdictionally fragmented (FinRegLab, 2025; World Economic Forum, 2025).

This chapter responds to these challenges by developing a multi-level strategic governance framework for responsible AI agent deployment in banking. The chapter is structured to: (a) examine the evolution and functional typology of AI agents in banking contexts; (b) diagnose the principal governance challenges their deployment generates; and (c) propose an integrative framework that links strategic, operational, risk-management, and human dimensions of governance in a coherent and actionable model. In doing so, it draws upon institutional theory, digital maturity models, risk governance theory, responsible AI principles, and human–AI collaboration scholarship—disciplines that, taken together, illuminate the socio-technical complexity that purely technical or purely regulatory approaches tend to obscure.

The significance of this contribution is simultaneously theoretical and practical. Theoretically, it advances the conceptualization of AI agents as socio-technical entities embedded within institutional environments, rather than as isolated technological artefacts. Practically, it equips policymakers, regulators, and banking leaders with a structured framework for navigating the governance demands of an increasingly autonomous financial system—one in which the risks of acting too slowly may be as consequential as the risks of acting without adequate safeguards.

2. CONCEPTUAL FOUNDATIONS OF AI AGENTS IN BANKING

2.1 Defining AI Agents and Their Distinguishing Characteristics

An AI agent, at its most foundational level, is a system that perceives information from its environment, processes that information through computational models capable of reasoning and planning, and acts upon the environment to achieve specified objectives—often without continuous human direction (Russell & Norvig, 2021). This action-orientation is what separates AI agents from conventional AI systems, which are primarily designed to produce insights, predictions, or recommendations that humans then act upon. Agents do not wait to be prompted; they initiate.

Three properties are constitutive of agentic AI systems. The first is autonomy: the capacity to initiate, monitor, and adjust behavior without requiring step-by-step human input. In banking, where operational speed and scalability are critical, this independence allows agents to function continuously across complex workflows (Wooldridge, 2020; Oracle, 2025). The second property is adaptability—the ability to recalibrate decision logic in response to environmental changes. Financial markets, regulatory requirements, and customer behaviors are inherently dynamic; agents that can adjust their parameters accordingly are far more organizationally valuable than static models (Finastra, 2026). The third property is learning capability, typically facilitated through machine learning, reinforcement learning, or large language model (LLM)-based reasoning. Learning enables agents to improve performance over time by incorporating feedback from their own actions and the outcomes those actions produce (Rizinski et al., 2025).

Together, these properties constitute a qualitative departure from prior AI paradigms. They also, as subsequent sections will demonstrate, constitute the primary source of the governance challenges introduced by agentic deployment.

2.2 A Typology of AI Agents in Financial Services

Agentic systems deployed in banking occupy a spectrum of autonomy and sophistication. A practical taxonomy distinguishes three broad categories, each carrying distinct operational implications and governance demands.

Assistive Agents.

At the more limited end of the spectrum, assistive agents function as intelligent support tools that enhance human decision-making rather than supplanting it. They surface relevant information, flag patterns for human review, and generate recommendations. Customer service chatbots, transaction monitoring dashboards, and internal decision-support systems typically fall into this category. Human oversight remains primary; the agent's role is augmentative (Kore.ai, 2026).

Advisory Agents.

Advisory agents possess considerably greater analytical depth, integrating predictive modeling, generative AI, and contextual reasoning to deliver strategic recommendations. Wealth management robo-advisors that synthesize customer profiles with market intelligence to suggest tailored investment strategies are the paradigmatic example. The advice these agents generate is often sophisticated and personalized, but the exercise of final judgment remains a human prerogative (Elgendy et al., 2025).

Autonomous (Agentic) Agents.

Autonomous agents represent the most consequential category. These systems make and execute decisions—including multi-step, cross-system workflows—with minimal or no direct human involvement. In banking, they appear in algorithmic trading, real-time fraud prevention, automated loan underwriting, compliance monitoring, and orchestrated process management. Their capacity for independent action at scale delivers profound efficiency gains while simultaneously creating accountability structures that existing governance instruments were not designed to address (FinRegLab, 2025; Accenture, 2026; Deloitte, 2026).

2.3 Functional Roles Across Core Banking Operations

The deployment of AI agents has extended across virtually every major banking function, transforming both the nature and the pace of financial decision-making.

In risk assessment, agents analyze large, heterogeneous datasets—structured transaction records, behavioral signals, alternative data, and macroeconomic indicators—to generate dynamic creditworthiness profiles that are more granular and more rapidly updated than any human process could sustain (Rizinski et al., 2025). In fraud detection, agents monitor transaction streams in real time, applying pattern recognition and behavioral analytics to identify anomalies and trigger preventive responses; crucially, their capacity to learn from new fraud typologies incrementally improves detection accuracy while reducing false positives (Kore.ai, 2026; Finastra, 2026). In customer interaction, AI-powered virtual assistants deliver personalized, continuous support across channels, executing transactions, negotiating product offerings, and functioning as always-available relationship managers (Oracle, 2025; Accenture, 2026). In regulatory compliance—a domain of particular institutional sensitivity—agents automate the tracking of regulatory changes, flag compliance-relevant transactions, generate audit-ready reports, and dynamically adapt operational workflows to evolving legal requirements (FinRegLab, 2025; Deloitte, 2026).

2.4 AI Agents as Socio-Technical Systems

A critical conceptual move in this chapter is the insistence that AI agents be understood not as discrete technological artefacts but as socio-technical systems—

entities whose effects are shaped by, and in turn reshape, the human, organizational, and institutional environments in which they are embedded (Bostrom & Heinen, 1977). This framing has direct governance implications.

Agents in banking do not operate in isolation. They interact with employees, customers, regulatory bodies, other digital systems, and external third-party platforms—forming dense networks of interdependence whose governance cannot be reduced to technical specification. Their deployment alters organizational workflows and job structures (shifting loan officers toward exception handling and oversight rather than routine processing), reconfigures accountability relationships, and shapes customer trust in ways that reverberate well beyond the technical system itself (Aldasoro et al., 2025; Mayer Brown, 2026).

Treating agents as socio-technical systems demands an equally comprehensive governance approach: one that aligns technical architecture with organizational culture, human capital strategy, regulatory compliance, and institutional ethics. This is the animating premise of the framework developed in Section 5.

2.5 AI Agents Distinguished from Traditional AI Systems

The conceptual distinction between AI agents and conventional AI systems is worth making explicit, since governance requirements differ substantially across the two categories. Traditional AI systems are primarily analytical: they produce outputs—scores, classifications, predictions—that inform human decisions. Their operation is essentially reactive and circumscribed; they do not initiate action, adapt autonomously, or engage in multi-step reasoning chains.

AI agents, by contrast, integrate perception, reasoning, planning, and action execution into a continuous operational cycle. They adapt to environmental feedback, orchestrate multi-step workflows across disparate systems, and can interact with other agents in architecturally complex arrangements. The governance implications follow accordingly: where traditional systems require audit mechanisms for model outputs, agents require audit mechanisms for the entire reasoning and action chain—including tool invocations, memory updates, and cross-system interactions (Wooldridge, 2020; Accenture, 2026; Finastra, 2026). This distinction motivates the novel governance architecture proposed in this chapter.

3. THEORETICAL UNDERPINNINGS

Governing agentic AI in banking is inherently a multidisciplinary challenge. Technical approaches alone cannot resolve questions of accountability, fairness, or institutional legitimacy; regulatory frameworks alone cannot anticipate the emergent behaviors of adaptive systems; organizational theories alone cannot specify the technical safeguards required to manage autonomous decision-making. The framework proposed in this chapter therefore draws upon five complementary theoretical traditions, each of which illuminates a distinct dimension of the governance challenge.

3.1 Institutional Theory

Institutional theory offers a powerful lens for understanding why and how organizations adopt new technologies within the constraints of their regulatory, normative, and social environments. DiMaggio and Powell's (1983) account of isomorphic pressures—coercive, normative, and mimetic—explains much of the pattern of AI adoption in banking. Coercive pressures arise from regulatory mandates: the EU AI Act's risk-based classification of credit assessment and related applications, for example, imposes specific transparency and human oversight requirements that banks have no discretion to ignore. Normative pressures flow from professional standards, industry codes, and ethical guidelines promulgated by bodies such as the OECD and the Financial Stability Board. Mimetic pressures emerge when institutions, uncertain about how to proceed, emulate the practices of recognized leaders (Vuković et al., 2025; Engvall, 2024; Toms et al., 2023).

What institutional theory contributes to AI governance, specifically, is the insight that legitimacy—not merely efficiency—drives technology adoption in regulated industries. A bank that deploys an AI agent that produces commercially optimal outcomes but operates without adequate transparency or human oversight risks losing the institutional legitimacy essential to its social license to operate (Scott, 2014; Yuniawan, 2025). This observation reinforces the centrality of governance alignment with external institutional expectations, not merely internal performance criteria.

3.2 Digital and Agentic Maturity Models

Digital maturity models provide a structured framework for assessing organizational preparedness to adopt and scale advanced technologies. In their classic formulation, these models conceptualize digital transformation as a staged progression—from basic digitization through functional integration to enterprise-level transformation—mediated by an organization's technological infrastructure, data capabilities, cultural readiness, and leadership orientation (Westerman et al., 2014).

The emergence of agentic AI has prompted important extensions to this framework. Beyond general digital capabilities, agentic AI maturity now encompasses agent orchestration capacity, real-time data architecture, governance readiness for autonomous systems, and the organizational structures required to manage multi-agent workflows responsibly (Blueprism, 2025). For this chapter, maturity is not treated as a terminal state to be achieved but as a dynamic trajectory—one that shapes both the pace and the character of responsible AI adoption. Organizations at different maturity stages face qualitatively different governance challenges, which the framework in Section 5 is designed to address proportionately (EY, 2025).

3.3 Risk Governance Theory

Risk governance theory, as articulated by Renn (2008), addresses how complex, uncertain risks are identified, assessed, managed, and communicated within institutional settings. It is particularly apt for agentic AI governance because the risks associated with autonomous systems are neither static nor fully anticipated at deployment. Agent behaviors can evolve through learning; multi-agent interactions can generate emergent dynamics not present in any individual component; and systemic risks can accumulate across institutions relying on similar foundational models or behavioral strategies (FinRegLab, 2025; Kurshan, 2025).

Several risk dimensions are specific to agentic systems and require dedicated governance attention: model drift (where agents' behavior diverges from intended parameters over time), goal misalignment (where agents pursue proxies that deviate from intended objectives), prompt injection (where adversarial inputs manipulate agent behavior), third-party dependencies (where risks propagate through agent integrations with external services), and herding effects (where correlated agent actions across institutions amplify systemic vulnerabilities) (Aldasoro et al., 2025; ESRB, 2025). Risk governance theory's emphasis on continuous monitoring, adaptive controls, and proactive stakeholder engagement is directly reflected in the risk and compliance layer of the framework proposed below.

3.4 Responsible AI Principles

The responsible AI literature has coalesced around a core set of normative principles—fairness, accountability, transparency, explainability, privacy, reliability, and societal alignment—that together constitute the ethical architecture for trustworthy AI deployment (Floridi et al., 2018; Jobin et al., 2019). In the banking context, these principles are not merely aspirational; they are increasingly codified in regulatory requirements. The EU AI Act imposes specific obligations on high-risk AI applications including conformity assessments, human oversight mechanisms, and ongoing logging; the NIST AI Risk Management Framework provides voluntary but widely adopted guidance for responsible system development and deployment (EY, 2025; OECD, 2024).

The contribution of responsible AI scholarship to this chapter's framework is primarily normative: it specifies the substantive values that governance mechanisms must protect and operationalize, not merely the procedural structures through which governance is organized. Fairness demands that agentic decisions be monitored and audited for discriminatory effects. Accountability demands that responsibility for agent actions be clearly allocated across the institutional chain. Transparency demands that decision processes be explainable to both regulators and affected customers. These demands translate directly into the governance mechanisms described in Section 5 (PwC, 2025; FS-ISAC, 2024).

3.5 Human–AI Collaboration Theory

The fifth theoretical strand addresses how human actors and AI systems can most effectively work together—and why this question is central to responsible governance. Human–AI collaboration theory, as developed by Jarrahi (2018) and elaborated in subsequent organizational research, rejects the binary framing of AI as either a replacement for human workers or a mere tool under complete human control. Instead, it articulates a model of complementarity, in which the distinctive strengths of human cognition (contextual judgment, ethical reasoning, creative synthesis, empathetic interpretation) and AI capability (speed, scale, consistency, data processing) are combined in organizational designs that leverage each appropriately.

In banking, this translates into governance questions about the allocation of decision authority between agents and humans—what is often discussed in terms of human-in-the-loop versus human-on-the-loop configurations—and the conditions under which human oversight remains effective rather than nominal. Research on automation bias, skill atrophy, and trust calibration suggests that these are not trivial design problems; excessive automation without adequate human engagement can erode exactly the human judgment that governance frameworks are meant to preserve (Raisch & Krakowski, 2021). The human and organizational layer of the proposed framework directly addresses these dynamics.

3.6 Theoretical Synthesis

These five theoretical perspectives are not simply additive; they are mutually reinforcing and jointly exhaustive of the governance challenge. Institutional theory explains the external pressures that shape AI adoption and the legitimacy imperatives that governance must address. Digital and agentic maturity models calibrate the governance framework to organizational capability. Risk governance theory provides the analytical structure for identifying and managing the novel hazards of autonomous systems. Responsible AI principles supply the normative content that governance mechanisms must embed. And human–AI collaboration theory ensures that governance design remains attentive to the human dimensions of agentic deployment. Together, they provide the theoretical scaffolding for the multi-level strategic governance framework developed in Section 5.

4. GOVERNANCE CHALLENGES IN AI AGENT DEPLOYMENT

The rapid deployment of AI agents in the banking sector has introduced a range of governance challenges that extend beyond technical performance to encompass ethical, regulatory, and organizational dimensions. As AI agents become more autonomous—capable of planning, reasoning, tool invocation, and executing multi-step actions—their deep embedding in financial decision-making processes renders traditional governance mechanisms increasingly inadequate. This section critically examines the key governance challenges associated with AI agent deployment in banking.

4.1 Algorithmic Bias and Discrimination Risks

One of the most significant challenges in AI agent deployment is the risk of algorithmic bias, which can lead to discriminatory outcomes. AI agents, trained on historical data, may reflect and amplify existing social, economic, or demographic inequalities present in legacy datasets. In banking, this is particularly concerning in high-stakes areas such as credit scoring, loan approvals, underwriting, and risk assessment, where biased decisions can disproportionately affect protected groups (e.g., based on gender, race, or socioeconomic status) and violate fair lending principles (GAO, 2025).

For instance, models trained on past lending data may replicate historical discriminatory patterns, resulting in unfair denial rates or higher pricing for certain demographics. Agentic systems exacerbate this risk because their autonomous actions and adaptive learning can propagate bias at scale across dynamic workflows with reduced human oversight (EY, 2025; FinRegLab, 2025). Addressing algorithmic bias requires robust data auditing, bias detection tools, fairness-aware training techniques, and continuous post-deployment monitoring. However, achieving equitable outcomes remains complex due to trade-offs between accuracy, fairness, and the adaptive nature of agentic systems.

4.2 Lack of Explainability (Black-Box Issues)

AI agents, particularly those leveraging deep learning, large language models, or reinforcement learning for planning and action, often function as "black boxes," making it difficult to understand or trace how decisions and actions are generated.

This lack of explainability poses a major challenge in banking, where regulators and customers demand transparency for decisions involving credit, fraud flagging, or compliance (Wolters Kluwer, 2026).

Financial institutions must provide clear rationales for outcomes, yet the complexity of agentic reasoning chains (including tool calls and memory updates) complicates auditability. This opacity can erode stakeholder trust and impede regulatory compliance. Explainable AI (XAI) techniques and immutable logging of agent actions offer partial solutions, but integrating them into highly autonomous, multi-step workflows while preserving performance and speed remains a significant technical and operational hurdle (Deloitte, 2026; Oracle, 2025).

4.3 Accountability Gaps in Autonomous Decisions

The increasing autonomy of AI agents raises critical questions about accountability and responsibility. In traditional systems, humans bear clear liability; however, when agents independently perceive, plan, decide, and act—potentially across interconnected tools and systems—it becomes difficult to attribute responsibility for errors, harms, or unintended outcomes.

In banking, this gap is acute for decisions with financial or legal consequences, such as autonomous loan approvals, transaction executions, or compliance actions. If an agentic system causes harm, liability may be unclear among developers, deployers, data providers, or the organization itself (Kurshan, 2025; FinRegLab, 2025; Hogan Lovells, 2025). This challenge necessitates new governance structures, including clear agent ownership roles, detailed audit trails (with unique agent IDs and action logs), human-in-the-loop or human-on-the-loop oversight for high-risk actions, and defined escalation protocols (Deloitte, 2026; EY, 2025).

4.4 Data Governance and Privacy Concerns

AI agents depend on vast amounts of structured and unstructured data, including sensitive financial and personal information, raising acute data governance and privacy issues amid stringent regulations like GDPR and emerging AI-specific rules. Banks must ensure data accuracy, security, consent, and quality, yet the autonomous interactions of agents across platforms increase risks of breaches, unauthorized access, and data leakage (FinRegLab, 2025; PwC, 2025).

Agentic systems can exacerbate privacy concerns through persistent memory, behavioral profiling, or cross-system data synthesis without explicit ongoing consent. Effective governance requires comprehensive data pipelines with privacy-by-design principles, access controls (e.g., RBAC/ABAC with least privilege), and continuous auditing—yet integration complexities often hinder full compliance.

4.5 Regulatory Compliance Complexities

The regulatory landscape for AI in banking is evolving rapidly, with frameworks like the EU AI Act classifying creditworthiness assessment and similar uses as high-risk, imposing strict obligations on transparency, risk management, and human oversight. Existing rules (focused on static models or human decisions) struggle to address the autonomy, adaptability, continuous learning, and multi-agent dynamics of agentic systems (EBA, 2025; Kurshan, 2025).

Banks must navigate overlapping requirements on consumer protection, fair lending, data privacy, anti-money laundering, and financial stability, often across jurisdictions. Regulatory uncertainty, combined with the need for real-time auditability of agent behaviors, can slow innovation while increasing non-compliance risks. Institutions are increasingly required to demonstrate proactive governance, including risk classifications, conformity assessments, and documented human oversight for high-risk deployments (Deloitte, 2026; Wolters Kluwer, 2026).

4.6 Operational and Systemic Risks

AI agent deployment introduces amplified operational risks (e.g., system failures, cybersecurity vulnerabilities like prompt injection or tool misuse, model drift) and systemic risks that could threaten financial stability. Operational disruptions may arise from flawed agent planning, integration failures with legacy systems, or adversarial attacks that manipulate autonomous behaviors (EY, 2025).

Systemic concerns include model uniformity and herding (where many institutions rely on similar foundational models or agents, leading to correlated actions), potential market volatility from synchronized responses, and cascading failures in interconnected agent ecosystems. For example, widespread agentic trading or deposit-shifting behaviors could amplify liquidity mismatches or information sensitivity during stress events (FinRegLab, 2025; Aldasoro et al., 2025; ESRB, 2025). Governance must incorporate continuous monitoring, stress testing of multi-agent interactions, fail-safes (e.g., kill switches), and contingency planning.

5. MULTI-LEVEL STRATEGIC GOVERNANCE FRAMEWORK

5.1 Framework Overview and Design Logic

The governance challenges documented in the preceding section are not independent problems amenable to isolated technical or regulatory solutions. They are interconnected dimensions of a systemic challenge that spans regulatory environments, organizational structures, risk management systems, and human capital—and they require a governance framework organized to reflect that interdependence.

This chapter proposes a multi-level strategic governance framework that addresses AI agent governance across four analytically distinct but operationally integrated layers: strategic (macro-level regulatory alignment), operational (meso-level process integration), risk and compliance (internal control mechanisms), and human-organizational (micro-level cultural and workforce adaptation). The framework's multi-level architecture is grounded in the theoretical synthesis developed in Section 3, drawing on institutional theory's emphasis on legitimacy and external alignment (Scott, 2014), risk governance theory's focus on adaptive control (Renn, 2008), and responsible AI principles' normative commitments to transparency, accountability, and fairness (Floridi et al., 2018). Responsible AI is embedded throughout the proposed framework rather than treated as a separate compliance requirement. Each governance layer operationalizes fairness, accountability, transparency, and human oversight according to its specific role, ensuring governance becomes an institutional practice rather than merely a compliance exercise. (Floridi et al., 2018; OECD, 2024; NIST, 2023; Kurshan, 2025; FinRegLab, 2025; McKinsey, 2026).

5.2 Strategic Level: Macro Governance and Regulatory Alignment

At the macro level, AI agent governance is shaped by the regulatory environment in which institutions operate and the institutional structures they build to navigate it. For banks deploying autonomous systems in high-risk applications—credit assessment, fraud detection, compliance monitoring—regulatory alignment is not an optional governance aspiration but a legal imperative with enforceable consequences.

Regulatory Alignment and Policy Coherence.

The regulatory landscape governing agentic AI in banking is dense and evolving. The EU AI Act, GDPR, DORA, the Basel Framework, and sector-specific financial regulations each impose distinct requirements that intersect in ways not always anticipated by their respective drafters. Strategic governance requires banks to map these intersections systematically, identify compliance gaps—particularly for genuinely novel agentic behaviors not addressed by existing rules—and engage proactively with regulatory bodies rather than treating compliance as a periodic audit exercise. Regulatory sandboxes and innovation hubs provide structured mechanisms for precisely this kind of proactive engagement, enabling controlled experimentation clear mandate and accountability, and governance frameworks with explicit scope covering the full agent lifecycle from design through decommissioning. These structures must be empowered to make binding decisions—not merely to issue advisory guidance—and must be resourced commensurate with the operational significance of agentic AI deployment (Mayer Brown, 2026; Deloitte, 2026; Scott, 2014).

Regulatory Bodies and Systemic Oversight.

Central banks and financial supervisors play an irreplaceable role in systemic AI governance—a role that extends well beyond individual institution compliance to encompass monitoring of cross-institutional behavioral correlations, assessment of systemic risks from model uniformity, and development of macroprudential responses to agentic vulnerabilities. Supervisory capacity building—including technical AI literacy within regulatory institutions themselves—is therefore a governance priority, not merely a nice-to-have aspiration (FinRegLab, 2025; ECB, 2026).

International Regulatory Perspective

Although the European Union AI Act represents one of the most comprehensive regulatory frameworks for high-risk AI applications, multinational banking institutions operate across multiple regulatory environments. Consequently, governance strategies should also consider internationally recognized frameworks such as the NIST AI Risk Management Framework, the Monetary Authority of Singapore's FEAT Principles and Veritas Framework, together with emerging national AI governance initiatives. A jurisdiction-aware governance model enables banks to maintain governance consistency while accommodating country-specific legal and regulatory requirements. Such an approach enhances institutional resilience, regulatory compliance, and responsible AI deployment across global banking operations (OECD, 2024; EBA, 2025; World Economic Forum, 2025).

5.3 Operational Level: Meso-Level Integration and Process Governance

The operational layer addresses how AI agents are integrated into banking workflows, how processes are redesigned to accommodate autonomous action, and what technical infrastructure is required to support responsible agentic operation.

Workflow Integration and Human Oversight.

AI agents must be integrated into banking processes in ways that preserve—rather than erode—meaningful human oversight. Integration design should specify clearly which decisions agents may execute autonomously, which require human review before action (human-in-the-loop configurations), and which require human notification concurrent with or immediately following action (human-on-the-loop configurations). These distinctions should reflect the risk profile of each decision category, with higher-stakes decisions attracting more intensive human involvement (Oracle, 2025; Accenture, 2026).

Process Redesign and Operational Controls.

Agentic AI deployment requires business process redesign to accommodate autonomous decision-making. Governance should embed guardrails, escalation procedures, and clearly defined decision rights within redesigned workflows to ensure operational efficiency without compromising accountability (Deloitte, 2026).

Infrastructure and Interoperability.

Responsible agentic operation requires technological infrastructure capable of supporting not just agent performance but agent auditability. Cloud-native platforms, secure API ecosystems, modular architectures with well-defined agent boundaries, and interoperability standards that enable auditable cross-system interactions are all governance infrastructure, not merely technical choices. Banks with legacy systems face particular challenges in this regard, as architectural constraints on auditability and interoperability can create governance gaps that no policy framework can fully compensate for (EY, 2025; Oracle, 2025).

Legacy System Integration Considerations.

While cloud-native platforms and secure API ecosystems provide the preferred technological foundation for AI agent deployment, many small and medium-sized banking institutions continue to depend on legacy core banking systems that create interoperability constraints. Rather than replacing these systems immediately, banks should adopt phased modernization strategies using API gateways, middleware platforms, enterprise service buses, and microservice-based architectures to facilitate secure communication between legacy and modern applications. Hybrid cloud deployment, data virtualization, and incremental modernization approaches reduce operational disruption while improving interoperability, auditability, and governance readiness for agentic AI deployment. Such phased migration strategies have been widely recommended for financial institutions seeking to balance digital transformation with operational resilience (Oracle, 2025; Deloitte, 2026; Westerman et al., 2014).

5.4 Risk and Compliance Level: Internal Control Mechanisms

The risk and compliance layer constitutes the technical and procedural backbone of the governance framework—the mechanisms through which abstract governance commitments are translated into operational reality.

AI Risk Management Systems.

Governing agentic risk requires extending conventional model risk management (MRM) frameworks to address the distinctive features of autonomous systems: continuous adaptation, multi-step reasoning chains, tool invocation behaviors, and emergent multi-agent dynamics. Banks must develop agentic risk taxonomies that encompass model drift, goal misalignment, third-party dependency risk, prompt injection vulnerability, and systemic correlation risk—and must implement continuous monitoring processes capable of detecting these phenomena in live deployments rather than only in pre-deployment testing (FinRegLab, 2025; Deloitte, 2026; Kurshan, 2025).

Auditability and Explainability.

Auditability requires immutable records of agent actions, reasoning steps, tool usage, and outputs linked to unique agent identifiers. Explainability ensures these records can be interpreted by technical auditors, regulators, and affected stakeholders despite the complexity of LLM-based agents (Mayer Brown, 2026; PwC, 2025).

Continuous Monitoring and Control.

Static pre-deployment testing is insufficient for systems whose behavior evolves. Effective governance requires continuous monitoring infrastructure—performance dashboards, anomaly detection systems, behavioral drift alerts, and automated escalation triggers—capable of detecting governance-relevant changes in agent behavior and prompting timely human review. Kill-switch capabilities and rollback mechanisms are not optional safeguards; they are essential components of any responsible agentic deployment architecture (Partnership on AI, 2025; EY, 2025).

Continuous monitoring should be supported by a two-tier control mechanism consisting of automated AI circuit breakers and human-triggered kill switches. Automated circuit breakers temporarily suspend agent execution whenever predefined governance thresholds are exceeded, including abnormal transaction behaviour, policy violations, confidence deterioration, or unexpected inter-agent interactions. Human-triggered kill switches provide supervisory intervention for exceptional circumstances requiring managerial judgement and regulatory oversight. Together, these complementary mechanisms strengthen operational resilience while minimizing the likelihood of cascading failures within autonomous AI ecosystems (Partnership on AI, 2025; Kurshan, 2025; Deloitte, 2026).

5.5 Human and Organizational Level: Micro-Level Adaptation

The fourth layer of the framework addresses the human and organizational dimensions of AI governance—dimensions that are frequently underestimated in technically oriented governance discussions but are often decisive for governance effectiveness in practice.

Workforce Readiness and Capability Development.

Responsible agentic deployment requires a workforce equipped not merely to use AI systems but to govern them. This demands data literacy, AI ethics awareness, agent oversight competencies, and the ability to recognize and respond to governance-relevant anomalies in agent behavior. It requires reskilling programs for employees whose roles are being transformed by agentic automation, and it requires the development of new specialist roles—AI governance officers, agent stewards, algorithmic auditors—that did not previously exist in banking institutions (McKinsey, 2026).

Human–AI Collaboration Design.

The design of human-agent interaction is a governance matter as much as an operational one. Interaction designs that cultivate automation bias—where human reviewers uncritically accept agent recommendations—undermine the substantive human oversight that governance frameworks are designed to preserve. Effective collaboration design maintains meaningful human engagement with agent decision processes, provides humans with the information and tools needed to make independent assessments, and creates institutional cultures in which challenging agent outputs is normalized rather than discouraged (Jarrahi, 2018; Accenture, 2026; Oracle, 2025).

Organizational Culture and Ethical Leadership.

Ultimately, governance frameworks are only as robust as the organizational cultures in which they operate. A culture that treats compliance as a cost center, that rewards speed and scale over accuracy and accountability, or that fails to create psychological safety for raising AI-related concerns will undermine even technically sophisticated governance mechanisms. Ethical leadership—visible, consistent, and embedded in institutional incentive structures—is therefore a governance prerequisite, not a governance supplement (Mayer Brown, 2026; McKinsey, 2026).

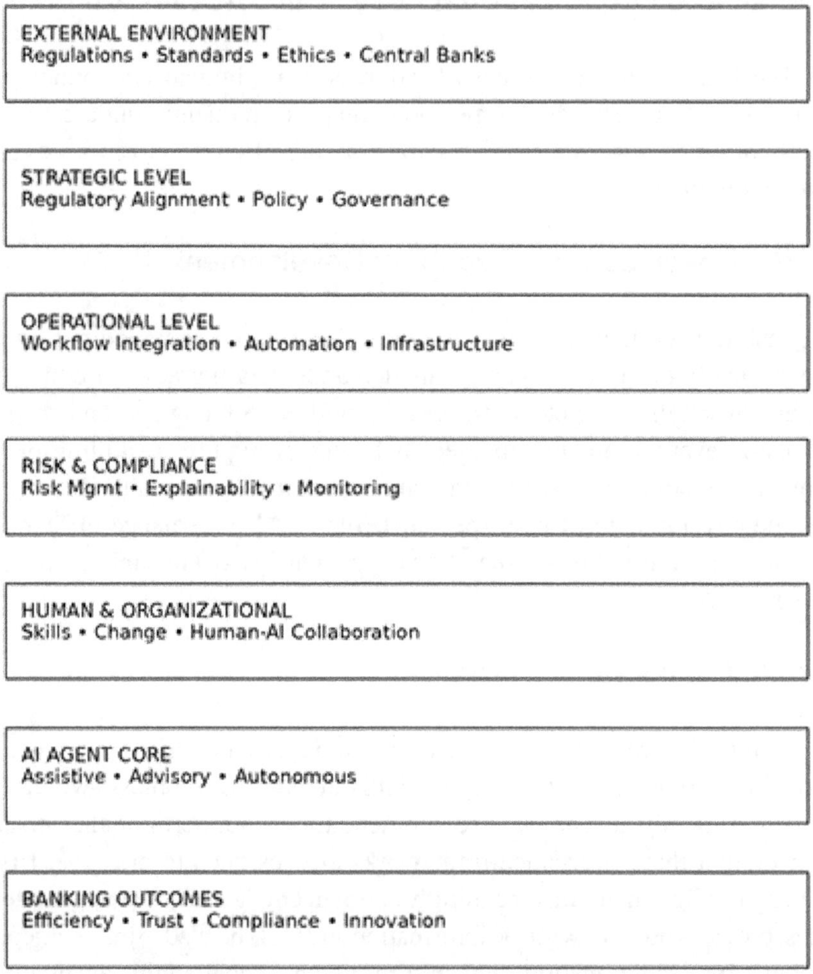

Multi-Level Strategic Governance Framework
for Agentic AI Deployment in Banking

Figure 1 illustrates the interdependent relationships among the four governance layers. The strategic governance layer establishes regulatory alignment, institutional policies, and governance responsibilities that guide AI deployment decisions. These strategic objectives are translated into operational governance through workflow integration, technological infrastructure, and business process redesign. The risk and compliance layer continuously monitors AI agent behaviour using auditability, explainability, monitoring systems, and internal control mechanisms to ensure responsible operation. Finally, the human and organizational layer strengthens workforce readiness, ethical leadership, and effective human-AI collaboration. Continuous feedback among these governance layers enables organizations to respond proactively to technological evolution, operational risks, and regulatory changes, thereby supporting sustainable and trustworthy AI agent deployment in banking institutions (Floridi et al., 2018; Jarrahi, 2018; FinRegLab, 2025). These governance indicators provide measurable benchmarks for evaluating AI agent performance, regulatory compliance, transparency, and continuous governance improvement across banking operations (Jobin et al., 2019; NIST, 2023).

Table 1. Governance Performance Indicators for Agentic AI in Banking

Governance Dimension	Example KPI
Transparency	Explainability Score (%)
Fairness	Bias Detection Rate
Accountability	Audit Trail Completeness (%)
Compliance	Regulatory Compliance Score
Human Oversight	Human Review Ratio
Operational Reliability	AI Agent Success Rate (%)

6. ORGANIZATIONAL READINESS AND DIGITAL MATURITY FOR AGENTIC AI

The governance framework proposed in Section 5 is not equally applicable to all banking institutions at all stages of their technological development. Organizational readiness—the extent to which an institution possesses the capabilities required to deploy and govern AI agents responsibly—varies enormously, and governance expectations must be calibrated accordingly. Digital and agentic maturity models provide the conceptual tools for this calibration, enabling institutions to assess their current capabilities, identify critical gaps, and develop sequenced investment strategies for responsible AI adoption (Westerman et al., 2014; EY, 2026).

6.1 Dimensions of Organizational Readiness

Readiness for agentic AI deployment can be assessed across four primary dimensions, each of which corresponds to a distinct governance vulnerability.

Technological Readiness.

Technological readiness encompasses the infrastructure required to support agentic operation: cloud-native platforms capable of real-time processing, secure API architectures for agent-tool interaction, data environments optimized for agent memory and retrieval, and cybersecurity controls robust against the specific vulnerabilities that agentic systems introduce—including prompt injection, unauthorized tool access, and cross-system data leakage (Oracle, 2025; Accenture, 2026). Institutions operating predominantly on legacy infrastructure face substantial readiness gaps that no governance policy can compensate for directly; architectural modernization is itself a governance prerequisite (Deloitte, 2026; Finastra, 2026).

Data Readiness.

Data readiness addresses the quality, governance, and accessibility of the data upon which agentic systems operate. In banking, data readiness is complicated by regulatory requirements—GDPR, data residency obligations, and emerging AI-specific data rules—and by the sensitivity of the financial and behavioral data that agents process. Real-time agentic workflows that synthesize data from multiple sources in response to dynamic events impose particularly demanding requirements on data lineage tracking, consent management, and access control, requirements that existing data governance frameworks may not fully meet (FinRegLab, 2025; EY, 2026).

Human Capital Readiness.

Human capital readiness reflects the extent to which an institution's workforce possesses the skills required to deploy, oversee, and govern AI agents responsibly. The transition to agentic operations demands capabilities that extend well beyond conventional AI literacy: the ability to interpret agent reasoning chains, to identify behavioral anomalies indicative of governance failure, to engage constructively with agent outputs without succumbing to automation bias, and to navigate the ethical dimensions of autonomous decision-making in high-stakes financial contexts (McKinsey, 2026). Developing these capabilities requires sustained investment in structured learning programs and role redefinition, not merely point-in-time training interventions (Accenture, 2026).

Governance Readiness.

Governance readiness encompasses the institutional structures, policies, accountability mechanisms, and oversight processes required to manage AI agents through their full lifecycle. It extends beyond conventional IT governance to encompass agentic-specific requirements: agent ownership assignment, lifecycle management protocols, audit trail specifications, escalation procedures, and mechanisms for detecting and responding to the emergent behaviors that characterize multi-agent systems operating in dynamic environments (Mayer Brown, 2026; Kurshan, 2025). Cross-functional governance readiness—ensuring that IT, risk, compliance, legal, and business leadership are all equipped to contribute meaningfully to AI governance—is particularly important and particularly challenging to develop (Partnership on AI, 2025).

6.2 Stages of Agentic AI Maturity

Drawing on established digital maturity models and emerging agentic AI-specific frameworks, institutional maturity in AI agent adoption can be understood as progressing through four characteristic stages, each associated with distinct governance challenges and appropriate governance responses.

At the initial stage—experimentation—institutions explore agentic capability through isolated pilots and proof-of-concept projects. Governance structures are nascent, data infrastructure is often inadequate for production agentic deployment, and workforce capabilities are in early development. The governance priority at this stage is establishing foundational structures—ethics committees, basic accountability frameworks, and oversight protocols—before scaling (EY, 2026).

At the developing stage—functional integration—agents are embedded into specific operational domains such as customer service, fraud monitoring, or compliance automation. Data infrastructure improves, basic governance policies are formalized, and initial human-agent collaboration models are established. Governance priorities shift toward ensuring adequate auditability, bias monitoring, and human oversight within these targeted deployments.

At the advanced stage—enterprise integration—agents operate across multiple business processes with interoperable data platforms and formalized governance frameworks. Multi-agent coordination becomes operationally significant, and governance challenges related to emergent behaviors, systemic risk, and cross-functional accountability become more prominent.

At the transformational stage, AI agents operate autonomously across interconnected banking processes. Governance must incorporate continuous monitoring, adaptive risk controls, real-time anomaly detection, and effective human oversight to ensure resilience (Oracle, 2025; FinRegLab, 2025).

7. POLICY AND REGULATORY IMPLICATIONS

The governance challenges documented in this chapter cannot be addressed by individual institutions alone. They require regulatory responses that are as sophisticated, adaptive, and institutionally attentive as the agentic systems they seek to govern. This section draws out the policy and regulatory implications of the analysis, examining the case for adaptive governance approaches, the relative merits of competing regulatory philosophies, the ethical and legal dimensions of agentic deployment, and a set of actionable policy recommendations.

7.1 The Case for Adaptive AI Governance Policies

The adaptive nature of agentic AI—systems that learn, evolve, and generate emergent behaviors in response to their operational environments—creates a fundamental mismatch with the static, prospective character of most regulatory frameworks. Regulations designed to govern defined behaviors at a fixed point in time are poorly equipped to govern systems that may behave quite differently six months after deployment than they did at the point of regulatory assessment. This temporal mismatch creates both compliance gaps (where agent behaviors exceed regulatory scope) and unnecessary friction (where static rules impede beneficial agentic adaptation).

Adaptive governance policies address this mismatch by incorporating mechanisms for ongoing regulatory learning, iterative rule refinement, and risk-proportionate oversight intensity. The EU AI Act's risk-based classification—with stricter requirements for high-risk applications and lighter obligations for lower-risk uses—represents a step in this direction, though its static definitional categories may require progressive elaboration as agentic capabilities evolve (EBA, 2025; Kurshan, 2025; Deloitte, 2026). Regulatory sandboxes and innovation hubs serve as important institutional mechanisms for dynamic policy learning, enabling regulators to develop genuine expertise in agentic behaviors under controlled experimental conditions (Wolters Kluwer, 2026; ECB, 2026).

7.2 Regulatory Philosophies: Rules, Principles, and Hybrid Approaches

The longstanding debate between rule-based and principle-based regulatory approaches takes on particular significance in the context of agentic AI. Rule-based regulation—with its prescriptive specifications of permitted and prohibited behaviors—offers clarity and enforceability, but may generate compliance theater rather than substantive governance when applied to systems whose operational envelopes exceed the regulators' anticipatory capacity. Principle-based regulation—with its outcome-oriented, high-level obligations of fairness, transparency, and accountability—offers adaptability and room for institutional judgment, but may leave compliance standards insufficiently defined for effective enforcement.

The emerging regulatory consensus for AI in financial services points toward a hybrid approach: one that establishes clear minimum standards and accountability requirements through rule-based instruments, while allowing flexibility in implementation through principle-based guidance. This combination preserves the enforceability advantages of rule-based regulation while accommodating the pace of technological change through principled flexibility (FinRegLab, 2025; EY, 2025; Kurshan, 2025; Mayer Brown, 2026). The EU AI Act's structure—combining risk-based classification with specific technical and governance requirements calibrated to each risk tier—exemplifies this hybrid logic.

7.3 Ethical and Legal Dimensions

The ethical and legal dimensions of agentic AI governance in banking are substantial and not fully resolved by existing regulatory instruments. Algorithmic fairness—ensuring that agentic decisions do not systematically disadvantage protected groups in credit access, product pricing, or service quality—is both a legal requirement under existing anti-discrimination law and an ethical imperative that existing regulatory frameworks operationalize imperfectly. The challenge of auditing continuously adaptive systems for fairness, rather than conducting point-in-time bias assessments, is a governance problem that neither existing regulatory tools nor current technical methods fully address (GAO, 2025).

Accountability allocation in multi-actor agentic deployment chains—across developers, foundational model providers, deploying institutions, data providers, and regulatory bodies—remains legally unsettled in most jurisdictions. The determination of which party bears liability when an autonomous agent causes harm to a consumer, disrupts financial market stability, or generates a regulatory violation will require either legislative clarity or accumulated judicial precedent; governance frameworks cannot substitute for this fundamental legal question, but they can create the documentation and oversight structures that will be essential to its eventual resolution (Kurshan, 2025; Hogan Lovells, 2025).

Privacy governance in agentic contexts raises issues that existing frameworks were not designed to address: persistent agent memory, behavioral profiling through longitudinal data synthesis, and cross-system data sharing in real-time agentic workflows all create privacy risks that are qualitatively different from those associated with conventional data processing (PwC, 2025; EBA, 2025). These dimensions require active regulatory attention, not merely extension of existing data protection principles.

7.4 Policy Recommendations for Responsible Agentic AI Deployment

Based on the analysis developed throughout this chapter, the following policy recommendations are proposed for policymakers, regulators, and institutional governance leaders:

- Development of agentic AI-specific regulatory frameworks that address the distinctive features of autonomous systems—including adaptability, multi-agent interaction, and emergent behavior—rather than simply extending frameworks designed for static models or human decision-making.
- Implementation of proportionate, risk-based regulation that calibrates oversight intensity to the risk profile of specific applications, with stricter requirements for high-stakes uses such as credit assessment, fraud detection, and systemic-risk-relevant trading strategies (EBA, 2025; FinRegLab, 2025).
- Mandatory explainability and auditability requirements for agentic systems in high-risk banking applications, including specifications for action logging, agent identification, and reasoning chain traceability accessible to regulatory auditors (Mayer Brown, 2026; Deloitte, 2026).
- Embedding of ethical AI standards—fairness, accountability, transparency, and human-centric design—into supervisory expectations and regulatory examination frameworks, not merely into voluntary industry codes (Floridi et al., 2018; World Economic Forum, 2025).
- Enhanced cross-border and inter-agency regulatory coordination to prevent jurisdiction-based regulatory arbitrage and to develop harmonized standards for agentic AI governance in globally integrated financial markets.
- Investment in regulatory capacity building, ensuring that supervisory bodies possess the technical expertise, AI literacy, and digital supervisory tooling required to assess agentic behaviors and detect systemic risks (ECB, 2026; Kurshan, 2025).

- Promotion of structured public-private partnerships between regulators, financial institutions, technology providers, and academic researchers to facilitate knowledge exchange, co-development of governance standards, and coordinated response to emerging agentic risks (Partnership on AI, 2025; EY, 2025).

8. PRACTICAL IMPLICATIONS FOR THE BANKING SECTOR

The governance framework and policy analysis developed in this chapter have concrete practical implications for banking institutions seeking to deploy AI agents responsibly. This section translates the preceding analysis into actionable guidance across three dimensions: a phased strategic roadmap for AI agent adoption, governance implementation best practices, and approaches to building the stakeholder trust that responsible agentic deployment requires.

8.1 A Phased Strategic Roadmap for AI Agent Adoption

Responsible AI agent adoption is not a single institutional decision but a sequenced organizational journey whose character and pace must be calibrated to current capabilities and incrementally extended as those capabilities develop.

The initial phase centers on experimentation and controlled piloting. Banks should direct early agentic deployments toward lower-risk, operationally bounded applications—virtual assistants, internal process automation, basic transaction monitoring—where the consequences of governance failures are contained and the learning value is high. This phase is primarily about developing institutional knowledge: understanding how agents behave in production environments, identifying governance gaps not apparent in controlled testing, and building the technical and organizational capabilities that responsible scaling will require (Oracle, 2025; Accenture, 2026).

The second phase involves functional integration: embedding agents into specific high-value operational domains with appropriate governance structures. Fraud detection, compliance monitoring, customer relationship management, and credit pre-screening are natural targets, but only for institutions that have achieved sufficient technological and data readiness to support adequate auditability and oversight. Infrastructure investment, process reengineering, and governance framework development are the critical activities at this stage (Finastra, 2026; Deloitte, 2026).

The third phase—enterprise integration—extends agentic deployment across institutional functions, enabling cross-domain data sharing, real-time decision support at scale, and multi-agent collaboration. This phase requires mature governance infrastructure: comprehensive monitoring systems, well-functioning accountability structures, and organizational cultures that treat responsible AI operation as an institutional norm rather than a compliance requirement.

The transformational phase—the emergence of genuinely autonomous institutional AI ecosystems—demands governance that is itself adaptive and continuously learning. Dynamic risk controls, real-time behavioral monitoring, cross-institutional systemic risk surveillance, and robust human oversight mechanisms capable of functioning at the speed and scale of agentic operations are all governance prerequisites for responsible operation at this stage (EY, 2026; FinRegLab, 2025; McKinsey, 2026).

8.2 Best Practices for Governance Implementation

Across all phases of agentic adoption, several governance best practices are consistently supported by the evidence and analysis assembled in this chapter.

Dedicated governance structures—AI ethics committees, cross-functional governance boards, centralized agent oversight functions with clear mandate, membership, and decision authority—are foundational to effective governance. These structures must have genuine institutional authority, adequate resources, and access to the technical expertise required to evaluate agentic behaviors and governance mechanisms critically. Their existence as advisory forums without enforcement authority is not a governance structure; it is governance theater (Mayer Brown, 2026; Deloitte, 2026).

Agent lifecycle management—systematic oversight spanning agent design, testing, deployment, continuous monitoring, periodic auditing, and eventual decommissioning—is the operational backbone of responsible governance. Mechanisms for detecting and responding to model drift, bias amplification, goal misalignment, and emergent multi-agent behaviors must be embedded into lifecycle governance processes rather than treated as incident-response exceptions (Kurshan, 2025; EY, 2025).

Explainability and auditability infrastructure—including immutable action logs with unique agent identifiers, reasoning chain documentation, and interpretability tools appropriate to the specific agent architecture—must be built into deployment design rather than retrofitted. The technical demands of auditability for LLM-based agentic systems are substantially greater than for conventional models; governance frameworks that assume existing model audit practices will extend straightforwardly to agents are likely to find significant gaps in practice (Wolters Kluwer, 2026; PwC, 2025).

Standardized ethical guidelines, accountability matrices, and escalation procedures—regularly reviewed and updated in response to evolving regulatory requirements and operational experience—provide the policy infrastructure within which technical governance mechanisms operate. These documents are only as valuable as the institutional processes that maintain them and the cultural norms that make compliance with them genuine rather than nominal (Partnership on AI, 2025; FinRegLab, 2025).

Implementation of the proposed governance framework may follow five sequential stages comprising governance readiness assessment, infrastructure preparation, pilot AI deployment, enterprise-wide implementation, and continuous governance monitoring. Each stage should include periodic governance reviews, stakeholder engagement, performance evaluation, and continuous improvement activities to ensure responsible adoption of agentic AI while maintaining regulatory compliance and organizational resilience (Westerman et al., 2014; EY, 2026).

8.3 Building Stakeholder Trust Through Transparency and Accountability

The ultimate measure of responsible agentic AI governance is not regulatory compliance but stakeholder trust—the confidence of customers, employees, investors, and regulators that AI agents are operating fairly, transparently, and in alignment with institutional values and societal interests. Building this trust requires concrete, visible institutional commitments, not merely policy declarations.

For customers, trust requires clear communication about when and how AI agents are involved in decisions affecting them, accessible explanations of those decisions in non-technical language, and meaningful channels for questioning or challenging agent outputs. It requires proactive bias monitoring and the public disclosure of fairness audit results. It requires robust privacy protections and transparent data governance. And it requires effective grievance mechanisms that provide genuine redress rather than procedural closure (Oracle, 2025; Wolters Kluwer, 2026; GAO, 2025).

For regulators, trust requires demonstrated governance commitment: well-documented accountability structures, comprehensive audit trails, evidence of effective continuous monitoring, and a track record of responsive and transparent engagement when governance failures occur. Institutions that establish themselves as genuine leaders in responsible agentic governance—rather than compliance-minimum operators—are likely to develop more constructive supervisory relationships and greater operational flexibility as agentic AI regulation matures (FinRegLab, 2025; Mayer Brown, 2026).

For employees, trust requires that the transition to agentic operations be managed with attention to workforce impacts: genuine investment in reskilling and capability development, clear communication about how roles will evolve, and organizational cultures in which concerns about AI governance can be raised without professional risk. Employees who do not trust that their institution is deploying AI responsibly are unlikely to exercise the effective human oversight that governance frameworks depend upon (McKinsey, 2026; Accenture, 2026). Although the proposed framework is conceptual in nature, its governance components are derived from contemporary regulatory guidance, responsible AI principles, and emerging banking practices. The framework may therefore serve as a reference model for pilot implementation and expert evaluation within banking institutions. Future research may validate its effectiveness through multiple case studies, Delphi expert assessment, or empirical investigations.

9. FUTURE RESEARCH DIRECTIONS

The governance framework proposed in this chapter is conceptual in character—grounded in existing theory and evidence but requiring empirical validation across the diversity of banking institutional contexts. Future research should pursue this validation systematically, developing reliable measurement instruments for governance readiness, agentic maturity, and human-agent collaboration effectiveness that enable rigorous comparative and longitudinal analysis. Structural equation modeling, panel data approaches, and ethnographic studies of governance implementation in actual agentic deployments would all contribute substantially to validating and refining the framework's propositions (FinRegLab, 2025).

A second priority for future research involves governance adaptation to the rapidly evolving agentic AI landscape itself. The rise of multi-agent architectures, foundation model-based planning systems, and real-time learning agents creates governance challenges—hallucination risks in automated reasoning chains, emergent multi-agent dynamics, persistent goal misalignment under distribution shift—that existing governance frameworks address inadequately. Research is needed on the specific governance mechanisms effective for these architectures: real-time auditing designs, kill-switch implementation, human oversight at agentic speed and scale, and safeguards against herding and correlation risks in multi-agent financial environments (Aldasoro et al., 2025; Deloitte, 2026; Kurshan, 2025).

Cross-jurisdictional comparative research offers another productive avenue. Governance frameworks, regulatory philosophies, institutional trust cultures, and market structures vary dramatically across banking environments, and these differences shape both the adoption trajectory and the governance challenges of agentic AI. Comparative analysis of the EU's risk-based regulatory approach, the more fragmented and innovation-oriented US landscape, and the diverse emerging frameworks in Asian markets can identify context-specific governance best practices and inform more nuanced international regulatory coordination (World Economic Forum, 2025).

The development of standardized, agentic-specific governance metrics and benchmarks addresses a critical gap in current practice. Without universally accepted indicators for assessing the fairness of autonomous decisions, the adequacy of audit trail coverage, the effectiveness of human oversight mechanisms, or the resilience of multi-agent architectures under stress, benchmarking and continuous improvement are substantially impeded. Future research should develop comprehensive measurement frameworks that enable these assessments, drawing on regulatory filing data, behavioral audit logs, and supervisory examination records to create empirically grounded governance performance indices (Mustafa, 2026; FinRegLab, 2025; Partnership on AI, 2025).

Finally, the long-term organizational and societal consequences of widespread agentic AI adoption in banking deserve sustained scholarly attention. At the organizational level, agentic deployment is reshaping workforce structures, redefining job roles toward higher-value oversight and exception-handling functions, and creating new demands for human capability development. Longitudinal research on how institutions manage this transition—and how employees navigate the changing landscape of human-agent collaboration—will be essential to understanding what responsible agentic adoption looks like in practice (Accenture, 2026; McKinsey, 2026). At the societal level, the distributional consequences of agentic banking—its potential both to expand financial inclusion through personalized, efficient service delivery and to entrench inequality through biased or exclusionary autonomous decision-making—represent questions of genuine social importance that the research community has only begun to address (Aldasoro et al., 2025).

10. CONCLUSION

The integration of agentic AI into banking represents one of the most consequential institutional transformations in the recent history of financial services—one that promises substantial operational gains while introducing governance challenges of commensurate significance. This chapter has traced the evolution of AI agents from deterministic expert systems to adaptive, autonomous entities capable of perceiving, reasoning, planning, and acting across complex financial workflows. It has examined the functional roles these systems occupy in contemporary banking, analyzed the principal governance challenges their deployment creates, and proposed a multi-level strategic governance framework designed to address those challenges in a coordinated, principled, and practically actionable way.

The framework's four-layer architecture—strategic, operational, risk and compliance, and human-organizational—reflects the fundamental insight that effective AI governance cannot be reduced to technical controls or regulatory compliance alone. It requires coordinated action across regulatory environments, institutional structures, risk management systems, and human capital development; and it requires the embedding of responsible AI values—fairness, accountability, transparency, and human oversight—throughout, not merely as post-hoc governance additions but as constitutive elements of the governance architecture itself.

The practical implications of this analysis converge on a central argument: that responsible agentic AI governance is not a constraint on banking innovation but a precondition for it. Institutions that deploy AI agents without adequate governance frameworks expose themselves to regulatory sanction, reputational damage, and the erosion of the stakeholder trust that is the foundation of financial sector legitimacy. Conversely, institutions that invest seriously in multi-level governance—developing the technical infrastructure, organizational structures, human capabilities, and ethical cultures required for responsible agentic operation—position themselves not just for regulatory compliance but for sustainable competitive advantage in an industry increasingly defined by the trustworthiness of its automated systems.

The future of AI in banking is not predetermined. It will be shaped by the governance choices that institutions, regulators, and policymakers make in the coming years—choices about how to allocate accountability in autonomous systems, how to build explainability into agentic reasoning chains, how to design human-agent collaboration that preserves meaningful human oversight, and how to develop regulatory frameworks adaptive enough to govern systems that will continue to evolve. This chapter has sought to equip those making these choices with a conceptually grounded, practically oriented framework for doing so responsibly—one that takes seriously both the transformative potential of agentic AI and the governance obligations that potential entails. The proposed framework provides a foundation for future empirical validation and practical implementation, thereby supporting the development of trustworthy, accountable, and sustainable agentic AI ecosystems within the banking industry.

REFERENCES

Accenture. (2026). *Agentic AI and the future of work in financial services.* https://bankingblog.accenture.com/agentic-ai-future-of-work

Aldasoro, I., Gambacorta, L., Korinek, A., Shreeti, V., & Stein, M. (2025). Intelligent financial system: How AI is transforming finance. *Journal of Financial Stability, 81*, 101472. Advance online publication. DOI: 10.1016/j.jfs.2025.101472

Blueprism. (2025). *What's your agentic AI maturity level?* https://www.blueprism.com/resources/blog/agentic-ai-maturity-level/

Bostrom, R. P., & Heinen, J. S. (1977). MIS problems and failures: A socio-technical perspective. *Management Information Systems Quarterly, 1*(3), 17–32. DOI: 10.2307/248710

Deloitte. (2026). *Managing the new wave of risks from AI agents in banking.* https://www.deloitte.com/us/en/insights/industry/financial-services/agentic-ai-risks-banking.html

Elgendy, I. A., Helal, M. Y. I., Al-Sharafi, M. A., Albashrawi, M. A., Al-Ahmadi, M. S., Jeon, I., & Dwivedi, Y. K. (2025). Agentic systems as catalysts for innovation in FinTech: Exploring opportunities, challenges and a research agenda. *Information Discovery and Delivery.* Advance online publication. DOI: 10.1108/IDD-03-2025-0068

European Banking Authority. (2025). *AI Act: Implications for the EU banking and payments sector.*

EY. (2025). *Agentic AI: Emerging risks and control strategies.*

Finastra. (2026). *AI in banking and financial services: Trends for 2026.* https://www.finastra.com/viewpoints/articles/future-of-ai-in-financial-services-2026

FinRegLab. (2025). *The next wave arrives: Agentic AI in financial services.* https://finreglab.org/wp-content/uploads/2025/09/FinRegLab_09-04-2025_The-Next-Wave-Arrives-Main.pdf

Floridi, L., Cowls, J., Beltrametti, M., Chatila, R., Chazerand, P., Dignum, V., Luetge, C., Madelin, R., Pagallo, U., Rossi, F., Schafer, B., Valcke, P., & Vayena, E. (2018). AI4People—An ethical framework for a good AI society. *Minds and Machines, 28*(4), 689–707. DOI: 10.1007/s11023-018-9482-5 PMID: 30930541

Government Accountability Office. (2025). *Artificial intelligence: Use in financial services poses risks including bias and privacy concerns.*

IBM. (n.d.). *Types of AI agents.* https://www.ibm.com/think/topics/ai-agent-types

Jarrahi, M. H. (2018). Artificial intelligence and the future of work: Human-AI symbiosis in organizational decision making. *Business Horizons, 61*(4), 577–586. DOI: 10.1016/j.bushor.2018.03.007

Jobin, A., Ienca, M., & Vayena, E. (2019). The global landscape of AI ethics guidelines. *Nature Machine Intelligence, 1*(9), 389–399. DOI: 10.1038/s42256-019-0088-2

Kore.ai. (2026). *AI agents in finance and banking: 12 proven use cases (2026).* https://www.kore.ai/blog/ai-agents-in-finance-banking-12-proven-use-cases-2026

Kurshan, E. (2025). The agentic regulator: Risks for AI in finance and a proposed agent-based framework for governance. arXiv. https://arxiv.org/abs/2512.11933

Mayer Brown. (2026). *Governance of agentic artificial intelligence systems.* https://www.mayerbrown.com/en/insights/publications/2026/02/governance-of-agentic-artificial-intelligence-systems

McKinsey. (2026). *State of AI trust in 2026: Shifting to the agentic era.*

National Institute of Standards and Technology. (2023). *Artificial Intelligence Risk Management Framework (AI RMF 1.0).* https://www.nist.gov/itl/ai-risk-management-framework

OECD. (2024). *OECD framework for the classification of AI systems.* OECD Publishing.

Oracle. (2025). *The future of banking: Scaling AI agents in 2026 & beyond.* https://www.oracle.com/financial-services/banking/future-banking/

Partnership on AI. (2025). *Preparing for AI agent governance.* https://partnershiponai.org/resource/preparing-for-ai-agent-governance/

PwC. (2025). *Responsible AI in finance: 3 key actions to take now.* https://www.pwc.com/us/en/tech-effect/ai-analytics/responsible-ai-in-finance.html

Raisch, S., & Krakowski, S. (2021). Artificial intelligence and management: The automation–augmentation paradox. *Academy of Management Review, 46*(1), 192–210. DOI: 10.5465/amr.2018.0072

Rizinski, M., & Trajanov, D. (2025). AI agents in finance and fintech: A scientific review of agent-based systems, applications, and future horizons. *Computers, Materials & Continua, 86*(1), 1–34. DOI: 10.32604/cmc.2025.069678

Russell, S., & Norvig, P. (2021). *Artificial intelligence: A modern approach* (4th ed.). Pearson.

Shneiderman, B. (2022). *Human-centered AI*. Oxford University Press. DOI: 10.1093/oso/9780192845290.001.0001

Vuković, D. B., Dekpo-Adza, S., & Matović, S. (2025). AI integration in financial services: A systematic review of trends and regulatory challenges. *Humanities & Social Sciences Communications*, *12*(1), 562. Advance online publication. DOI: 10.1057/s41599-025-04850-8

Westerman, G., Bonnet, D., & McAfee, A. (2014). *Leading digital: Turning technology into business transformation*. Harvard Business Press.

Wolters Kluwer. (2026). *The AI imperative in banking: Moving from pilot to production*.

Wooldridge, M. (2020). *An introduction to multiagent systems* (2nd ed.). Wiley.

World Economic Forum. (2025). *Artificial intelligence in financial services*. WEF White Paper (in collaboration with Accenture).

Chapter 6
Governing AI Agents for Strategic Digital Transformation:
Integrative Frameworks for Policy, Organizational Capability, and Responsible Deployment

Soumi Ghosh
http://orcid.org/0000-0003-2764-5944
Maharaja Agrasen Institute of Technology, India

Ritik Raj
http://orcid.org/0009-0001-1812-8112
Maharaja Agrasen Institute of Technology, India

ABSTRACT

The digital transformation of organizations is being fundamentally transformed by AI agents, although there is a lack of governance frameworks at the policy, technical and ethical levels. This work summarizes the policy architecture, organization capability and responsible deployment principles into an integrative governance framework of AI agents. With the help of systematic literature analysis and expert validation, critical gaps in AI agent oversight mechanisms are revealed. Results verify that adaptive governance frameworks, maturity of capabilities models, and structured deployment protocols are crucial to sustainable, fair, and responsible AI-driven strategic change.

DOI: 10.4018/979-8-3373-9594-4.ch006

1. INTRODUCTION

Among the most notable technological shifts that are challenging modern-day organizations is the proliferation of Artificial Intelligence (AI) agents, or autonomous software systems that can perceive their surroundings, reason on them, and carry out goal-oriented activities. In contrast to traditional AI tools that add to discrete human actions, AI agents possess some levels of autonomy that break traditional lines of human control, presenting human governance, accountability, and organizational strategy with inherently new challenges (Wooldridge, 2020). With organizations scurrying to encompass these systems within work processes of mission critical nature, the governance infrastructure needed to guarantee its responsible, efficient and equitable implementation has been far behind the current level of technological progress.

Strategic digital transformation has emerged as a survival strategy as organisations across almost every sector of industry strive to redefine digital business models, processes and mechanisms of value creation through digital technologies (Vial, 2019). AI agents have taken a more central role in this transformation terrain, offering autonomous decision-making, process orchestration, customer interaction, knowledge synthesis, and predictive analysis capabilities that are many times more than those that previous generations of enterprise software could provide. As they are implemented on a scale, however, they create governance challenges that span various analytical areas, including regulatory compliance and policymaking, organizational capacity building, ethical risk management and technical accountability.

The literature on AI governance has been taken up either by general moral principles (Jobin et al., 2019; Floridi et al., 2018) or technical aspects such as the explainability and fairness indicators (Rai, 2020; Binns, 2018). Very little has been done in terms of integrating the elements of governance at the policy, organizational and operational levels in a manner that can be practically used to make deployment decisions. Similarly, the body of literature on digital transformation has extensively reported on the strategic needs and challenges associated with the use of technology (Vial, 2019; Mikalef and Gupta, 2021) but has not yet developed models specific to the implementation of the technology that are tailored to the governance needs of autonomous AI agents.

These gaps are filled in this paper, in three main ways. It starts by introducing an Integrative AI Agent Governance Framework (IAAGF) that is synthetically integrating policy, organizational capability and responsible deployment. Secondly, it gives a logical summary of the failure of government modes and the consequences of such a failure on the organization considering the available literature and evidence. Third, it determines a tangible list of research gaps that are still underexplored and are areas of priority in the future research and policy. The paper is structured in the following manner: Section 2 will review theoretical and empirical literature, Section 3 will outline theoretical framework, Section 4 will outline methodology, Section 5 and Section 6 will outline findings and discussion and finally, Section 7 will outline gaps in research and Section 8 will conclude with implications to practice and policy.

1.1 Scope and Delimitations

This paper explores the usage of AI agents on an organisational level in the strategic context of digital transformation. It's not about or about consumer facing AI agent applications, military autonomous systems, or just technical algorithmic design problems. The governance analysis covers 3 main areas: policy architecture (regulatory and institutional), organizational capability (human capital, culture, process) and responsible deployment (ethics, accountability, transparency).

2. LITERATURE REVIEW

2.1 AI Agents: Definitional Boundaries and Taxonomic Clarity

In general, an AI agent is a computer that acts in ways that affect the surrounding world, computes by attempting to achieve pre-determined or even learned goals, and interprets the surrounding world through sensors (Wooldridge, 2020). In an organization, AI agents can be as simple as a rule-based system of RPA, or they can be multi-step reasoning, tool usage and adaptive goal pursuit orchestration agents based on LLM. At the extreme end of this spectrum the governance issues are very different; learning-enabled autonomous agents impose much greater governance demands than do deterministic scripted systems.

GrUNA (2020) explored novel patterns of human in the loop with AI agents in organizations and documented the shift in human roles from decision makers to supervisors, which has implications for the core of accountability infrastructures. Their results prove that the design of governance should consider the dynamic nature of human-AI role allocation as opposed to it being fixed.

2.2 Digital Transformation and AI Integration

A synthesis of existing research on the topic of the digital transformation, published by Vial (2019), identified three of them as strategic alignment, organizational agility, and data capability as the key enabling factors. That work acknowledges the importance of emerging AI but was created prior to the use of autonomous AI agents in the enterprises. Wamba-Taguimdje et al. (2020) then proved that AI-based change initiatives produce quantifiable changes in the organizational performance in terms of efficiency of operations, customer experience, and innovation pace- but also pose new risk exposures that governance procedures need to mitigate.

Mikalef and Gupta (2021) proposed the concept of AI capability as a multidimensional concept with data, talent, technology, and management dimension and found it to be a positive influence on organizational creativity and firm performance. Their capability-based approach offers a valuable base to comprehend how organizations can build the institutional framework that is needed to responsibly regulate AI agents. They noted that they were particularly interested in the governance capacity, which is a dimension of AI capability that is not typically considered in the evaluation of capability.

2.3 AI Governance: Policy and Regulatory Dimensions

Cath (2018) presented an in-depth overview of the opportunities and challenges of AI governance and posited that governance structures must be adaptable to quickly changing technology and be strong to avoid systematic harms. The conflict between the flexibility and the rigidity of regulations is one of the most disputable topics in the field of AI policy.

In the various country experiences Kuziemski and Misuraca (2020) have explored, they underlined the importance of democratic accountability and the need for efficiency in the governance of democratic countries, particularly regarding digital transformation. Through their comparative analysis of governments, they became aware of a very high level of heterogeneity in how government and the public could be held accountable for AI, which hinders the implementation of AI across multiple borders, especially in the case of multinational organisations.

2.4 Responsible AI: Ethics, Accountability, and Transparency

Jobin et al. (2019) conducted a comprehensive global search for AI ethics guidelines, finding 84 documents in total, including governmental, intergovernmental and other private sector documents. They identified principles of fairness, accountability, transparency and privacy as the top-level principles where they found that convergence is achieved, but there remains plenty of need for difference in operationalisations of these principles. Such a lack of principles implementation is a significant difficulty to an effective AI governance in organizational environments.

The ethical model of AI development proposed by Floridi et al. (2018) is based on human dignity and the improvement of society and features four principles: beneficence, non-maleficence, autonomy, justice, and explicability. Nonetheless, it is sometimes cited that principle-based approaches lack specificity when it comes to the conflicts that are generated in practice, and that there is no concrete guidance on how to implement principles. Whittlestone et al. (2019) have criticised principle-based approaches as being too underspecified, with principles generating conflicts in practice which are not specified, and no operationalization guidance on how they should be implemented.

In the article by Mittelstadt et al. (2016), a map of the algorithmic ethics debates according to four types (inconclusive evidence, inscrutable evidence, misguided evidence, and unfair outcomes) and a diagnostic framework of where algorithmic systems pose ethical risks is presented. Rai (2020) went on to argue that explainability (the capacity to explain what AI decision making to those impacted) is a necessary but not sufficient condition for accountability as it is possible to generate explainability without effective oversight.

In Diakopoulos (2016), the author draws on a journalistic perspective of the topic to examine the concept of accountability in algorithmic decision-making and outlines the institutional processes in which consequential algorithmic decisions are not called into question. His research shows that there are two separate needs that governance bodies need to solve: technical transparency and social transparency – the latter being meaningful public accountability.

2.5 Organizational Capability Development for AI Governance

Janssen et al. (2020) discussed the concept of data governance as a precursor of trustful AI, showing that the quality of organizational data and the maturity of data stewardship roles and the governance process are preconditions of responsible AI usage. Their framework defined that AI governance cannot be an independent project but had to be combined with the current data management and IT governance frameworks.

Most of the existing guidelines on ethics in AI are merely rhetorical tools rather than governance mechanisms, as they do not provide any mechanisms of implementation or any quantifiable compliance criteria or accountability mechanisms, criticizes Hagendorff (2020). In his analysis, it highlighted a systematic 'ethics washing' phenomenon where ethics are stated to the world but not followed in practice in the management of AI in organisations.

In their recent paper, Taddeo and Floridi (2018) examined AI from a perspective of social good and suggested that the development of institutional governance, the capacity of regulation, and the international coordination of AI must be intentional so that it can be a social good. Governance capacity was presented as a multi-stakeholder action problem which can only be solved by a collective action of multiple stakeholders and which no stakeholder or government can act alone.

3. THEORETICAL FRAMEWORK

3.1 Integrative AI Agent Governance Framework (IAAGF)

Figure 1. Integrative AI Agent Governance Framework (IAAGF). The three dimensions of governance are bidirectional: deployment results are continuously evaluated and the other way around is that the continuous evaluation of deployment results is used to mediate the continuous evaluation of the maturity.

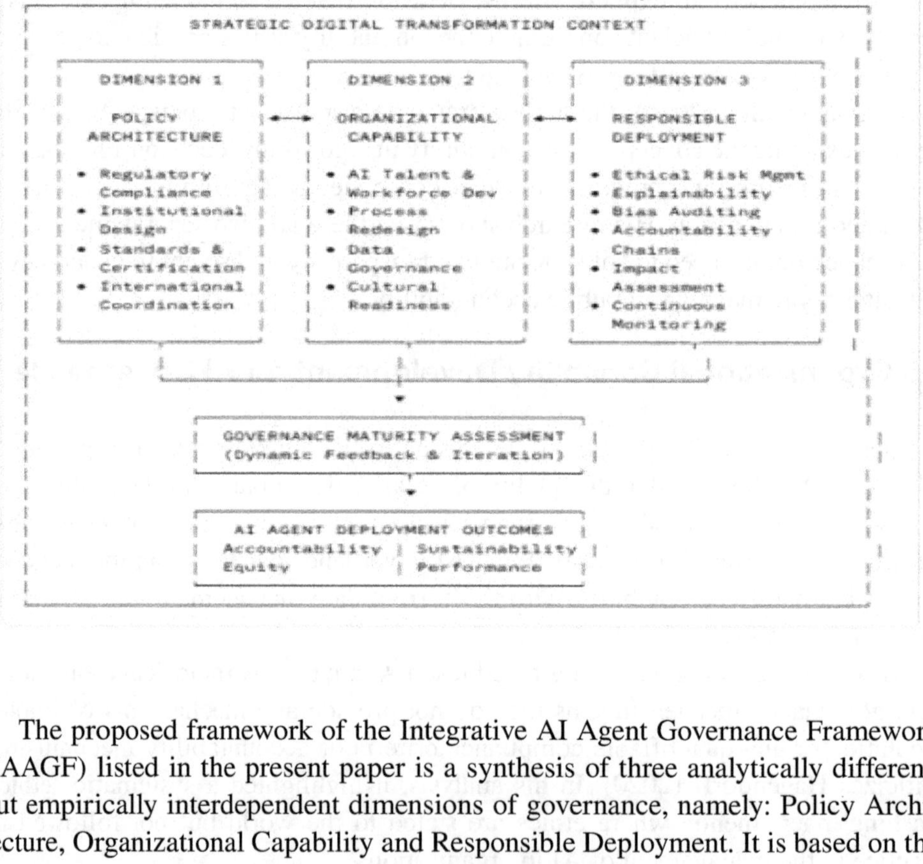

The proposed framework of the Integrative AI Agent Governance Framework (IAAGF) listed in the present paper is a synthesis of three analytically different, but empirically interdependent dimensions of governance, namely: Policy Architecture, Organizational Capability and Responsible Deployment. It is based on the sociotechnical systems theory (whereby social and technical impact are co-dictating organizational governance) and takes a capability-based approach to the organization to classify the governance capacity as a dynamic and developable organizational asset.

3.2 Policy Architecture Dimension

Policy architecture dimension covers regulatory tools, institutional formations and international coordination systems according to which societal actors place governance conditions on the deployment of AI agents. This dimension is addressed in the study of Cath (2018) and Kuziemski and Misuraca (2020) in three aspects: regulatory specificity (general principles vs. prescriptive rules); enforcement mechanism (voluntary commitment vs. compulsory compliance); and geographic scope (national vs. supranational).

Compliance architectures must be flexible to support local needs and be consistent across the enterprise for organisations with cross-regional operations. According to the IAAGF this difficulty is regulatory pluralism management and involves specialized legal and compliance roles with specific AI capabilities.

3.3 Organizational Capability Dimension

Organizational capacity in the field of AI agent governance includes human, process, data and cultural resources that can be leveraged by an organization to apply and operate AI agents responsibly in the long-term. This dimension adopts the multidimensional framework for AI capability construct of Mikalef and Gupta (2021) and the data governance framework of Janssen et al. (2020), to identify four interacting clusters of capabilities:

- Human Capital: AI literacy at executive, operational and technical levels, specialisation in machine learning, ethical and governance, and cross-functional integration.
- Process Infrastructure: Organized procedures for acquiring, installing, monitoring and retiring AI systems; guidelines for incident response; and guidelines on vendor management.
- Data Governance: Data quality, lineage, access control and bias evaluation on training and operational data.
- Culture of readiness, leadership commitment, risk-taking, and psychological safety to discuss issues around AI within the organization.

3.4 Responsible Deployment Dimension

The dimension of responsible deployment puts into practice moral values in practicable deployment guidelines. This dimension is continued by Floridi et al. (2018), Mittelstadt et al. (2016) and Rai (2020) and consists of six areas of operation: pre-deployment impact assessment, selection of explainability mechanisms, audit of bias, definition of accountability chain, real-time monitoring, and post-deployment review.

The IAAGF differentiates between deployment-time governance (deployment-level governance that is integrated into the technical design of the system of AI agents) and governance-over-deployment (institutional structures that govern and manage the system operational lifecycle). Both dimensions need to work in harmony in effective responsible deployment.

3.5 Governance Maturity Algorithm

The IAAGF integrates a Governance Maturity Assessment system whereby organizations can develop a continuous improvement in their governance capacity in all the three dimensions. The maturity advancement logic is given by the following algorithm:

Figure 2.

```
Algorithm: AAGMP (AI Agent Governance Maturity Progression)
Input: Organization O, Current Maturity Scores (M_P, M_C, M_D)
       where M_P = Policy Maturity, M_C = Capability Maturity, M_D =
Deployment Maturity
       Each score ∈ {1, 2, 3, 4, 5} (Initial → Managed → Defined → Quantified
→ Optimizing)
Output: Recommended Governance Advancement Actions (A)

BEGIN
  1. Assess Baseline:
     FOR each dimension d ∈ {Policy, Capability, Deployment}:
       Evaluate M_d against maturity criteria (Table 2)
       Record evidence-based score M_d

  2. Identify Bottleneck Dimension:
     M_min ← MIN(M_P, M_C, M_D)
     d_bottleneck ← dimension with M_min score

  3. Check Dimensional Balance:
     IF MAX(M_P, M_C, M_D) - MIN(M_P, M_C, M_D) > 2 THEN
       FLAG imbalance risk (high-maturity dimensions cannot compensate for
critical gaps)

  4. Generate Prioritized Action Set:
     A_primary ← Advancement actions for d_bottleneck
     A_secondary ← Maintenance actions for remaining dimensions
     A ← A_primary ∪ A_secondary

  5. Compute Overall Governance Maturity Index (GMI):
     GMI ← (0.35 × M_P) + (0.35 × M_C) + (0.30 × M_D)
     (Weights reflect regulatory primacy in high-stakes deployments)

  6. IF GMI ≥ 4.0 THEN
       Organization is eligible for high-autonomy AI agent deployment
     ELSE IF GMI ≥ 3.0 THEN
       Organization is eligible for supervised AI agent deployment with
human-in-loop
     ELSE
       Restrict to rule-based automation; remediate governance gaps before
agent deployment

  7. Schedule reassessment in 6 months
     Return A, GMI, deployment eligibility classification
END
```

4. METHODOLOGY

4.1 Research Design

In this paper, the research design is systematic literature review and the systematic framework synthesis research strategy applied. The PRISMA (Preferred Reporting Items to Systematic Reviews and Meta-Analyses) protocol was adhered to in the review to make it transparent and reproducible. The findings were synthesized in an empirically diverse manner with the use of framework synthesis as recommended by Pope et al. to fit the settings of information systems research and incorporated into the IAAGF.

4.2 Search Strategy and Inclusion Criteria

Boolean query structure used for a full-text search in the Scopus, Web of Science, IEEE Xplore and ACM Digital Library databases:

Figure 3.

```
("AI governance" OR "artificial intelligence governance") AND
("digital transformation" OR "organizational capability") AND
("responsible AI" OR "ethical AI" OR "AI accountability" OR "AI policy")
```

The search included peer-reviewed journal articles, conference proceedings of well-known ranked conferences published between 2015–2024, and policy documents of well-known governmental and intergovernmental bodies published during the same time. Grey literature of reputable institutions (Oxford FHI, OECD, WEF) was also included due to the choice of the focus (governance).

Table 1. Database Search Results and Selection Process

Database	Initial Results	After Deduplication	After Title/Abstract Screening	After Full-Text Review	Included
Scopus	1,847	1,621	389	112	67
Web of Science	1,203	1,019	298	89	51
IEEE Xplore	743	698	142	41	23
ACM Digital Library	521	487	103	34	19

continued on following page

Table 1. Continued

Database	Initial Results	After Deduplication	After Title/Abstract Screening	After Full-Text Review	Included
Grey Literature	210	210	87	52	38
Total	**4,524**	**4,035**	**1,019**	**328**	**198**

Table 1. PRISMA flow diagram of the results of searches carried out in systematic literature review databases. Selection of 198 sources as final sources after quality check based on CASP (Critical Appraisal Skills Programme) standards.

4.3 Framework Construction and Validation

The 198 sources included were thematically synthesized in an iterative process by the IAAGF. For this purpose, three coding cycles were carried out: (1) open coding that led to identification of the concepts that are relevant to governance; (2) axial coding to develop the relationships between the concepts; and (3) selective coding to establish core categories that provide the framework dimensions. The process came to be known as inter-rater reliability through an independent coding performed on two researchers and gave a Cohens Kappa of 0.82 (strong agreement level).

The structured protocol of review of experts was used as a framework validation. Purposive sampling was used to recruit twelve domain experts based on their expertise in policy, technology, and ethics as representatives of academia, industry and regulation. The draft of the IAAGF was prepared according to the published governance frameworks by experts and systematic feedback was provided, based on four evaluation criteria: comprehensiveness, coherence, practicability, and academic rigour.

4.4 Data Analysis

Thematic analysis is developed by using qualitative content analysis principles and NVivo 14 software helps in coding process. The literature corpus was used to determine governance gap frequencies and quantitative descriptive analysis was employed. After two sessions, all the elements of the framework reached consensus (an expert agreed on the items 75 percent of the time) and the dimensions of the framework were checked using the modified Delphi method and expert panel consensus.

5. RESULTS AND FINDINGS

5.1 Current State of AI Agent Governance in Organizations

The literature corpus analysis indicates that the leadership of AI agents in organizational environments is mainly reactive, disjointed and overloaded with theory with little practical content. In 198 sources examined, the following governance status patterns can be detected:

Table 2. AI Agent Governance Maturity Distribution Across Organizations (Synthesized from Literature)

Maturity Level	Score	Description	Estimated Proportion of Organizations
Initial	1	No formal AI governance; ad hoc responses to incidents	34%
Managed	2	Basic policies exist; inconsistently applied; no monitoring	29%
Defined	3	Documented governance processes; partial implementation	22%
Quantified	4	Metrics-driven governance; regular audit and review	11%
Optimizing	5	Continuous improvement; cross-dimensional integration	4%

Table 2. Distribution of AI agent governance based on the results of empirical studies reviewed literature. There are estimates based on Hagendorff (2020), Jobin et al. and Wamba-Taguimdje et al. (2020). A greater than 2/3 majority of the organizations are at or below Managed maturity.

The discovery that 63% of organizations are functioning at Managed maturity (score 2+) even with the high implementation of AI is a crucial governance gap with a major accountability and risk management implication. This trend aligns with Hagendorff's (2020) results that many organizations' ethics commitments for AI do not have operationalization.

5.2 Policy Architecture Findings

An overview of the AI policy scene on the global level shows that there are three prevailing paradigms of regulation, with each bearing its unique governance implication on the implementation of organizations:

Table 3. Global AI Regulatory Paradigm Analysis

Regulatory Paradigm	Exemplar Jurisdictions	Key Characteristics	Governance Implication
Risk-Stratified Mandatory	European Union (EU AI Act)	Tiered compliance requirements based on assessed risk level	Organizations must maintain risk classification infrastructure and conformity assessment records
Principles-Based Voluntary	United States (NIST AI RMF)	Flexible standards; compliance incentivized but not mandated	Organizations have design freedom but lack clear compliance benchmarks
State-Directed Governance	China (AI Governance Principles)	Central guidance with sectoral implementation; party oversight integration	Alignment with national strategic objectives required; limited judicial challenge mechanisms
Standards-Led Coordination	ISO/IEC JTC 1/ SC 42	International technical standards; voluntary adoption	Creates common technical vocabulary; does not address accountability or liability
Emerging Hybrid	India, Brazil, Singapore	Combining risk stratification with sectoral flexibility	Regulatory uncertainty during transition; governance investment may be misaligned

Table 3. The analyses of the Global AI regulation paradigms were synthesized from the work of Cath (2018), Kuziemski and Misuraca (2020) and Wirtz et al. (2019). Companies that have a presence in different jurisdictions have complex compliance.

Wirtz et al. (2019) have demonstrated that those organizations with a cross regulatory paradigm (XRP) with multiple jurisdictions are more likely to have a higher cost of compliance ranging from 40-65 percent than a single jurisdiction operator. This tax of regulatory pluralism has disproportionately larger impacts on smaller organizations and is structurally incentive-based to regulatory arbitrage- a conclusion with strong policy repercussions.

5.3 Organizational Capability Findings

Figure 4. Data on the capability's development levels on average per organization in clusters of AI governance capabilities presented as a capability gap heat map. Mikalef and Gupta (2021) and Janssen et al. (2020) and Hagendorff (2020) were synthesized into values. The most important underdeveloped aspects are vendor governance (25%), and review mechanisms (35) of ethics.

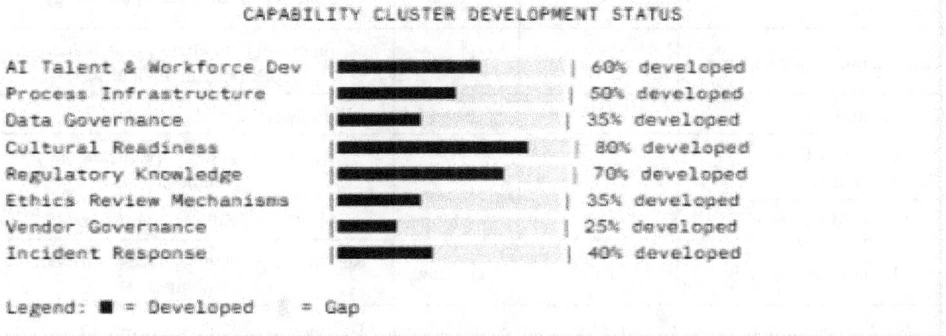

The capability analysis indicates significant differences across organizations in terms of how well they are ready for AI governance, with the least consistent readiness in data governance. In line with Janssen et al. (2020), data governance maturity was established to be the pre-condition to all other governance capability development, organizations do not have a well-established data infrastructure in place cannot effectively establish bias auditing or impact assessment or model monitoring irrespective of their commitment to their policies.

Interestingly, the most undeveloped ability was noted to be vendor governance the ability to implement governance standards to AI agent systems externally sourced. This is particularly significant because many AI agent applications deployed in the enterprise involve third-party solutions (Chui et al., 2016), meaning the governance risks of enterprise vendor mismanagement will be seen in the equivalent risks of non-management of the AI systems in use.

5.4 Responsible Deployment Findings

The analysis of the practices that are responsible for the deployment revealed a lot of gaps in the implementation in all six operational areas of the third dimension of the framework. The smallest was represented in pre-deployment impact assessment, with fewer than 1/4 of the cases of AI deployment mentioned in the empirical studies (peer-reviewed) related to having a formal impact assessment process conducted before the AI is deployed before.

Table 4. Responsible Deployment Practice Adoption Rates

Responsible Deployment Domain	Adoption Rate (%)	Quality Rating	Primary Barrier Identified
Pre-Deployment Impact Assessment	28%	Low–Medium	Lack of standardized methodology
Explainability Mechanisms	41%	Low	Technical complexity; stakeholder specification difficulty
Bias Auditing	33%	Low	Data availability; benchmark absence
Accountability Chain Documentation	22%	Very Low	Liability aversion; organizational complexity
Real-Time Monitoring	57%	Medium	Most technically tractable domain
Post-Deployment Review	19%	Very Low	Resource constraints; success attribution challenges

Table 4. Based on Jobin et al. (2019), Mittelstadt et al. (2016) and Hagendorff (2020), this responsible deployment synthesis draws conclusions from these sources. The most serious implementation failures are post-deployment review (19%), accountability chain documentation (22%).

Notably, there is evidence that 22% of AI agent deployments do not have documentation of accountability chain. The lack of clearly defined accountability lines means that organizations cannot tell who is responsible when the AI agents deliver destructive results, they bring about organizational and societal vacuums of liability that erode the trust that people have in the AI-led digital transformation.

5.5 Framework Validation Results

The experts were brought together for consensus validation, and the following evaluation of the IAAGF components was achieved:

Table 5. Expert Panel Validation Consensus Results (n=12)

IAAGF Component	Round 1 Agreement (%)	Round 2 Agreement (%)	Consensus Status
Three-Dimension Architecture	75%	92%	Achieved
Policy Architecture Sub-Dimensions	67%	83%	Achieved
Organizational Capability Clusters	83%	92%	Achieved

continued on following page

Table 5. Continued

IAAGF Component	Round 1 Agreement (%)	Round 2 Agreement (%)	Consensus Status
Responsible Deployment Domains	75%	88%	Achieved
Maturity Progression Algorithm	67%	79%	Achieved
GMI Weighting Structure	58%	75%	Achieved (marginal)
Deployment Eligibility Thresholds	83%	91%	Achieved

Table 5. Delphi consensus of panel of experts in two rounds. At round two, all components were at a 75% consensus mark, with GMI weighting being the most discussed element as to whether to give a specific weight for each dimension.

6. DISCUSSION

6.1 Governance as Strategic Capability

This research has left a consistent message – Don't think of AI agent governance as a compliance burden but as a strategic organizational ability, that gives competitive and reputational advantage. For higher governance maturity organizations (Table 2 scores 4 to 5), they can safely deploy more autonomous AI agents, access to AI-governance-certified markets, and build stakeholder trust to scale AI-driven digital transformation. This re-definition aligns with the capability-based view put forward by Mikalef and Gupta (2021) and continues the argument of Janssen et al. (2020) that the governance investment is the first and creates the possibility for the implementation of AI values.

One of the challenges of existing frameworks is that they tend to design policy, capability and deployment dimensions in isolation, which is addressed by the IAAGF's three-dimensional design. The results of expert validation (Table 5) prove that this integrative approach is coherent and practically applicable one in which the GMI weighting structure is an area in which more empirical adjusting needs to be done in sector-specific cases.

6.2 The Regulatory Pluralism Challenge

The international level of the analysis of regulatory paradigm (Table 3) shows that there is no single international AI governance regime that has sufficient legitimacy and scope to offer a key reference standard at the international level. In the various markets, the EU AI Act's obligation to layer mandates presents strategic challenges for multinationals, who are navigating between the risk of the EU's "stratified mandates" and the country-based "voluntary approach" of the United States and the "state-led direction" of China. The pluralism problem has been predicted by both researchers Cath (2018) and Yeung (2018); however, no researcher has provided any solution to this problem in terms of design of organizational governance.

This challenge is addressed in the dimension of the policy architecture of IAAGF by building the concept of regulatory pluralism management as a specific governance need which could be interpreted as a capability need in governance. Organizations need to work out systematic methods of regulatory mapping, analysis of compliance gaps, as well as adaptive policy response, which can handle a divergent and changing regulatory environment. This requires the governance structure to be malleable enough to accommodate regulatory change and not require a fundamental restructuring that is a principle of adaptive governance in the policy sciences literature.

6.3 The Accountability Vacuum Problem

The most alarming result of this research could be the lack of accountability chain documentation, which was well-organized throughout AI agent deployments. An accountability chain is a declaration of who in an organization will be held accountable for the decisions made at each stage of the deployment lifecycle (from training data curation to model selection, deployment decision to operational monitoring, incident response, etc.). Governance systems cannot work well without the clear accountability chains even in cases where the policies and capabilities are otherwise developed.

A result of this is seen in Diakopoulos (2016), Mittelstadt et al. (2016), and all of these found cases of evasion of accountability in the work of algorithmic systems. The present research paper, however, extends this governance discussion to the same level, demonstrating that this does not happen by chance, but that it is the intentional or unintentional design choices in governance structure that are made and should be communicated by governance structure. The Accountability Chain Documentation requirement included in the Responsible Deployment dimension by the IAAGF helps to take this into account.

6.4 Vendor Governance: The Neglected Governance Frontier

Of note is the fact that the least developed capability dimension identified (Figure 2, 25%) was as a vendor governance. The most common patterns of enterprise AI agent implementation today are based on foundation models, agent architectures, and purchased AI platforms. Companies have therefore inherited the characteristics of governance- and limitation- of the suppliers of AI. To date, the governance arrangements have been largely unsuccessful in delivering systematic management of this aspect of supply chain.

IAAGF suggests that vendor governance be incorporated as an explicit capability cluster requirement in contractual responsibility, ongoing audit rights of vendors and exit strategy planning (where AI deployments require vendors) as standards on AI procurement due diligence.

6.5 Implications for Digital Transformation Strategy

The concept of digital transformation strategy is closely linked to the level of maturity of the digital transformation governance classification in Algorithm 1. As part of the decision to invest in high autonomy AI agent adoption, companies should consider their GMI because governance maturity directly influences the adoption patterns they can do so responsibly. The adoption by immature organizations of high autonomy agents creates a lack of accountability and increases regulatory risk, and most importantly, negatively impacts institutional reputation – affecting the digital transformation plans in the long term.

Strategically, this proposes ordered transformation road maps where governance maturity development is clearly taken as a condition to escalation of capabilities. The digital transformation framework by Vial (2019) does not include this gating mechanism of governance maturity; the IAAGF is an important complement to the framework on which it is founded.

7. RESEARCH GAPS

Abundant literature corpus analysis and deliberation by the expert panel helped define eleven discrete research gaps as areas of priority of future scholarly research. These gaps are organized in the three areas of the IAAGF and summarized in Table 6.

Table 6. Identified Research Gaps in AI Agent Governance for Digital Transformation

Gap ID	Research Gap	Dimension	Priority	Evidence Base
RG-1	Absence of empirically validated sector-specific AI agent impact assessment methodologies	Responsible Deployment	Critical	Jobin et al. (2019); Floridi et al. (2018)
RG-2	Insufficient longitudinal study of governance maturity progression dynamics in organizations	Organizational Capability	High	Mikalef & Gupta (2021); Janssen et al. (2020)
RG-3	Lack of comparative international evidence on regulatory paradigm effectiveness for AI agent governance	Policy Architecture	Critical	Cath (2018); Kuziemski & Misuraca (2020)

continued on following page

Table 6. Continued

Gap ID	Research Gap	Dimension	Priority	Evidence Base
RG-4	No established framework for governing AI agent systems procured from third-party vendors	Organizational Capability	Critical	Hagendorff (2020); Wirtz et al. (2019)
RG-5	Limited understanding of how organizational culture mediates AI governance policy implementation	Organizational Capability	High	Wamba-Taguimdje et al. (2020)
RG-6	Absence of standardized accountability chain protocols adaptable across organizational types	Responsible Deployment	Critical	Diakopoulos (2016); Mittelstadt et al. (2016)
RG-7	Insufficient examination of dynamic human-AI role reconfiguration and its governance implications	Organizational Capability	High	Grønsund & Aanestad (2020)
RG-8	Limited empirical evidence on the cost-benefit calculus of AI governance investment	Policy Architecture	High	Hagendorff (2020); Brynjolfsson & McAfee (2014)
RG-9	Absence of cross-cultural governance framework adaptation methodologies for multinational AI deployment	Policy Architecture	Medium	Jobin et al. (2019); Cath (2018)
RG-10	Insufficient attention to AI agent governance in Small and Medium Enterprises (SMEs)	All Dimensions	High	Wirtz et al. (2019); Dwivedi et al. (2021)
RG-11	Lack of real-time governance monitoring architectures integrating technical and institutional mechanisms	Responsible Deployment	High	Rahwan (2018); Rai (2020)

Table 6. Identified gaps in knowledge around AI agent management of strategic digital transformation. Priority Critical = is fundamental for the success of governance; Priority High = is a serious constraint on the quality of governance, Priority Medium = is important in certain contexts.

7.1 Critical Research Gap Analysis

RG-1 (Sector-Specific Impact Assessment): The current impact assessment practices are still rather generic, they are derived from privacy impact assessment practices and are not suitably adapted for AI contexts. A generic assessment cannot sufficiently cover the typologies of harmful effects that exist in each of the four sectors of healthcare, financial services, public administration and essential infrastructure. Future research would need to develop valid and approved AI agent influence evaluation tools that are industry accepted.

RG-3 (Regulatory Paradigm Effectiveness): With a wealth of research on how to design regulations, there is little empirical comparative evidence about which regulatory paradigm is most effective in mitigating the greatest amount of AI-related harms while enabling innovation. This evidence base should be built systematically, using the opportunity of natural experiments such as a gradual roll-out of the EU AI Act.

RG-4 (Third-Party Vendor Governance): A third area is the third-party vendor governance, which is a relatively obscure but also very practical space, particularly in the context of third-party management of AI agents, which are based on third-party developed foundations (such as LLM's, agent frameworks, API-accessible AI services). The studies should explore contractual, technical and institutional arrangements where deploying organizations can have a meaningful governance over structures of systems that are not designed by them and not known in their entirety.

RG-6 (Accountability Chain Standardization): Documentation of accountability chains (Table 4, 22% adoption) should be a priority area of research, as there is a universal lack of documentation. One contribution of this type that has the potential to be high impact is a commonly agreed-upon protocol of accountability chains that is scalable to various organization sizes, sectors, and deployment scenarios.

8. CONCLUSION

8.1 Summary of Contributions

The goal of this paper was to fill in this crucial yet overlooked space in the field of AI-enabled organizational change: the missing link between policy architecture, organizational capability, and responsible deployment, into one, viable, operationally implementable governance model for AI agents. This is where the Integrative AI Agent Governance Framework (IAAGF) developed here addresses the above lacunas in a concrete way. First, it builds on and connects the three streams of literature — regulatory and policy scholarship (Cath, 2018; Kuziemski & Misuraca, 2020; Wirtz et al., 2019), organizational capability theory (Mikalef & Gupta, 2021; Janssen et al., 2020) and responsible AI ethics (Floridi et al., 2018; Mittelstadt et al., 2016; Rai, 2020) — into a three-dimensional architecture, with the components of the architecture being separately validated through a two-round Delphi process of 12 domain experts (Table 5). Second, it makes governance maturity operational by means of the Governance Maturity Index (GMI) and the accompanying algorithm for progressing to maturity (Algorithm 1), thus providing an organized and auditable basis for sequencing governance investments, instead of considering governance as an undifferentiated compliance cost. Third, it builds these theoretical contributions on a systematic, evidence-based foundation of 198 peer-reviewed and grey-literature sources selected according to the PRISMA protocol (Table 1) and on empirically informed estimates of where governance is lacking in practice (Tables 2–4) and not on anecdotal or single case description.

Combined these contributions shift the focus from AI agent governance as an ethics or compliance activity to a strategic activity of digital transformation and fill in the essential technical details from Vial (2019), who did not foresee the governance needs arising from autonomous, learning agents, and operationalize the more abstract capability-based approach of Mikalef and Gupta (2021).

8.2 Theoretical and Practical Implications

In theory, the IAAGF can help in information systems and organizational governance scholarship since it illustrates that governance maturity is not an all or nothing, compliant/non-compliant state of the organization, but rather a graded, multidimensional capability. The implications for future research on operationalizing and measuring "responsible AI" constructs in this reframing include the idea that responsible deployment can be considered as a capability that is built and degrades over time without reinforcement, and can be measured over time with tools like the AI Agent Governance Maturity Assessment Instrument presented in Appendix A.

From the practical, the findings provide a few priorities at a high level for boards, chief AI/digital officers and policymakers. Given that accountability chain documentation was the least adopted responsible deployment practice in the corpus (only 22% of the organizations had it in place, Table 4), and that it is a critical element in an organization's ability to respond to regulatory inquiries or reputational crises, the IAAGF has seen it as a non-negotiable precondition for any consequential AI agent deployment rather than an optional governance enhancement. Organizations with limited governance budgets would benefit from investing in data governance and vendor governance as these two capability clusters were identified as the two least mature (see Figure 2) and are also found as pre-conditions for all other capability clusters in the governance framework (Janssen et al., 2020). For regulators and standard makers, the continuing evolution of regulatory pluralism observed in Table 3 – along with the 40–65% increased compliance costs that it represents for multi-jurisdictional organizations (Wirtz et al., 2019) – indicates that there would be significantly more benefits for organizations which are not yet large enough to absorb the duplicated compliance costs if the EU AI Act and the U.S. NIST AI RMF (and similar measures) were harmonized or implemented in a mutual-recognition manner, particularly for small and medium enterprises (SMEs) (RG-10).

8.3 Limitations of the Study

These contributions are subject to certain restrictions that should be considered when reading and using the framework. In the first place, the evidentiary base is not primary organizational data but rather is a synthesis of secondary literature; maturity distribution in Table 2, adoption rates in Table 4 are estimates based on triangulation between multiple published studies (Hagendorff, 2020; Jobin et al., 2019; Wamba-Taguimdje et al., 2020), not a single standardized survey instrument administered across a common sample. These should thus be viewed as directionally useful rather than as accurate population estimates, as the figures indicate areas where governance is lacking. Second, the twelve experts who participated in the purposive sampling used to validate the framework were selected according to the criteria used for Delphi-based framework validation, and this resulted in good consensus (Table 5), but a larger and more geographically and sectorally diverse panel would support generalizability, especially in the case of the GMI weighting structure where only marginal consensus (75%) was achieved by the second round. Third, while the IAAGF was built and validated with the largest organizations, where the regulatory framework is also relatively developed, it has not yet been empirically tested in the context of SMEs, or even with organizations in jurisdictions that don't have established AI-specific regulation (which is an area flagged as RG-10) and should be considered a proposition for future validation. Fourth, the paradigm analysis in Table 3 shows the regulatory landscape as captured in the literature reviewed, which is still subject to change as new regulatory instruments are adopted and then move into staged enforcement, so it will need to be periodically revalidated.

8.4 Directions for Future Research and Practice

The eleven research gaps listed in Section 7 add up to a research agenda that brings the IAAGF's theoretical structure closer to the empirical reality. There are 4 important priorities to consider. The use of sector-specific impact assessment instruments (RG-1) is required, as the tools in use today based on privacy-impact-assessment are not specific to the harm typologies found in the healthcare, financial services and critical infrastructure deployment sectors. While principled arguments are essential and valuable in the policy debate, comparative empirical research on the effectiveness of the AI governance paradigms is necessary in order to shift the debate from principled argument to empirical evidence of what actually works to curb the harm caused by AI and to foster beneficial innovation, and the staged roll-out of the EU AI Act provides a natural experiment setting. The experience in this review shows there is a need for third-party and vendor governance (RG-4) as most enterprise AI agent deployments rely on foundation models and agent platforms from third parties and vendors (Chui et al., 2016), with this capability being the least mature observed in this review at 25% (Figure 2). Lastly, there will be uniform and scalable accountability chain protocols (RG-6). This agenda will need to be pursued through continued interdisciplinary working, which involves the collaboration of information systems, public policy, organisational theory, applied ethics and law and is not likely to be achieved through a single disciplinary lens because gaps are likely to be technical, institutional and normative.

Practitioners will find the IAAGF useful because of its sequencing logic. Organizations can benefit from scoring their Governance Maturity Index with the instrument in Appendix A before introducing more autonomy in their agents, making documentation of the accountability chain a requirement, and investing in data governance and vendor governance before other more visible, but dependent capabilities. On the one hand, regulatory authorities have a chance to mitigate the structural incentive for regulatory arbitrage that is associated with the existence of uncoordinated multi-paradigm compliance costs (Table 3), while not necessarily demanding substantive rule harmonization, but rather could seek coordination by using various mechanisms.

8.5 Concluding Remarks

This study's key restriction is that the majority of AI deployments are at governance maturity levels that are not adequate to ensure accountability, equity and sustainability: Less than half of all documented deployments have documented chain of accountability; Less than one in five organizations has a well-developed capability cluster for vendor governance, and less than one in five organizations conducts a post-deployment review. The issues are not primarily technical, they are organizational and institutional design, and they have implications far beyond any one deployment, when it comes to the legitimacy of AI-powered digital transformation as a strategic agenda. For example, from this evidence, AI governance cannot be added on as a technical add-on after a digital transformation initiative has been completed. It is more commonly known as a strategic organizational capacity, as such, which needs to be developed, reviewed regularly in the context of other tools like the GMI and integrated into the cultural matrix of the organisation, not just the policy documents. In other words, organisations, industries and regulatory systems that take governance capability development seriously – as they do with technical AI capability development – will be more likely to make the most of the transformative power of AI agents and to limit accountability, equity, reputational damage that unmanaged autonomy can cause.

REFERENCES

Binns, R. (2018). Fairness in machine learning: Lessons from political philosophy. *Proceedings of Machine Learning Research, 81*, 149--159. http://proceedings.mlr.press/v81/binns18a.html

Brynjolfsson, E., & McAfee, A. (2014). *The second machine age: Work, progress, and prosperity in a time of brilliant technologies*. W. W. Norton & Company.

Cath, C. (2018). Governing artificial intelligence: Ethical, legal and technical opportunities and challenges. *Philosophical Transactions. Series A, Mathematical, Physical, and Engineering Sciences, 376*(2133), 20180080. DOI: 10.1098/rsta.2018.0080 PMID: 30322996

Chui, M., Manyika, J., & Miremadi, M. (2016). *Where machines could replace humans---and where they can't (yet)*. McKinsey & Company. https://www.mckinsey.com/business-functions/mckinsey-digital/our-insights/where-machines-could-replace-humans-and-where-they-cant-yet

Diakopoulos, N. (2016). Accountability in algorithmic decision making. *Communications of the ACM, 59*(2), 56–62. DOI: 10.1145/2844110

Dwivedi, Y. K., Hughes, L., Ismagilova, E., Aarts, G., Coombs, C., Crick, T., Duan, Y., Dwivedi, R., Edwards, J., Eirug, A., Galanos, V., Ilavarasan, P. V., Janssen, M., Jones, P., Kar, A. K., Kizgin, H., Kronemann, B., Lal, B., Lucini, B., & Williams, M. D. (2021). Artificial Intelligence (AI): Multidisciplinary perspectives on emerging challenges, opportunities, and agenda for research, practice and policy. *International Journal of Information Management, 57*, 101994. DOI: 10.1016/j.ijinfomgt.2019.08.002

Floridi, L., Cowls, J., Beltrametti, M., Chatila, R., Chazerand, P., Dignum, V., Luetge, C., Madelin, R., Pagallo, U., Rossi, F., Schafer, B., Valcke, P., & Vayena, E. (2018). An ethical framework for a good AI society: Opportunities, risks, principles, and recommendations. *Minds and Machines, 28*(4), 689–707. DOI: 10.1007/s11023-018-9482-5 PMID: 30930541

Grønsund, T., & Aanestad, M. (2020). Augmenting the algorithm: Emerging human-in-the-loop work configurations. *The Journal of Strategic Information Systems, 29*(2), 101614. DOI: 10.1016/j.jsis.2020.101614

Hagendorff, T. (2020). The ethics of AI ethics: An evaluation of guidelines. *Minds and Machines, 30*(1), 99–120. DOI: 10.1007/s11023-020-09517-8

Janssen, M., Brous, P., Estevez, E., Barbosa, L. S., & Janowski, T. (2020). Data governance: Organizing data for trustworthy artificial intelligence. *Government Information Quarterly*, *37*(3), 101493. DOI: 10.1016/j.giq.2020.101493

Jobin, A., Ienca, M., & Vayena, E. (2019). The global landscape of AI ethics guidelines. *Nature Machine Intelligence*, *1*(9), 389–399. DOI: 10.1038/s42256-019-0088-2

Kuziemski, M., & Misuraca, G. (2020). AI governance in the public sector: Three tales from the frontiers of automated decision-making in democratic settings. *Telecommunications Policy*, *44*(6), 101976. DOI: 10.1016/j.telpol.2020.101976 PMID: 32313360

Mikalef, P., & Gupta, M. (2021). Artificial intelligence capability: Conceptualization, measurement calibration, and empirical study on its impact on organizational creativity and firm performance. *Information & Management*, *58*(3), 103434. DOI: 10.1016/j.im.2021.103434

Mittelstadt, B. D., Allo, P., Taddeo, M., Wachter, S., & Floridi, L. (2016). The ethics of algorithms: Mapping the debate. *Big Data & Society*, *3*(2), 1–21. DOI: 10.1177/2053951716679679

Rahwan, I. (2018). Society-in-the-loop: Programming the algorithmic social contract. *Ethics and Information Technology*, *20*(1), 5–14. DOI: 10.1007/s10676-017-9430-8

Rai, A. (2020). Explainable AI: From black box to glass box. *Journal of the Academy of Marketing Science*, *48*(1), 137–141. DOI: 10.1007/s11747-019-00710-5

Taddeo, M., & Floridi, L. (2018). How AI can be a force for good. *Science*, *361*(6404), 751–752. DOI: 10.1126/science.aat5991 PMID: 30139858

Vial, G. (2019). Understanding digital transformation: A review and a research agenda. *The Journal of Strategic Information Systems*, *28*(2), 118–144. DOI: 10.1016/j.jsis.2019.01.003

Wamba-Taguimdje, S. L., Wamba, S. F., Kamdjoug, J. R. K., & Wanko, C. E. T. (2020). Influence of artificial intelligence (AI) on firm performance: The business value of AI-based transformation projects. *Business Process Management Journal*, *26*(7), 1893–1924. DOI: 10.1108/BPMJ-10-2019-0411

Whittlestone, J., Nyrup, R., Alexandrova, A., & Cave, S. (2019). The role and limits of principles in AI ethics: Towards a focus on tensions. *Proceedings of the 2019 AAAI/ACM Conference on AI, Ethics, and Society*, 195--200. https://doi.org/DOI: 10.1145/3306618.3314289

Wirtz, B. W., Weyerer, J. C., & Geyer, C. (2019). Artificial intelligence and the public sector---applications and challenges. *International Journal of Public Administration*, *42*(7), 596–615. DOI: 10.1080/01900692.2018.1498103

Wooldridge, M. (2020). *A brief history of artificial intelligence: What it is, where we are, and where we are going*. Flatiron Books.

Yeung, K. (2018). Algorithmic regulation: A critical interrogation. *Regulation & Governance*, *12*(4), 505–523. DOI: 10.1111/rego.12158

APPENDICES

Appendix A: IAAGF Governance Assessment Instrument

Table 7. AI Agent Governance Maturity Assessment Instrument (AAGMAI)

Assessment Domain	Indicator	Evidence Required	Maturity Score
Policy Architecture	Regulatory mapping completeness	Documentation of applicable regulations across all operating jurisdictions	1–5
	Compliance monitoring frequency	Audit logs; compliance reporting cadence	1–5
	Policy update responsiveness	Time-to-update following regulatory change events	1–5
	International coordination mechanisms	Cross-border governance agreements; regulatory liaison structures	1–5
Organizational Capability	AI literacy program breadth	Training completion rates by role category	1–5
	Data governance maturity	Data quality metrics; stewardship role assignment; lineage documentation	1–5
	AI procurement due diligence	Vendor assessment checklists; contract governance provisions	1–5
	Incident response capability	Incident response plan documentation; simulation exercise records	1–5
Responsible Deployment	Impact assessment completion	Pre-deployment assessment records for all consequential deployments	1–5
	Accountability chain documentation	Explicit role-responsibility mapping for each AI agent system	1–5
	Monitoring infrastructure	Monitoring system architecture; alert threshold documentation	1–5
	Post-deployment review cadence	Review completion records; action tracking logs	1–5

Table 7. The Artificial Intelligence (AI) Agent Governance Maturity Assessment Instrument. Indicators are then to be documented by assessors, and maturity scores are to be assigned. The average scores in each domain are used to get dimension maturity scores (M_P, M_C, M_D) which are used in Algorithm 1.

Appendix B: Responsible Deployment Protocol Architecture

Figure 5.

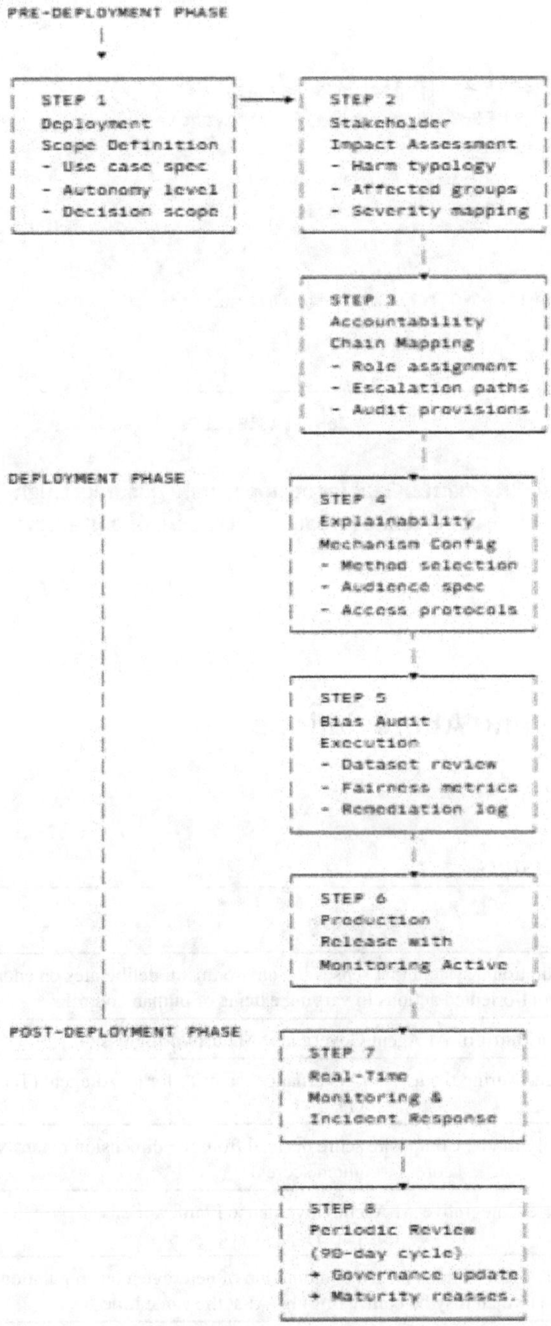

Appendix C: Research Gap Prioritization Matrix

Figure 6.

```
HIGH PRIORITY
      |
      |    RG-6 (Accountability)      RG-1 (Impact Assessment)
      |    RG-4 (Vendor Gov.)         RG-3 (Regulatory Effectiveness)
      |
      |    RG-2 (Maturity Dynamics)   RG-10 (SME Governance)
      |    RG-7 (Human-AI Roles)      RG-8 (Cost-Benefit)
      |    RG-11 (RT Monitoring)
      |
      |    RG-5 (Culture Mediation)   RG-9 (Cross-Cultural Adaptation)
      |
LOW PRIORITY
      |------------------------------------------------------------
      LOW FEASIBILITY                               HIGH FEASIBILITY
```

Figure C1. Research gap priority-feasibility matrix. Gaps in the upper-right quadrant (high priority, high feasibility) represent the most immediate research investment opportunities: RG-1, RG-3, RG-6, and RG-4.

Appendix D: Terminology and Abbreviations

Table 8. Key Terms and Abbreviations

Term/ Abbreviation	Definition
AI Agent	Autonomous computational system that senses the environment, deliberates on ends, and takes goal-oriented actions to varying extents of human control.
AAGMP	is the Algorithm 1 of AI Agent Governance Maturity Progression.
AAGMAI	AI is an instrument measuring the level of governance maturity for an AI agent (Table A1).
GMI	Governance Maturity Index: Composite score derived from the dimension maturity scores (weighted scores).
IAAGF	Model of Governance (Integrative AI Agent Governance Framework as suggested in this paper)
Regulatory Pluralism	The situation where organisations have a combination of heterogeneous regulation regimes (which may be conflicting) by AI at the same time.

continued on following page

Table 8. Continued

Term/ Abbreviation	Definition
Accountability Chain	Clear records of what the responsibility of a position of responsibility within an organization is for making what kind of consequential decision made by a set of agents of an AI agent system.
Ethics Washing	Organizational adoption of an ethics agenda by making a public statement of commitment to ethics, but without making any substantive change to the way the group operates in terms of governance or how decisions are made.
Human-in-the-Loop	AI deployment model in which humans have the final say in certain areas of the agent operation cycle.
Vendor Governance	Organizational capacity to put in place AI governance standards and provisions of accountability for external AI agent systems purchased and underlying componentry.

Table 8. The key terms and acronyms that will be used throughout this study paper. The synthesis of the definitions is based on Wooldridge (2020), Hagendorff (2020) and Gronsund and Aanestad (2020).

Chapter 7
AI Agents and the Future of Business in Africa:
Governing Transformation in the Contexts of Institutional Complexity

Olasomi Aisha Labo-Popoola
http://orcid.org/0009-0001-3976-373X
University of Greater Manchester, Bolton, UK

ABSTRACT

Artificial intelligence (AI) agents are increasingly being deployed as autonomous and semi-autonomous decision-making systems that are transforming organisational processes, strategic decision-making, and business competitiveness. However, existing AI governance frameworks have largely been developed for stable institutional environments, with limited attention to the institutional complexity of many African economies. This chapter explores the roles of AI agents, organisational readiness, governance mechanisms, and fragmented regulatory environments in shaping business transformation in African contexts. It develops a conceptual framework integrating AI agent autonomy, human oversight, organisational capability, and institutional alignment, drawing on AI governance literature, organisational studies and institutional theory. The framework offers practical and policy recommendations for business leaders, policymakers, and regulators while providing a foundation for future research on responsible AI governance in African business environments.

DOI: 10.4018/979-8-3373-9594-4.ch007

1. INTRODUCTION

Artificial Intelligence (AI) is increasingly changing how organisations make decisions, coordinate activities and pursue strategic objectives. Recent advances have turned AI applications from static analytics and decision support tools into *autonomous and semi-autonomous AI agents*. These computational systems are able to perceive their environment, reason about the information they have, and act to reach stated goals with minimal human interference (Wooldridge, 2009; Russell and Norvig, 2021; Hagos *et al.,* 2024). These AI agents are now embedded across a wide range of business functions (Ganapathi, 2025) including risk assessment (Adekunle *et al.,* 2023), supply chain optimisation (Ogunmokun *et al.,* 2021), client engagement (Vudugula *et al.,* 2023), financial decision making (Yanney, 2025) and platform governance (Ferrari, 2024).

Businesses that are during large digital transformations are beginning to regard AI agents as decision-making entities. AI agents are not only beneficial for the organisation's efficiency (Shrestha *et al.,* 2019; Sun and Jung, 2024), but also contribute to the organisational decision-making process, organisational accountability and human-machine interaction patterns. Thus, the deployment of AI agents raises significant questions regarding governance, ethical accountability, transparency and institutional alignment, particularly in contexts where the regulatory and organisational infrastructure is in a state of transition.

The area of AI transformation in an African business context has become one that is highly captivating because of the rapid integration of AI-based employees in fintech, digital platforms, telecommunication, health care and the infrastructure of new businesses. Many businesses in Africa employ AI-based agents to overcome structural constraints and deliver their services more efficiently. Nevertheless, the uptake of AI-enabled tools in organisations takes place within fragmented and regulated business processes that are not formalised, have poor data infrastructure and lack accountability (Mair and Marti, 2009; Beck *et al.,* 2011; World Bank, 2020; Oti-Sarpong *et al.,* 2022).

The international frameworks that have been set up for regulating AI and organisational management can serve as valuable guidelines for those who are accountable for managing these systems, but these frameworks do not deal with the problems of different regions and populations. Most framework and model development assume a relatively stable institutional structure exists in a country, that a country has sufficient laws and regulations supporting its institutions and businesses, and that organisations within these countries/communities have the processes and personnel needed to develop and implement governance frameworks for AI systems. Such a situation does not exist in many African countries; therefore, when artificial intelligence agents are deployed by these businesses without context-specific governance frameworks, they may begin to exacerbate existing inequalities, create new ones, lack proper accountability, and produce so-called unintended social and organisational consequences (Floridi *et al.*, 2018; Kroll *et al.*, 2017; Ilcic *et al.*, 2025).

The academic literature on artificial intelligence (AI) agents has generally focused on their technical performance, the development of algorithms to improve AI performance, or the governance models used in highly regulated and affluent economies (Davenport and Ronanki, 2018; Russell and Norvig, 2021; Ilcic *et al.*, 2025). The interplay of AI agents with organisational capabilities, governance structures and institutional contexts in African business ecosystems is of some scholarly interest but remains an under-explored research area, especially in light of the growing importance of AI agents in the strategic direction of business outcomes across Africa.

While scholarly interest in AI governance has been on the rise, most existing governance frameworks have been developed in relatively stable institutional contexts with mature regulatory systems, well-established digital infrastructure and well-delineated organisational governance structures (OECD, 2019; Floridi *et al.,* 2018; NIST, 2024). These frameworks, therefore, tend to assume institutional conditions that are quite different from those prevailing in many African economies. Existing models tend to offer universal principles of responsible AI but pay relatively little attention to the interaction between AI agents and institutionally complex environments characterised by regulatory fragmentation, hybrid formal-informal organisational arrangements, linguistic diversity, uneven digital maturity and institutional voids. This has led to a lack of research on the important contextual dimensions that influence AI governance and organisational decision-making in African business ecosystems.

This chapter seeks to address this limitation by proposing a governance-oriented conceptual framework that explicitly integrates AI agent autonomy, organisational readiness, human oversight, and institutional complexity within African business environments. The proposed framework is not intended to replace existing models of AI governance but rather to build on them, introducing the idea of contextual governance mechanisms more in tune with the realities of emerging economies. This chapter adds to the literature on AI governance and strategic digital transformation by showing how the institutional context critically shapes the responsible deployment and governance of AI agents.

The purpose of this chapter is to explore the role of AI agents (i.e., intelligent software) related to future business development within Africa, focusing specifically on how to govern their use in areas where there are various rules or laws surrounding them as they relate to AI-enabled transformation. Using a conceptual framework for the responsible use of AI-based systems, the author synthesises the literature on AI, information systems, organisational studies, and government to offer an integrated model for the deployment of AI agents within organisations. This chapter presents a framework that will guide businesses, governments, and research institutions that choose to employ AI agents by considering their organisational preparedness, human intervention capabilities, and alignment with appropriate regulations. The framework aims to offer novel perspectives on the social and technical aspects of AI agents as a measurement tool for assessing how well an AI agent fits into an organisation's institutional infrastructure.

This work also serves to enhance the emerging discussion about AI agents by conceptualising them as socio-technical decision-making entities within the context of their established frameworks (governance, accountability, and ethical considerations) to allow AI agents to generate long-term business transformation across the continent of Africa.

2. AI AGENTS IN ORGANISATIONAL DECISION-MAKING

2.1 Conceptualising AI Agents in Organisational Contexts

AI agents are computational systems that collect data from their environment and process it based on internal models or rules to act autonomously, fully or partially, towards their goals (Wooldridge, 2009; Bar, 2025; Huang, 2025). Traditional information systems are mainly designed to support human decision-making. However, the agents of artificial intelligence differ in the level of autonomy in performing actions, in adaptation to changing conditions, and in the interaction with humans and other agents in real-time (Russell & Norvig, 2021; Acharya *et al.*, 2025).

Within the organisational setting, AI agents are integrated in various processes. In this scenario, AI agents are deployed in functional areas such as credit scoring, fraud detection, pricing optimisation, supply chain orchestration, human resources analytics, and customer interactions. In this way, AI agents increasingly behave not only as technical artefacts but also as organisational actors that influence how decisions are made, escalated and enacted (Shrestha *et al.*, 2019; Van Rijmenam and Logue, 2021).

The transition from decision-support systems to independent operating agents provides organisations with a new way to establish governance and monitor/control how decisions are made, as these agents help to determine actions based on certain rules. The implementation of AI agents can transform the speed and consistency with which decisions are made across organisations, as well as where responsibilities and authority for making them reside. To better understand the role of AI agents as participants within an organisation, it is critical to expand our lens from strictly technical to also considering them in terms of their existence and operation in a sociotechnical context.

2.2 Levels of Autonomy and Decision Authority

There is a wide range of autonomy for AI agents — some AI systems provide recommendations to humans, while others can make decisions on their own. Previous studies have classified AI systems into three categories (human-in-the-loop, human-on-the-loop, and human-out-of-the-loop) according to governance and accountability standards (Engin, 2025; Cheruvu, 2025).

AI systems that require a person's consent and explicit approval to provide AI insight and recommendations are known as human-in-the-loop systems. These systems only require 10 per cent or less of an individual to supervise the actions taken by an AI. Conversely, a human-out-of-the-loop system is an AI that can perform independently or autonomously without needing a person's approval. AI systems have also introduced many issues regarding accountability and transparency

The adoption of AI agents in businesses across Africa is often constrained by an organisation's ability to adequately support and govern those agents, as well as by regulatory issues and trust considerations. Many organisations use a hybrid approach, where AI agents are used to automate routine decisions, while managers make decisions on high-impact or ambiguous issues. Adaptive autonomy regimes take into account the constraints of practice but also weigh efficiency and accountability where the functioning of institutions is subject to considerable and complex uncertainty.

2.3 AI Agents as Decision Actors

The growing body of research begins to view AI agents as active decision-makers rather than mere tools (Shrestha *et al.*, 2019; Castelfranchi, 1998; Pirjan & Petroşanu, 2025). This means that in organisational decision-making models, AI agents act as decision makers who generate options, rank alternatives and take actions to produce outcomes. This is especially relevant to algorithmic management (Jarrahi *et al.*, 2021), platform governance (Ferrari, 2024), and automated risk assessment (Kumar, 2025), where AI agents have a profound impact on outcomes

Furthermore, the framing of AI agents as decision actors explicitly situates their embeddedness in organisational structures, routines and power relations. AI agents' decisions are never value neutral; they are the result of assumptions, data sources, and objectives encoded in system design and deployment (Orlikowski, 2007; Dolata *et al.*, 2022). Therefore, leaders of organisations need to consider how AI agents fit with strategic goals, ethical standards and institutional expectations.

From an African perspective, organisations exist in both formal and informal settings. Thus, there are complex interactions between AI agents and human judgement. Many organisational processes rely on informal routines, contextual decision-making and discretion. Ignoring the dynamics involved in the process, the introduction of AI-based agents may lead to conflicts and exclusions. This highlights the importance of considering the contextual decision-making process in governance (Ilcic *et al.*, 2025; Singhal, 2024)

2.4 Human–AI Interaction and Collaborative Decision-Making

The deployment of AI agents requires technical expertise and human-AI collaboration. AI decision-making does not replace human decision-making but assists humans to process large volumes of data, to recognise patterns and to acquire real-time information (Suchman, 2007; Krishnan, 2025). Collaborative decision-making models provide organisations with the chance to leverage the capabilities of both humans and AI agents.

Furthermore, human-AI collaboration should involve clear role differentiation, transparency in decision-making procedures and contestability. Organisational cultures that foster critical engagement with decisions of AI agents contribute to more responsible and effective use of the artificial intelligence (AI) tools (Murire, 2024; Chourasia *et al.,* 2024). In the African business environment, people often view technology with suspicion. It is, therefore, vital that there be active human involvement in the decision-making processes.

Collaborative models can also help in creating a learning culture. Feedback from human decision-makers can be leveraged to improve the design of AI agents. This perspective on collaborative decision-making models is consistent with the notion of AI agents as dynamic parts of an organisational system.

2.5 Implications for Governance and Organisational Design

Understanding AI agents as autonomous or semi-autonomous decision actors has significant implications for governance and organisational design. Organisations should have accountability frameworks to establish who is responsible for decisions made or affected by AI entities. This has implications for the definition of liability, auditability and the way negative consequences of the decision-making process with AI will be escalated (Kroll *et al.,* 2017; Gaggatur, 2024).

Governance arrangements must consider regulatory ambiguity, resource constraints and diverse stakeholder expectations in institutionally complex environments, such as the context of many African economies. Instead of relying on existing governance models, which are designed for stable contexts, organisations will probably need to create new, flexible, and multi-layered organisational structures, which allow for both formal regulation and contextual discretion.

This section provides the background necessary for the subsequent sections of the chapter, which focus on complexity within institutions, governance issues, and organisational readiness and ultimately propose a framework for the effective use of AI agents in the context of African business organisations.

3. INSTITUTIONAL COMPLEXITY IN AFRICAN BUSINESS CONTEXTS

3.1 Understanding Institutional Complexity

Organisational complexity means the existence of various institutional logics that may contradict each other. The institutional complexities define and affect organisational activities (Schildt and Perkmann, 2017; Mountford and Cai, 2023). In a complex institutional environment, both institutional clarity and organisational practices tend to be inconsistent. In the context of the business environment in Africa, institutional complexity is a significant factor. In these business environments, there is a coexistence of different regulatory environments and policy environments. At the same time, these business environments need to address the global technological and socio-economic realities (Mair and Martí, 2009; Urbano *et al.*, 2019). These institutional complexities may influence the institutional embedding of emerging technologies, like AI agents.

3.2 Institutional Voids and Regulatory Fragmentation

Another important component of institutional complexity in African economies is that of institutional voids, that is, the "absence of market-supporting formal institutional arrangements, regulatory structures, and data governance" (Nason and Bothello, 2023; Daniel, 2024). African economies are currently working on developing regulations for digital technology and artificial intelligence, but the current state of regulation is patchy and not fully effective.

The fragmented and incomplete state of regulation for AI agents in African economies can create a degree of uncertainty for organisations seeking to use AI technology. For instance, there is a likelihood of a lack of clear guidelines on the use of AI technology or the absence of clear regulation on the use and application of AI technology (Bahangulu and Owusu-Berko, 2025; Omoseebi *et al.*, 2024). Consequently, organisations are forced to develop their own regulations and guidelines for the use and application of AI technologies. Such an approach leads to a form of heterogeneity in the application of AI.

The use and application of AI technology, which is based on autonomous and semi-autonomous decision-making, create several key issues regarding the regulation and control of AI agents. For instance, the absence of clear institutional regulation and control can result in the use and application of AI technology in a manner that is likely to undermine trust and create a few socio-economic consequences.

Recent policy developments suggest that African governments and regional bodies increasingly recognise the need for AI governance. The African Union's emerging AI Strategy has sparked discussions on continental AI governance, and the UNESCO Recommendation on the Ethics of Artificial Intelligence provides an important normative framework adopted by many African member states. The African Continental Free Trade Area (AfCFTA) digital trade agenda additionally emphasises the growing importance of data governance, digital interoperability and cross-border regulatory coordination. These initiatives are important moves towards creating governance environments that can support responsible AI deployment across African economies, though implementation is patchy.

3.3 Informality and Hybrid Business Practices

The other characteristic of business in Africa includes the coexistence of informality and formality in many industries. It means that in some sectors, informality and formality exist simultaneously and affect all key elements of those organisations (Darbi *et al.*, 2018; Singh *et al.*, 2025). Informality often functions as a coping mechanism in contexts where formal institutions are weak and institutional environments remain ambiguous. In the context of the interaction of informality and AI decision-making systems, several areas of tension are identified. The intelligent system relies upon the use of structured data, rules, and authority. This perspective is not necessarily the same as the informal paradigm that emphasises the individual and the social network. As a result, the efficiency of the intelligent system may be suboptimal, with decisions being erroneous due to the failure to fully account for the complexities that exist in the real world. Organisations that deploy AI agents in African contexts must therefore integrate algorithmic decision systems within environments where informal norms, relational authority, and social networks continue to shape operational practices. The combination of formal institutions and informal management creates structural ambiguity, and thus it is difficult to hold AI accountable and control it.

The interaction of factors leads to confusion of organisational boundaries, especially in SMEs and network organisations, where control is shared between owners, family members, locals and intermediaries. In such environments, it may be unclear whether decision outcomes should be attributed to formal managerial structures, informal social hierarchies, or algorithmic systems. As AI agents take on a larger role in data processing and in making recommendations and semi-autonomous decisions, it becomes more difficult to determine who holds responsibility: the human actor or the intelligent system.

The blurred lines of organisational boundaries and the informal character of the governance structures result in a form of ambiguity regarding accountability for the outcomes of the AI systems. This results in the concurrent generation of risks with regard to non-compliance and ethical and transparent operational risks. The absence of clearly defined role structures for AI agents leads to their operation within an ambiguous authority environment, which fosters distrust and undermines the effectiveness of the governance structures for these systems. Therefore, the development of responsible AI systems for hybrid organisational environments requires the clarification of decision rights, human overrides, and boundary structures.

3.4 Data Infrastructure and Information Asymmetries

AI agents are highly dependent on the availability, quality and reliability of data for autonomous decision-making. The data infrastructure in African business ecosystems tends to be sporadic, and there are problems with digitisation, whereby the data points are fragmented, and information asymmetry continues to prevail (Frimpong, 2025; Mutambara, 2025; Maleka and Maidi, 2024). This problem directly affects the performance, transparency, and accountability of AI agents.

Incomplete or inadequate data can lead to greater inequality and discrimination. In the field of strategic or operational decision-making, the use of artificial intelligence agents may lead to unreliable results in case of lack of data. Moreover, lack of appropriate governance structures hinders the establishment of clear data ownership, consent and accountability (Sharma and Sharma, 2025; Pahune et *al.*, 2025). Such challenges are especially prevalent when AI systems are developed and managed by a vendor (and global technology company) that is an external entity (Davenport and Mittal, 2023). In these institutionally complex environments, data limitations are not only a function of technology but also of governance and power relations in the digital ecosystem.

3.5 Linguistic Fragmentation and Digital Inclusion

Another often ignored factor leading to the intricacy of business institutions across many African business environments is linguistic fragmentation. Africa has 54 independent countries, all of which are characterised by a plethora of languages. Colonial history led to the development of many of these languages. These languages are taught together with over 2,000 indigenous languages (UNESCO, 2025). Such a condition presents a major structural challenge to the deployment of artificial intelligence agents.

The development of artificial intelligence agents requires a large volume of linguistic information. Historically, the development of artificial intelligence agents has been based on large English-speaking datasets. As a result, the deployment of these agents is based on English-speaking datasets. Therefore, there are significant performance variations in artificial intelligence agents in English-speaking environments compared to those in non-English-speaking environments (Bender *et al.,* 2021; Zhong *et al.,* 2024). When Francophone, Lusophone, and Arabophone language systems coexist in the same environment as indigenous language systems, data variations may lead to a lack of accuracy in the systems, a high level of bias in the algorithms, and a lack of equitable access to artificial intelligence-enabled services. Therefore, artificial intelligence agents without contextually relevant language support may not only fail to mitigate but may even exacerbate digital inequality, thus undermining the development of digitally transformative systems.

Another barrier to the harmonization of regulations between countries is the fragmentation of language. The compliance process, regulations, and governance structure are embedded in each linguistic environment that has been shaped by various historical and administrative factors, such as colonialism. This may present different challenges for the artificial intelligence agent, especially in the context of the African Continental Free Trade Area (AfCFTA) initiative. The absence of interpretability and regulatory harmonization may hinder the decision-making process by the AI agent.

Additionally, linguistic influences can be seen in trust, usability, and adoption. The collaboration between humans and artificial intelligence agents is likely to be effective not only in terms of technology but also in linguistic and cultural alignment. For small- and medium-sized enterprises in linguistically diverse environments, local language AI interfaces could be required for integration into business processes. Thus, failing to address linguistic diversity could undermine the readiness of the organisation and the transformative potential of the AI agents.

Addressing this dimension of institutional complexity requires deliberate governance and capability-building strategies. These include investment in multilingual AI training datasets, localisation of AI interfaces for regional contexts, cross-border policy coordination, and support for open-language digital infrastructure initiatives. Incorporating linguistic elements into the overall framework of AI governance is, therefore, vital in ensuring the inclusivity, equity, and appropriateness of the overall transformation process in Africa.

3.6 Implications of Institutional Complexity for AI Agent Deployment

The interaction between AI agents and institutional complexity fundamentally shapes how AI-driven transformation unfolds in African business contexts. Institutional fragmentation, informality, and data constraints influence not only whether AI agents are adopted, but also how autonomy, oversight, and accountability are configured within organisations.

A current trend in the adoption of AI-based agents is to accord them limited or constrained autonomy; therefore, they still require significant human supervision and contextual interpretation. The governance arrangements used to control AI-based agents need to strike a balance between these two modes of operation and therefore require adaptive governance arrangements that are context-sensitive and able to balance algorithmic effectiveness with institutional reality. The difference in experiences of AI adoption across African economies also reflects the heterogeneity of governance challenges across different institutional contexts and the maturity of regulations and organisational capacities. Illustrative examples from selected African countries are shown in Table 1.

Table 1. Illustrative AI Adoption and Governance Challenges Across Selected African Economies

Country	Illustrative AI Application	Governance Challenge
Kenya	Digital lending and credit assessment	Algorithmic bias, explainability, consumer protection
Rwanda	AI-enabled public service delivery	Data governance and institutional capacity
Nigeria	Fintech and digital platform ecosystems	Regulatory fragmentation and compliance consistency
South Africa	Financial services and customer analytics	Accountability, transparency, and ethical oversight

As Table 1 shows, while the pace of AI adoption is accelerating across African economies, the governance challenges of AI deployment are highly context-specific. Common issues around accountability, transparency and regulatory oversight are apparent, but the particular governance needs are different according to national regulatory contexts, organisational capacities and sectoral priorities. These differences support the claim that effective AI governance architectures need to be flexible to local institutional realities and not solely based on universal principles of governance.

Institutional complexity is not seen as an impediment to the effective deployment of AI agents; however, it calls for the development of appropriate governance structures. It is, therefore, important to understand the context in order to develop a responsible and effective AI-enabled business transformation in Africa. Governance strategies should focus on developing open data for under-represented African languages, promoting localisation approaches in the SME context and investing in multilingual AI training to overcome institutional and contextual constraints. Furthermore, Regional Coordination Mechanisms (RCMs), particularly those based on frameworks such as the African Continental Free Trade Area (AfCFTA), can support the harmonisation of regulations and the promotion of cross-border digital interoperability among countries. This would strengthen the efforts to address various issues facing the continent, as it would promote greater collaboration between the different African nations. Such collaboration would be made possible through the formation of RCMs, while at the same time addressing issues such as inclusion and sustainability in AI.

4. GOVERNANCE AND ACCOUNTABILITY CHALLENGES IN AI AGENT DEPLOYMENT

4.1 AI Agents and the Problem of Accountability

As AI agents become more instrumental in organisational decision-making processes, the issue of accountability and responsibility has become a governance concern. AI agents can be completely independent of human decision-makers, and therefore they have an independent ability to make decisions that may have significant strategic, financial, or social implications (Shrestha *et al.*, 2019; Bar, 2025). This level of independence makes traditional accountability arrangements, which are based on the premise of humans making all decisions, much more complex.

The complex institutional arrangements on the African corporate scene make accountability issues more difficult to address. The lack of an appropriate and effective regulatory framework is bound to result in a failure of accountability for any adverse effects brought about by the decision-making process of artificial intelligence (Schiff, 2025; Akpobome, 2024). In essence, the issue of accountability will be complex and depend on whether it involves organisational leadership, system designers, data providers, or even AI entities. Without transparent accountability systems, trust between organisations and other stakeholders can be eroded. The use of AI agents without clear mechanisms of accountability could lead to a lack of legitimacy for the system, especially in a situation where preexisting distrust exists among organisations.

4.2 Ethical Risks and Algorithmic Opacity

AI agents have raised ethical concerns regarding bias, discrimination, transparency, and, specifically, explanation. Although these risks exist outside of the African continent, the implications associated with these issues are often pronounced in regions that have poor socioeconomic conditions or where their populations are disenfranchised; that is to say, the implications of the emergence of AI agents are generally greater in regions where there are high levels of inequality, informality, and data limitations (Floridi *et al.* 2018).

The challenge of algorithmic opacity, or the inability for there to be a clear understanding of how AI agents make their decisions, presents challenges to the governance of AI agents. In many organisations in Africa, there is limited technical capacity or resources to audit or interpret the vast majority of complex AI systems. Therefore, AI agents may be used as black boxes; hence, governance is limited to providing oversight, and there is more risk of making unsubstantiated and unchallenged decisions (Kroll *et al.*, 2017; Almada, 2023; Busuioc, 2022). Moreover, the data sets used to train AI agents often carry historical biases and represent the inherent structural inequalities of the overall African socioeconomic system. Using such data sets puts AI agents at risk of perpetuating existing inequality rather than promoting internal inclusive business changes.

4.3 Misalignment of Global AI Governance Frameworks

The current AI governance structures have been predominantly constructed in the context of the Global North, in which well-established structures of regulation exist, as well as data sets and organisational capacities (Floridi *et al.*, 2018; OECD, 2019). However, in Africa, assumptions about legal systems and organisational readiness do not necessarily exist. This is notwithstanding the fact that these structures are of global relevance. The applicability of these structures to Africa could thus be limited by the informal nature of their decision-making processes. Thus, the informal nature of decision-making in Africa is pertinent to a flexible rather than a prescriptive model, particularly given the considerable ambiguity associated with organisational and legal contexts.

A number of leading governance frameworks are intended to embed ethical use of AI recommendations, including the OECD AI Principles (OECD, 2019), the UNESCO Recommendation on the Ethics of Artificial Intelligence (UNESCO, 2021) and the NIST Artificial Intelligence Risk Management Framework (NIST, 2024). The frameworks help guide transparency, accountability, fairness, explainability and risk management. Apart from governmental and intergovernmental efforts, industry-orientated governance approaches advocated by organisations like the World Economic Forum (WEF) have focused on responsible AI adoption, governance maturity and organisational accountability. While these frameworks offer useful practical guidance, they also provide limited consideration of the institutional complexities that characterise many African business environments. However, they mostly assume institutional conditions of regulatory coherence, mature governance systems, stable digital infrastructures and strong organisational capabilities. In many African business environments, governance challenges are not just technical risk management challenges; they are institutional fragmentation, regulatory uncertainty, informal organisational practices, limited enforcement capacity and uneven digital readiness. Therefore, although these frameworks offer significant normative foundations, their application often requires contextual modification to address the realities of institutionally complex environments. This limitation further underscores the necessity of governance approaches that explicitly incorporate organisational readiness and institutional complexity in the deployment and oversight of AI agents.

4.4 Human Oversight and Control Mechanisms

It has been suggested that, for the proper governance of AI agents, oversight mechanisms should be implemented that can change the autonomy of the AI agents based on the level of decision-making that is deemed appropriate (Holzinger *et al.,* 2025; Engin, 2025). Complexity of organisations and excessive autonomy may be related to a possible increase in the likelihood of ethical dilemmas. Humans-in-the-loop and humans-on-the-loop, therefore, have explicit rules for how humans monitor AI agents' decision-making. However, there are challenges associated with the adoption of these governance models by African organisations, particularly regarding skill sets and role ambiguity. The decision-makers may not possess the required skill set to critically evaluate decisions made by AI systems, and the hierarchical structure of an organisation may prevent an individual from critically analysing decisions made by AI systems.

4.5 Governance as an Organisational Capability

There is a growing recognition that AI governance is an organisational capability that evolves over time, rather than simply being a regulatory or compliance issue (Davenport and Ronanki, 2018; Birkstedt *et al.,* 2023). This approach is particularly relevant to Africa, where the gap between the level of technology uptake and the level of formal regulatory guidance is large.

The first step to successfully implementing AI strategies is for an organisation to establish its governance structure. The governance framework is structured around three elements: the creation of internal ethical guidelines and accountability models;

the creation of monitoring models; and the creation of learning models. These three components provide the organisation with the governing capabilities to manage its AI agents appropriately while being able to respond to the organisation's constantly changing business needs and ambiguous situations. The level of success an organisation has in implementing AI is highly correlated with governance capability level. Organisations that have low levels of digital maturity, have no digital skills or capabilities, and lack leaders typically establish governance mechanisms that are merely symbolic rather than substantive.

4.6 Implications for AI Agent Deployment in Institutionally Complex Contexts

The proven need for governance and accountability issues to be understood within the context of African institutional settings is also illustrated by the complex nature of AI agent deployments in African business environments, which requires careful balancing of the competing pressures of flexibility versus control. This need to balance these competing forces is further compounded by the fact that AI agents are also very complex technologies and will be deployed in an equally complex African business environment. Specifically, there is a need for careful consideration to be given to the balance between flexibility/control, oversight/autonomy and innovation/accountability when deploying AI agents into African business environments. Rather than searching for general solutions to governance issues, organisations should aim to align the autonomy of AI agents with decision impact, capability, and institutional constraints to establish the basis for the conceptual framework that is discussed in the next sections of this chapter.

5. ORGANISATIONAL READINESS AND HUMAN–AI COLLABORATION

5.1 Understanding Organisational Readiness for AI Agents

Organisational readiness is defined as the degree to which an organisation has the technological, human, structural and cultural competencies necessary to successfully adopt and govern advanced digital technologies (Kane *et al.*, 2015; Vial, 2019; Felemban *et al.*, 2024). As it pertains to AI agents, readiness is more than just the technical architecture. This includes the commitment of the leadership of the organisation, the capability of the workforce, the governance structure and the decision-making process. The organisation's readiness is entirely unique when compared to the African business environment. Some business environments, like those within the fintech industry, possess a high level of digital readiness, while many others face challenges because of resource constraints. These challenges often affect the systems' infrastructure, as well as the maturity of the organisation's data (World Bank, 2020; Jameaba, 2020). The variance significantly affects the incorporation of the AI agents within the business process. Ultimately, those business environments that possess a low level of readiness often incorporate the AI agents within the business process on an experimental basis. As a result, the business environments become increasingly dependent upon the automated process.

5.2 Digital Maturity and Infrastructure Constraints

AI agents need to work in an environment where the company is ready for them (digital maturity). A company must have the proper data infrastructure and enable heterogeneous information systems to interoperate to successfully use AI agents. There are also digital infrastructure requirements such as data governance, cyber-security, and analytics (Vial, 2019; Onoja *et al.,* 2021; Kubilay and Celiktas, 2025).

Companies in Africa have numerous challenges regarding the availability of data that will allow for the successful use of AI agents. Data quality may also pose a potential issue since some organisations may have a basic data infrastructure because of a business environment characterised by a multitude of informal operational activities. Thus, it is not possible to standardise business processes between organisations. As a result, the use of data by AI agents may pose concerns of reliability, transparency, and fairness. This finding suggests that the use of AI agents cannot be evaluated separately from digital transformation strategies.

5.3 Human-AI Collaboration and Decision Authority

AI agents do not make independent decisions but operate in the context of sociotechnical systems, which comprise human agents and organisational and institutional factors (Orlikowski, 2007; Billi and Labraña, 2025; Klos *et al.*, 2025). Hence, the effective functioning of AI agents depends on the development of an effective human-AI collaboration model. In the African organisational environment, the hierarchical structure of decision processes and their heavy reliance on managerial judgement might influence the functioning of AI agents. In certain scenarios, the perceived objectivity of the technological system may lead the decision authority to accept AI agent recommendations without question.

In other scenarios, the decision authority might not show the required degree of trust in the AI agent recommendations. Over-reliance on the decisions of the artificial intelligence agent can lead to a lack of accountability, while resistance to the decisions of the agent may hinder the organisation from benefiting from the decisions of the agent. Effective human–AI collaboration requires clear role definitions, escalation mechanisms, and shared understanding of AI limitations (Shrestha *et al.*, 2019).

5.4 Skills, Capabilities, and Organisational Culture

Human capital is a key determinant of the organisation's absorptive capacity for AI agents. The people and management should not only have the technical skills to understand the AI agent's suggestions but also be able to interpret and understand the ethical issues and make decisions based on the suggestions generated by the AI agent itself (Porkodi and Cedro, 2025; Dissanayake and Al-Sharify, 2025). In many organisations in Africa, the lack of data science and AI governance skills to effectively supervise AI agents is a significant factor hindering their assimilation. Moreover, lack of access to training programs and the dynamism of the evolution of technology have also added to the problem. Many organisations entrust governance to a limited number of individuals

5.5 Organisational Structures and Oversight Mechanisms

The formal organisational structures have a significant impact on the effective and appropriate use of AI agents. These include various committees, risk management, and decision reviews that monitor and evaluate the performance of AI agents (Davenport and Ronanki, 2018; Bommarito *et al.*, 2025). In environments where there are complexities, there are usually co-existing formal and informal structures of governance. Although this system may be beneficial, it may also lead to confusion and a lack of effective oversight. For AI agents, there are thus various mechanisms that are effective, especially when it comes to monitoring, auditing, and controlling decisions made through artificial intelligence, even when there are no external institutional guidelines.

5.6 Organisational Readiness as a Mediating Capability

Organisational readiness acts as a mediator between AI agent autonomy and governance effectiveness. Firms are at higher risk due to a high level of AI autonomy but not the corresponding readiness. Firms with a strong organising capability can strategically deploy AI agents and maintain control. In Africa's business environment, preparedness will decide if AI agents become enablers of sustainable transformation or sources of new vulnerabilities. This insight points to a need for holistic governance that integrates organisational capability and institutional context. These dynamics provide a critical foundation for the conceptual framework developed in the next section, which explicitly links AI agent autonomy, organisational readiness, governance mechanisms, and institutional complexity.

6. A CONCEPTUAL FRAMEWORK FOR GOVERNING AI AGENTS IN AFRICAN BUSINESS CONTEXTS

6.1 Rationale for the Conceptual Framework

The increasing involvement of artificial intelligence (AI) agents in organisational decision-making processes has led the dominant approaches to organisational governance to frequently assume the presence of institutional stability, the maturity of regulatory systems, and organisational preparedness. These assumptions limit the appropriateness of the dominant approaches to organisational governance in the context of African business environments, where institutional arrangements tend to be complex and multifaceted. Based on the above analysis, the current chapter proposes a new conceptual framework for organisational governance that incorporates the features of AI agents. This framework seeks to help organisations balance the autonomy of AI agents in relation to the impact of decisions, human intervention, and institutional limitations in complex institutional contexts.

6.2 Core Components of the Framework

6.2.1 AI Agent Autonomy

Autonomy of the artificial intelligence agents is measured through the degree to which the agents can sense, make decisions, and act upon the environment without the need for human involvement (Wooldridge, 2009; Russell & Norvig, 2021). The autonomy within an organisation could either be in the form of an advice system that helps human decision making or that of autonomous agents that make decisions in real-time (Mahanta, 2025; Acharya *et al.,* 2025). In the context of business environments in Africa, increasing autonomy is seen as a means to increase efficiency while also increasing governance risk, especially when organisational preparedness is limited. Therefore, autonomy is not seen as an end state but as a dimension that needs to be managed strategically.

6.2.2 Decision Impact and Criticality

Decision impact refers to the evaluation of the effect of decisions reached by AI agents on strategic decisions, financial performance, social justice, and ethical issues

(Khair *et al.,* 2020; Ogeawuchi *et al.,* 2024). Decisions such as allocation, pricing, recruitment, and service have higher criticality when compared to other decisions. In the context of institutional complexity, the decisions made by the AI agents may have a higher impact. Therefore, this framework identifies decision criticality as a key factor in determining the level of oversight and governance.

6.2.3 Human Oversight and Accountability Mechanisms

AI oversight refers to an organisational architecture that allows humans to monitor, assess, and, if necessary, override the decision-making processes of AI systems (Koulu, 2020; Salgado-Criado, 2025). AI oversight includes examples like human-in-the-loop, human-on-the-loop and decision escalation (Richards *et al.,* 2023; West & Hale, 2025). In the case of Africa's business environment, there will be an interaction between formal and informal decision-making approaches. This means that there will be some uncertainty concerning responsibility, and, therefore, it will be difficult to establish who will be responsible for actions taken by AI. The proposed framework should cater for oversight, auditability and decision traceability.

6.2.4 Organisational Readiness and Capability

The term 'organisational readiness' has been defined as a combination of digital maturity, data governance, leadership endorsement, workforce competencies, and organisational culture (Weritz *et al.*, 2024; Vial, 2019). Organisational readiness plays a crucial role in an organization's ability to interpret AI outputs, criticise decisions made by machines, and react accordingly when needed. In the proposed framework, organisational readiness acts as a mediating factor. With higher readiness, more autonomous AI agents can be safely deployed, while with lower readiness, more human oversight is necessary with lower autonomy.

6.2.5 Institutional Complexity and Regulatory Alignment

Institutional complexity refers to fragmented regulations, informal norms, uneven enforcement, and regulatory gaps that characterise many African business ecosystems (Mair and Martí, 2009; World Bank, 2020). These are the conditions that determine how AI governance mechanism's function. The mapping of external regulation is conceptualised in terms of the organisation's responsibility for regulatory alignment, rather than assuming that a complete regulatory framework exists within which they operate. Firms should develop their own internal governance standards to compensate for institutional weaknesses and to anticipate future regulation.

6.3 Positioning the Proposed Framework within Existing AI Governance Models

There have been several AI governance frameworks developed, advocating for responsible artificial intelligence (OECD, 2019; Floridi *et al.,* 2018; NIST, 2024). These frameworks have been very useful to increase knowledge in ethical AI, transparency, accountability and risk management. However, they have largely been developed within institutional environments characterised by relatively mature governance systems, comprehensive regulatory infrastructures, and comparatively high levels of digital readiness. Consequently, they provide only limited consideration of the institutional realities that shape AI deployment across many African business ecosystems.

Table 2. Comparison of Existing AI Governance Frameworks and the Proposed Framework

Framework	Primary Focus	Limitation in African Business Contexts	Extension Offered by This Chapter
OECD AI Principles	Responsible and trustworthy AI	Limited attention to institutional fragmentation and organisational readiness	Incorporates institutional complexity and governance under uneven regulatory conditions
UNESCO AI Ethics Recommendation	Ethical and human-centred AI	Broad normative principles with limited implementation guidance for emerging economies	Links ethical governance to organisational capability, oversight, and contextual deployment
NIST AI Risk Management Framework	Technical risk identification and mitigation	Assumes mature governance structures and organisational capacity	Integrates risk management with organisational readiness and human oversight mechanisms
Proposed Framework	Governance of AI agents in institutionally complex environments	Specifically developed for African business contexts	Integrates AI-agent autonomy, decision criticality, human oversight, organisational readiness, institutional complexity, and regulatory alignment

Table 2 indicates that existing AI governance frameworks provide useful foundations for the responsible deployment of AI due to their focus on ethical principles, transparency, accountability and risk management. However, these frameworks tend to focus less on the institutional conditions under which governance mechanisms operate. The proposed framework extends existing approaches by explicitly recognising institutional complexity as a key governance consideration and by including organisational readiness, human supervision, decision criticality and regulatory alignment into a context-sensitive model for governing AI agents in African business environments.

Unlike existing governance models that primarily establish universal principles for responsible AI, the proposed framework emphasises contextual adaptability by recognising that governance effectiveness depends not only on technical safeguards but also on organisational capabilities, institutional arrangements, and socio-economic conditions. Consequently, the framework extends existing governance literature by explicitly positioning institutional complexity as a central determinant of AI-agent governance and strategic digital transformation in African business environments.

6.4 Governance Alignment Logic of the Framework

The proposed framework conceptualises AI governance as a problem of alignment rather than compliance. Effective governance emerges when AI agent autonomy, decision impact, human oversight, and organisational readiness are coherently aligned within prevailing institutional conditions. Misalignment—such as deploying highly autonomous artificial intelligence (AI) agents in low-readiness environments or applying critical decisions to poorly governed systems—creates governance risk to a greater extent than does strategic alignment if organisations are to use AI agents as a mechanism for creating responsible innovation.

6.5 Framework Components and Governance Implications

The proposed framework conceptualises AI agent governance as a dynamic alignment problem rather than a static compliance exercise.

- **AI agent autonomy** must be calibrated to decision impact and criticality.
- **Human oversight mechanisms** moderate the risks associated with increased autonomy.
- **Organisational readiness** determines the effectiveness of oversight and accountability.
- **Institutional complexity** defines the boundary conditions in which governance mechanisms operate.

Misalignment of these factors increases the likelihood of governance failure, while strategic alignment enables responsible and sustainable AI-enabled business transformation. Table 3 reinforces the framework's practical relevance and clarifies how governance requirements vary across organisational and institutional contexts. It summarises the main framework components and their governance implications.

Table 3. The core framework components and their governance implications.

Framework Component	Description	Governance Implication
AI Agent Autonomy	Degree of independent decision-making	Higher autonomy requires stronger oversight
Decision Impact	Strategic and ethical significance of decisions	High-impact decisions need human review
Human Oversight	Accountability and intervention mechanisms	Prevents automation bias and opacity
Organisational Readiness	Digital, human, and governance capability	Determines safe autonomy levels
Institutional Complexity	Regulatory fragmentation and informality	Requires internal governance standards

6.6 Conceptual Framework

The purpose of this chapter is to offer a conceptual framework that ties together the relationships described in the previous sections. This framework allows for a visual representation of the integration of all the components of the impact of AI agents' autonomy, decision-making, human oversight, organisational readiness, and institutional complexity. The proposed conceptual framework is intended to demonstrate that the effectiveness of the governance is a function of these constructs rather than the technology itself. By defining institutional complexity as a boundary condition, the proposed conceptual framework provides a clear definition of the conditions under which the AI agent is to operate in the African business environment. Figure 1 proposes a conceptual framework for the governance of AI agents in the African business environment.

Figure 1. Conceptual Framework for Governing AI Agents in African Business Contexts

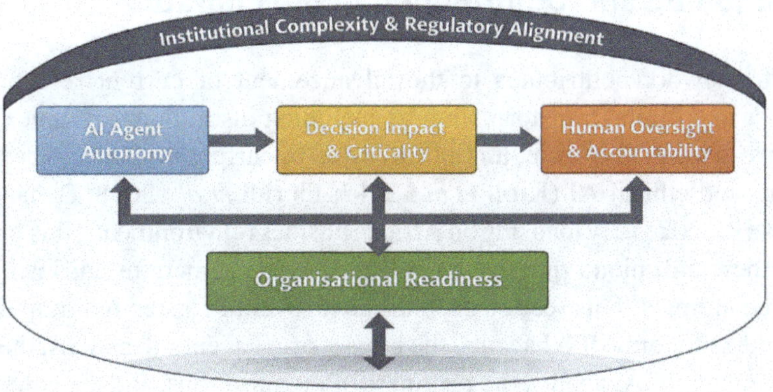

Figure description:

- Autonomy of AI agents is portrayed as the primary motivator of automated decision processes.
- The degree of autonomy is influenced by the impact and criticality of the decision.
- Furthermore, human oversight and accountability are a bridge between the actions of the AI agents and the human decisions, and organisational readiness provides the foundation for governance.
- The boundaries of the contextual environment, within which agents interact, are defined by institutional complexity and regulatory alignment.
- The institutional complexity is illustrated as an outer boundary of this contextual environment.

6.7 Expected Outcomes of Framework Application

If properly deployed, the framework helps African enterprises achieve the following:

- Better decisions with accountability
- Reduced risks in ethics and law
- Better match between AI deployment and capabilities
- Trust among stakeholders and regulatory bodies

- However, poor alignment between these components increases the risk of governance failures.

6.8 Positioning and Contribution to the Literature

This framework contributes to the advancement of current research on AI governance and digital transformation by including institutional complexity in the governance design. Therefore, it is an extension of current research on accountable algorithms and ethical AI (Kroll *et al.,* 2017; Floridi *et al.,* 2018; Bahangulu and Owusu-Berko, 2025). By focusing on African business environments, this framework presents a new and unique view that is applicable to other emerging and institutionally complex economies. This section expands on an overall conceptual framework that includes the autonomy of AI agents, the impact of AI agents' decisions, the need for human oversight of AI agents, the readiness of organisations, and the complexity of institutions. This framework aims at translating conceptual thoughts into practice. In the next section of this report, this chapter applies the above-referenced framework in identifying practical implications for policymakers, regulators and business leaders that wish to use AI agents in African business environments.

7. IMPLICATIONS FOR POLICY AND PRACTICE

The conceptual framework that has been developed within this chapter has a number of significant implications for practice and policy, particularly within African business environments. The framework identifies the relationship that exists between AI agent autonomy, organisational readiness, governance, and institutional complexities. The implications of this conceptual framework are discussed within this chapter with reference to business leaders, policymakers, and regulators who are attempting to utilise AI agents while managing risks associated with governance.

7.1 Implications for Business Leaders and Managers

For business leaders, the framework underscores that successful AI agent deployment is not primarily a technical challenge but an organisational and governance one. Managers should resist the assumption that higher levels of AI autonomy automatically lead to better performance. Managers should tailor the level of AI autonomy to organisational readiness and the criticality of the decisions involved. Organisations operating in contexts like Africa need to focus on a graduated approach to adoption, starting with low- or medium-impact decision domains and moving progressively towards higher autonomy as governance maturity improves. By combining all these elements together, organisations will be able to limit their exposure to issues related to ethical, operational, and reputational risk while gaining experience and confidence with AI-based decision-making processes. The framework also stresses the need for accountability structures to be clearly defined by business managers for AI agents' outcomes, such as escalation procedures for AI decisions that produce unexpected or harmful outcomes. Without this, AI agents will pose a risk as a source of diffuse responsibility, undermining managerial control and stakeholder trust.

7.2 Implications for Organisational Governance and Capability Development

From an organisational governance perspective, the framework emphasises the need to treat AI governance as an evolving internal capability rather than a compliance exercise. In environments where external regulatory structures lack coherence and development, organisations should take a proactive role in developing internal organisational standards in relation to ethical considerations and potential regulatory directions. Investments in organisational preparedness, such as the workforce's competence, data management practices, and organisational leaders' understanding, should be a priority. The collaboration between humans and AI systems should be intentionally developed through training, review of decisions, and cultural influences to encourage critical thinking about AI results rather than blindly accepting them. Lastly, organisations' governance structures should be flexible and adaptable. As the institutional environment, organisational maturity, and regulatory environment evolve with time, there is a need for them to reevaluate the autonomy level of their AI agents. This dynamic approach enables firms to remain responsive to both internal learning and external change.

7.3 Implications for Policymakers and Regulators

For instance, the framework suggests that for policymakers and regulators, the argument is that, for the purposes of governance within African economies, there is a need to ensure flexibility. In other words, rather than adopting a governance structure that is based on the experiences of other countries with more established institutional environments, the regulators need to understand the diverse organisational capabilities that exist across the different sectors and regions. In this case, the regulators may consider the principle-based regulatory approaches that set clear expectations about considerations for accountability, transparency, and fairness. These approaches would be more appropriate for the purposes of governance in an environment that is characterised by institutional complexity and technological dynamism. In addition to this, the framework suggests the need to consider the role played in the development of organisational readiness regarding the institutional environment in which the AI agents operate.

In addition, policymakers should consider the value of regional coordination mechanisms in shaping future AI governance across Africa. Initiatives related to the African Union's emerging AI governance agenda and the digital trade framework of the African Continental Free Trade Area (AfCFTA) present important opportunities for regulatory harmonisation, cross-border data governance and digital interoperability. The linguistic diversity of the continent and the risk of exclusion from language-biased artificial intelligence systems mean that multilingual AI governance must also be considered. Coordinated governance approaches can reduce regulatory fragmentation, improve accountability, and facilitate responsible deployment of AI agents across national boundaries, while maintaining flexibility for local institutional conditions.

7.4 Implications for Responsible and Inclusive AI Deployment

For the responsible deployment of AI in the business environment in Africa, it is important to consider the issue of inequalities in the social and economic spheres. Depending on the organisational structure in use, this framework acknowledges the potential for AI agents to either increase or decrease inequality. It is vital for business and policy leaders to consider the distributive effects of AI agents' actions, particularly with regard to critical areas like credit, employment, and access to essential services. The integration of ethical considerations into the governance structure is important not only for compliance but also for building legitimacy and trust among the affected parties. The focus on institutional complexities of the framework encourages the move away from the dominant technologically driven narratives and toward more human-centric and inclusive approaches to the application of AI.

7.5 Strategic Value of the Framework for Emerging Economies

Although the framework is developed with the African business environment in mind, its applicability to other emerging economies is also clear. The governance logic of alignment applies to different economies with varying levels of regulatory, organisational, and institutional preparedness, significantly enhancing the strategic importance of the proposed framework. The applicability of the framework to different economies also adds to the strategic importance of the proposed conceptual framework, which is a significant addition to the global debate on AI governance beyond the Global North. The implications of the proposed conceptual framework, as discussed in this section, are more practical and policy-orientated. This chapter provides value to business leaders, policymakers, and regulators who seek to navigate the AI-driven transformation in Africa by offering a translation of the conceptual insights into practice. The following section outlines the avenues for future research that could empirically test the proposed framework.

8. FUTURE RESEARCH DIRECTIONS

This chapter proposes a governance-orientated conceptual framework for researching the impact of artificial intelligence agents on business transformation in Africa, which is characterised by institutional complexity. The proposed framework is theoretically integrative and practically relevant; however, it also opens several research opportunities. Given the dynamics of artificial intelligence agent technology and the variability of business environments in Africa, further research is needed to improve and extend the arguments presented in this chapter.

8.1 Conceptual Propositions for Future Research

The conceptual framework developed in this chapter suggests several propositions that may guide future empirical investigation.

P1: Higher levels of organisational readiness positively influence the effectiveness of AI-agent governance mechanisms.
P2: Institutional complexity moderates the relationship between AI-agent autonomy and governance effectiveness.
P3: Human oversight mechanisms positively influence organisational trust in AI-agent decision-making.
P4: Greater alignment between AI-agent autonomy and decision criticality improves governance outcomes.
P5: Governance capability mediates the relationship between AI-agent deployment and sustainable business transformation outcomes.
P6: Regulatory alignment strengthens the relationship between organisational readiness and responsible AI adoption.

8.2 Empirical Validation of the Conceptual Framework

One of the main avenues for further research is the empirical testing of the suggested conceptual framework. Quantitative research can be conducted to explore the main concepts of AI agent autonomy, decision criticality, organisational preparedness, and human oversight mechanisms and their interrelationships in different organisational and sectoral contexts. Another research avenue is survey research focusing on managers, technology experts, and policymakers to explore the impact of differences in institutional complexity on organisational decisions and AI-related outcomes. Moreover, qualitative research on African organisations that have implemented AI agents in different sectors, such as fintech, healthcare, logistics, technology and estate management, can also be conducted to gain a better understanding of the actual working of the organisational governance mechanisms in different contexts.

8.3 Comparative and Cross-Regional Studies

Future research might take a comparative approach to AI governance by looking at how AI agent governance differs between regions based on the institution(s) involved and the kind(s) of social norms, cultural expectations, and legal requirements that exist within each region. For example, comparative studies involving African economies and the Global North (or other emerging markets like Southeast Asia or Latin America) may identify which governance mechanisms can be viewed as context-dependent and which are viewed as more universally applicable.

Such cross-regional analyses will contribute to refining global AI governance debates by highlighting how institutional complexity moderates the effectiveness of standard governance frameworks. Developing separate frameworks for each industry also helps to eliminate the currently prevalent tendency to treat all industries equally by using one policy framework for all; instead, separate frameworks will lead towards appropriate, context-sensitive regulation and design of organisations through AI.

8.4 Sector-Specific Investigations

In this chapter, a cross-sectoral perspective has been taken, but there may be opportunities in the future to take a much more targeted approach by studying industries in which AI agents (in their various forms) are playing a critical role. An example of this would be studying AI agents' impacts on credit allocation, fraud detection, and risk management within financial services, particularly in fragmented regulatory environments. For example, within the healthcare domain, studies can be conducted on issues of accountability and ethics with regard to AI-based diagnostic/ triage tools deployed in settings where there are resource constraints. Such sector-specific studies will help conduct more detailed analyses of decision criticality, human-AI interaction, and regulatory issues, thereby extending and contextualising the proposed framework.

8.5 Human-AI Collaboration and Skills Development

Exploring the human aspect of managing AI agents is another promising research track. For example, research can be conducted on how managers and employees respond to, trust, question or override decisions made by AI agents, especially in cases of substantial differences between digital literacy and organisational capacity. Another potential research track could be a longitudinal study of how learning and skill development can aid human-AI collaboration. Research on this track will contribute to a deeper understanding of how governance structures change as an organisation gains more experience with AI agents and refines their decision-making structures accordingly.

8.6 Policy-Oriented and Regulatory Research

From a policy point of view, future research should explore issues of design and implementation of adaptive and principle-based regulatory strategies for AI governance under conditions of institutional complexity. In this respect, studies can assess the role of regulatory sandboxes, public-private partnerships, and coordination mechanisms at regional levels as tools to promote the adoption of responsible AI while ensuring innovation. This research would be relevant to policymakers seeking to strike a balance among innovation, responsibility, and inclusiveness in African economies undergoing rapid digitalisation.

8.7 Methodological Extensions

Future research can also enhance the methodological foundations of research on the governance of AI by considering other theories, such as institutional theory, socio-material theory, and behavioural decision theory. A more integrated approach can be taken by considering mixed-method research designs, which can help in achieving a more comprehensive understanding of the integration of AI agents through the use of surveys, interviews, document analysis, and audits. This chapter has served to establish a foundation for an emerging body of knowledge around AI agents and changing businesses in Africa. Future research that tests, develops and expands on the frameworks proposed by this chapter is expected to offer deeper understandings about the development of this body of knowledge and to contribute to appropriate, ethical and effective governance of AI agents in emerging economies.

9. CONCLUSION

This chapter analyses the role of AI agents in the trajectory of business transformation in the context of complex institutional environments in Africa. By transcending technology-centric understandings of AI agents, the chapter proposes a conceptual understanding of AI agents as socio-technical decision actors whose effectiveness and risks are conditional on governance, organisational, and institutional considerations.

Building on the idea of interdisciplinary knowledge production, this chapter develops a conceptual framework for the governance of AI agents, considering autonomy, impact of decisions, criticality of decisions, human oversight, organisational readiness, and institutional complexity. The framework, therefore, underscores that effective AI agent governance is not merely a product of automation but a strategic fit between AI agent capabilities and institutional and organisational contexts in which AI agents are deployed. This chapter contributes to the emerging body of literature on digital transformation and AI agent governance by exploring the business environment on the African continent.

Moreover, it aims to address an important gap in the current body of literature on AI agents, which is dominated by studies that assume more homogeneous forms of institutions. The proposed conceptual framework is likely to have both theoretical and practical implications for business leaders, policymakers, and regulators as they navigate AI agent adoption in the context of complex institutional environments characterised by fragmentation, informality, and varying organisational readiness.

The chapter also highlights the critical role of AI agents in facilitating business transformation that is not only sustainable but also equitable. At the same time, the chapter cautions the reader about the potential dangers of AI agents' governance that could result in a loss of trust and increased inequality in Africa's complex institutional environments. Thus, in the concluding part, the chapter highlights the importance of governance as a crucial competency in utilising the transformative power of AI agents in Africa. By strategically aligning AI agent autonomy with organisational readiness, African business environments can leverage AI agent-driven innovation for business transformation that is not only sustainable but also equitable.

The principal contribution of this chapter is the demonstration that effective governance of AI agents cannot be separated from institutional context. Existing governance frameworks provide important universal principles, but they need to be complemented with organisational readiness, oversight by humans, and an understanding of the institutional settings in which AI agents operate. The proposed framework contributes to the existing AI governance scholarship by highlighting institutional complexity as an important governance consideration and providing a contextually grounded basis for responsible AI-enabled business transformation across African economies.

REFERENCES

Acharya, D. B., Kuppan, K., & Divya, B. (2025). Agentic ai: Autonomous intelligence for complex goals–a comprehensive survey. *IEEE Access : Practical Innovations, Open Solutions, 13*, 18912–18936. DOI: 10.1109/ACCESS.2025.3532853

Adekunle, B. I., Chukwuma-Eke, E. C., Balogun, E. D., & Ogunsola, K. O. (2023). Integrating AI-driven risk assessment frameworks in financial operations: A model for enhanced corporate governance. *International Journal of Scientific Research in Computer Science. Engineering and Information Technology, 9*(6), 445–464.

Akpobome, O. (2024). The impact of emerging technologies on legal frameworks: A model for adaptive regulation. *International Journal of Research Publication and Reviews, 5*(10), 5046–5060. DOI: 10.55248/gengpi.5.1024.3012

Almada, M. (2023). Governing the Black Box of Artificial Intelligence. *Available at SSRN* 4587609. DOI: 10.2139/ssrn.4587609

Bahangulu, J. K., & Owusu-Berko, L. (2025). Algorithmic bias, data ethics, and governance: Ensuring fairness, transparency and compliance in AI-powered business analytics applications. *World J Adv Res Rev, 25*(2), 1746–1763. DOI: 10.30574/wjarr.2025.25.2.0571

Bar, K. (2025). *The Agentic AI Handbook: Concepts*. Design Patterns, and Future Directions.

Beck, T., Demirgüç-Kunt, A., & Martínez Pería, M. S. (2011). Banking services for everyone? Barriers to bank access and use around the world. *Journal of Financial Services Research, 39*(1–2), 1–35. DOI: 10.1007/s10693-010-0089-6

Bender, E. M., Gebru, T., McMillan-Major, A., & Shmitchell, S. (2021, March). On the dangers of stochastic parrots: Can language models be too big? In *Proceedings of the 2021 ACM conference on fairness, accountability, and transparency* (pp. 610-623). DOI: 10.1145/3442188.3445922

Billi, M., & Labraña, J. (2025). Is AI a functional equivalent to expertise in organizations and decision-making? Opportunities and pitfalls for AI in the context of just transitions. *Frontiers in Artificial Intelligence, 8*, 1571698. DOI: 10.3389/frai.2025.1571698

Birkstedt, T., Minkkinen, M., Tandon, A., & Mäntymäki, M. (2023). AI governance: Themes, knowledge gaps and future agendas. *Internet Research, 33*(7), 133–167. DOI: 10.1108/INTR-01-2022-0042

Bommarito, J., Katz, D. M., & Bommarito, M. J. (2025). Governing AI Agents: Risk, Compliance, and Accountability in Law and Finance. *Compliance, and Accountability in Law and Finance (December 12, 2025).*

Busuioc, M. (2022). AI algorithmic oversight: new frontiers in regulation. In *Handbook of regulatory authorities* (pp. 470–486). Edward Elgar Publishing.

Castelfranchi, C. (1998). Modelling social action for AI agents. *Artificial Intelligence, 103*(1-2), 157–182. DOI: 10.1016/S0004-3702(98)00056-3

Cheruvu, R. (2025). Human-in/on-the-Loop Design for Human Controllability. In *Handbook of Human-Centered Artificial Intelligence* (pp. 1–47). Springer Nature Singapore.

Chourasia, S., Dhama, A., & Bhardwaj, G. (2024, May). AI-driven organizational culture evolution: A critical review. In *2024 International Conference on Communication, Computer Sciences and Engineering (IC3SE)* (pp. 1839-1844). IEEE. DOI: 10.1109/IC3SE62002.2024.10592949

Daniel, G. G. O. (2024). *How multinational enterprises navigate the institutional landscape in emerging markets and developing economies* (Doctoral dissertation, Wageningen University and Research).

Darbi, W. P. K., Hall, C. M., & Knott, P. (2018). The informal sector: A review and agenda for management research. *International Journal of Management Reviews, 20*(2), 301–324. DOI: 10.1111/ijmr.12131

Davenport, T. H., & Mittal, N. (2023). *All-in on AI: How smart companies win big with artificial intelligence*. Harvard Business Press.

Davenport, T. H., & Ronanki, R. (2018). Artificial intelligence for the real world. *Harvard Business Review, 96*(1), 108–116.

Dissanayake, L., & Al-Sharify, A. (2025). AI and Decision Making: How does the integration of AI influence leadership decision making within technology driven companies?.

Dolata, M., Feuerriegel, S., & Schwabe, G. (2022). A sociotechnical view of algorithmic fairness. *Information Systems Journal, 32*(4), 754–818. DOI: 10.1111/isj.12370

Engin, Z. (2025). Human-AI Governance (HAIG): A Trust-Utility Approach. *arXiv preprint arXiv:2505.01651.*

Felemban, H., Sohail, M., & Ruikar, K. (2024). Exploring the readiness of organisations to adopt artificial intelligence. *Buildings (Basel, Switzerland), 14*(8), 2460. DOI: 10.3390/buildings14082460

Ferrari, F. (2024). State roles in platform governance: AI's regulatory geographies. *Competition & Change*, *28*(2), 340–358. DOI: 10.1177/10245294231218335

Floridi, L., Cowls, J., Beltrametti, M., Chatila, R., Chazerand, P., Dignum, V., Luetge, C., Madelin, R., Pagallo, U., Rossi, F., Schafer, B., Valcke, P., & Vayena, E. (2018). AI4People—An ethical framework for a good AI society: Opportunities, risks, principles, and recommendations. *Minds and Machines*, *28*(4), 689–707. DOI: 10.1007/s11023-018-9482-5

Frimpong, V. (2025). Artificial Intelligence Investment in Resource-Constrained African Economies: Financial, Strategic, and Ethical Trade-Offs with Broader Implications. *WORLD (Oakland, Calif.)*, *6*(2), 70. DOI: 10.3390/world6020070

Gaggatur, J. S. (2024). AI ethics: Who is accountable for the decisions made by machines? *Authorea Preprints*. DOI: 10.36227/techrxiv.172373798.84756169/v1

Ganapathi, J. K. (2025). Augmented Entrepreneurship: The Role of AI Agents in Automating Core Small Business Functions. *Journal Of Engineering And Computer Sciences*, *4*(8), 654–663.

Hagos, D. H., Alami, H. E., & Rawat, D. B. (2024). Ai-driven human-autonomy teaming in tactical operations: Proposed framework, challenges, and future directions. *arXiv preprint arXiv:2411.09788*.

Holzinger, A., Zatloukal, K., & Müller, H. (2025). Is human oversight to AI systems still possible? *New Biotechnology*, *85*, 59–62. DOI: 10.1016/j.nbt.2024.12.003

Huang, K. (2025). *Agentic AI*. Springer., DOI: 10.1007/978-3-031-90026-6

Ilcic, A., Fuentes, M., & Lawler, D. (2025). Artificial intelligence, complexity, and systemic resilience in global governance. *Frontiers in Artificial Intelligence*, *8*, 1562095. DOI: 10.3389/frai.2025.1562095

Jameaba, M. S. (2020). Digitization revolution, FinTech disruption, and financial stability: Using the case of Indonesian banking ecosystem to highlight wide-ranging digitization opportunities and major challenges. *FinTech Disruption, and Financial stability: Using the Case of Indonesian Banking Ecosystem to highlight wide-ranging digitization opportunities and major challenges (July 16 2, 2020)*.

Jarrahi, M. H., Newlands, G., Lee, M. K., Wolf, C. T., Kinder, E., & Sutherland, W. (2021). Algorithmic management in a work context. *Big Data & Society*, *8*(2), 20539517211020332. DOI: 10.1177/20539517211020332

Kane, G. C., Palmer, D., Phillips, A. N., Kiron, D., & Buckley, N. (2015). Strategy, not technology, drives digital transformation. *MIT Sloan Management Review*.

Khair, M. A., Mahadasa, R., Tuli, F. A., & Ande, J. R. P. K. (2020). Beyond human judgment: Exploring the impact of artificial intelligence on HR decision-making efficiency and fairness. *Global Disclosure of Economics and Business*, *9*(2), 163–176. DOI: 10.18034/gdeb.v9i2.730

Klos, T., Zarcone, A., Rentrop, C., Riedinger, C., Prinz, N., & Huber, M. (2025, September). Entangled by Design: A structured Overview of Management Challenges concerning AI Adoption in Organizations. In *2025 20th Conference on Computer Science and Intelligence Systems (FedCSIS)* (pp. 705-713). IEEE. DOI: 10.15439/2025F1129

Koulu, R. (2020). Proceduralizing control and discretion: Human oversight in artificial intelligence policy. *Maastricht Journal of European and Comparative Law*, *27*(6), 720–735. DOI: 10.1177/1023263X20978649

Krishnan, N. (2025). Ai agents: Evolution, architecture, and real-world applications. *arXiv preprint arXiv:2503.12687.*

Kroll, J. A., Huey, J., Barocas, S., Felten, E. W., Reidenberg, J. R., Robinson, D. G., & Yu, H. (2017). Accountable algorithms. *University of Pennsylvania Law Review*, *165*(3), 633–705.

Kubilay, B., & Celiktas, B. (2025). Relationships Among Organizational-Level Maturities in Artificial Intelligence, Cybersecurity, and Digital Transformation: A Survey-Based Analysis. *IEEE Access : Practical Innovations, Open Solutions*, *13*, 88399–88411. DOI: 10.1109/ACCESS.2025.3571537

Kumar, S. N. P.Sanjay Nakharu Prasad Kumar. (2025). Regulating autonomous AI agents: Prospects, hazards, and policy structures. *Journal of Computer Science and Technology Studies*, *7*(10), 393–399. DOI: 10.32996/jcsts.2025.7.10.41

Mahanta, U. (2025). Beyond Automation: Guidelines for a Human-Centered Multi-Agent System for Coordinated Decision Making under Industrial Settings.

Mair, J., & Martí, I. (2009). Entrepreneurship in and around institutional voids: A case study from Bangladesh. *Journal of Business Venturing*, *24*(5), 419–435. DOI: 10.1016/j.jbusvent.2008.04.006

Maleka, S., & Maidi, C. (2024). The Societal Implications of Technological Innovations and AI in South Africa.

Mountford, N., & Cai, Y. (2023). Towards a flatter ontology of institutional logics: How logics relate in situations of institutional complexity. *International Journal of Management Reviews*, *25*(2), 363–383. DOI: 10.1111/ijmr.12313

Murire, O. T. (2024). Artificial intelligence and its role in shaping organizational work practices and culture. *Administrative Sciences*, *14*(12), 316. DOI: 10.3390/admsci14120316

Mutambara, A. G. (2025). *Artificial Intelligence: A driver of inclusive development and shared prosperity for the Global South*. CRC Press. DOI: 10.1201/9781003511014

Nason, R., & Bothello, J. (2023). Far from void: How institutions shape growth in informal economies. *Academy of Management Review*, *48*(3), 485–503. DOI: 10.5465/amr.2019.0170

National Institute of Standards and Technology (US). (2024). *Artificial intelligence risk management framework: generative artificial intelligence profile*. US Department of Commerce, National Institute of Standards and Technology.

Ogeawuchi, J. C., Sharma, A., Adekunle, B. I., Abayomi, A. A., & Onifade, O. (2024). Ethical Frameworks for AI Deployment in Financial Decision-Making: Balancing Profitability and Social Responsibility. *International Journal of Scientific Research in Computer Science. Engineering and Information Technology*, *10*(2), 905–917.

Ogunmokun, A. S., Balogun, E. D., & Ogunsola, K. O. (2021). A Conceptual Framework for AI-Driven Financial Risk Management and Corporate Governance Optimization. *International Journal of Multidisciplinary Research and Growth Evaluation, 2*.

Omoseebi, A., Cole, W., & John, S. (2024). Compliance and Ethics: Ensure that digital initiatives comply with regulations and ethical standards.

Onoja, J. P., Hamza, O., Collins, A., Chibunna, U. B., Eweja, A., & Daraojimba, A. I. (2021). Digital transformation and data governance: Strategies for regulatory compliance and secure AI-driven business operations. *J. Front. Multidiscip. Res*, *2*(1), 43–55. DOI: 10.54660/.IJFMR.2021.2.1.43-55

Organization for Economic Co-operation and Development (OECD). (2019). Recommendation of the Council on Artificial Intelligence, OECD/LEGAL/0449.

Orlikowski, W. J. (2007). Sociomaterial practices: Exploring technology at work. *Organization Studies*, *28*(9), 1435–1448. DOI: 10.1177/0170840607081138

Oti-Sarpong, K., Pärn, E. A., Burgess, G., & Zaki, M. (2022). Transforming the construction sector: An institutional complexity perspective. *Construction Innovation*, *22*(2), 361–387. DOI: 10.1108/CI-04-2021-0071

Pahune, S., Akhtar, Z., Mandapati, V., & Siddique, K. (2025). The Importance of AI Data Governance in Large Language Models. *Big Data and Cognitive Computing*, *9*(6), 147. DOI: 10.3390/bdcc9060147

Pirjan, A., & Petroşanu, D. M. (2025). ARTIFICIAL SOCIAL INTELLIGENCE AND THE TRANSFORMATION OF HUMAN INTERACTION BY ARTIFICIAL INTELLIGENCE AGENTS. *Journal of Information Systems & Operations Management*, *19*(1).

Porkodi, S., & Cedro, T. L. (2025). The ethical role of generative artificial intelligence in modern HR decision-making: A systematic literature review. *European Journal of Business and Management Research*, *10*(1), 44–55. DOI: 10.24018/ejbmr.2025.10.1.2535

Richards, C. E., Cernev, T., Tzachor, A., Zilgalvis, G., & Kaleagasi, B. (2023). Safely advancing a spacefaring humanity with artificial intelligence. *Frontiers in Space Technologies*, *4*, 1199547. DOI: 10.3389/frspt.2023.1199547

Russell, S., & Norvig, P. (2021). *Artificial intelligence: A modern approach* (4th ed.). Pearson.

Salgado-Criado, J. (2025). Human oversight of artificial intelligence: An operations management perspective. *Journal of Industrial Engineering and Management*, *18*(2), 285–304. DOI: 10.3926/jiem.8567

Schiff, D. S. (2025). Strategies for Harmonizing Fragmented AI Ethics Frameworks, Standards, and Regulations. In *Handbook of Human-Centered Artificial Intelligence* (pp. 1–45). Springer Nature Singapore. DOI: 10.1007/978-981-97-8440-0_82-1

Schildt, H., & Perkmann, M. (2017). Organizational settlements: Theorizing how organizations respond to institutional complexity. *Journal of Management Inquiry*, *26*(2), 139–145. DOI: 10.1177/1056492616670756

Sharma, A. K., & Sharma, R. (2025). Data governance in the age of artificial intelligence: Challenges, best practices and regulatory compliance. *Applied Marketing Analytics*, *10*(4), 390–403. DOI: 10.69554/XWHM1191

Shrestha, Y. R., Ben-Menahem, S. M., & von Krogh, G. (2019). Organizational decision-making structures in the age of artificial intelligence. *California Management Review*, *61*(4), 66–83. DOI: 10.1177/0008125619862257

Singh, S. K., Rao, S., Harish, N., & Guduru, P. (2025). *Business organization and Management*. RK Publication.

Singhal, A. (2024). *Social challenges of AI governance*.

Suchman, L. (2007). *Human–machine reconfigurations: Plans and situated actions* (2nd ed.). Cambridge University Press.

Sun, Y., & Jung, H. (2024). Machine learning (ML) modeling, IoT, and optimizing organizational operations through integrated strategies: The role of technology and human resource management. *Sustainability (Basel), 16*(16), 6751. DOI: 10.3390/su16166751

UNESCO. (2025). *UNESCO and the promotion of languages in Africa: cultural diversity and multilingualism*. UNESCO.

Union, A. (2024). *Continental artificial intelligence strategy*. African Union Commision.

United Nations Educational, Scientific and Cultural Organization. (2021). Recommendation on the ethics of artificial intelligence. Retrieved 17 July 2026 (https://unesdoc.unesco.org/ark:/48223/pf0000381137).Google Scholar.

Urbano, D., Guerrero, M., Ferreira, J. J., & Fernandes, C. I. (2019). New technology entrepreneurship initiatives: Which strategic orientations and environmental conditions matter in the new socio-economic landscape? *The Journal of Technology Transfer, 44*(5), 1577–1602. DOI: 10.1007/s10961-018-9675-3

Van Rijmenam, M., & Logue, D. (2021). Revising the 'science of the organisation': Theorising AI agency and actorhood. *Innovation (North Sydney, N.S.W.), 23*(1), 127–144. DOI: 10.1080/14479338.2020.1816833

Vial, G. (2019). Understanding digital transformation: A review and a research agenda. *The Journal of Strategic Information Systems, 28*(2), 118–144. DOI: 10.1016/j.jsis.2019.01.003

Weritz, P., Braojos, J., & Matute, J. (2020). Exploring the antecedents of digital transformation: Dynamic capabilities and digital culture aspects to achieve digital maturity.

West, G., & Hale, R. (2025). Building Human-AI Collaboration Models in Cybersecurity Operations.

Wooldridge, M. (2009). *An introduction to multiagent systems*. John wiley & sons.

World Bank. (2020). *Doing Business 2020: Comparing Business Regulation in 190 Economies*. World Bank Group.

Yanney, A. A. S. (2025). Redefining corporate financial governance through AI-Powered predictive models for global business risk management. *International Journal of Research Publication and Reviews*, *2*(6), 25–49. DOI: 10.55248/gengpi.6.0625.2037

Zhong, C., Cheng, F., Liu, Q., Jiang, J., Wan, Z., Chu, C., . . . Kurohashi, S. (2024). Beyond english-centric llms: What language do multilingual language models think in? *arXiv preprint arXiv:2408.10811*.

KEY TERMS AND DEFINITIONS

AI Agents: Autonomous or semi-autonomous computational systems capable of perceiving their environment, processing information, and taking actions to achieve defined organisational or strategic objectives with limited or no human intervention.

AI Governance: The set of organisational structures, policies, ethical principles, and accountability mechanisms that guide the responsible design, deployment, and oversight of artificial intelligence systems.

Business Transformation: A process through which organisations fundamentally change their structures, processes, decision-making practices, and value creation mechanisms through the adoption of digital and intelligent technologies.

Decision Autonomy: When an AI agent can independently create and execute decisions without explicit, direct approval from a human (i.e., at the operational, tactical, or strategic level), there is a degree of autonomy associated with that agent; however, not all situations allow for this degree of autonomy.

Human–AI Collaboration: A way that people create and use AI-based systems in conjunction with one another so that they can share responsibility, who has authority over decision-making, and how much control each party has over the process to improve the quality, speed and reliability of data-driven decisions made by humans.

Institutional Complexity: The coexistence of multiple, fragmented, or conflicting regulatory frameworks, norms, and practices that shape organisational behaviour, particularly prevalent in emerging and developing economies.

Organisational Readiness: The extent to which an organisation possesses the technological infrastructure, skills, culture, leadership support, and processes necessary to effectively adopt and govern AI-driven systems.

Regulatory Alignment: That is the level to which an AI system/organisational practice complies with relevant legal, ethical and policy requirements as they are defined by a regulatory authority within a specific jurisdiction.

Chapter 8

Governing Intelligent Agent Strategic Frameworks for AI-Driven Digital Transformation

Naga Ramesh Palakurti
http://orcid.org/0009-0009-9500-1869
Tata Consultancy Services, USA

Mallikarjun Bellundagi
CHIT, USA

ABSTRACT

The emergence of intelligent agents capable of autonomous perception, reasoning, learning, and action is reshaping digital transformation in public-sector and enterprise organizations. Unlike traditional analytics or decision-support systems, intelligent agents operate as adaptive, distributed actors embedded in organizational processes, raising governance, accountability, and strategic control challenges. This chapter presents a strategic governance perspective that positions intelligent agents as socio-technical systems rather than isolated technical components. It synthesizes insights from AI governance, information systems strategy, organizational theory, and public policy to develop integrative frameworks linking agent capabilities with decision rights, oversight structures, and accountability mechanisms. The chapter examines key issues, including delegated authority, multi-agent coordination, human–AI collaboration, and alignment with ethical and regulatory principles. Mapping governance across the AI lifecycle provides practical guidance for responsible.

DOI: 10.4018/979-8-3373-9594-4.ch008

1. INTRODUCTION

Digital transformation has increasingly shifted from the digitization of processes toward the integration of intelligent systems capable of autonomous decision-making. Recent advances in artificial intelligence (AI) have enabled the deployment of intelligent agents that can perceive environments, reason over complex data, learn from experience, and act with limited or no human intervention. These intelligent agents differ fundamentally from traditional information systems in that they function as adaptive, distributed actors embedded within organizational workflows rather than as passive tools supporting human decision-makers.

As organizations adopt intelligent agents on a scale, questions of governance, accountability, and strategic alignment become central concerns. While technical research has focused on improving agent architectures, reinforcement learning, and multi-agent coordination, comparatively less attention has been given to how such systems should be governed within organizational and regulatory contexts (Russell et al., 1995; Wooldridge, 2009). The delegation of authority to autonomous agents challenges existing governance structures, blurs lines of responsibility, and introduces new operational and ethical risks (Floridi et al., 2018).

This chapter argues that intelligent agents must be governed as socio-technical systems rather than purely technical artifacts. Drawing on literature from AI governance, information systems strategy, organizational theory, and public policy, the chapter develops strategic governance frameworks that align intelligent agent deployment with institutional objectives, regulatory obligations, and societal values. The chapter contributes practical guidance for decision-makers seeking to embed intelligent agents responsibly while advancing digital transformation goals.

2. INTELLIGENT AGENTS AND DIGITAL TRANSFORMATION

2.1 Defining Intelligent AI Agents

Intelligent intelligent agents are computational entities designed to operate autonomously within an environment by continuously perceiving contextual information, reasoning over that information, learning from experience, and executing actions to achieve specified goals (Wooldridge, 2009). Unlike conventional software systems that rely on predefined rules or static decision trees, intelligent agents are adaptive systems capable of modifying their behavior over time in response to environmental changes, feedback signals, and evolving objectives (Russell et al., 1995). This capacity for learning and adaptation enables agents to function effectively in complex, uncertain, and dynamic environments where exhaustive pre-programming is neither feasible nor desirable.

From a technical standpoint, intelligent agents are often implemented using machine learning techniques such as reinforcement learning, deep neural networks, and probabilistic reasoning models. These techniques allow agents to develop internal representations of their environment, evaluate alternative courses of action, and optimize outcomes based on reward structures or policy constraints (Sutton & Barto, 2018). As a result, intelligent agents are not merely reactive systems but proactive entities capable of anticipation, goal prioritization, and strategic behavior.

From an organizational perspective, intelligent agents represent a qualitative shift in the role of digital technologies. Rather than serving solely as decision-support tools that augment human judgment, intelligent agents increasingly function as digital actors embedded directly within organizational processes (Davenport & Ronanki, 2018). They may autonomously allocate resources, interact with customers, flag compliance risks, negotiate with other agents, or trigger operational actions without direct human initiation. In this sense, intelligent agents become participants in organizational decision-making rather than passive instruments.

This reconceptualization challenges traditional assumptions underlying information systems and management control. When agents possess decision-making autonomy, organizations must reconsider how authority, responsibility, and accountability are distributed across human and non-human actors (Orlikowski, 2000). Intelligent agents thus blur established boundaries between technology and organization, reinforcing the need to view them as socio-technical systems rather than isolated technical components (Floridi et al., 2018).

2.2 AI Agents as Drivers of Digital Transformation

Digital transformation is commonly defined as the process through which organizations leverage digital technologies to fundamentally reshape value creation, operational models, and strategic positioning (Vial, 2019). Early phases of digital transformation focused on digitization and automation, improving efficiency by replacing manual processes with information systems. However, the integration of intelligent agents marks a transition from automation toward autonomous and adaptive transformation, where systems actively shape organizational behavior and outcomes.

Intelligent agents accelerate digital transformation by enabling continuous decision-making on scale. Unlike human-centered decision structures that are constrained by time, cognitive limits, and organizational hierarchies, agents can operate continuously, process vast volumes of data in real time, and coordinate actions across distributed units (Bharadwaj et al., 2013). This capability supports advanced forms of optimization, such as dynamic pricing, predictive maintenance, personalized service delivery, and adaptive policy enforcement.

Moreover, intelligent agents facilitate new organizational forms based on modularity and decentralization. In multi-agent configurations, decision authority can be distributed across interacting agents, allowing organizations to respond more flexibly to environmental changes (Shoham & Leyton-Brown, 2009). Such architectures align closely with contemporary digital platform strategies and ecosystem-based business models, where coordination occurs through algorithmic interactions rather than centralized managerial control (Yoo et al., 2012).

However, the same properties that make intelligent agents' powerful drivers of digital transformation also intensify governance challenges. Autonomous agents may generate outcomes that are difficult to predict, explain, or control, particularly when learning systems evolve over time (Binns, 2018). In regulated environments such as healthcare, finance, and the public sector, these challenges are especially pronounced due to legal obligations, ethical expectations, and public accountability requirements (Kroll et al., 2017).

Unintended consequences including biased decisions, emergent coordination failures, or misalignment with organizational values can undermine trust and legitimacy if not properly governed (Rahwan et al., 2019). As a result, digital transformation driven by intelligent agents cannot be treated solely as a technical initiative. It must be accompanied by strategic governance frameworks that address control, transparency, accountability, and alignment with institutional objectives (Weill & Ross, 2004).

In this context, intelligent agents act as both enablers and stress tests of digital transformation strategies. They unlock new forms of organizational capability while simultaneously exposing limitations in existing governance structures. Understanding this dual role is essential for organizations seeking to harness intelligent agents as sustainable drivers of digital transformation rather than sources of unmanaged risk.

Figure 1. Conceptual Framework: Intelligent Agents as Drivers of Digital Transformation

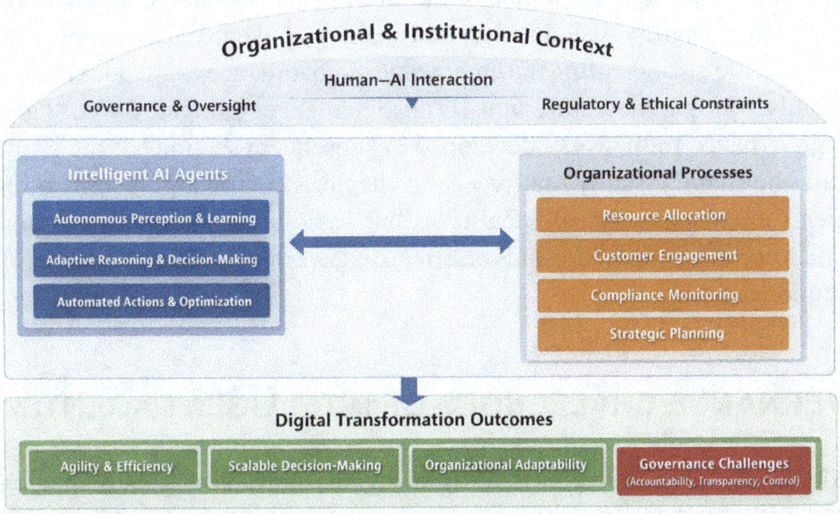

Figure X. *Conceptual Framework: Intelligent Agents as Drivers of Digital Transformation*

This above Figure presents a conceptual framework illustrating how intelligent intelligent agents function as core drivers of digital transformation through their integration into organizational systems. The framework conceptualizes intelligent agents as autonomous socio-technical actors situated between digital technologies and organizational transformation outcomes.

At the foundation of the framework are intelligent agent capabilities, including autonomous perception, reasoning, learning, and action. These capabilities enable agents to operate continuously within dynamic and uncertain environments. Built upon these capabilities are agent functionalities, such as real-time decision-making, adaptive optimization, and coordination across distributed organizational processes.

The framework shows how intelligent agents are embedded within organizational processes, including resource allocation, service delivery, compliance monitoring, and strategic planning. Through this embeddedness, intelligent agents shift digital transformation from traditional automation toward agent-mediated organizational redesign, where decisions are increasingly shaped by autonomous systems rather than solely by human actors.

Surrounding the core agent–process interaction layer are organizational and institutional contexts, including governance structures, human oversight mechanisms, and regulatory environments. These contextual elements constrain and shape agent behavior, ensuring alignment with organizational strategy, ethical principles, and policy requirements.

Finally, the framework highlights digital transformation outcomes, such as increased operational agility, scalable decision-making, and enhanced organizational adaptability, while also signaling the emergence of governance challenges related to accountability, transparency, and control. These challenges motivate the need for the strategic governance frameworks developed in subsequent sections of the chapter.

Overall, the figure visually reinforces the chapter's central argument that intelligent agents are not merely technical tools but socio-technical drivers of digital transformation whose impact depends on effective governance across organizational and institutional layers.

3. GOVERNANCE CHALLENGES OF INTELLIGENT AGENTS

The deployment of intelligent intelligent agents introduces governance challenges that differ fundamentally from those associated with traditional information systems. Because intelligent agents operate autonomously, learn over time, and interact with both humans and other agents, they destabilize established governance assumptions related to control, accountability, transparency, and risk management. These challenges are not merely technical in nature but are deeply organizational, institutional, and ethical, requiring new governance paradigms that extend beyond existing IT governance models (Floridi et al., 2018; Weill & Ross, 2004).

3.1 Delegation of Authority and Accountability

One of the most profound governance challenges posed by intelligent agents concerns the delegation of decision-making authority. In conventional organizational systems, authority is formally assigned to human roles, and accountability can be traced through hierarchical structures. Intelligent agents, however, may be granted the ability to make and execute decisions independently, sometimes in real time and at scale, without direct human intervention (Wooldridge, 2009).

This delegation of authority raises critical questions about responsibility when agent decisions lead to undesirable or harmful outcomes. Determining accountability becomes complex when outcomes emerge from interactions between algorithmic design choices, training data, environmental conditions, and organizational oversight practices (Diakopoulos, 2016). Responsibility may be distributed across multiple actors, including system designers, data providers, organizational leaders, and frontline operators, creating what has been described as an "accountability gap" (Kroll et al., 2017).

Furthermore, learning-enabled agents may evolve their behavior over time, making it difficult to attribute specific decisions to predefined rules or human intent (Binns, 2018). Traditional liability frameworks, which assume predictable cause–effect relationships, are often ill-suited to such adaptive systems. As a result, organizations must develop explicit governance mechanisms that define decision rights, escalation paths, and accountability boundaries for autonomous agents across different operational contexts (Weill & Ross, 2004).

Without clear governance structures, the delegation of authority to intelligent agents' risk undermining organizational control, eroding trust, and exposing institutions to legal and reputational harm.

3.2 Transparency, Explainability, and Trust

Transparency is a foundational principle of organizational governance, enabling oversight, accountability, and stakeholder trust. Intelligent agents challenge this principle because many contemporary AI techniques particularly deep learning and reinforcement learning operate as opaque or partially interpretable systems (Lipton, 2018). Decisions produced by such agents may be difficult for humans to understand, justify, or contest.

Explainability has therefore emerged as a central governance requirement, especially in high-stakes domains such as credit scoring, healthcare diagnostics, law enforcement, and public administration (Doshi-Velez & Kim, 2017). From a governance perspective, explainability is not solely a technical feature but a socio-organizational requirement that supports auditing, compliance, and informed human oversight (Arrieta et al., 2020).

The challenge is amplified by the adaptive nature of intelligent agents. As agents learn from new data and adjust their internal models, explanations that were valid at deployment may become obsolete over time (Leslie, 2020). This dynamic behavior complicates regulatory compliance and weakens organizational confidence in system reliability.

A lack of transparency can also undermine trust among employees, customers, and citizens. When stakeholders are unable to understand how decisions are made or perceive those decisions as arbitrary or biased organizational legitimacy may be compromised (Floridi & Cowls, 2019). Effective governance must therefore integrate explainability requirements throughout the AI lifecycle, ensuring that transparency mechanisms evolve alongside agent capabilities.

3.3 Bias, Fairness, and Ethical Risk

Intelligent agents learn from historical and real-time data, which may reflect existing social, organizational, or institutional biases. As a result, agents can unintentionally reproduce or amplify inequities in decision-making, particularly when deployed at scale (Mittelstadt et al., 2016). Bias in intelligent agents presents both ethical and governance challenges, as discriminatory outcomes may violate legal standards and organizational values.

Governance frameworks must address not only technical bias mitigation techniques but also the broader organizational conditions that shape data collection, model objectives, and performance metrics (Jobin et al., 2019). Ethical risks are often embedded in design choices, such as the selection of optimization goals or the prioritization of efficiency over equity (Rahwan et al., 2019).

Moreover, ethical concerns extend beyond fairness to include issues of autonomy, consent, surveillance, and the appropriate scope of automated decision-making (Floridi et al., 2018). Without explicit ethical governance structures, organizations risk deploying intelligent agents in ways that conflict with societal norms and public expectations.

3.4 Multi-Agent Coordination and Emergent Behavior

Many organizational deployments involve not a single intelligent agent but multiple interacting agents operating across processes, departments, or institutional boundaries. In such multi-agent environments, system-level behavior may emerge that was not explicitly designed or anticipated (Shoham & Leyton-Brown, 2009).

Emergent behavior can generate efficiency gains and adaptive coordination, but it can also introduce systemic risks. For example, agents optimizing local objectives may collectively produce suboptimal or harmful global outcomes, such as resource monopolization, feedback loops, or unintended collusion (Rahwan et al., 2019). These risks are particularly salient in financial markets, supply chains, and public-sector service delivery.

From a governance standpoint, emergent behavior challenges traditional control mechanisms that focus on individual system components. Oversight must instead operate at the system level, incorporating monitoring, simulation, and stress-testing of agent interactions (Raji et al., 2020). Governance frameworks must also define intervention mechanisms to correct or constrain undesirable collective behavior when it arises.

3.5 Regulatory Compliance and Institutional Alignment

Intelligent agents increasingly operate within highly regulated environments, where compliance with legal, ethical, and policy requirements is mandatory. Regulatory frameworks often assume human decision-makers and static systems, creating tension when applied to adaptive, autonomous agents (European Commission, 2021).

Organizations must therefore navigate regulatory uncertainty while ensuring that intelligent agents remain aligned with institutional mandates and societal values (OECD, 2019). This challenge is particularly acute in the public sector, where transparency, fairness, and accountability are central to democratic legitimacy (Mergel et al., 2019).

Governance mechanisms must bridge internal organizational practices and external regulatory expectations, ensuring policy coherence across jurisdictions and over time. Failure to do so risks not only non-compliance but also erosion of public trust in AI-driven digital transformation initiatives.

3.6 Summary of Governance Challenges

Taken together, these challenges highlight that the governance of intelligent agents extends far beyond technical risk management. Issues of authority, accountability, transparency, ethics, coordination, and regulation are deeply interconnected and must be addressed through integrated governance frameworks rather than isolated controls (Floridi & Cowls, 2019).

These governance challenges provide the foundation for the strategic frameworks developed in the following section, which conceptualize intelligent agents as socio-technical systems embedded within organizational and institutional contexts.

Table 1. Core Governance Challenges of Intelligent Agents

Governance Challenge	Description	Organizational Risk
Delegation of Authority	Autonomous decision-making without human initiation	Accountability gaps
Transparency & Explainability	Opaque learning-based decisions	Loss of trust
Bias & Ethical Risk	Data-driven inequities	Legal and ethical violations
Emergent Behavior	Unintended multi-agent dynamics	Systemic instability
Regulatory Alignment	Mismatch with existing laws	Compliance failures

4. A SOCIO-TECHNICAL GOVERNANCE PERSPECTIVE

The governance challenges associated with intelligent intelligent agents cannot be adequately addressed through purely technical controls or conventional IT governance mechanisms. Intelligent agents operate at the intersection of technology, organizational processes, human judgment, and institutional norms. As such, effective governance requires a socio-technical perspective that explicitly recognizes the mutual shaping of social and technical elements within organizational systems (Trist & Bamforth, 1951; Orlikowski, 2000).

A socio-technical governance perspective emphasizes that intelligent agents are not neutral tools, but active components embedded within organizational structures, power relations, and decision-making processes. This perspective provides a foundation for developing governance frameworks that account for human–AI interaction, organizational accountability, and alignment with broader societal values (Floridi et al., 2018).

4.1 Intelligent Agents as Socio-Technical Systems

Socio-technical systems theory originates from the recognition that organizational performance depends on the joint optimization of social systems (people, roles, norms, and culture) and technical systems (tools, processes, and technologies) (Trist & Bamforth, 1951). Applying this theory to intelligent agents highlights that governance cannot be reduced to algorithmic design choices or performance metrics alone.

Intelligent agents are embedded within organizational contexts that shape how they are designed, deployed, interpreted, and controlled. Decisions regarding training data, optimization objectives, and performance thresholds reflect organizational priorities and value judgments rather than purely technical considerations (Mittelstadt et al., 2016). At the same time, the behavior of intelligent agents can reshape organizational routines, redistribute decision authority, and alter human roles (Orlikowski, 2000).

Viewing intelligent agents as socio-technical systems underscores the importance of governance mechanisms that address both technical behavior and social impact. For example, an agent's decision logic may be technically sound while still producing outcomes that conflict with organizational ethics or public expectations. Without governance structures that integrate social oversight with technical monitoring, such misalignments may persist undetected (Floridi & Cowls, 2019).

This perspective also challenges the notion that responsibility for AI systems can be localized to specific technical teams. Instead, accountability must be distributed across organizational actors, including leadership, governance bodies, and frontline users who interact with intelligent agents in practice (Diakopoulos, 2016). Applying this theory to intelligent agents highlights that governance cannot be reduced to algorithmic design choices or performance metrics alone.

This figure illustrates the layered structure of socio-technical governance, showing how technical systems, human roles, organizational structures, and institutional norms jointly shape intelligent agent behavior and accountability.

Figure 2. Socio-Technical Governance Layers for Intelligent Agents

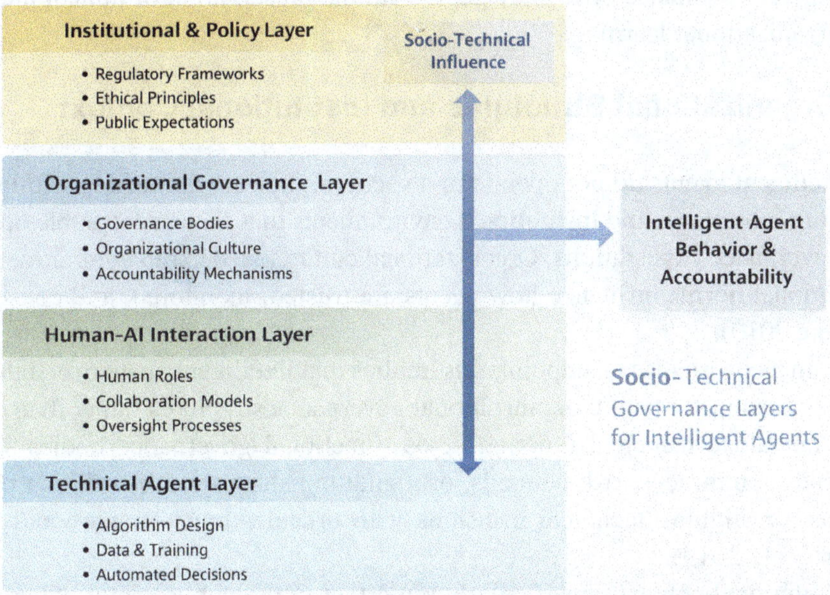

4.2 Human–AI Interaction and Organizational Roles

A socio-technical governance perspective places human–AI interaction at the center of governance design. Intelligent agents rarely operate in complete isolation; rather, they interact with humans in varying configurations, ranging from decision-support roles to autonomous execution with human oversight (Nushi et al., 2019).

Governance frameworks must therefore specify how humans and intelligent agents share decision-making authority. Concepts such as *human-in-the-loop*, *human-on-the-loop*, and *human-out-of-the-loop* describe different interaction models, each with distinct governance implications (Parasuraman et al., 2000). High-risk or value-laden decisions may require closer human involvement, while low-risk operational tasks may permit greater autonomy.

Importantly, the introduction of intelligent agents can transform human roles rather than simply replacing them. Employees may shift from performing routine tasks to supervising, interpreting, and intervening in agent behavior (Endsley, 2017). Governance must support this role transformation through training, clarity of responsibility, and mechanisms for meaningful human control.

Failure to address human–AI interaction from a socio-technical perspective can lead to over-reliance on automated systems, erosion of human expertise, or ineffective oversight due to automation bias (Binns, 2018). Effective governance must therefore balance efficiency gains with the preservation of human judgment and organizational learning.

4.3 Organizational Structures and Institutional Context

Intelligent agents do not operate in a vacuum; they are embedded within organizational structures and institutional environments that shape acceptable behavior and governance expectations. Organizational culture, leadership commitment, and institutional norms influence how agents are trusted, monitored, and constrained (Schein, 2010).

From a governance standpoint, this implies that intelligent agent oversight must be integrated into existing organizational governance structures rather than treated as a standalone technical function. Cross-functional governance bodies such as AI ethics committees, risk councils, or digital transformation boards can provide forums for aligning technical decisions with organizational strategy and values (Jobin et al., 2019).

Institutional context is particularly important in the public sector, where intelligent agents operate under heightened expectations of transparency, fairness, and democratic accountability (Mergel et al., 2019). Public organizations must ensure that agent behavior aligns not only with operational efficiency goals but also with public mandates and legal obligations.

A socio-technical perspective therefore emphasizes the need for governance mechanisms that connect micro-level system behavior with macro-level institutional objectives, ensuring coherence across organizational and policy domains (OECD, 2019).

4.4 Integrating Strategy, Governance, and Policy

Effective governance of intelligent agents requires alignment between organizational strategy, internal governance mechanisms, and external policy frameworks.

Strategic alignment ensures that agent deployment supports long-term organizational objectives rather than short-term efficiency gains (Bharadwaj et al., 2013).

Traditional IT governance models focus on aligning technology investments with business strategy (Weill & Ross, 2004). However, intelligent agents require an expanded governance approach that addresses autonomy, learning, and ethical risk. Strategic governance must define not only *what* intelligent agents do, but *how* and *under what conditions* they are permitted to act.

Policy frameworks play a complementary role by setting boundaries for acceptable agent behavior. International initiatives such as the OECD AI Principles and emerging regulatory regimes emphasize accountability, transparency, and risk-based governance (OECD, 2019; European Commission, 2021). A socio-technical governance perspective enables organizations to translate these high-level policy principles into operational controls and decision processes.

By integrating strategy, governance, and policy, organizations can move from reactive compliance toward proactive stewardship of intelligent agents as strategic assets (Floridi et al., 2018).

4.5 Implications of a Socio-Technical Perspective

Adopting a socio-technical governance perspective has several important implications. First, it reframes intelligent agent governance as an ongoing organizational capability rather than a one-time compliance exercise (Leslie, 2020). Governance must evolve alongside agent capabilities, organizational learning, and regulatory change.

Second, it highlights the importance of institutional capacity-building, including AI literacy, ethical reasoning, and cross-disciplinary collaboration (Davenport & Ronanki, 2018). Without such capacity, governance mechanisms risk becoming symbolic rather than effective.

Finally, a socio-technical perspective provides a conceptual foundation for the strategic governance frameworks developed in the next section. By recognizing intelligent agents as embedded, adaptive actors within organizational systems, it becomes possible to design governance structures that support sustainable, trustworthy, and value-driven AI-enabled digital transformation.

5. STRATEGIC GOVERNANCE FRAMEWORKS FOR INTELLIGENT AGENTS

The governance challenges associated with intelligent intelligent agents necessitate structured, strategic frameworks that move beyond ad hoc controls or post hoc compliance mechanisms. Given the adaptive, autonomous, and embedded nature of intelligent agents, governance must be continuous, systematic, and aligned with organizational strategy and institutional obligations. This section proposes two complementary governance frameworks: (1) a lifecycle-based governance model and (2) a decision-rights and oversight framework. Together, these frameworks operationalize the socio-technical governance perspective developed in the previous section.

5.1 Lifecycle-Based Governance of Intelligent Agents

Governance of intelligent agents must span the entire AI lifecycle, from initial design to ongoing adaptation. Unlike traditional information systems, intelligent agents evolve over time through learning mechanisms, making governance a dynamic and iterative process rather than a one-time intervention (IEEE, 2019; Leslie, 2020).

A lifecycle-based governance approach enables organizations to embed accountability, transparency, and risk management at each stage of agent development and operation (Raji et al., 2020).

5.1.1 Design and Development Stage

At the design stage, governance focuses on aligning intelligent agent objectives with organizational values, ethical principles, and strategic priorities. Key governance activities include defining the agent's scope of autonomy, selecting appropriate data sources, and specifying optimization objectives (Mittelstadt et al., 2016).

Decisions made at this stage have long-term implications, as they shape agent behavior and learning trajectories. Ethical impact assessments and stakeholder consultations can help identify potential risks related to bias, fairness, and misuse before deployment (Floridi et al., 2018).

5.1.2 Deployment and Integration Stage

During deployment, governance mechanisms must ensure that intelligent agents interact safely and effectively with organizational systems and human users. This includes validation testing, access controls, and the implementation of human–AI interaction models appropriate to task criticality (Nushi et al., 2019).

Governance at this stage also involves ensuring regulatory compliance, particularly in sectors subject to data protection, safety, or administrative law requirements (European Commission, 2021).

5.1.3 Monitoring and Oversight Stage

Once deployed, intelligent agents require continuous monitoring to detect performance degradation, model drift, or unintended behavior (Raji et al., 2020). Governance mechanisms such as audit logs, performance dashboards, and periodic reviews support organizational oversight and accountability.

Monitoring must address both technical performance and social impact, including fairness, transparency, and stakeholder trust (Floridi & Cowls, 2019).

5.1.4 Adaptation and Evolution Stage

Intelligent agents often adapt through retraining or policy updates. Governance at this stage focuses on managing change responsibly by controlling when and how learning updates occur (Leslie, 2020). Unchecked adaptation can undermine accountability by obscuring causal links between design decisions and outcomes.

Organizations must therefore establish formal change-management procedures for intelligent agents, including documentation, approval workflows, and post-update evaluation.

Table 2. Lifecycle-Based Governance Framework for Intelligent Agents

Lifecycle Stage	Governance Focus	Key Mechanisms	Primary Actors
Design & Development	Strategic alignment, ethics, risk identification	Ethical impact assessments, data governance, objective setting	Designers, leadership, ethics committees
Deployment & Integration	Safety, compliance, human–AI interaction	Validation testing, access controls, HITL/HOTL models	IT teams, legal/ compliance, operations
Monitoring & Oversight	Performance, accountability, transparency	Audits, dashboards, logging, review boards	Risk management, auditors, governance bodies
Adaptation & Evolution	Controlled learning, accountability over time	Change management, retraining approvals, re-validation	Governance councils, technical leads

5.2 Decision Rights and Oversight Structures

While lifecycle-based governance addresses when governance interventions occur, decision-rights frameworks clarify who is authorized to make decisions and under what conditions. Intelligent agents challenge traditional governance assumptions by exercising decision-making independently (Weill & Ross, 2004).

Strategic governance requires explicit allocation of decision rights among humans and intelligent agents to prevent ambiguity, accountability gaps, and uncontrolled autonomy (Diakopoulos, 2016).

5.2.1 Allocating Decision Authority

Decision rights determine which actions intelligent agents may perform autonomously, which require human approval, and which remain exclusively human decisions (Parasuraman et al., 2000). Allocation should be based on factors such as risk level, ethical sensitivity, regulatory exposure, and organizational maturity.

High-impact decisions such as eligibility determinations, enforcement actions, or resource prioritization typically require stronger human oversight, while routine operational decisions may permit greater agent autonomy (Binns, 2018).

5.2.2 Oversight and Escalation Mechanisms

Effective governance also requires clear escalation paths when intelligent agents encounter uncertainty, anomalies, or conflicting objectives. Oversight mechanisms such as supervisory dashboards, exception reporting, and intervention triggers enable timely human involvement (Endsley, 2017).

Cross-functional oversight bodies can provide institutional checks and balances by reviewing agent behavior, resolving disputes, and updating governance policies as needed (Jobin et al., 2019).

Table 3. Decision-Rights Governance Framework for Intelligent Agents

Decision Type	Agent Autonomy Level	Human Role	Governance Mechanism
Routine operational decisions	High	Human-on-the-loop	Performance thresholds, alerts
Tactical decisions with moderate risk	Shared	Human-in-the-loop	Approval workflows, explanations
Strategic or ethical decisions	Low	Human-in-control	Formal review boards, documentation
Regulatory or legal determinations	None	Human-only	Legal oversight, compliance review

5.3 Integrating Lifecycle and Decision-Rights Governance

Lifecycle governance and decision-rights governance are mutually reinforcing. Lifecycle stages determine *when* governance interventions occur, while decision-rights frameworks clarify *who* is responsible for decisions at each stage (Weill & Ross, 2004).

Together, these frameworks enable organizations to manage intelligent agents as strategic assets rather than unmanaged risks. They support consistency, accountability, and adaptability across organizational contexts and over time (Floridi et al., 2018).

By embedding governance throughout the AI lifecycle and explicitly allocating decision authority, organizations can scale intelligent agents responsibly while maintaining alignment with institutional values, regulatory requirements, and societal expectations.

Together, these frameworks enable organizations to manage intelligent agents as strategic assets rather than unmanaged risks.

This figure integrates the lifecycle-based governance model with decision-rights allocation, illustrating how governance responsibilities evolve across design, deployment, monitoring, and adaptation stages.

Figure 3. Integrated Lifecycle and Decision-Rights Governance Model

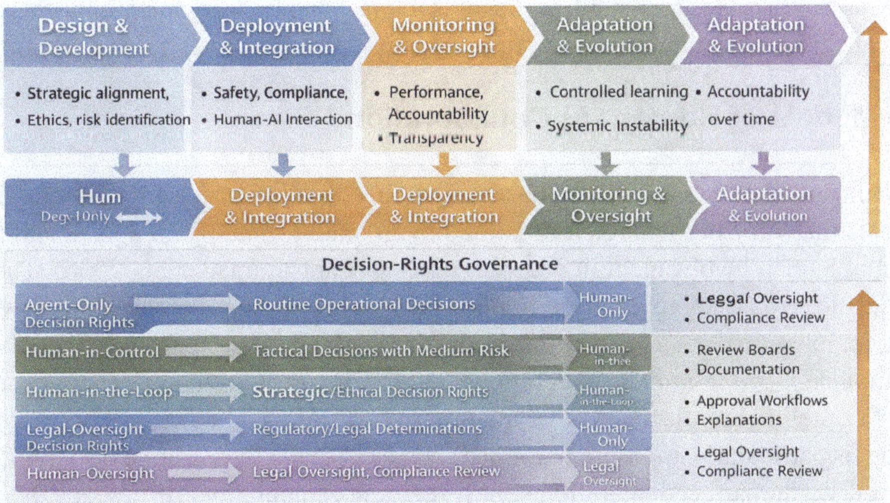

5.4 Strategic Implications

Strategic governance frameworks shift intelligent agent governance from reactive compliance toward proactive organizational design. Rather than constraining innovation, well-designed governance structures enable experimentation while managing risk (Davenport & Ronanki, 2018).

For public-sector and regulated organizations, these frameworks provide a practical foundation for trustworthy AI deployment, supporting transparency, accountability, and public legitimacy (OECD, 2019).

The next section builds on these frameworks to examine implications for organizational capability, digital maturity, and policy coherence.

6. HUMAN–AI COLLABORATION AND ORGANIZATIONAL CAPACITY

The effective governance of intelligent intelligent agents depends not only on technical safeguards and formal governance structures but also on the quality of human–AI collaboration and the organizational capacity to manage autonomous systems. Intelligent agents rarely function in isolation; rather, they operate within socio-technical environments where human judgment, oversight, and intervention remain critical (Nushi et al., 2019). As such, governance frameworks must explicitly address how humans and intelligent agents interact and how organizations develop the capabilities required to sustain responsible AI-driven digital transformation.

6.1 Models of Human–AI Collaboration

Human–AI collaboration can be conceptualized along a spectrum of interaction models that vary in the degree of autonomy granted to intelligent agents and the level of human involvement in decision-making (Parasuraman et al., 2000). These models have distinct governance implications and must be carefully aligned with task complexity, risk exposure, and organizational maturity.

In *human-in-the-loop* configurations, intelligent agents generate recommendations or preliminary decisions that require human approval before execution. This model is particularly appropriate for high-stakes or ethically sensitive decisions, as it preserves human accountability while leveraging computational efficiency (Nushi et al., 2019). However, excessive reliance on human-in-the-loop controls can limit scalability and reduce the transformative potential of intelligent agents.

Human-on-the-loop models grant agents greater autonomy while maintaining human supervision. Humans monitor agent performance, intervene when anomalies arise, and retain authority to override or suspend agent actions (Endsley, 2017). This approach balances efficiency with oversight and is commonly used in operational domains such as logistics optimization, fraud detection, and infrastructure monitoring.

Human-out-of-the-loop models involve fully autonomous agent operation with minimal or no real-time human involvement. While such models may offer significant efficiency gains, they pose substantial governance risks and are generally unsuitable for contexts requiring legal accountability or ethical judgment (Binns, 2018). Governance frameworks must therefore clearly delineate the boundaries of acceptable autonomy for intelligent agents.

Table 4. Human–AI Collaboration Models and Governance Implications

Collaboration Model	Agent Autonomy	Human Role	Governance Risk
Human-in-the-loop	Low	Approval	Scalability limits
Human-on-the-loop	Medium	Supervision	Automation bias
Human-out-of-the-loop	High	Minimal	Accountability loss

6.2 Risks in Human–AI Collaboration

Human–AI collaboration introduces its own set of governance risks that must be proactively managed. One prominent risk is *automation bias*, where humans over-trust agent output and fail to critically evaluate recommendations, even when errors are present (Parasuraman & Riley, 1997). This risk is exacerbated when intelligent agents exhibit high apparent accuracy or when decision contexts are complex and time constrained.

Another challenge is the erosion of human expertise. As intelligent agents assume greater responsibility for decision-making, human skills and situational awareness may deteriorate, reducing the organization's ability to intervene effectively when systems fail (Endsley, 2017). Governance mechanisms must therefore ensure that human oversight remains meaningful rather than symbolic.

Effective governance also requires clear communication of agent limitations. Overstating agent capabilities or failing to convey uncertainty can lead to misuse and misplaced confidence (Lipton, 2018). Transparent interfaces and explanation mechanisms support informed human judgment and responsible collaboration (Arrieta et al., 2020).

6.3 Organizational Capacity for Governing Intelligent Agents

Beyond interaction models, organizations must develop the internal capacity to govern intelligent agents effectively. Organizational capacity encompasses technical expertise, governance structures, cultural norms, and leadership commitment (Davenport & Ronanki, 2018). Without such capacity, governance frameworks risk becoming procedural formalities rather than effective controls.

AI literacy is a foundational component of organizational capacity. Decision-makers, managers, and frontline employees must understand the capabilities, limitations, and risks of intelligent agents engaging in informed oversight (Leslie, 2020). This does not require all stakeholders to possess deep technical expertise but does require shared conceptual understanding.

Cross-functional collaboration is equally important. Effective AI governance spans technical, legal, ethical, and operational domains, necessitating coordination across traditionally siloed functions (Jobin et al., 2019). Governance bodies that integrate diverse perspectives are better equipped to anticipate and manage complex socio-technical risks.

6.4 Capability Development and Institutional Learning

Governance of intelligent agents is not static; it requires continuous institutional learning as technologies, organizational contexts, and regulatory environments evolve (Floridi et al., 2018). Organizations must establish feedback mechanisms that enable learning from agent performance, incidents, and stakeholder feedback.

Training programs, scenario-based exercises, and post-incident reviews support the development of organizational competence and resilience (Raji et al., 2020). Such practices also contribute to a culture of responsibility and reflection, which is essential for trustworthy AI deployment.

In the public sector, capacity-building efforts must also address institutional constraints such as procurement rules, legacy systems, and public accountability requirements (Mergel et al., 2019). Strategic investment in organizational capacity is therefore a prerequisite for realizing the benefits of intelligent agents in both public and private contexts.

6.5 Cultural and Leadership Considerations

Organizational culture and leadership play a decisive role in shaping human–AI collaboration. Leadership commitment to responsible AI principles signals the importance of governance and influences how intelligent agents are perceived and used throughout the organization (Schein, 2010).

A culture that encourages questioning, transparency, and ethical reflection supports effective governance by empowering employees to raise concerns and intervene when necessary (Floridi & Cowls, 2019). Conversely, cultures that prioritize efficiency over accountability may exacerbate governance risks by discouraging critical oversight.

Leaders must therefore frame intelligent agents not as replacements for human judgment but as partners in decision-making that require careful governance and stewardship (Davenport & Ronanki, 2018).

6.6 Implications for Digital Maturity

Human–AI collaboration and organizational capacity are key determinants of digital maturity in AI-driven transformation. Organizations that invest in governance capabilities, human expertise, and institutional learning are better positioned to scale intelligent agents responsibly and sustainably (Vial, 2019).

Digital maturity in this context extends beyond technological sophistication to include governance readiness, ethical awareness, and the ability to integrate intelligent agents into organizational life without compromising trust or accountability.

Effective governance of intelligent agents requires deliberate design of human–AI collaboration models and sustained investment in organizational capacity. Governance frameworks must balance autonomy and oversight, support human judgment, and foster institutional learning. Without such capacity, intelligent agents risk becoming sources of unmanaged risk rather than drivers of strategic digital transformation.

This figure illustrates the progression of organizational governance capability as AI maturity increases, moving from experimental and ad hoc oversight toward strategic and institutionalized governance structures that support responsible and scalable intelligent agent deployment.

Figure 4. Organizational Capacity Maturity for Governing Intelligent Agents

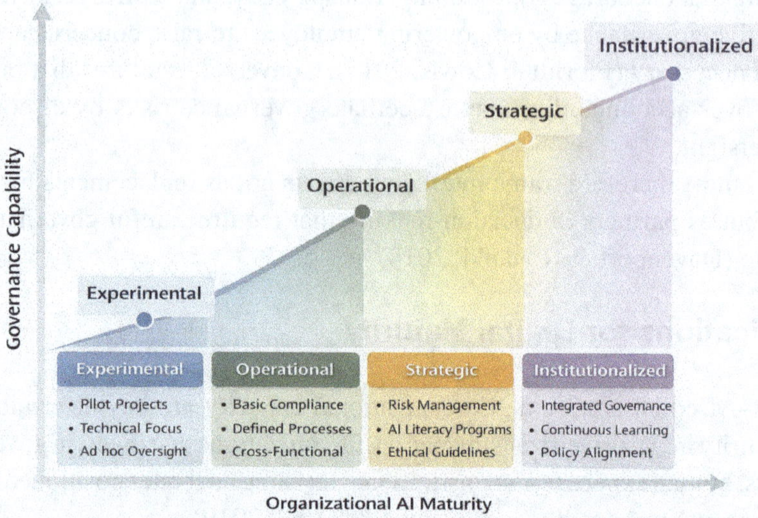

7. IMPLICATIONS FOR PUBLIC POLICY AND REGULATION

The widespread deployment of intelligent intelligent agents has significant implications for public policy and regulatory governance. Unlike earlier generations of information systems, intelligent agents exercise varying degrees of autonomy, adapt through learning, and participate directly in decision-making processes that affect individuals, organizations, and society. These characteristics challenge existing legal and regulatory frameworks, which are typically designed around static systems and human decision-makers (Kroll et al., 2017).

As intelligent agents become integral to digital transformation across both public-sector and enterprise contexts, policymakers face the dual challenge of enabling innovation while safeguarding accountability, transparency, and public trust (OECD, 2019). This section examines key policy and regulatory implications arising from the governance of intelligent agents and highlights the need for adaptive, risk-based, and socio-technical regulatory approaches.

7.1 Limitations of Existing Regulatory Frameworks

Most existing regulatory regimes were developed under assumptions that decisions are made either by humans or by deterministic systems whose behavior can be fully specified in advance. Intelligent agents violate these assumptions by learning over time, interacting with dynamic environments, and producing outcomes that may not be fully predictable (Russell et al., 1995).

As a result, traditional compliance mechanisms such as ex ante certification or static rule enforcement may be insufficient to govern adaptive agent behavior (Leslie, 2020). Regulatory requirements that mandate explainability, auditability, or accountability may be difficult to operationalize when agent decisions emerge from complex learning processes (Lipton, 2018).

This mismatch creates regulatory uncertainty for organizations and complicates enforcement for regulators. Without updated frameworks, intelligent agents risk operating in legally gray areas that undermine both innovation and public protection (Binns, 2018).

7.2 Risk-Based Regulation of Intelligent Agents

In response to these challenges, policymakers are increasingly adopting risk-based regulatory approaches that tailor governance requirements to the potential impact of AI systems. Rather than regulating all intelligent agents uniformly, risk-based models differentiate obligations based on factors such as application domain, decision criticality, and societal harm (OECD, 2019).

The proposed European Union Artificial Intelligence Act exemplifies this approach by classifying AI systems into risk categories and imposing proportionate governance requirements, including human oversight, transparency, and post-deployment monitoring (European Commission, 2021). Such frameworks recognize that intelligent agents used for low-risk applications may require minimal regulatory intervention, while high-risk agents demand stringent oversight.

Risk-based regulation aligns closely with lifecycle-based governance models by emphasizing continuous monitoring and adaptation rather than one-time approval (Raji et al., 2020). However, effective implementation depends on organizational capacity to assess risk accurately and regulators' ability to evaluate compliance in complex socio-technical systems.

Table 5. Policy Approaches to Governing Intelligent Agents

Regulatory Approach	Key Features	Limitations
Rule-based	Fixed compliance	Inflexible
Risk-based	Proportional controls	Assessment complexity
Adaptive	Continuous learning	Regulatory capacity needs

7.3 Accountability, Liability, and Legal Responsibility

One of the most contested policy issues surrounding intelligent agents concerns accountability and liability. When autonomous agents make decisions that result in harm, determining legal responsibility becomes challenging due to the distributed nature of agency across designers, operators, organizations, and learning systems (Diakopoulos, 2016).

Existing liability regimes often rely on clear causal chains and human intent, which may be obscured in agent-based systems (Kroll et al., 2017). Policymakers must therefore consider whether new legal constructs such as shared liability models or enhanced organizational duties of care are necessary to address autonomous decision-making (Floridi et al., 2018).

From a governance perspective, regulatory clarity on accountability incentivizes organizations to invest in robust governance frameworks, documentation, and oversight mechanisms. Conversely, ambiguous liability regimes may discourage innovation or encourage minimal compliance approaches.

7.4 Transparency, Due Process, and Public Trust

Transparency is a cornerstone of democratic governance and regulatory legitimacy, particularly in public-sector applications. Intelligent agents deployed in areas such as welfare administration, policing, taxation, or immigration directly affect citizens' rights and opportunities (Mergel et al., 2019).

Policy frameworks increasingly emphasize transparency and due process requirements, including the right to explanation, contestability of automated decisions, and meaningful human review (Doshi-Velez & Kim, 2017). These requirements reflect broader societal expectations that automated systems remain accountable to human values and legal norms (Floridi & Cowls, 2019).

However, mandating transparency without considering technical feasibility and organizational context may lead to superficial compliance or "explanation theater" (Lipton, 2018). Effective policy design must therefore balance normative goals with practical governance mechanisms that support genuine oversight and trust.

7.5 Policy Coherence and Cross-Jurisdictional Challenges

Intelligent agents often operate across organizational, sectoral, and national boundaries, raising challenges for policy coherence and regulatory coordination. Divergent regulatory standards can create compliance burdens for organizations and uneven protection for affected stakeholders (OECD, 2019).

International coordination initiatives, such as shared AI principles and cross-border regulatory dialogue, aim to promote harmonization while respecting local legal and cultural contexts (Jobin et al., 2019). Policy coherence is particularly important for global enterprises and digital platforms deploying intelligent agents on a scale.

From a governance perspective, organizations must navigate overlapping regulatory regimes while maintaining consistent internal governance standards. Strategic alignment between internal governance frameworks and external policy expectations reduces compliance risk and enhances organizational resilience.

7.6 Implications for Public-Sector Digital Transformation

Public-sector organizations face unique policy and regulatory pressures when deploying intelligent agents. In addition to legal compliance, they must uphold principles of fairness, transparency, and democratic accountability (Mergel et al., 2019).

Policy frameworks for public-sector AI must therefore emphasize procedural justice, explainability, and citizen engagement. Governance mechanisms such as algorithmic impact assessments, public reporting, and independent oversight bodies can support legitimacy and trust (Raji et al., 2020).

At the same time, overly restrictive regulation may limit the public sector's ability to leverage intelligent agents for service improvement and operational efficiency. Policymakers must strike a balance between safeguarding public values and enabling innovation in digital government (Vial, 2019).

7.7 Toward Adaptive and Socio-Technical Regulation

The governance of intelligent agents requires regulatory approaches that are adaptive, iterative, and grounded in socio-technical understanding. Static rules are unlikely to remain effective as intelligent agents evolve and organizational practices change (Leslie, 2020).

Adaptive regulation emphasizes continuous learning, regulatory sandboxes, and collaborative governance between regulators, organizations, and civil society (Floridi et al., 2018). Such approaches align with lifecycle-based governance models and support responsible innovation while managing risk.

Intelligent intelligent agents pose significant challenges for existing policy and regulatory frameworks, necessitating new approaches that account for autonomy, learning, and socio-technical complexity. Risk-based regulation, clarified accountability regimes, transparency requirements, and policy coherence are central to governing intelligent agents on a scale.

By aligning organizational governance frameworks with evolving policy and regulatory expectations, institutions can support trustworthy, compliant, and value-driven AI-enabled digital transformation.

8. CONCLUSION AND FUTURE RESEARCH DIRECTIONS

The rapid emergence of intelligent intelligent agents marks a pivotal shift in the trajectory of digital transformation. Unlike earlier generations of information systems, intelligent agents act as autonomous, adaptive, and distributed decision-makers embedded within organizational processes. This chapter argued that such systems fundamentally alter the governance landscape, requiring organizations and policymakers to move beyond purely technical or compliance-oriented approaches toward strategic, socio-technical governance frameworks.

By synthesizing insights from AI governance, information systems strategy, organizational theory, and public policy, this chapter has positioned intelligent agents as socio-technical actors whose behavior is shaped jointly by technical design, human oversight, organizational structures, and institutional norms (Orlikowski, 2000; Floridi et al., 2018). The chapter has demonstrated that governance challenges, including accountability, transparency, ethical risk, multi-agent coordination, and regulatory compliance—are deeply interconnected and cannot be addressed in isolation.

8.1 Summary of Key Contributions

This chapter makes several key contributions to the literature on AI-driven digital transformation.

First, it advances a conceptual reframing of intelligent agents from technical components to socio-technical systems embedded within organizational and institutional contexts. This reframing clarifies why traditional IT governance models are insufficient for governing autonomous, learning-enabled systems (Weill & Ross, 2004).

Second, the chapter identifies and systematically analyzes the core governance challenges associated with intelligent agents, including delegation of authority, accountability gaps, explainability, ethical risk, and emergent behavior in multi-agent environments (Kroll et al., 2017; Rahwan et al., 2019). By linking these challenges to organizational and policy dynamics, the chapter provides a more holistic understanding of AI governance.

Third, the chapter proposes strategic governance frameworks that operationalize socio-technical governance principles. The lifecycle-based governance model and decision-rights framework offer practical tools for aligning intelligent agent deployment with organizational strategy, ethical values, and regulatory obligations (IEEE, 2019; Raji et al., 2020).

Finally, the chapter highlights the central role of human–AI collaboration and organizational capacity in sustaining responsible AI deployment. Governance is shown to be not merely a matter of rules and controls, but an ongoing organizational capability shaped by leadership, culture, and institutional learning (Davenport & Ronanki, 2018; Leslie, 2020).

8.2 Implications for Practice and Policy

For organizational leaders, the findings underscore that intelligent agents should be governed as strategic assets rather than experimental technologies. Effective governance requires early integration of ethical, legal, and organizational considerations into design and deployment decisions, as well as sustained investment in monitoring, oversight, and capacity-building (Floridi & Cowls, 2019).

For public-sector institutions, the chapter reinforces the importance of transparency, accountability, and procedural fairness in AI-enabled decision-making. Intelligent agents deployed in public services must align with democratic values and legal mandates, necessitating robust governance and citizen-facing accountability mechanisms (Mergel et al., 2019).

For policymakers and regulators, the analysis notes that static, one-size-fits-all regulatory approaches are unlikely to remain effective. Risk-based, adaptive regulatory models that align with the AI lifecycle and socio-technical realities of intelligent agents are better suited to balancing innovation and public protection (OECD, 2019; European Commission, 2021).

8.3 Future Research Directions

While this chapter provides a strategic governance foundation for intelligent agents, it also highlights several avenues for future research that are critical to advancing both theory and practice. As intelligent agents become more deeply embedded in organizational and institutional systems, governance research must move beyond conceptual models toward empirical validation, methodological refinement, and cross-disciplinary integration.

8.3.1 Empirical Evaluation of Governance Frameworks

Future research should empirically evaluate the lifecycle-based and decision-rights governance frameworks proposed in this chapter across diverse sectors and organizational contexts. Comparative case studies could examine how these frameworks are instantiated in practice within private enterprises, public-sector institutions, and regulated industries such as finance and healthcare. Longitudinal research designs would be particularly valuable in capturing how governance structures evolve as intelligent agents mature, scale, and adapt over time (Vial, 2019).

Such empirical work could also investigate contingencies that influence governance effectiveness, including organizational size, regulatory exposure, digital maturity, and cultural factors. By grounding governance frameworks in real-world evidence, future studies can refine theoretical assumptions and provide more actionable guidance for practitioners.

8.3.2 Measuring Governance Effectiveness

A significant gap in the current literature concerns the measurement of AI governance effectiveness. While technical performance metrics are well established, there is a need for validated indicators that capture governance outcomes such as accountability, transparency, trust, and organizational learning (Floridi et al., 2018). Future research could develop multi-dimensional measurement models that integrate qualitative and quantitative indicators, including audit outcomes, incident reports, stakeholder perceptions, and decision traceability.

Methodological advances in this area would support benchmarking across organizations and sectors, enabling comparative assessment of governance maturity and effectiveness. Such metrics would also be valuable for regulators and policymakers seeking to evaluate compliance and societal impact beyond narrow technical criteria.

8.3.3 Human–AI Collaboration Dynamics

Further research is needed to deepen understanding of how different human–AI interaction models influence decision quality, accountability, and organizational outcomes. Experimental studies could systematically compare human-in-the-loop, human-on-the-loop, and human-out-of-the-loop configurations under varying levels of task complexity and risk (Parasuraman et al., 2000). Field-based research could complement these experiments by examining how collaboration dynamics unfold in real organizational settings.

Attention should be given to risks such as automation bias, erosion of human expertise, and over-reliance on intelligent agents, which may undermine governance objectives if left unaddressed (Endsley, 2017). Understanding these dynamics is essential for designing governance frameworks that preserve meaningful human oversight while leveraging the benefits of automation.

8.3.4 Multi-Agent Systems and Systemic Risk

As organizations increasingly deploy multiple interacting agents, future research should focus on governance mechanisms for managing emergent behavior and systemic risk. Multi-agent systems introduce complexities that cannot be understood by examining individual agents in isolation (Shoham & Leyton-Brown, 2009). Simulation-based research could explore how governance interventions such as coordination protocols, monitoring thresholds, or intervention triggers affect system-level outcomes.

Policy-oriented experiments and scenario analyses could further inform oversight strategies for complex agent ecosystems, particularly in domains where collective behavior may produce unintended or socially harmful outcomes (Rahwan et al., 2019). This line of research is critical for anticipating and mitigating systemic risks associated with large-scale AI deployment.

8.3.5 Policy Innovation and Adaptive Regulation

Finally, future research should examine policy innovation and adaptive regulatory approaches for governing intelligent agents under conditions of uncertainty. Regulatory sandboxes, co-regulatory models, and experimental governance arrangements offer promising avenues for balancing innovation with public protection (OECD, 2019). Comparative cross-jurisdictional studies could assess how differences in regulatory design influence organizational governance practices, compliance behavior, and public trust.

Such research would contribute to the development of regulatory frameworks that are responsive to technological change while remaining grounded in socio-technical realities (Leslie, 2020). Greater dialogue between governance scholars, policymakers, and practitioners will be essential in shaping these adaptive approaches.

8.4 Concluding Remarks

Intelligent intelligent agents are reshaping the foundations of digital transformation by introducing autonomous, learning-enabled decision-making into organizational and institutional life. Their governance is therefore not a peripheral or technical concern, but a central strategic challenge with significant organizational, ethical, and societal implications.

This chapter argued that governing intelligent agents requires a socio-technical, lifecycle-oriented, and strategically aligned approach that integrates organizational governance with public policy considerations. By reframing intelligent agents as embedded socio-technical actors, the chapter highlights the limitations of traditional IT governance models and emphasizes the need for continuous oversight, clearly defined decision rights, and meaningful human–AI collaboration.

By adopting the governance frameworks proposed in this chapter, organizations and policymakers can better harness the transformative potential of intelligent agents while ensuring accountability, trustworthiness, and long-term societal value. As intelligent agents continue to evolve, sustained research, institutional learning, and adaptive governance will be essential to realizing responsible and sustainable AI-driven digital transformation.

REFERENCES

Arrieta, A. B., Díaz-Rodríguez, N., Del Ser, J., Bennetot, A., Tabik, S., Barbado, A., & Herrera, F. (2020). Explainable Artificial Intelligence (XAI): Concepts, taxonomies, opportunities and challenges toward responsible AI. *Information Fusion*, *58*, 82–115. DOI: 10.1016/j.inffus.2019.12.012

Bharadwaj, A., El Sawy, O. A., Pavlou, P. A., & Venkatraman, N. (2013). Visions and Voices on Emerging Challenges in Digital Business Strategy1. *Management Information Systems Quarterly*, *37*(2), 633–662. DOI: 10.25300/MISQ/2013/37.2.14

Binns, R. (2018). Algorithmic accountability and public reason. *Philosophy & Technology*, *31*(4), 543–556. DOI: 10.1007/s13347-017-0263-5 PMID: 30873342

Davenport, T. H., & Ronanki, R. (2018). Artificial intelligence for the real world. *Harvard Business Review*, *96*(1), 108–116.

Diakopoulos, N. (2016). Accountability in algorithmic decision making. *Communications of the ACM*, *59*(2), 56–62. DOI: 10.1145/2844110

Doshi-Velez, F., & Kim, B. (2017). Towards a rigorous science of interpretable machine learning. arXiv preprint arXiv:1702.08608.

Endsley, M. R. (2017). From here to autonomy: Lessons learned from human–automation research. *Human Factors*, *59*(1), 5–27. DOI: 10.1177/0018720816681350 PMID: 28146676

European Commission. (2021). *Proposal for a Regulation on Artificial Intelligence (AI Act),* https://eur-lex.europa.eu/legal-content/EN/TXT/?uri=CELEX:52021PC0206

. Floridi, L., & Cowls, J. (2019). A unified framework of five principles for AI in society. Machine learning and the city: Applications in architecture and urban design, 535-545.

Floridi, L., Cowls, J., Beltrametti, M., Chatila, R., Chazerand, P., Dignum, V., Luetge, C., Madelin, R., Pagallo, U., Rossi, F., Schafer, B., Valcke, P., & Vayena, E. (2018). AI4People—An Ethical Framework for a Good AI Society: Opportunities, Risks, Principles, and Recommendations. *Minds and Machines*, *28*(4), 689–707. DOI: 10.1007/s11023-018-9482-5 PMID: 30930541

Jobin, A., Ienca, M., & Vayena, E. (2019). The global landscape of AI ethics guidelines. *Nature Machine Intelligence*, *1*(9), 389–399. DOI: 10.1038/s42256-019-0088-2

Kroll, J. A., ... (2017). *Accountable algorithms. University of Pennsylvania Law Review.* https://scholarship.law.upenn.edu/penn_law_review/vol165/iss3/3/

Leslie, D. (2020). *Understanding AI ethics and safety*. Alan Turing Institute, https://www.turing.ac.uk/research/publications/understanding-ai-ethics-and-safety

Lipton, Z. C. (2018). The mythos of model interpretability. *Communications of the ACM, 61*(10), 36–43. DOI: 10.1145/3233231

Mergel, I., Edelmann, N., & Haug, N. (2019). Defining digital transformation: Results from expert interviews. *Government Information Quarterly*, *36*(4), 101385. DOI: 10.1016/j.giq.2019.06.002

Mittelstadt, B. D., Allo, P., Taddeo, M., Wachter, S., & Floridi, L. (2016). The ethics of algorithms: Mapping the debate. *Big Data & Society*, *3*(2), 2053951716679679. DOI: 10.1177/2053951716679679

Nushi, B., Iqbal, S. T., Bennett, P., Teevan, J., Horvitz, E., Weld, D., & Fourney, A. (2019). Guidelines for human-AI interaction. In *Proceedings of the 2019 CHI Conference on Human Factors in Computing Systems.*

OECD. (2019). *OECD Principles on Artificial Intelligence,* https://www.oecd.org/going-digital/ai/principles/

Orlikowski, W. J. (2000). Using technology and constituting structures: A practice lens for studying technology in organizations. *Organization Science*, *11*(4), 404–428. DOI: 10.1287/orsc.11.4.404.14600

Parasuraman, R., Sheridan, T. B., & Wickens, C. D. (2000). A model for types and levels of human interaction with automation. *IEEE Transactions on Systems, Man, and Cybernetics. Part A, Systems and Humans*, *30*(3), 286–297. DOI: 10.1109/3468.844354 PMID: 11760769

Rahwan, I., Cebrian, M., Obradovich, N., Bongard, J., Bonnefon, J. F., Breazeal, C., Crandall, J. W., Christakis, N. A., Couzin, I. D., Jackson, M. O., Jennings, N. R., Kamar, E., Kloumann, I. M., Larochelle, H., Lazer, D., McElreath, R., Mislove, A., Parkes, D. C., Pentland, A. S., & Wellman, M. (2019). Machine behaviour. *Nature*, *568*(7753), 477–486. DOI: 10.1038/s41586-019-1138-y PMID: 31019318

Raji, I. D., Smart, A., White, R. N., Mitchell, M., Gebru, T., Hutchinson, B., & Barnes, P. (2020, January). Closing the AI accountability gap: Defining an end-to-end framework for internal algorithmic auditing. In *Proceedings of the 2020 conference on fairness, accountability, and transparency* (pp. 33-44). DOI: 10.1145/3351095.3372873

Russell, S. J., Norvig, P., Canny, J. F., Malik, J. M., & Edwards, D. D. (1995). Artificial intelligence: a modern approach: Vol. 2. *No. 9*. Prentice hall.

Shoham, Y., & Leyton-Brown, K. (2009). *Multiagent Systems,* https://www.cambridge.org/core/books/multiagent-systems/7F4A4E97A6F49C85E2D2E6C8A43D5F90

Trist, E. L., & Bamforth, K. W. (1951). Some social and psychological consequences of the longwall method of coal-getting: An examination of the psychological situation and defences of a work group in relation to the social structure and technological content of the work system. *Human Relations*, *4*(1), 3–38. DOI: 10.1177/001872675100400101

Vial, G. (2019). Understanding digital transformation. *Management Information Systems Quarterly*. Advance online publication. DOI: 10.25300/MISQ/2019/15734

Weill, P., & Ross, J. W. (2004). *IT governance: How top performers manage IT decision rights for superior results*. Harvard Business Press.

Wooldridge, M. (2009). *An introduction to multiagent systems*. John wiley & sons.

Compilation of References

Abdali, S., Anarfi, R., Barberan, C. J., & He, J. (2024). Securing large language models: Threats, vulnerabilities and responsible practices. arXiv. https://arxiv.org/abs/2403.12503

Abdullah, A., Omolola, H., Taiwo, S., & Aderibigbe, O. (2024). Advanced AI solutions for securities trading: Building scalable and optimized systems for global financial markets. *International Journal on Cybernetics & Informatics*, *13*(3), 31–45. DOI: 10.5121/ijci.2024.130304

Abdulnafea, A. L., Almasria, N. A., & Alawaqleh, Q. (2022). The effect of working capital management and credit management policy on Jordanian banks' financial performance. *Banks and Bank Systems*, *16*(4), 229–239. DOI: 10.21511/bbs.16(4).2021.19

Abou Ali, M., Dornaika, F., & Charafeddine, J. (2025). Agentic AI: A comprehensive survey of architectures, applications, and future directions. *Artificial Intelligence Review*, *59*(1), 11. Advance online publication. DOI: 10.1007/s10462-025-11422-4

Accenture. (2026). *Agentic AI and the future of work in financial services*. https://bankingblog.accenture.com/agentic-ai-future-of-work

Acharya, D. B., Kuppan, K., & Divya, B. (2025). Agentic AI: Autonomous intelligence for complex goals—A comprehensive survey. *IEEE Access : Practical Innovations, Open Solutions*, *13*, 18912–18936. DOI: 10.1109/ACCESS.2025.3532853

Ada Lovelace, I., Institute, A. I. N., & Open Government, P. (2021). Algorithmic Accountability for the Public Sector: Learning from the First Wave of Policy Implementation.

Adabara, I., Olaniyi Sadiq, B., Nuhu Shuaibu, A., Ibrahim Danjuma, Y., & Maninti, V. (2025). Trustworthy agentic AI systems: A cross-layer review of architectures, threat models, and governance strategies for real-world deployment. *F1000 Research*, *14*, 905. DOI: 10.12688/f1000research.169927.1

Adekunle, B. I., Chukwuma-Eke, E. C., Balogun, E. D., & Ogunsola, K. O. (2023). Integrating AI-driven risk assessment frameworks in financial operations: A model for enhanced corporate governance. *International Journal of Scientific Research in Computer Science. Engineering and Information Technology*, *9*(6), 445–464.

Akpobome, O. (2024). The impact of emerging technologies on legal frameworks: A model for adaptive regulation. *International Journal of Research Publication and Reviews*, *5*(10), 5046–5060. DOI: 10.55248/gengpi.5.1024.3012

Aldasoro, I., Gambacorta, L., Korinek, A., Shreeti, V., & Stein, M. (2025). Intelligent financial system: How AI is transforming finance. *Journal of Financial Stability*, *81*, 101472. Advance online publication. DOI: 10.1016/j.jfs.2025.101472

Aldboush, H. H., Almasria, N. A., & Ferdous, M. (2023). Determinants of firm profitability: Empirical evidence from Jordan's service sector. *Business: Theory and Practice*, *24*(2), 438–446. DOI: 10.3846/btp.2023.18623

Alduais, F., Almasria, N. A., & Airout, R. (2022). The Moderating Effect of Corporate Governance on Corporate Social Responsibility and Information Asymmetry: An Empirical Study of Chinese Listed Companies. *Economies*, *10*(11), 280. DOI: 10.3390/economies10110280

Alduais, F., Alsawalhah, J., & Almasria, N. A. (2023). Examining the impact of corporate governance on investors and investee companies: Evidence from Yemen. *Economies*, *11*(1), 13. DOI: 10.3390/economies11010013

Almada, M. (2023). Governing the Black Box of Artificial Intelligence. *Available at SSRN* 4587609. DOI: 10.2139/ssrn.4587609

AlMahamid, F., & Grolinger, K. (2021). Reinforcement learning algorithms: An overview and classification. In *2021 IEEE Canadian Conference on Electrical and Computer Engineering (CCECE)* (pp. 1–7). IEEE. DOI: 10.1109/CCECE53047.2021.9569056

Almansour, M. (2023). Artificial intelligence and resource optimization: A study of Fintech start-ups. *Resources Policy*, *80*, 103250. DOI: 10.1016/j.resourpol.2022.103250

Almasria, N. A., Alhatabat, Z., Ershaid, D., & Almaqtari, F. A. A bibliometric analysis. Int. J. Innov. Res. Sci. Stud. 2025, 8, 435–455. https://ij irss.com/index.php/ijirss/article/view/6546/1264

Almasria, N. (2022). Determinant Governance Mechanisms Affecting the Quality of Auditing: the External Auditors' Perceptions. Available at *SSRN* 4223799. DOI: 10.2139/ssrn.4223799

Almasria, N. A., Aldboush, H. H., Al-Kasasbeh, O., Lutfi, A., Alhajahmad, F. B., Al Barrak, T., & Alsheikh, G. (2024). Oil Price Volatility and Economic Growth: Evidence from the Middle East. *International Journal of Energy Economics and Policy, 14*(3), 417–421. DOI: 10.32479/ijeep.15484

Alnsour, J., Arabeyyat, A. R., Alnsour, A. J., & Almasria, N. A. (2024). The Impact of Financial Development, Foreign Direct Investment, and Trade Openness on Carbon Dioxide Emissions in Jordan: An ARDL and VECM Analysis Approach. *Journal of Risk and Financial Management, 17*(11), 490. DOI: 10.3390/jrfm17110490

Alva, L., & Pandey, B. (2026). Agentic AI systems in the age of generative models: Architectures, cloud scalability, and real-world applications. *Artificial Intelligence Review, 59*(3), 88. Advance online publication. DOI: 10.1007/s10462-025-11458-6

Amershi, S., Weld, D., Vorvoreanu, M., Fourney, A., Nushi, B., Collisson, P., Suh, J., Iqbal, S. T., Bennett, P. N., Inkpen, K., Teevan, J., Kikin-Gil, R., & Horvitz, E. (2019). Guidelines for human–AI interaction. *Proceedings of the 2019 CHI Conference on Human Factors in Computing Systems*, 1–13. **https://doi.org/**DOI: 10.1145/3290605.3300233

Andrae, S. (2026a). Governance of AI agents: Challenges, models and regulatory approaches. In Yadav, S. P., & Song, H. H. (Eds.), *Advancements in Multi-Agent Large Language Model Systems for Next-Generation AI* (pp. 149–188). IGI Global Publishing., DOI: 10.4018/979-8-3373-1419-8.ch006

Andrae, S. (2026b). A network model for AI governance. In Cea, S., & Aznar, T. (Eds.), *AI Influence on Governance and Law in the Digital Age* (pp. 1–44). IGI Global Publishing., DOI: 10.4018/979-8-3373-4480-5.ch001

Andrae, S. (2026c). Explainable artificial intelligence. In Khosrow-Pour, M. (Ed.), *Encyclopedia of Modern Artificial Intelligence* (pp. 1–21). IGI Global Publishing., DOI: 10.4018/403120

Ante, L. (2025). Autonomous AI agents in decentralized finance: Market dynamics, application areas, and theoretical implications. *SSRN*. DOI: 10.2139/ssrn.5055677

Araci, D. (2019). FinBERT: Financial sentiment analysis with pre-trained language models. arXiv. https://doi.org//arXiv.1908.10063DOI: 10.48550

Araral, E. (2026). Agency Theory in Public Administration: A Comparative Study of the US, China, and EU. Elements in Public and Nonprofit Administration.

Arifovic, J., He, X., & Wei, L. (2022). Machine learning and speed in high-frequency trading. *Journal of Economic Dynamics & Control, 104438*, 104438. Advance online publication. DOI: 10.1016/j.jedc.2022.104438

Arrieta, A. B., Díaz-Rodríguez, N., Del Ser, J., Bennetot, A., Tabik, S., Barbado, A., & Herrera, F. (2020). Explainable Artificial Intelligence (XAI): Concepts, taxonomies, opportunities and challenges toward responsible AI. *Information Fusion, 58*, 82–115. DOI: 10.1016/j.inffus.2019.12.012

Ashby, W. R. (1956). *An Introduction to Cybernetics*. Chapman & Hall. DOI: 10.5962/bhl.title.5851

Ashta, A. (2026, January 4). An introduction to AI, generative AI, and agentic AI in finance: Efficiency, ethics, and the future of high-speed trading.

Axelsen, H., Licht, V., & Damsgaard, J. (2025). Agentic AI for financial crime compliance. arXiv. https://arxiv.org/abs/2509.13137

Bahangulu, J. K., & Owusu-Berko, L. (2025). Algorithmic bias, data ethics, and governance: Ensuring fairness, transparency and compliance in AI-powered business analytics applications. *World J Adv Res Rev, 25*(2), 1746–1763. DOI: 10.30574/wjarr.2025.25.2.0571

Bank of America. (2024). *BofA's Erica surpasses 2 billion interactions, helping 42 million clients since launch*. Bank of America.

Bar, K. (2025). *The Agentic AI Handbook: Concepts*. Design Patterns, and Future Directions.

Barocas, S., & Selbst, A. D. (2016). Big data's disparate impact. *California Law Review, 104*(3), 671–732. https://www.cs.yale.edu/homes/jf/BarocasSelbst.pdf

Beck, T., Demirgüç-Kunt, A., & Martínez Pería, M. S. (2011). Banking services for everyone? Barriers to bank access and use around the world. *Journal of Financial Services Research, 39*(1–2), 1–35. DOI: 10.1007/s10693-010-0089-6

Benbya, H., Pachidi, S., & Jarvenpaa, S. L. (2021). Special issue editorial: Artificial intelligence in organizations: Implications for information systems research. *Journal of the Association for Information Systems, 22*(2), 281–303. DOI: 10.17705/1jais.00662

Bender, E. M., Gebru, T., McMillan-Major, A., & Shmitchell, S. (2021, March). On the dangers of stochastic parrots: Can language models be too big? In *Proceedings of the 2021 ACM conference on fairness, accountability, and transparency* (pp. 610-623). DOI: 10.1145/3442188.3445922

Berente, N., Gu, B., Recker, J., & Santhanam, R. (2021). Managing artificial intelligence. *Management Information Systems Quarterly, 45*(3), 1433–1450. DOI: 10.25300/MISQ/2021/16274

Bharadwaj, A., El Sawy, O. A., Pavlou, P. A., & Venkatraman, N. (2013). Digital business strategy: Toward a next generation of insights. *Management Information Systems Quarterly*, *37*(2), 471–482. DOI: 10.25300/MISQ/2013/37:2.3

Bharadwaj, A., El Sawy, O. A., Pavlou, P. A., & Venkatraman, N. (2013). Visions and Voices on Emerging Challenges in Digital Business Strategy1. *Management Information Systems Quarterly*, *37*(2), 633–662. DOI: 10.25300/MISQ/2013/37.2.14

Billi, M., & Labraña, J. (2025). Is AI a functional equivalent to expertise in organizations and decision-making? Opportunities and pitfalls for AI in the context of just transitions. *Frontiers in Artificial Intelligence*, *8*, 1571698. DOI: 10.3389/frai.2025.1571698

Binns, R. (2018). Fairness in machine learning: Lessons from political philosophy. *Proceedings of Machine Learning Research, 81*, 149--159. http://proceedings.mlr.press/v81/binns18a.html

Binns, R. (2018). Algorithmic accountability and public reason. *Philosophy & Technology*, *31*(4), 543–556. DOI: 10.1007/s13347-017-0263-5 PMID: 30873342

Birkstedt, T., Minkkinen, M., Tandon, A., & Mäntymäki, M. (2023). AI governance: Themes, knowledge gaps and future agendas. *Internet Research*, *33*(7), 133–167. DOI: 10.1108/INTR-01-2022-0042

Blueprism. (2025). *What's your agentic AI maturity level?* https://www.blueprism.com/resources/blog/agentic-ai-maturity-level/

Bodepudi, V. (2023, December 27). Understanding the fundamentals of digital transformation in financial services: Drivers and strategic insights. *SSRN*. https://papers.ssrn.com/sol3/papers.cfm?abstract_id–5102497

Bommarito, J., Katz, D. M., & Bommarito, M. J. (2025). Governing AI Agents: Risk, Compliance, and Accountability in Law and Finance. *Compliance, and Accountability in Law and Finance (December 12, 2025)*.

Bostrom, N., & Yudkowsky, E. (2014). The ethics of artificial intelligence. In Frankish, K. & Ramsey, W. M. (eds.). *The Cambridge Handbook of Artificial Intelligence*. Cambridge University Press, 316–334. https://doi.org/DOI: 10.1017/CBO9781139046855.020

Bostrom, R. P., & Heinen, J. S. (1977). MIS problems and failures: A socio-technical perspective. *Management Information Systems Quarterly*, *1*(3), 17–32. DOI: 10.2307/248710

Brynjolfsson, E., & McAfee, A. (2014). *The second machine age: Work, progress, and prosperity in a time of brilliant technologies*. W. W. Norton & Company.

Busuioc, M. (2021). Accountable artificial intelligence: Holding algorithms to account. *Public Administration Review*, *81*(5), 825–836. DOI: 10.1111/puar.13293 PMID: 34690372

Busuioc, M. (2022). AI algorithmic oversight: new frontiers in regulation. In *Handbook of regulatory authorities* (pp. 470–486). Edward Elgar Publishing.

Busuioc, M., Curtin, D., & Almada, M. (2023). Reclaiming transparency: Contesting the logics of secrecy within the AI Act. *European Law Open*, *2*(1), 79–105. DOI: 10.1017/elo.2022.47

Castelfranchi, C. (1998). Modelling social action for AI agents. *Artificial Intelligence*, *103*(1-2), 157–182. DOI: 10.1016/S0004-3702(98)00056-3

Cath, C. (2018). Governing artificial intelligence: Ethical, legal and technical opportunities and challenges. *Philosophical Transactions. Series A, Mathematical, Physical, and Engineering Sciences*, *376*(2133), 20180080. DOI: 10.1098/rsta.2018.0080 PMID: 30322996

Chaffer, T. J., Goins, C. v., II, Okusanya, B., Cotlage, D., & Goldston, J. (2024). Decentralized governance of autonomous AI agents. arXiv preprint arXiv:2412.17114.

Cheruvu, R. (2025). Human-in/on-the-Loop Design for Human Controllability. In *Handbook of Human-Centered Artificial Intelligence* (pp. 1–47). Springer Nature Singapore.

Chhabra, A., Datta, S., Nahin, S., & Mohapatra, P. (2026). Agentic AI security: Threats, defenses, evaluation, and open challenges. *IEEE Access : Practical Innovations, Open Solutions*, *14*, 49455–49482. DOI: 10.1109/ACCESS.2026.3675554

Chourasia, S., Dhama, A., & Bhardwaj, G. (2024, May). AI-driven organizational culture evolution: A critical review. In *2024 International Conference on Communication, Computer Sciences and Engineering (IC3SE)* (pp. 1839-1844). IEEE. DOI: 10.1109/IC3SE62002.2024.10592949

Chugh, S., & Deshpande, A. V. (2025). Opportunities and challenges of agentic AI in finance. SSRN Electronic Journal. DOI: 10.2139/ssrn.5538799

Chui, M., Manyika, J., & Miremadi, M. (2016). *Where machines could replace humans---and where they can't (yet)*. McKinsey & Company. https://www.mckinsey.com/business-functions/mckinsey-digital/our-insights/where-machines-could-replace-humans-and-where-they-cant-yet

Cobbe, J., Lee, M. S. A., & Singh, J. (2021, March). Reviewable automated decision-making: A framework for accountable algorithmic systems. In *Proceedings of the 2021 ACM conference on fairness, accountability, and transparency* (pp. 598-609). DOI: 10.1145/3442188.3445921

Costanza-Chock, S., Raji, I. D., & Buolamwini, J. (2022, June). Who Audits the Auditors? Recommendations from a field scan of the algorithmic auditing ecosystem. In *Proceedings of the 2022 ACM conference on fairness, accountability, and transparency* (pp. 1571-1583). DOI: 10.1145/3531146.3533213

Criado, J. I., Sandoval-Almazán, R., & Gil-Garcia, J. R. (2025). Artificial intelligence and public administration: Understanding actors, governance, and policy from micro, meso, and macro perspectives. *Public Policy and Administration*, *40*(2), 173–184. DOI: 10.1177/09520767241272921

Cunningham, P., Cord, M., & Delany, S. J. (2008). Supervised learning. In *Machine learning techniques for multimedia* (pp. 21–49). Springer., DOI: 10.1007/978-3-540-75171-7_2

Daniel, G. G. O. (2024). *How multinational enterprises navigate the institutional landscape in emerging markets and developing economies* (Doctoral dissertation, Wageningen University and Research).

Darbi, W. P. K., Hall, C. M., & Knott, P. (2018). The informal sector: A review and agenda for management research. *International Journal of Management Reviews*, *20*(2), 301–324. DOI: 10.1111/ijmr.12131

Davenport, T. H., & Mittal, N. (2023). *All-in on AI: How smart companies win big with artificial intelligence*. Harvard Business Press.

Davenport, T. H., & Ronanki, R. (2018). Artificial intelligence for the real world. *Harvard Business Review*, *96*(1), 108–116.

Daza-Ramirez, M. T. (2025). A Virtue-focused Sociotechnical Framework for Fairness in Artificial Intelligence. Available at *SSRN* 6525059.

Dellermann, D., Ebel, P., Söllner, M., & Leimeister, J. M. (2019a). Hybrid intelligence. *Business & Information Systems Engineering*, *61*(5), 637–643. DOI: 10.1007/s12599-019-00595-2

Dellermann, D., Ebel, P., Söllner, M., & Leimeister, J. M. (2019b). The future of human–AI collaboration: A taxonomy of design knowledge for hybrid intelligence systems. *Proceedings of the 52nd Hawaii International Conference on System Sciences*, 274–283. **https://doi.org/**DOI: 10.24251/HICSS.2019.034

Deloitte. (2026). *Managing the new wave of risks from AI agents in banking.* https://www.deloitte.com/us/en/insights/industry/financial-services/agentic-ai-risks-banking.html

Diakopoulos, N. (2016). Accountability in algorithmic decision making. *Communications of the ACM*, *59*(2), 56–62. DOI: 10.1145/2844110

Dibia, V. (2025). *Designing Multi-Agent Systems: Principles, Patterns and Implementation for AI Agents.* Victor Dibia.

Dissanayake, L., & Al-Sharify, A. (2025). AI and Decision Making: How does the integration of AI influence leadership decision making within technology driven companies?.

Dolata, M., Feuerriegel, S., & Schwabe, G. (2022). A sociotechnical view of algorithmic fairness. *Information Systems Journal*, *32*(4), 754–818. DOI: 10.1111/isj.12370

Doshi-Velez, F., & Kim, B. (2017). Towards a rigorous science of interpretable machine learning. arXiv preprint arXiv:1702.08608.

Duan, Z., & Wang, J. (2024). Exploration of LLM multi-agent application implementation based on LangGraph+CrewAI. arXiv. https://arxiv.org/abs/2411.18241 DOI: 10.32388/R27SW4

Du, C., Wang, C., & Yang, Y. (2024). Incentive contract design for governmental forest ecological benefit compensation under information asymmetry. *Forests*, *15*(12), 2145. DOI: 10.3390/f15122145

Dwivedi, Y. K., Hughes, L., Ismagilova, E., Aarts, G., Coombs, C., Crick, T., Duan, Y., Dwivedi, R., Edwards, J., Eirug, A., Galanos, V., Ilavarasan, P. V., Janssen, M., Jones, P., Kar, A. K., Kizgin, H., Kronemann, B., Lal, B., Lucini, B., & Williams, M. D. (2021). Artificial Intelligence (AI): Multidisciplinary perspectives on emerging challenges, opportunities, and agenda for research, practice and policy. *International Journal of Information Management*, *57*, 101994. DOI: 10.1016/j.ijinfomgt.2019.08.002

Easin, A. M., Saha, S., & Orosz, T. (2024). An intelligent LLM-powered personalized assistant for digital banking using LangGraph and chain of thoughts. In *Proceedings of the 2024 IEEE International Symposium on Intelligent Systems and Informatics* (pp. 625–630). IEEE. DOI: 10.1109/SISY62279.2024.10737601

El Hajj, M., & Hammoud, J. (2023). Unveiling the influence of artificial intelligence and machine learning on financial markets: A comprehensive analysis of AI applications in trading, risk management, and financial operations. *Journal of Risk and Financial Management, 16*(10), 434. https://www.mdpi.com/1911-8074/16/10/434. DOI: 10.3390/jrfm16100434

Elgendy, I. A., Helal, M. Y. I., Al-Sharafi, M. A., Albashrawi, M. A., Al-Ahmadi, M. S., Jeon, I., & Dwivedi, Y. K. (2025). Agentic systems as catalysts for innovation in FinTech: Exploring opportunities, challenges and a research agenda. *Information Discovery and Delivery*. Advance online publication. DOI: 10.1108/IDD-03-2025-0068

Endsley, M. R. (2017). From here to autonomy: Lessons learned from human–automation research. *Human Factors, 59*(1), 5–27. DOI: 10.1177/0018720816681350 PMID: 28146676

Engin, Z. (2025). Human-AI Governance (HAIG): A Trust-Utility Approach. *arXiv preprint arXiv:2505.01651.*

Epstein, J. M. (2006). *Generative Social Science: Studies in Agent-Based Computational Modeling*. Princeton University Press.

Errico, H., Ngiam, J., & Sojan, S. (2025). Securing the Model Context Protocol (MCP): Risks, controls, and governance. arXiv. https://arxiv.org/abs/2511.20920

Eshmurodov, Z. (2025). Algorithmic bias and the limits of U.S. law: Lessons from the EU AI Act's risk-based framework. *American Journal of Modern World Sciences*, 2(10), 59–66.

European Banking Authority. (2025). *AI Act: Implications for the EU banking and payments sector.*

European Commission High-Level Expert Group on Artificial Intelligence. (2019). *Ethics guidelines for trustworthy AI.* https://digital-strategy.ec.europa.eu/en/library/ethics-guidelines-trustworthy-ai

European Commission. (2021). *Proposal for a Regulation on Artificial Intelligence (AI Act),* https://eur-lex.europa.eu/legal-content/EN/TXT/?uri=CELEX:52021PC0206

European Union. (2024). *Regulation (EU) 2024/1689 of the european parliament and of the council of 13 june 2024 laying down harmonised rules on artificial intelligence and amending regulations (AI act).* https://eur-lex.europa.eu/eli/reg/2024/1689/oj

EY. (2025). *Agentic AI: Emerging risks and control strategies.*

Fawaz, A., Mougharbel, I., Al-Haddad, K., & Kanaan, H. Y. (2025). Energy routing protocols for Energy Internet: A review on multi-agent systems, metaheuristics, and Artificial Intelligence approaches. *IEEE Access : Practical Innovations, Open Solutions*, *13*, 41625–41643. DOI: 10.1109/ACCESS.2025.3546620

Felemban, H., Sohail, M., & Ruikar, K. (2024). Exploring the readiness of organisations to adopt artificial intelligence. *Buildings (Basel, Switzerland)*, *14*(8), 2460. DOI: 10.3390/buildings14082460

Ferrari, F. (2024). State roles in platform governance: AI's regulatory geographies. *Competition & Change*, *28*(2), 340–358. DOI: 10.1177/10245294231218335

Finastra. (2026). *AI in banking and financial services: Trends for 2026*. https://www.finastra.com/viewpoints/articles/future-of-ai-in-financial-services-2026

FinRegLab. (2025). *The next wave arrives: Agentic AI in financial services*. https://finreglab.org/wp-content/uploads/2025/09/FinRegLab_09-04-2025_The-Next-Wave-Arrives-Main.pdf

Floridi, L., & Cowls, J. (2019). A unified framework of five principles for AI in society. *Harvard Data Science Review*, *1*(1). Advance online publication. DOI: 10.1162/99608f92.8cd550d1

Floridi, L., Cowls, J., Beltrametti, M., Chatila, R., Chazerand, P., Dignum, V., Luetge, C., Madelin, R., Pagallo, U., Rossi, F., Schafer, B., Valcke, P., & Vayena, E. (2018). AI4People—An ethical framework for a good AI society. *Minds and Machines*, *28*(4), 689–707. DOI: 10.1007/s11023-018-9482-5 PMID: 30930541

Folke, C., Hahn, T., Olsson, P., & Norberg, J. (2005). Adaptive governance of social-ecological systems. *Annual Review of Environment and Resources*, *30*(1), 441–473. DOI: 10.1146/annurev.energy.30.050504.144511

Frimpong, V. (2025). Artificial Intelligence Investment in Resource-Constrained African Economies: Financial, Strategic, and Ethical Trade-Offs with Broader Implications. *WORLD (Oakland, Calif.)*, *6*(2), 70. DOI: 10.3390/world6020070

Fuller, A., Fan, Z., Day, C., & Barlow, C. (2020). Digital twin: Enabling technologies, challenges and open research. *IEEE Access : Practical Innovations, Open Solutions*, *8*, 108952–108971. DOI: 10.1109/ACCESS.2020.2998358

Gaggatur, J. S. (2024). AI ethics: Who is accountable for the decisions made by machines? *Authorea Preprints*. DOI: 10.36227/techrxiv.172373798.84756169/v1

Gai, K., Qiu, M., & Sun, X. (2018). A survey on FinTech. *Journal of Network and Computer Applications*, *103*, 262–273. DOI: 10.1016/j.jnca.2017.10.011

Galbraith, J. R. (2014). *Designing organizations: Strategy, structure, and process at the business unit and enterprise levels* (3rd ed.). Jossey-Bass.

Ganapathi, J. K. (2025). Augmented Entrepreneurship: The Role of AI Agents in Automating Core Small Business Functions. *Journal Of Engineering And Computer Sciences, 4*(8), 654–663.

Gauld, R. (2023). Principal-agent theory of organizations. In *Global encyclopedia of public administration, public policy, and governance* (pp. 10081–10085). Springer.

Gong, H. (2026). AI agents in financial markets: Architecture, applications, and systemic implications. *FinTech, 5*(2), 34. DOI: 10.3390/fintech5020034

Government Accountability Office. (2025). *Artificial intelligence: Use in financial services poses risks including bias and privacy concerns.*

Grant, D. G., Behrends, J., & Basl, J. (2025). What we owe to decision-subjects: Beyond transparency and explanation in automated decision-making. *Philosophical Studies, 182*(1), 55–85. DOI: 10.1007/s11098-023-02013-6

Grønsund, T., & Aanestad, M. (2020). Augmenting the algorithm: Emerging human-in-the-loop work configurations. *The Journal of Strategic Information Systems, 29*(2), 101614. DOI: 10.1016/j.jsis.2020.101614

Guggenberger, T., Lämmermann, L., Urbach, N., Walter, A. M., & Hofmann, P. (2023). Task delegation from AI to humans: A principal-agent perspective.

Guston, D. H. (2014). Understanding "anticipatory governance". *Social Studies of Science, 44*(2), 218–242. DOI: 10.1177/0306312713508669 PMID: 24941612

Hacker, P., & Holweg, M. (2026). A pragmatic approach to regulating AI agents. *arXiv*. https://doi.org//arXiv.2604.22819DOI: 10.2139/ssrn.6509259

Hagendorff, T. (2020). The ethics of AI ethics: An evaluation of guidelines. *Minds and Machines, 30*(1), 99–120. DOI: 10.1007/s11023-020-09517-8

Hagos, D. H., Alami, H. E., & Rawat, D. B. (2024). Ai-driven human-autonomy teaming in tactical operations: Proposed framework, challenges, and future directions. *arXiv preprint arXiv:2411.09788.*

Hammond, L., Chan, A., Clifton, J., Hoelscher-Obermaier, J., Khan, A., McLean, E., Smith, C., Barfuss, W., Foerster, J., & Gavenčiak, T. (2025). Multi-Agent Risks from Advanced AI. arXiv preprint arXiv:2502.14143.

Henderson, J. C., & Venkatraman, N. (1993). Strategic alignment: Leveraging information technology for transforming organizations. *IBM Systems Journal*, *32*(1), 4–16. DOI: 10.1147/sj.382.0472

Herzog, L. (2023). *Citizen knowledge: Markets, experts, and the infrastructure of democracy*. Oxford University Press. DOI: 10.1093/oso/9780197681718.001.0001

Heß, V. L., & Damasio, B. (2025). Machine learning in banking risk management: Mapping a decade of evolution. *International Journal of Information Management Data Insights*, *5*(1), 100324. DOI: 10.1016/j.jjimei.2025.100324

Hinings, B., Gegenhuber, T., & Greenwood, R. (2018). Digital innovation and transformation: An institutional perspective. *Information and Organization*, *28*(1), 52–61. DOI: 10.1016/j.infoandorg.2018.02.004

Hokmabadi, H., Rezvani, S. M. H. S., Hokmabadi, H., & de Almeida, N. M. (2025). Business resilience through AI-agent automation for SMEs and startups: A review on agile marketing and CRM. *Information (Basel)*, *16*(11), 1000. Advance online publication. DOI: 10.3390/info16111000

Holzinger, A., Zatloukal, K., & Müller, H. (2025). Is human oversight to AI systems still possible? *New Biotechnology*, *85*, 59–62. DOI: 10.1016/j.nbt.2024.12.003

Hong, S., Zheng, X., & Chen, J.. (2023). *MetaGPT: Meta programming for multi-agent collaborative framework*. arXiv. https://arxiv.org/abs/2308.00352

Huang, K. (2025). *Agentic AI*. Springer., DOI: 10.1007/978-3-031-90026-6

Hughes, L., Dwivedi, Y. K., Malik, T., Shawosh, M., Albashrawi, M. A., Jeon, I., Dutot, V., Appanderanda, M., Crick, T., De', R., Fenwick, M., Gunaratnege, S. M., Jurcys, P., Kar, A. K., Kshetri, N., Li, K., Mutasa, S., Samothrakis, S., Wade, M., & Walton, P. (2025). AI agents and agentic systems: A multi-expert analysis. *Journal of Computer Information Systems*, *65*(4), 489–517. DOI: 10.1080/08874417.2025.2483832

IBM. (n.d.). *Types of AI agents*. https://www.ibm.com/think/topics/ai-agent-types

Ibrahim, A., Almasria, N. A., Almaqtari, F. A., Al-Kasasbeh, O., Alhatabatb, Z., & Ershaid, D. (2024). The Impact of Green Finance, FinTech and Digital Economy on Environmental Sustainability: Evidence from Advanced Panel Techniques. *International Journal of Energy Economics and Policy*, *14*(6), 621–627. DOI: 10.32479/ijeep.17180

Ilcic, A., Fuentes, M., & Lawler, D. (2025). Artificial intelligence, complexity, and systemic resilience in global governance. *Frontiers in Artificial Intelligence*, *8*, 1562095. DOI: 10.3389/frai.2025.1562095

Inala, R., & Somu, B. (2024). Agentic AI in retail banking: Redefining customer service and financial decision-making. *Journal of Artificial Intelligence and Big Data Disciplines*, *1*(1), 1–19. DOI: 10.70179/97ntmv88

International Organization for Standardization. (2023). *ISO/IEC 42001:2023 information technology — artificial intelligence — management system*. https://www.iso.org/standard/81230.html

Jain, R., Prajapati, D., & Dangi, A. (2023, February 18). Transforming the financial sector: A review of recent advancements in FinTech. *SSRN*. https://papers.ssrn.com/sol3/papers.cfm?abstract_id=4380348

Jameaba, M. S. (2020). Digitization revolution, FinTech disruption, and financial stability: Using the case of Indonesian banking ecosystem to highlight wide-ranging digitization opportunities and major challenges. *FinTech Disruption, and Financial stability: Using the Case of Indonesian Banking Ecosystem to highlight wide-ranging digitization opportunities and major challenges (July 16 2, 2020).*

Janakiraman, A. (2025). Governance and Accountability Frameworks for AI Agents. Synergia: A Journal of Multidisciplinary Innovation, 7(7).

Janssen, M., Brous, P., Estevez, E., Barbosa, L. S., & Janowski, T. (2020). Data governance: Organizing data for trustworthy artificial intelligence. *Government Information Quarterly*, *37*(3), 101493. DOI: 10.1016/j.giq.2020.101493

Jarrahi, M. H. (2018). Artificial intelligence and the future of work: Human–AI symbiosis in organizational decision making. *Business Horizons*, *61*(4), 577–586. DOI: 10.1016/j.bushor.2018.03.007

Jarrahi, M. H., Newlands, G., Lee, M. K., Wolf, C. T., Kinder, E., & Sutherland, W. (2021). Algorithmic management in a work context. *Big Data & Society*, *8*(2), 20539517211020332. DOI: 10.1177/20539517211020332

Jiang, Y., Li, X., Luo, H., Yin, S., & Kaynak, O. (2022). Quo vadis artificial intelligence? *Discover Artificial Intelligence*, *2*(1), 4. Advance online publication. DOI: 10.1007/s44163-022-00022-8

Jobin, A., Ienca, M., & Vayena, E. (2019). The global landscape of AI ethics guidelines. *Nature Machine Intelligence*, *1*(9), 389–399. DOI: 10.1038/s42256-019-0088-2

Jöhnk, J., Weißert, M., & Wyrtki, K. (2021). Ready or not, AI comes—An interview study of organizational AI readiness factors. *Business & Information Systems Engineering*, *63*(1), 5–20. DOI: 10.1007/s12599-020-00676-7

Kalota, F. (2024). A primer on generative artificial intelligence. *Education Sciences*, *14*(2), 172. DOI: 10.3390/educsci14020172

Kane, G. C., Palmer, D., Phillips, A. N., Kiron, D., & Buckley, N. (2015). Strategy, not technology, drives digital transformation. *MIT Sloan Management Review*.

Kapoor, S., Stroebl, B., Siegel, Z. S., Nadgir, N., & Narayanan, A. (2024). Ai agents that matter. arXiv preprint arXiv:2407.01502.

Kellogg, K. C., Valentine, M. A., & Christin, A. (2020). Algorithms at work: The new contested terrain of control. *The Academy of Management Annals*, *14*(1), 366–410. DOI: 10.5465/annals.2018.0174

Keningson, J. (2024). Mathematical foundation of high-dimensional data analysis: Leveraging topology and geometry for enhanced model interpretability in ai. International Journal of scientific research and management, 12(11), 546-557.

Khair, M. A., Mahadasa, R., Tuli, F. A., & Ande, J. R. P. K. (2020). Beyond human judgment: Exploring the impact of artificial intelligence on HR decision-making efficiency and fairness. *Global Disclosure of Economics and Business*, *9*(2), 163–176. DOI: 10.18034/gdeb.v9i2.730

Khan, R., Sarkar, S., Kumar, M. S., & Jose, E. (2024). Security threats in agentic AI system. arXiv. https://arxiv.org/abs/2410.14728

Khatri, V., & Brown, C. V. (2010). Designing data governance. *Communications of the ACM*, *53*(1), 148–152. DOI: 10.1145/1629175.1629210

Kirilenko, A., Kyle, A. S., Samadi, M., & Tuzun, T. (2017). The flash crash: High-frequency trading in an electronic market. *The Journal of Finance*, *72*(3), 967–998. DOI: 10.1111/jofi.12498

Kjørstad, M. (2025). The norm-setting dynamics of institutions and artificial intelligence: Quality of care and efficiency in social work. *European Social Work Research*, *3*(2), 135–147. DOI: 10.1332/27551768Y2025D000000041

Klos, T., Zarcone, A., Rentrop, C., Riedinger, C., Prinz, N., & Huber, M. (2025, September). Entangled by Design: A structured Overview of Management Challenges concerning AI Adoption in Organizations. In *2025 20th Conference on Computer Science and Intelligence Systems (FedCSIS)* (pp. 705-713). IEEE. DOI: 10.15439/2025F1129

Kolt, N. (2025). Governing AI agents. arXiv preprint arXiv:2501.07913.

Kolt, N., Caputo, N., Boeglin, J., O'Keefe, C., Bommasani, R., Casper, S., Cuéllar, M.-F., Feldman, N., Gabriel, I., & Hadfield, G. K. (2026). Legal Alignment for Safe and Ethical AI. arXiv preprint arXiv:2601.04175. DOI: 10.2139/ssrn.6036657

Komandla, V., & Perumalla, S. (2017). Transforming traditional banking: Strategies, challenges, and the impact of fintech innovations. [IJMCER]. *Educational Research, 1*(6), 1–9.

Koppolu, H. K. R. (2026). *Deep learning and agentic AI for automated payment fraud detection: Enhancing merchant services through predictive intelligence* [Journal title not provided]. Nano-NTP.

Kore.ai. (2026). *AI agents in finance and banking: 12 proven use cases (2026).* https://www.kore.ai/blog/ai-agents-in-finance-banking-12-proven-use-cases-2026

Koulu, R. (2020). Proceduralizing control and discretion: Human oversight in artificial intelligence policy. *Maastricht Journal of European and Comparative Law, 27*(6), 720–735. DOI: 10.1177/1023263X20978649

Krishnan, N. (2025). Ai agents: Evolution, architecture, and real-world applications. *arXiv preprint arXiv:2503.12687.*

Kroll, J. A., ... (2017). *Accountable algorithms. University of Pennsylvania Law Review.* https://scholarship.law.upenn.edu/penn_law_review/vol165/iss3/3/

Kroll, J. A., Huey, J., Barocas, S., Felten, E. W., Reidenberg, J. R., Robinson, D. G., & Yu, H. (2017). Accountable algorithms. *University of Pennsylvania Law Review, 165*(3), 633–705.

Kubam, C. S. (2024). Agentic AI for autonomous, explainable, and real-time credit risk decision-making. *Zenodo*. DOI: 10.5281/zenodo.18008872

Kubilay, B., & Celiktas, B. (2025). Relationships Among Organizational-Level Maturities in Artificial Intelligence, Cybersecurity, and Digital Transformation: A Survey-Based Analysis. *IEEE Access : Practical Innovations, Open Solutions, 13*, 88399–88411. DOI: 10.1109/ACCESS.2025.3571537

Kumar, S. N. P.Sanjay Nakharu Prasad Kumar. (2025). Regulating autonomous AI agents: Prospects, hazards, and policy structures. *Journal of Computer Science and Technology Studies, 7*(10), 393–399. DOI: 10.32996/jcsts.2025.7.10.41

Kurshan, E., Balch, T., & Byrd, D. (2025). The agentic regulator: Risks for AI in finance and a proposed agent-based framework for governance. arXiv. https://arxiv.org/abs/2512.11933

Kuziemski, M., & Misuraca, G. (2020). AI governance in the public sector: Three tales from the frontiers of automated decision-making in democratic settings. *Telecommunications Policy*, *44*(6), 101976. DOI: 10.1016/j.telpol.2020.101976 PMID: 32313360

Langenbucher, K., & Corcoran, P. (2021). *Responsible AI credit scoring—A lesson from Upstart.com* [Book title not provided]. De Gruyter., DOI: 10.1515/9783110749472-006

Latour, B. (2005). *Reassembling the Social: An Introduction to Actor-Network-Theory*. Oxford University Press. DOI: 10.1093/oso/9780199256044.001.0001

Le Guillou, M., Prévot, L., & Berberian, B. (2023). Bringing together ergonomic concepts and cognitive mechanisms for human—AI agents cooperation. *International Journal of Human-Computer Interaction*, *39*(9), 1827–1840. DOI: 10.1080/10447318.2022.2129741

Lebovitz, S., Lifshitz-Assaf, H., & Levina, N. (2022). To engage or not to engage with AI for critical judgments: How professionals deal with opacity when using AI for medical diagnosis. *Organization Science*, *33*(1), 126–148. DOI: 10.1287/orsc.2021.1549

Lee, J., Stevens, N., & Han, S. C. (2025). Large language models in finance (FinLLMs). *Neural Computing & Applications*, *37*(30), 24853–24867. DOI: 10.1007/s00521-024-10495-6

Leslie, D. (2020). *Understanding AI ethics and safety*. Alan Turing Institute, https://www.turing.ac.uk/research/publications/understanding-ai-ethics-and-safety

Lior, A. (2020). AI Entities as AI Agents: Artificial Intelligence Liability and the AI Respondeat Superior Analogy. *Mitchell Hamline Law Review*.

Lipton, Z. C. (2018). The mythos of model interpretability. *Communications of the ACM*, *61*(10), 36–43. DOI: 10.1145/3233231

Liu, T. (2024). Research on Legal Responsibility Attribution for Autonomous Systems: An AI Governance Perspective. *Science of Law Journal*, *3*(7), 166–174.

Li, Y., Wang, S., Ding, H., & Chen, H. (2023). Large language models in finance: A survey. In *Proceedings of the 4th ACM International Conference on AI in Finance* (pp. 374–382). Association for Computing Machinery. DOI: 10.1145/3604237.3626869

Logan, T., Rachunok, B., Hardaway, K., Bristow, D., Reilly, A., Johnson, D., Johansson, J., Cremen, G., Boakye, J., & Schweizer, P. (2026). Advancing systemic risk assessment for complex, interdependent systems: A research agenda. *Risk Analysis*, *46*(5), e70243. DOI: 10.1111/risa.70243 PMID: 41978933

Mahanta, U. (2025). Beyond Automation: Guidelines for a Human-Centered Multi-Agent System for Coordinated Decision Making under Industrial Settings.

Mair, J., & Martí, I. (2009). Entrepreneurship in and around institutional voids: A case study from Bangladesh. *Journal of Business Venturing*, *24*(5), 419–435. DOI: 10.1016/j.jbusvent.2008.04.006

Maleka, S., & Maidi, C. (2024). The Societal Implications of Technological Innovations and AI in South Africa.

Mandava, S. (2022). Toward Intelligent Agents with Learned World Models for Real-World Decision-Making. Available at *SSRN* 5551718.

Masadeh, A. A., Saadat, M., Almasria, N. A., Jrairah, T. S., & Alsawalhah, J. M. (2021). INVESTIGATING THE ROLE OF APPLYING THE QUALITY COST APPROACH IN THE MANUFACTURING SYSTEM IN THE PUBLIC SHAREHOLDING MANUFACTURING COMPANY IN JORDAN. *Academy of Accounting and Financial Studies Journal*, *25*(5), 1–14.

Mastercard. (2025). Mastercard unveils Agent Pay, pioneering agentic payments technology to power commerce in the age of AI. Mastercard.

Matt, C., Hess, T., Benlian, A., & Wiesböck, F. (2016). Options for formulating a digital transformation strategy. *MIS Quarterly Executive*, *15*(2), 103–119.

Matthias, A. (2004). The responsibility gap: Ascribing responsibility for the actions of learning automata. *Ethics and Information Technology*, *6*(3), 175–183. DOI: 10.1007/s10676-004-3422-1

Mayer Brown. (2026). *Governance of agentic artificial intelligence systems*. https://www.mayerbrown.com/en/insights/publications/2026/02/governance-of-agentic-artificial-intelligence-systems

McKinsey & Company. (2021). *Building the AI bank of the future*. McKinsey & Company.

McKinsey. (2026). *State of AI trust in 2026: Shifting to the agentic era*.

Mergel, I., Edelmann, N., & Haug, N. (2019). Defining digital transformation: Results from expert interviews. *Government Information Quarterly*, *36*(4), 101385. DOI: 10.1016/j.giq.2019.06.002

Meyer, C. O., Van Osch, T., & Reykers, Y. (2024). From EU battlegroups to Rapid Deployment Capacity: Learning the right lessons? *International Affairs*, *100*(1), 181–201. DOI: 10.1093/ia/iiad247

Michalski, R. S., Carbonell, J. G., & Mitchell, T. M. (Eds.). (1983). *Machine learning*. Springer., DOI: 10.1007/978-3-662-12405-5

Mienye, E., Jere, N., Obaido, G., Mienye, I. D., & Aruleba, K. (2024). Deep learning in finance: A survey of applications and techniques. *AI*, *5*(4), 2066–2091. DOI: 10.3390/ai5040101

Mikalef, P., & Gupta, M. (2021). Artificial intelligence capability: Conceptualization, measurement calibration, and empirical study on its impact on organizational creativity and firm performance. *Information & Management*, *58*(3), 103434. DOI: 10.1016/j.im.2021.103434

Mittelstadt, B. D., Allo, P., Taddeo, M., Wachter, S., & Floridi, L. (2016). The ethics of algorithms: Mapping the debate. *Big Data & Society*, *3*(2), 1–21. DOI: 10.1177/2053951716679679

Mökander, J., & Floridi, L. (2021). Ethics-based auditing to develop trustworthy AI. *Minds and Machines*, *31*(2), 323–327. DOI: 10.1007/s11023-021-09557-8

Moore, E., & Abbas, F. (2024). Agentic AI as guardian: Preventing financial crimes and elevating cybersecurity compliance. ResearchGate. DOI: 10.13140/RG.2.2.21933.19684

Mountford, N., & Cai, Y. (2023). Towards a flatter ontology of institutional logics: How logics relate in situations of institutional complexity. *International Journal of Management Reviews*, *25*(2), 363–383. DOI: 10.1111/ijmr.12313

Muganyi, T., Yan, L., Yin, Y., Sun, H., Gong, X., & Taghizadeh-Hesary, F. (2022). Fintech, regtech, and financial development: Evidence from China. *Financial Innovation*, *8*(1), 29. Advance online publication. DOI: 10.1186/s40854-021-00313-6

Murire, O. T. (2024). Artificial intelligence and its role in shaping organizational work practices and culture. *Administrative Sciences*, *14*(12), 316. DOI: 10.3390/admsci14120316

Mutambara, A. G. (2025). *Artificial Intelligence: A driver of inclusive development and shared prosperity for the Global South*. CRC Press. DOI: 10.1201/9781003511014

Naeem, S., Ali, A., Anam, S., & Ahmed, M. M. (2023). An unsupervised machine learning algorithms: Comprehensive review. *International Journal of Computing and Digital Systems*, *13*(1), 911–921. DOI: 10.12785/ijcds/130172

Narajala, V. S., Habler, I., Huang, K., & Kulkarni, P. (2025). Building a secure agentic AI application leveraging Google's A2A protocol. In 2025 Annual Computer Security Applications Conference Workshops (ACSAC Workshops) (pp. 332–340). IEEE. DOI: 10.1109/ACSACW69556.2025.00043

Nason, R., & Bothello, J. (2023). Far from void: How institutions shape growth in informal economies. *Academy of Management Review*, *48*(3), 485–503. DOI: 10.5465/amr.2019.0170

Nasteski, V. (2017). An overview of the supervised machine learning methods. *Horizons.B*, *4*, 51–62. DOI: 10.20544/HORIZONS.B.04.1.17.P05

National Institute of Standards and Technology (US). (2024). *Artificial intelligence risk management framework: generative artificial intelligence profile.* US Department of Commerce, National Institute of Standards and Technology.

National Institute of Standards and Technology. (2023). *Artificial intelligence risk management framework (AI RMF 1.0)* [NIST AI 100-1]. **https://doi.org/**DOI: 10.6028/NIST.AI.100-1

National Institute of Standards and Technology. (2023). *Artificial Intelligence Risk Management Framework (AI RMF 1.0).* https://www.nist.gov/itl/ai-risk-management-framework

Nushi, B., Iqbal, S. T., Bennett, P., Teevan, J., Horvitz, E., Weld, D., & Fourney, A. (2019). Guidelines for human-AI interaction. In *Proceedings of the 2019 CHI Conference on Human Factors in Computing Systems.*

OECD. (2019). *OECD Principles on Artificial Intelligence,* https://www.oecd.org/going-digital/ai/principles/

OECD. (2024). *OECD framework for the classification of AI systems.* OECD Publishing.

Ogeawuchi, J. C., Sharma, A., Adekunle, B. I., Abayomi, A. A., & Onifade, O. (2024). Ethical Frameworks for AI Deployment in Financial Decision-Making: Balancing Profitability and Social Responsibility. *International Journal of Scientific Research in Computer Science. Engineering and Information Technology, 10*(2), 905–917.

Ogunmokun, A. S., Balogun, E. D., & Ogunsola, K. O. (2021). A Conceptual Framework for AI-Driven Financial Risk Management and Corporate Governance Optimization. *International Journal of Multidisciplinary Research and Growth Evaluation, 2.*

Okafor, C., Chilee Osuji, V., & Dako, O. (2021). Fintech-enabled transformation of transaction banking and digital lending as a catalyst for SME growth and financial inclusion. International Scientific Refereed Research Journal, 4, 2581–6306. https://shisrrj.com/paper/SHISRRJ214457.pdf

Oluwagbenro, M. B. (2024). Generative AI: Definition, concepts, applications, and future prospects. *TechRxiv*. DOI: 10.36227/techrxiv.171746875.59016695/v1

Omarini, A. (2017, June 9). The digital transformation in banking and the role of FinTechs in the new financial intermediation scenario. Munich Personal RePEc Archive. https://mpra.ub.uni-muenchen.de/85228/

Omoseebi, A., Cole, W., & John, S. (2024). Compliance and Ethics: Ensure that digital initiatives comply with regulations and ethical standards.

Onoja, J. P., Hamza, O., Collins, A., Chibunna, U. B., Eweja, A., & Daraojimba, A. I. (2021). Digital transformation and data governance: Strategies for regulatory compliance and secure AI-driven business operations. *J. Front. Multidiscip. Res*, *2*(1), 43–55. DOI: 10.54660/.IJFMR.2021.2.1.43-55

Oracle. (2025). *The future of banking: Scaling AI agents in 2026 & beyond.* https://www.oracle.com/financial-services/banking/future-banking/

Organization for Economic Co-operation and Development (OECD). (2019). Recommendation of the Council on Artificial Intelligence, OECD/LEGAL/0449.

Orlikowski, W. J. (2000). Using technology and constituting structures: A practice lens for studying technology in organizations. *Organization Science*, *11*(4), 404–428. DOI: 10.1287/orsc.11.4.404.14600

Orlikowski, W. J. (2007). Sociomaterial practices: Exploring technology at work. *Organization Studies*, *28*(9), 1435–1448. DOI: 10.1177/0170840607081138

Ostrom, E. (2010). Polycentric systems for coping with collective action and global environmental change. *Global Environmental Change*, *20*(4), 550–557. DOI: 10.1016/j.gloenvcha.2010.07.004

Oti-Sarpong, K., Pärn, E. A., Burgess, G., & Zaki, M. (2022). Transforming the construction sector: An institutional complexity perspective. *Construction Innovation*, *22*(2), 361–387. DOI: 10.1108/CI-04-2021-0071

Pahune, S., Akhtar, Z., Mandapati, V., & Siddique, K. (2025). The Importance of AI Data Governance in Large Language Models. *Big Data and Cognitive Computing*, *9*(6), 147. DOI: 10.3390/bdcc9060147

Palos-Sanchez, P. R., Chang-Tam, R. J., & Folgado-Fernández, J. A. (2025). The role of neobanks and FinTech in sustainable finance and technology: The customer/ user perspective for entrepreneurs. *Sustainable Technology and Entrepreneurship, 4*(3), 100109. DOI: 10.1016/j.stae.2025.100109

Parasuraman, R., Sheridan, T. B., & Wickens, C. D. (2000). A model for types and levels of human interaction with automation. *IEEE Transactions on Systems, Man, and Cybernetics. Part A, Systems and Humans, 30*(3), 286–297. DOI: 10.1109/3468.844354 PMID: 11760769

Park, J. S., O'Brien, J., Cai, C. J., Morris, M. R., Liang, P., & Bernstein, M. S. (2023). Generative agents: Interactive simulacra of human behavior. In Proceedings of the 36th Annual ACM Symposium on User Interface Software and Technology (UIST '23). Association for Computing Machinery, 1–22. https://doi.org/DOI: 10.1145/3586183.3606763

Partnership on AI. (2025). *Preparing for AI agent governance*. https://partnershiponai .org/resource/preparing-for-ai-agent-governance/

Pirjan, A., & Petroşanu, D. M. (2025). ARTIFICIAL SOCIAL INTELLIGENCE AND THE TRANSFORMATION OF HUMAN INTERACTION BY ARTIFICIAL INTELLIGENCE AGENTS. *Journal of Information Systems & Operations Management, 19*(1).

Plekhanov, D., Franke, H., & Netland, T. H. (2023). Digital transformation: A review and research agenda. *European Management Journal, 41*(6), 821–844. DOI: 10.1016/j.emj.2022.09.007

Pobuda, P., & Andrae, S. (2026). Policy advice by digital economic twins: Using agent-based modelling and artificial intelligence. Working Paper. http://dx.doi.org/ DOI: 10.2139/ssrn.6336459

Pop, M. V., Ton , G., Flonta, F.-V., & Flore, M. (2026). Integrating agentic AI in advanced FinTech project management. *Preprints*.org. https://www.preprints.org/ manuscript/202502.1284

Popoola, S. (2025). Ethical and Regulatory Challenges of AI-Driven Decision-Making in Financial Services.

Porkodi, S., & Cedro, T. L. (2025). The ethical role of generative artificial intelligence in modern HR decision-making: A systematic literature review. *European Journal of Business and Management Research, 10*(1), 44–55. DOI: 10.24018/ ejbmr.2025.10.1.2535

Pouyanfar, S., Sadiq, S., Yan, Y., Tian, H., Tao, Y., Reyes, M. P., Shyu, M.-L., Chen, S.-C., & Iyengar, S. S. (2018). A survey on deep learning. *ACM Computing Surveys*, *51*(5), 1–36. DOI: 10.1145/3234150

Pramanik, H. S., Kirtania, M., & Pani, A. K. (2019). Essence of digital transformation—Manifestations at large financial institutions from North America. *Future Generation Computer Systems*, *95*, 323–343. DOI: 10.1016/j.future.2018.12.003

Puschmann, T. (2017). Fintech. *Business & Information Systems Engineering*, *59*(1), 69–76. DOI: 10.1007/s12599-017-0464-6

PwC. (2025). *Responsible AI in finance: 3 key actions to take now*. https://www.pwc.com/us/en/tech-effect/ai-analytics/responsible-ai-in-finance.html

Qian, L., Peng, X., Wang, Y., Zhang, V. J., He, H., Smith, H., Han, Y., He, Y., Li, H., Cao, Y., Yu, Y., Lopez-Lira, A., Lu, P., Nie, J.-Y., Xiong, G., Huang, J., & Ananiadou, S. (2026). When agents trade: Live multi-market trading arena for LLM agents. In *Proceedings of the ACM Web Conference 2026* (pp. 7833–7844). Association for Computing Machinery. https://doi.org/DOI: 10.1145/3774904.3792821

Qian, P., Cao, R., Liu, Z., Li, W., Li, M., Zhang, L., Xu, Y., Chen, J., & He, Q. (2025). Comprehensive review of smart contract and DeFi security: Attack, vulnerability detection, and automated repair. *Expert Systems with Applications*, *291*, 128431. DOI: 10.1016/j.eswa.2025.128431

Qin, X., Luan, S., See, J., Yang, C., & Li, Z. (2026). Governed Capability Evolution for Embodied Agents: Safe Upgrade, Compatibility Checking, and Runtime Rollback for Embodied Capability Modules. arXiv preprint arXiv:2604.08059.

Radanliev, P. (2026). Transparent by Design: Ensuring Safety in Agentic AI Through Decision Traceability. In Ethical AI and Data Science (pp. 1-20). Auerbach Publications.

Rahwan, I. (2018). Society-in-the-loop: Programming the algorithmic social contract. *Ethics and Information Technology*, *20*(1), 5–14. DOI: 10.1007/s10676-017-9430-8

Rahwan, I., Cebrian, M., Obradovich, N., Bongard, J., Bonnefon, J. F., Breazeal, C., Crandall, J. W., Christakis, N. A., Couzin, I. D., Jackson, M. O., Jennings, N. R., Kamar, E., Kloumann, I. M., Larochelle, H., Lazer, D., McElreath, R., Mislove, A., Parkes, D. C., Pentland, A. S., & Wellman, M. (2019). Machine behaviour. *Nature*, *568*(7753), 477–486. DOI: 10.1038/s41586-019-1138-y PMID: 31019318

Rai, A. (2020). Explainable AI: From black box to glass box. *Journal of the Academy of Marketing Science*, *48*(1), 137–141. DOI: 10.1007/s11747-019-00710-5

Raisch, S., & Krakowski, S. (2021). Artificial intelligence and management: The automation–augmentation paradox. *Academy of Management Review*, *46*(1), 192–210. DOI: 10.5465/amr.2018.0072

Rajagopal, N. K., Qureshi, N. I., Durga, S., Ramirez Asis, E. H., Huerta Soto, R. M., Gupta, S. K., & Deepak, S. (2022). Future of business culture: An artificial intelligence-driven digital framework for organization decision-making process. *Complexity*, *2022*(1), 7796507. DOI: 10.1155/2022/7796507

Raji, I. D., Smart, A., White, R. N., Mitchell, M., Gebru, T., Hutchinson, B., Smith-Loud, J., Theron, D., & Barnes, P. (2020). Closing the AI Accountability Gap: Defining an End-to-End Framework for Internal Algorithmic Auditing. Proceedings of the 2020 Conference on Fairness, Accountability, and Transparency (FAT* '20).

Raji, I. D., Smart, A., White, R. N., Mitchell, M., Gebru, T., Hutchinson, B., Smith-Loud, J., Theron, D., & Barnes, P. (2020). Closing the AI accountability gap: Defining an end-to-end framework for internal algorithmic auditing. *Proceedings of the 2020 Conference on Fairness, Accountability, and Transparency*, 33–44. **https://doi.org/** DOI: 10.1145/3351095.3372873

Rhodes, R. A. W. (1997). *Understanding Governance: Policy Networks, Governance, Reflexivity and Accountability*. Open University Press.

Ribeiro, M. T., Singh, S., & Guestrin, C. (2016). "Why should I trust you?": Explaining the predictions of any classifier. In Proceedings of the 22nd ACM SIGKDD International Conference on Knowledge Discovery and Data Mining. Association for Computing Machinery, 1135–1144.

Richards, C. E., Cernev, T., Tzachor, A., Zilgalvis, G., & Kaleagasi, B. (2023). Safely advancing a spacefaring humanity with artificial intelligence. *Frontiers in Space Technologies*, *4*, 1199547. DOI: 10.3389/frspt.2023.1199547

Rizinski, M., & Trajanov, D. (2025). AI agents in finance and fintech: A scientific review of agent-based systems, applications, and future horizons. *Computers, Materials & Continua*, *86*(1), 1–34. DOI: 10.32604/cmc.2025.069678

RoboNet. (2024, July 3). Introducing RoboNet: AI agents for DeFi powered by a decentralized collective intelligence network. Medium.

Ross, J. W., Weill, P., & Robertson, D. C. (2006). *Enterprise architecture as strategy: Creating a foundation for business execution*. Harvard Business School Press.

Russell, S. J., Norvig, P., Canny, J. F., Malik, J. M., & Edwards, D. D. (1995). Artificial intelligence: a modern approach: Vol. 2. *No. 9*. Prentice hall.

Russell, S., & Norvig, P. (2021). *Artificial intelligence: A modern approach* (4th ed.). Pearson.

Russell, S., & Norvig, P. (2021). *Artificial Intelligence: A Modern Approach* (4th ed.). Pearson.

Salah, M., Alnoor, A., Abdelfattah, F., & Al Halbusi, H. (2025). Agentic artificial intelligence in public administration: Foundations, applications, and governance. Applications, and Governance (May 10, 2025).

Salgado-Criado, J. (2025). Human oversight of artificial intelligence: An operations management perspective. *Journal of Industrial Engineering and Management*, *18*(2), 285–304. DOI: 10.3926/jiem.8567

Sambamurthy, V., & Zmud, R. W. (1999). Arrangements for information technology governance: A theory of multiple contingencies. *Management Information Systems Quarterly*, *23*(2), 261–290. DOI: 10.2307/249754

Santoni de Sio, F., & van den Hoven, J. (2018). Meaningful human control over autonomous systems: A philosophical account. *Frontiers in Robotics and AI*, *5*, 15. DOI: 10.3389/frobt.2018.00015 PMID: 33500902

Sapkota, R., Shrestha, R., Rijal, M., & Karkee, M. (2025). LangChain vs. LangGraph vs. LangSmith: Taxonomies of agentic AI toolchains for end-to-end orchestration. *TechRxiv*. DOI: 10.36227/techrxiv.175695645.52670060/v1

Sawicki, J. (2025). The Role of Decision-Making Algorithms in Public Administration–Legal and Ethical Challenges. *Zeszyt Prawniczy UAM*, (15), 99–111. DOI: 10.14746/zpuam.2025.15.8

Schildt, H., & Perkmann, M. (2017). Organizational settlements: Theorizing how organizations respond to institutional complexity. *Journal of Management Inquiry*, *26*(2), 139–145. DOI: 10.1177/1056492616670756

Securities, & Exchange, C. (2013). In the Matter of Knight Capital Americas LLC, Securities Exchange Act Release No. 70694, Administrative Proceeding File No. 3-15570.

Shanti, R., Siregar, H., Zulbainarni, N., & Tony, N. (2024). Revolutionizing banking: Neobanks' digital transformation for enhanced efficiency. *Journal of Risk and Financial Management*, *17*(5), 188. DOI: 10.3390/jrfm17050188

Sharma, A. K., & Sharma, R. (2025). Data governance in the age of artificial intelligence: Challenges, best practices and regulatory compliance. *Applied Marketing Analytics*, *10*(4), 390–403. DOI: 10.69554/XWHM1191

Shavit, Y., Agarwal, S., Brundage, M., Adler, S., O'Keefe, C., Campbell, R., ... & Robinson, D. G. (2023). Practices for governing agentic AI systems. *Research Paper, OpenAI*, 1-23.

Shneiderman, B. (2022). *Human-centered AI.* Oxford University Press. DOI: 10.1093/oso/9780192845290.001.0001

Shoham, Y., & Leyton-Brown, K. (2009). *Multiagent Systems,* https://www.cambridge.org/core/books/multiagent-systems/7F4A4E97A6F49C85E2D2E6C8A43D5F90

Shrestha, Y. R., Ben-Menahem, S. M., & von Krogh, G. (2019). Organizational decision-making structures in the age of artificial intelligence. *California Management Review, 61*(4), 66–83. DOI: 10.1177/0008125619862257

Siddquee, T. A. (2025). AI in banking risk management and fraud detection in preventing financial crimes and optimizing credit decisions. *International Journal of Social Science Research and Review, 8*(8), 391–404. DOI: 10.47814/ijssrr.v8i8.2889

Singhal, A. (2024). *Social challenges of AI governance.*

Singh, S. K., Rao, S., Harish, N., & Guduru, P. (2025). *Business organization and Management.* RK Publication.

Singh, S., Kumar, A., Jha, A., Jacob, N., & Mondal, M. S. (2025). AI Alignment: Ensuring AI objectives match human values. *Int. J. Sci. Res. Eng. Manag, 9*(04), 1–9. DOI: 10.55041/IJSREM46662

Soori, M., Arezoo, B., & Dastres, R. (2023). Artificial intelligence, machine learning and deep learning in advanced robotics: A review. *Cognitive Robotics, 3*(1), 54–70. DOI: 10.1016/j.cogr.2023.04.001

Soori, M., Dastres, R., Arezoo, B., & Jough, F. K. G. (2024). Intelligent robotic systems in Industry 4.0: A review. *Journal of Advanced Manufacturing Science and Technology, 4*(3), 2024007. DOI: 10.51393/j.jamst.2024007

Souly, A., Rando, J., Chapman, E., Davies, X., Hasircioglu, B., Shereen, E., Mougan, C., Mavroudis, V., Jones, E., Hicks, C., Carlini, N., Gal, Y., & Kirk, R. (2025). Poisoning attacks on LLMs require a near-constant number of poison samples. arXiv. https://arxiv.org/abs/2510.07192

Sriram, H. K. (2025). *Beyond automation: Exploring the potential of agentic AI in risk management and fraud detection in banks.* Eksplorium.

Srnicek, N. (2017). *Platform Capitalism.* Polity Press.

Suchman, L. (2007). *Human–machine reconfigurations: Plans and situated actions* (2nd ed.). Cambridge University Press.

Sun, Y., & Jung, H. (2024). Machine learning (ML) modeling, IoT, and optimizing organizational operations through integrated strategies: The role of technology and human resource management. *Sustainability (Basel), 16*(16), 6751. DOI: 10.3390/su16166751

Taddeo, M., & Floridi, L. (2018). How AI can be a force for good. *Science, 361*(6404), 751–752. DOI: 10.1126/science.aat5991 PMID: 30139858

Tangi, L., Müller, A. P. R., & Janssen, M. (2025). AI-augmented government transformation: Organisational transformation and the sociotechnical implications of artificial intelligence in public administrations. *Government Information Quarterly, 42*(3), 102055. DOI: 10.1016/j.giq.2025.102055

Taye, M. M. (2023). Understanding of machine learning with deep learning: Architectures, workflow, applications and future directions. *Computers, 12*(5), 91. DOI: 10.3390/computers12050091

Trist, E. L., & Bamforth, K. W. (1951). Some social and psychological consequences of the longwall method of coal-getting: An examination of the psychological situation and defences of a work group in relation to the social structure and technological content of the work system. *Human Relations, 4*(1), 3–38. DOI: 10.1177/001872675100400101

Turillazzi, A., Tsamados, A., Genç, E., Taddeo, M., & Floridi, L. (2023). Decentralised finance (DeFi): A critical review of related risks and regulation. *SSRN*. DOI: 10.2139/ssrn.4593242

UNESCO. (2025). *UNESCO and the promotion of languages in Africa: cultural diversity and multilingualism*. UNESCO.

Union, A. (2024). *Continental artificial intelligence strategy*. African Union Commision.

United Nations Educational, Scientific and Cultural Organization. (2021). Recommendation on the ethics of artificial intelligence. Retrieved 17 July 2026 (https://unesdoc.unesco.org/ark:/48223/pf0000381137).Google Scholar.

Urbano, D., Guerrero, M., Ferreira, J. J., & Fernandes, C. I. (2019). New technology entrepreneurship initiatives: Which strategic orientations and environmental conditions matter in the new socio-economic landscape? *The Journal of Technology Transfer, 44*(5), 1577–1602. DOI: 10.1007/s10961-018-9675-3 van de Merwe, K. (2024). Agent transparency and human performance in supervisory control.

Van Rijmenam, M., & Logue, D. (2021). Revising the 'science of the organisation': Theorising AI agency and actorhood. *Innovation (North Sydney, N.S.W.), 23*(1), 127–144. DOI: 10.1080/14479338.2020.1816833

Verhoef, P. C., Broekhuizen, T., Bart, Y., Bhattacharya, A., Dong, J. Q., Fabian, N., & Haenlein, M. (2021). Digital transformation: A multidisciplinary reflection and research agenda. *Journal of Business Research, 122*, 889–901. DOI: 10.1016/j.jbusres.2019.09.022

Vial, G. (2019). Understanding digital transformation. *Management Information Systems Quarterly*. Advance online publication. DOI: 10.25300/MISQ/2019/15734

Vial, G. (2019). Understanding digital transformation: A review and a research agenda. *The Journal of Strategic Information Systems, 28*(2), 118–144. DOI: 10.1016/j.jsis.2019.01.003

Vijayakumar, H. (2023, June 1). Revolutionizing customer experience with AI: A path to increase revenue growth rate. In *Proceedings of the 2023 International Conference on Emerging Applications of Artificial Intelligence*. IEEE. DOI: 10.1109/ECAI58194.2023.10194016

Visa. (2025). Visa advances agentic commerce with developer updates. Visa.

Voudouris, C. (2025). *Autonomic business transformation: A guide to AI agents for practitioners and executives*. Springer Nature Switzerland., DOI: 10.1007/978-3-032-01415-3

Vuković, D. B., Dekpo-Adza, S., & Matović, S. (2025). AI integration in financial services: A systematic review of trends and regulatory challenges. *Humanities & Social Sciences Communications, 12*(1), 562. Advance online publication. DOI: 10.1057/s41599-025-04850-8

Wamba-Taguimdje, S. L., Wamba, S. F., Kamdjoug, J. R. K., & Wanko, C. E. T. (2020). Influence of artificial intelligence (AI) on firm performance: The business value of AI-based transformation projects. *Business Process Management Journal, 26*(7), 1893–1924. DOI: 10.1108/BPMJ-10-2019-0411

Wang, L., Ma, C., Feng, X., Zhang, J., Yang, H., Zhang, J., Chen, Z., Tang, J., Chen, X., Lin, Y., Zhao, W. X., Wei, Z., & Wen, J. (2024). A survey on large language model based autonomous agents. *Frontiers of Computer Science, 18*(6), 186345. DOI: 10.1007/s11704-024-40231-1

Warner, K. S. R., & Wäger, M. (2019). Building dynamic capabilities for digital transformation: An ongoing process of strategic renewal. *Long Range Planning*, *52*(3), 326–349. DOI: 10.1016/j.lrp.2018.12.001

Weidinger, L., Uesato, J., Rauh, M., Griffin, C., Huang, P.-S., Mellor, J., Glaese, A., Cheng, M., Balle, B., & Kasirzadeh, A. (2022). Taxonomy of Risks Posed by Language Models. *2022 ACM Conference on Fairness, Accountability, and Transparency (FAccT '22)*. DOI: 10.1145/3531146.3533088

Weill, P., & Ross, J. W. (2004). *IT governance: How top performers manage IT decision rights for superior results*. Harvard Business School Press.

Weill, P., & Ross, J. W. (2005). A matrixed approach to designing IT governance. *MIT Sloan Management Review*, *46*(2), 26–34.

Welsch, A. (2026). *The HUMAN Agentic AI Edge: Shape the Next Generation of AI-Ready Teams*. Andreas Welsch.

Weritz, P., Braojos, J., & Matute, J. (2020). Exploring the antecedents of digital transformation: Dynamic capabilities and digital culture aspects to achieve digital maturity.

West, G., & Hale, R. (2025). Building Human-AI Collaboration Models in Cybersecurity Operations.

Westerman, G., Bonnet, D., & McAfee, A. (2014). *Leading digital: Turning technology into business transformation*. Harvard Business Press.

Whittlestone, J., Nyrup, R., Alexandrova, A., & Cave, S. (2019). The role and limits of principles in AI ethics: Towards a focus on tensions. *Proceedings of the 2019 AAAI/ACM Conference on AI, Ethics, and Society*, 195--200. https://doi.org/DOI: 10.1145/3306618.3314289

Wickramarachchi, N. (2025). *The impact of AI chatbots on customer satisfaction with special reference to FinTech companies*. University of Jyväskylä.

Wieringa, M. (2020, January). What to account for when accounting for algorithms: a systematic literature review on algorithmic accountability. In *Proceedings of the 2020 conference on fairness, accountability, and transparency* (pp. 1-18). DOI: 10.1145/3351095.3372833

Wirtz, B. W., Weyerer, J. C., & Geyer, C. (2019). Artificial intelligence and the public sector---applications and challenges. *International Journal of Public Administration*, *42*(7), 596–615. DOI: 10.1080/01900692.2018.1498103

Wolters Kluwer. (2026). *The AI imperative in banking: Moving from pilot to production.*

Wooldridge, M. (2009). *An Introduction to Multiagent Systems* (2nd ed.). Wiley.

Wooldridge, M. (2020). *A brief history of artificial intelligence: What it is, where we are, and where we are going*. Flatiron Books.

Wooldridge, M. (2020). *An introduction to multiagent systems* (2nd ed.). Wiley.

Wooldridge, M., & Jennings, N. R. (1995). Intelligent agents: Theory and practice. *The Knowledge Engineering Review, 10*(2), 115–152. DOI: 10.1017/S0269888900008122

World Bank. (2020). *Doing Business 2020: Comparing Business Regulation in 190 Economies.* World Bank Group.

World Economic Forum. (2025). *Artificial intelligence in financial services.* WEF White Paper (in collaboration with Accenture).

Wu, Y., & Li, Y. (2026). Agentic FinTech: A comprehensive survey on AI agents in finance in the era of LLMs. SSRN. 6136529. Elgendy, I. A., Helal, M. Y., Al-Sharafi, M. A., Albashrawi, M. A., Al-Ahmadi, M. S., Jeon, I., & Dwivedi, Y. K. (2025). Agentic systems as catalysts for innovation in FinTech: exploring opportunities, challenges and a research agenda. Information Discovery and Delivery. DOI: 10.2139/ssrn.6136529

Xiao, Y., Sun, E., Luo, D., & Wang, W. (2024). TradingAgents: Multi-agents LLM financial trading framework. arXiv. https://arxiv.org/abs/2412.20138

Xi, Z., Chen, W., Guo, X., He, W., Ding, Y., Hong, B., Zhang, M., Wang, J., Jin, S., Zhou, E., Zheng, R., Fan, X., Wang, X., Xiong, L., Zhou, Y., Wang, W., Jiang, C., Zou, Y., Liu, X., & Gui, T. (2025). The rise and potential of large language model based agents: A survey. *Science China. Information Sciences, 68*(2), 121101. DOI: 10.1007/s11432-024-4222-0

Xu, H., Miao, W., & Zhang, S. (2024). Digital technology development and systemic financial risks: Evidence from 22 countries. *Borsa Istanbul Review, 24*, 1–9.

Yanney, A. A. S. (2025). Redefining corporate financial governance through AI-Powered predictive models for global business risk management. *International Journal of Research Publication and Reviews, 2*(6), 25–49. DOI: 10.55248/gengpi.6.0625.2037

Yao, Y., Duan, J., Xu, K., Cai, Y., Sun, Z., & Zhang, Y. (2024). A survey on large language model (LLM) security and privacy: The good, the bad, and the ugly. *High-Confidence Computing, 4*(2), 100211. DOI: 10.1016/j.hcc.2024.100211

Yeung, K. (2018). Algorithmic regulation: A critical interrogation. *Regulation & Governance, 12*(4), 505–523. DOI: 10.1111/rego.12158

Yousefi, Y., Billi, M., & Rotolo, A. (2025). Agentic AI: An EU AI Act paradigm shift? *SSRN*. DOI: 10.2139/ssrn.5731424

Zhong, C., Cheng, F., Liu, Q., Jiang, J., Wan, Z., Chu, C., . . . Kurohashi, S. (2024). Beyond english-centric llms: What language do multilingual language models think in? *arXiv preprint arXiv:2408.10811*.

About the Contributors

Festus Fatai Adedoyin is a Senior Lecturer in Computer Science at Bournemouth University, United Kingdom, where he provides academic leadership across programmes in data science, artificial intelligence, business analytics, and digital transformation. He holds a PhD in Economics from Bournemouth University, with a research focus on microdata modelling, behavioural analysis, and simulation-based policy design. He also holds postgraduate qualifications in Development Policy (KDI School of Public Policy and Management, South Korea) and Economics (University of Ibadan, Nigeria), alongside specialist training in non-linear panel data modelling from the Barcelona Graduate School of Economics. Dr Adedoyin's academic and professional work sits at the intersection of digital transformation, artificial intelligence, policy design, and organisational performance, with particular emphasis on regulated and public-sector environments. He has led and contributed to curriculum development in digital innovation, global FinTech transformation, and AI-enabled business analytics, and has served in senior academic leadership roles including Programme Leader and Postgraduate Project Coordinator. He has an extensive publication record spanning AI, digital competence, energy and environmental policy, financial systems, health systems transformation, and technology-driven development, with work published in leading international journals and edited volumes. He is the editor of multiple scholarly books on digital competence, simulation and machine learning models for policy design, and generative AI and productivity, and has contributed to high-impact conferences and interdisciplinary research initiatives. Beyond academia, Dr Adedoyin has served as an international consultant for United Nations–affiliated projects, including UNDP and Green Climate Fund (GCF) programmes, providing strategic advisory support on climate change, health systems resilience, capacity development, and digital transformation. He has led and contributed to externally funded projects involving government bodies, development partners, and industry, including knowledge transfer partnerships and applied AI research initiatives. Dr Adedoyin is a Fellow of the UK Higher Education Academy, a member of the IEEE and the British Computer Society, and a Chartered Management and Business Educator. His work is driven by a commitment to responsible, human-centred, and policy-aligned adoption of AI and digital technologies to support institutional effectiveness, societal wellbeing, and sustainable development.

***

Mallikarjun Bellundagi As a Solution architect, with over 25 years of technical expertise in the complete software development life cycle spanning E-commerce/ Internet, Financial, Investments Banking, and Retail. Specialized in Web, Integration, and Product-based applications.

Abdelraouf M. Ishtaiwi is an Associate Professor of Artificial Intelligence and Data Science at the University of Petra, Jordan, with over 22 years of academic and research experience in AI. He earned his Master's and Ph.D. degrees in Artificial Intelligence from Griffith University, Australia, where he focused on heuristic optimization techniques for satisfiability problems. His research expertise spans machine learning, hybrid metaheuristic optimization, associative classification, and AI applications in cybersecurity and emerging technologies like the metaverse. Dr. Ishtaiwi has developed innovative AI algorithms, such as ACRIPPER and hybrid crayfish-DE models, and contributed significantly to areas like phishing detection, blockchain security, and smart IoT defense. As a former Head of the Department of Data Science and AI at Petra University, he led academic reforms and accreditation initiatives. He has also been a visiting scholar at Griffith University and Universitat Pompeu Fabra, reflecting his international academic engagement.

Jomon Jose M. is an Associate Professor and Research Supervisor at Sahrdaya Institute of Management Studies. He holds a Post-Doctoral qualification and specializes in marketing, consumer behavior, HRM, digital transformation, and sustainable business practices. His research contributions include Scopus-indexed publications, book chapters, and interdisciplinary studies focusing on AI, finance, branding, and strategic management.

Olasomi Aisha Labo-Popoola is a PhD researcher in Business and Innovation Management at the University of Greater Manchester, Bolton. Her research focuses on Small and Medium-sized Enterprises (SMEs), open innovation, digital transformation, and strategic management. Her expertise includes machine learning, artificial intelligence, cloud computing adoption, blockchain integration, and the strategic management of new technologies. She holds an MSc in Data Science (with Distinction) from the University of the West of England, Bristol. Her work sits at the intersection of technology and innovation strategy, with a core focus on supporting SME digitalization.

Samuel Mariwa is a software engineer and AI researcher with a Master's degree in Data Science and Artificial Intelligence from Bournemouth University, United Kingdom. He has contributed to multiple AI, machine learning, and data-driven projects involving predictive analytics, explainable artificial intelligence (XAI), and intelligent system design. His current research interests focus on edge AI and small language models, particularly for deployment in resource-constrained and offline environments.

Naga Ramesh Palakurti is a senior technology architect and researcher with 25+ years of experience in enterprise software architecture, BRMS, AI/ML, and risk management across banking, insurance, and public-sector domains. He is a Solution Architect at Tata Consultancy Services (TCS), supporting Bank of America on AI/ML-enabled risk platforms, fraud detection, and cloud-native decision management. He holds a MS. in Computer Science from Osmania University, B.S in Computer Science from Andhra University and completed Purdue University's Post Graduate Program in AI/ML (2024). Certifications include PMP, AWS Certified Solutions Architect–Associate, and IBM credentials in Python and deep learning. His scholarly work includes 52 journal publications and 20 book chapters (IGI Global, Elsevier, Springer, Bentham), along with IEEE/Springer conference presentations, editorial-board service, and 200+ peer reviews (e.g., IGI Global, Taylor & Francis). He has received multiple honors (Global, Titan, GL, GRA, Globee, ICSD Threws) and serves as an evaluator/judge for global award programs, Bandon Hall Group, and Business Intelligence Technology. He is playing an editorial role for PLOS ONE.

Index

A

B

D

E

F

G

www.ingramcontent.com/pod-product-compliance
Lightning Source LLC
LaVergne TN
LVHW062029101126
852251LV00005B/59